Get the eBook FREE!

(PDF, ePub, Kindle, and liveBook all included)

We believe that once you buy a book from us, you should be able to read it in any format we have available. To get electronic versions of this book at no additional cost to you, purchase and then register this book at the Manning website.

Go to https://www.manning.com/freebook and follow the instructions to complete your pBook registration.

That's it!
Thanks from Manning!

Privacy-Preserving Machine Learning

Privacy-Preserving Machine Learning

J. MORRIS CHANG
DI ZHUANG
DUMINDU SAMARAWEERA

MANNING
SHELTER ISLAND

For online information and ordering of this and other Manning books, please visit
www.manning.com. The publisher offers discounts on this book when ordered in quantity.
For more information, please contact

Special Sales Department
Manning Publications Co.
20 Baldwin Road
PO Box 761
Shelter Island, NY 11964
Email: orders@manning.com

Manning Publications Co.
20 Baldwin Road
PO Box 761
Shelter Island, NY 11964

Development editor:	Dustin Archibald
Technical development editor:	Al Krinker
Technical editor:	Wilko Henecka
Review editor:	Aleksandar Dragosavljević
Production editor:	Keri Hales
Copy editor:	Andy Carroll
Proofreader:	Katie Tennant
Technical proofreader:	Karsten Strøbæk
Typesetter:	Gordan Salinovic
Cover designer:	Marija Tudor

ISBN 9781617298042
Printed in the United States of America

brief contents

v

contents

preface

Given the popularity of social media and online streaming services, you have probably experienced how far machine learning (ML) can go in delivering personalized services. Even though this exciting field opens doors to many new possibilities and has become an indispensable part of our lives, training ML models requires the use of significant amounts of data collected in various ways. When this data is processed through ML models, it is essential to preserve the confidentiality and privacy of individuals and to maintain the trust of those who use these models.

While preserving privacy in ML is essential, it is also challenging. In late 2014, Dr. Chang and his former PhD student, Dr. Mohammad Al-Rubaie, started to investigate the problem of privacy leakage in ML techniques and explored the possibilities of mitigating such leaks. As they continued their research, the Defense Advanced Research Projects Agency (DARPA) initiated a new research program in early 2015 called "Brandeis" (BAA-15-29) with a $50 million initial budget. The program was named after Louis Brandeis, a US Supreme Court Justice who published the "Right to Privacy" paper in the *Harvard Law Review* journal in 1890. The main goal of the Brandeis program was to seek and develop the technical means to protect private information by enabling safe and predictable sharing of data in which privacy is preserved. Dr. Chang and his team participated in the Brandeis program and developed several privacy-preserving technologies based on compressive privacy and differential privacy techniques.

In 2019, with another research award from US Special Operations Command (USSOCOM), Drs. Chang, Zhuang, and Samaraweera and their team tried to put these privacy and security-enhancing technologies for ML into practical applications by utilizing the latest ML models and tools. With their years of hands-on experience participating in the Brandeis program and many other DoD-sponsored research programs since 2015, they believe it's now time to put together the techniques they've developed. Thus, this book is different from other technical books: it discusses the fundamental concepts of ML and the privacy-preserving techniques for ML, and it offers intuitive examples and implementation code showing how to use them in practice.

They believe this book is the first to provide comprehensive coverage of privacy-preserving ML. Herein, they take you on an exciting journey that covers all the essential concepts, techniques, and hands-on details. If you want to know more after reading this book, you can follow up with the references cited in each chapter and listed at the end of the book.

acknowledgments

A big thanks goes to the DARPA Brandeis program and the project managers with whom we had the pleasure of working on developing new paradigms of privacy-preserving machine learning. We are also very grateful to our team, who worked on the Brandeis project, especially Dr. Sun-Yuan Kung and Dr. Pei-yuan Wu. Furthermore, this book would not have been possible if not for the former and current PhD students of Dr. Chang's research group at the University of South Florida, especially Dr. Mohammad Al-Rubaie and Sen Wang.

Another huge thanks goes to the editorial and production staff at Manning for all their hard work in producing this book. Finally, we would like to thank all the reviewers for their support and valuable feedback on improving the discussions in the manuscript: Abe Taha, Aditya Kaushik, Alain Couniot, Bhavani Shankar Garikapati, Clifford Thurber, Dhivya Sivasubramanian, Erick Nogueira do Nascimento, Frédéric Flayol, Harald Kuhn, Jaganadh Gopinadhan, James Black, Jeremy Chen, Joseph Wang, Kevin Cheung, Koushik Vikram, Mac Chambers, Marco Carnini, Mary Anne Thygesen, Nate Jensen, Nick Decroos, Pablo Roccatagliata, Raffaella Ventaglio, Raj Sahu, Rani Sharim, Richard Vaughan, Rohit Goswami, Satej Sahu, Shankar Garikapati, Simeon Leyzerzon, Simon Tschöke, Simone Sguazza, Sriram Macharla, Stephen Oates, Tim Kane, Vidhya Vinay, Vincent Ngo, Vishwesh Ravi Shrimali, and Xiangbo Mao—your suggestions helped make this a better book.

about this book

Privacy-Preserving Machine Learning is a comprehensive guide written to help machine learning (ML) enthusiasts avoid data privacy leakages through their ML applications. It begins with some practical use cases and scenarios involving privacy considerations in modern data-driven applications. Then it introduces different techniques for building privacy-assured ML applications.

Who should read this book

Privacy-Preserving Machine Learning is designed for intermediate-level data science enthusiasts of ML (i.e., people with some experience in ML) and people who would like to learn about privacy-preserving techniques for ML so they can integrate them into their applications. Although privacy and security concepts are generally mathematical and hard to follow, this book tries to dismantle complex algorithms into pieces to make them easy to follow, and it provides a series of hands-on exercises and examples.

How this book is organized: A road map

The book has three parts with 10 chapters.

Part 1 explains what privacy-preserving ML is and how differential privacy can be used in practical use cases:

- Chapter 1 discusses privacy considerations in ML with an emphasis on how severe the privacy threats are when private data is exposed.

- Chapter 2 introduces the core concepts of differential privacy and formulates the widely adopted differential privacy mechanisms in use today that have served as essential building blocks in various privacy-preserving algorithms and applications.
- Chapter 3 mainly covers the advanced design principles of differentially private ML algorithms. Toward the latter part of the chapter, we introduce a case study that walks you through the process of designing and analyzing a differentially private algorithm.

Part 2 extends the discussion with another level of differential privacy called local differential privacy and discusses how to generate synthetic data for privacy assurance purposes:

- Chapter 4 introduces the core concepts and definitions of local differential privacy.
- Chapter 5 covers the advanced mechanisms of local differential privacy by considering various data types and real-world application scenarios. We also provide a case study on local differential privacy that guides you through the process of designing and analyzing the algorithm.
- Chapter 6 introduces the concepts and techniques involved in synthetic data generation by discussing how to design a privacy-preserving synthetic data generation scheme for ML tasks.

Part 3 covers the next-level core concepts required to build privacy-assured ML applications:

- Chapter 7 introduces the importance of privacy preservation in data mining applications, widely used privacy-protection mechanisms, and their characteristics in data mining operations.
- Chapter 8 extends the discussion of privacy assurance in data mining by covering common privacy models, their characteristics in data mining operations when processing and publishing data, and various threats and vulnerabilities.
- Chapter 9 introduces compressive privacy for ML and its design and implementation.
- Chapter 10 puts these concepts together to design a privacy-enhanced platform for research data protection and sharing.

In general, we encourage you to read the first few chapters carefully so you understand the core concepts and the importance of privacy preservation for ML applications. The remainder of the chapters discuss different levels of the core concepts and best practices, and they can mostly be read out of order, based on your particular needs. At the end of each core topic, a case study is introduced with a more comprehensive and thorough analysis of a selected algorithm, which will be of particular interest to readers who want to know more about the process of designing and analyzing privacy-enhanced ML algorithms.

About the code

This book contains many examples of source code, both in numbered listings and in line with normal text. In both cases, the source code is formatted in a `fixed-width font like this` to separate it from ordinary text. Most of the code is written in the Python language, but some of the use case experiments are presented in Java. Readers are expected to know the basic syntax and how to write and debug Python and Java code. Readers must also be familiar with certain Python scientific computations and machine learning packages, such as NumPy, scikit-learn, PyTorch, TensorFlow, and so on.

In many cases, the original source code has been reformatted; we've added line breaks and reworked indentation to accommodate the available page space in the book. In some cases, even this was not enough, and listings include line-continuation markers (➡). Additionally, comments in the source code have often been removed from the listings when the code is described in the text. Code annotations accompany many of the listings, highlighting important concepts.

You can get executable snippets of code from the liveBook (online) version of this book at https://livebook.manning.com/book/privacy-preserving-machine-learning. The complete code for the examples in the book is available for download from the Manning website at https://www.manning.com/books/privacy-preserving-machine-learning, and from GitHub at https://github.com/nogrady/PPML/.

liveBook discussion forum

Purchase of *Privacy-Preserving Machine Learning* includes free access to liveBook, Manning's online reading platform. Using liveBook's exclusive discussion features, you can attach comments to the book globally or to specific sections or paragraphs. It's a snap to make notes for yourself, ask and answer technical questions, and receive help from the authors and other users. To access the forum, go to https://livebook.manning.com/book/privacy-preserving-machine-learning/discussion. You can also learn more about Manning's forums and the rules of conduct at https://livebook.manning.com/discussion.

Manning's commitment to our readers is to provide a venue where a meaningful dialogue between individual readers and between readers and the authors can take place. It is not a commitment to any specific amount of participation on the part of the authors, whose contributions to the forum remains voluntary (and unpaid). We suggest you try asking them some challenging questions lest their interest stray! The forum and the archives of previous discussions will be accessible from the publisher's website as long as the book is in print.

about the authors

J. MORRIS CHANG has been a professor in the electrical engineering department at University of South Florida since 2016, with prior faculty positions at Iowa State University (2001–2016), Illinois Institute of Technology (1995–2001), and Rochester Institute of Technology (1993–1995). Before joining academia, he was employed as a computer engineer at AT&T Bell Labs (1988–1990). His recent research efforts cover a broad spectrum of cybersecurity subject areas, from authentication to malware detection, privacy-enhancing technologies, and security in machine learning, and were funded by different Department of Defense (DoD) agencies. Dr. Chang received his PhD in computer engineering from North Carolina State University. He received the IIT University Excellence in Teaching Award in 1999, and was inducted into the NC State University ECE Alumni Hall of Fame in 2019. Over the past 10 years, he has served as the lead principal investigator on various projects funded by DoD agencies. Morris has over 196 publications in refereed journals and conference proceedings. In addition, he has also served in the Institute of Electrical and Electronics Engineers (IEEE) in various positions, including associate editor in chief of IEEE's *IT Professional* magazine (2014–2018), associate editor of the *IEEE Transactions on Reliability* journal (2022), and Program Chairs in Chief of COMPSAC 2019 (IEEE Computer Society signature conference on Computers, Software, and Applications, 2019).

DI ZHUANG is a security engineer at Snap Inc. His degrees include a bachelor of information security and a bachelor of laws from Nankai University, Tianjin, China, and a PhD in electrical engineering from the University of South Florida. He is an energetic, skilled security and privacy researcher with interest, expertise, and experience in privacy by design, differential privacy, privacy-preserving machine learning, social network science, and network security. He conducted privacy-preserving machine learning research under the DARPA Brandeis program from 2015 to 2018.

DUMINDU SAMARAWEERA is an assistant research professor at the University of South Florida. Dumindu received his BS in computer systems and networking from Curtin University, Australia; a BS in information technology from Sri Lanka Institute of Information Technology, Sri Lanka; and an MS in enterprise application development from Sheffield Hallam University, UK. He obtained his PhD in electrical engineering from the University of South Florida (USF), concentrating his research on cybersecurity and data science. His doctoral dissertation, "Security and Privacy Enhancement Technologies in the Deep Learning Era," addresses the privacy and security issues identified in today's data-driven applications and provides in-depth solutions to mitigate such problems. Over the years, he has worked with multiple large-scale US Department of Defense–funded cybersecurity research projects. Before joining USF, he worked in the industry as a software engineer/electrical engineer for more than six years, managing and deploying enterprise-level solutions.

The technical editor for this book, WILKO HENECKA, is a senior software engineer at Ambiata, building privacy-preserving software. He holds a PhD in mathematics from Adelaide University and a master's degree in IT security from Ruhr-University Bochum.

about the cover illustration

The figure on the cover of *Privacy-Preserving Machine Learning* is "Femme Acadienne," or "Acadian Woman," taken from a collection by Jacques Grasset de Saint-Sauveur, published in 1788. Each illustration is finely drawn and colored by hand.

In those days, it was easy to identify where people lived and what their trade or station in life was just by their dress. Manning celebrates the inventiveness and initiative of the computer business with book covers based on the rich diversity of regional culture centuries ago, brought back to life by pictures from collections such as this one.

Part 1

Basics of privacy-preserving machine learning with differential privacy

Part 1 covers the basics of privacy-preserving machine learning and differential privacy. Chapter 1 discusses privacy considerations in machine learning with an emphasis on the dangers of private data being exposed. Chapter 2 introduces the core concepts of differential privacy along with some widely adopted differential privacy mechanisms that serve as building blocks in various privacy-preserving algorithms and applications. Chapter 3 covers the advanced design principles of differentially private machine learning algorithms and presents a case study.

Privacy considerations in machine learning

1

This chapter covers

- The importance of privacy protection in the era of big data artificial intelligence
- Types of privacy-related threats, vulnerabilities, and attacks in machine learning
- Techniques that can be utilized in machine learning tasks to minimize or evade privacy risks and attacks

Our search queries, browsing history, purchase transactions, watched videos, and movie preferences are a few types of information that are collected and stored daily. Advances in artificial intelligence have increased the ability to capitalize on and benefit from the collection of private data.

This data collection happens within our mobile devices and computers, on the streets, and even in our own offices and homes, and the data is used by a variety of machine learning (ML) applications in different domains, such as marketing, insurance, financial services, mobility, social networks, and healthcare. For instance, more and more cloud-based data-driven ML applications are being developed by different service providers (who can be classified as the *data users*, such as Facebook, LinkedIn, and Google). Most of these applications leverage the vast amount of data collected from each individual (the *data owner*) to offer users valuable services. These services often give users some commercial or political advantage by facilitating various user recommendations, activity recognition, health monitoring, targeted advertising, or even election predictions. However, on the flip side, the same data could be repurposed to infer sensitive (private) information, which would jeopardize the privacy of individuals. Moreover, with the increased popularity of Machine Learning as a Service (MLaaS), where cloud-based ML and computing resources are bundled together to provide efficient analytical platforms (such as Microsoft Azure Machine Learning Studio, AWS Machine Learning, and Google Cloud Machine Learning Engine), it is necessary to take measures to enforce privacy on those services before they are used with sensitive datasets.

1.1 Privacy complications in the AI era

Let's first visit a real-world example of private data leakage to visualize the problem. During the Facebook–Cambridge Analytica scandal in April 2018, data from about 87 million Facebook users was collected by a Facebook quiz app (a cloud-based data-driven application) and then paired with information taken from those users' social media profiles (including their gender, age, relationship status, location, and "likes") without any privacy-preserving operations being taken other than anonymization. How did this happen?

The quiz, called "This Is Your Digital Life," was originally created by Aleksandr Kogan, a Russian psychology professor at the University of Cambridge. The quiz was designed to collect personality information, and around 270,000 people were paid to take part. However, in addition to what the quiz was created to collect, it also pulled data from the participants' friends' profiles, making a large data pile. Later, Kogan shared this information in a commercial partnership with Cambridge Analytica, which harvested personal information from this dataset, such as where users lived and what pages they liked, eventually helping Cambridge Analytica to build psychological profiles and infer certain sensitive information about each individual, such as their identity, sexual orientation, and marital status, as summarized in figure 1.1.

That was just one incident! In 2020, after another privacy scandal, Facebook agreed to pay $550 million to settle a class-action lawsuit over its use of ML-based facial recognition technology, which again raised questions about the social network's data-mining practices. The suit said the company violated an Illinois biometric privacy law by harvesting facial data for tag suggestions from the photos of millions of users in the state without their permission and without telling them how long the data would be kept. Eventually, Facebook disabled the tag-suggestion feature amid privacy concerns.

These unprecedented data leak scandals raised the alarm about privacy concerns in cloud-based data-driven applications. People began to think twice before submitting

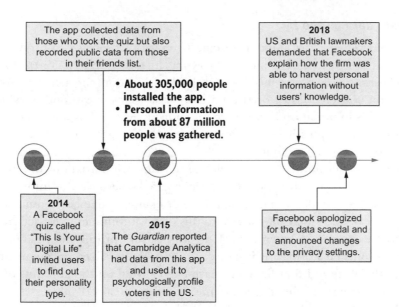

The app collected data from those who took the quiz but also recorded public data from those in their friends list.

- **About 305,000 people installed the app.**
- **Personal information from about 87 million people was gathered.**

2018
US and British lawmakers demanded that Facebook explain how the firm was able to harvest personal information without users' knowledge.

2014
A Facebook quiz called "This Is Your Digital Life" invited users to find out their personality type.

2015
The *Guardian* reported that Cambridge Analytica had data from this app and used it to psychologically profile voters in the US.

Facebook apologized for the data scandal and announced changes to the privacy settings.

Figure 1.1   The Facebook–Cambridge Analytica scandal raised the alarm about privacy concerns.

any data to cloud-based services. Thus, data privacy has become a hotter topic than ever before among academic researchers and technology companies, which have put enormous efforts into developing privacy-preserving techniques to prevent private data leaks. For instance, Google developed Randomized Aggregatable Privacy-Preserving Ordinal Response (RAPPOR), a technology for crowdsourcing statistics from end-user client software. Apple also claimed it first introduced its well-developed privacy techniques with iOS 11, for crowdsourcing statistics from iPhone users regarding emoji preferences and usage analysis. In 2021 Google introduced its privacy sandbox initiative to the Chrome web browser by replacing third-party cookies and putting boundaries around how advertising companies could interact with private data used in the browser. When people use the internet, publishers and advertisers want to provide content, including ads, that is relevant and interesting to them. People's interests are often gauged on today's web by observing what sites or pages they visit, relying on third-party cookies or less transparent and undesirable mechanisms like device fingerprinting. With this privacy sandbox initiative, Google introduced a new way to provide relevant content and ads by clustering large groups of people with similar browsing patterns, hiding individuals in the crowd and keeping their web histories on their browsers, without using third-party cookies.

1.2   *The threat of learning beyond the intended purpose*

ML can be seen as the capability of an algorithm to mimic intelligent human behavior, performing complex tasks by looking at data from different angles and analyzing it across domains. This learning process is utilized by various applications in our day-to-day life, from product recommendation systems in online web portals to sophisticated intrusion detection mechanisms in internet security applications.

1.2.1 Use of private data on the fly

ML applications require vast amounts of data from various sources to produce high confidence results. Web search queries, browsing histories, transaction histories of online purchases, movie preferences, and individual location check-ins are some of the information collected and stored on a daily basis, usually without users' knowledge. Some of this information is private to the individuals, but it is uploaded to high-end centralized servers mostly in clear-text format so ML algorithms can extract patterns and build ML models from it.

The problem is not limited to the collection of this private data by different ML applications. The data is also exposed to insider attacks because the information is available to workers at data-mining companies. For example, database administrators or application developers may have access to this data without many restrictions. This data may also be exposed to external hacking attacks, with private information being revealed to the outside world. For instance, in 2015 Twitter fired an engineer after intelligence officials found that he might have been spying on the accounts of Saudi dissidents by accessing user details such as phone numbers and IP addresses. According to the *New York Times*, the accounts belonged to security and privacy researchers, surveillance specialists, policy academics, and journalists. This incident is yet another example of how big the problem is. Most importantly, it is possible to extract additional information from private data even if it is transformed to a different embedding (anonymized), or if datasets and ML models are inaccessible and only the testing results are revealed.

1.2.2 How data is processed inside ML algorithms

To understand the relationship between data privacy and ML algorithms, knowing how ML systems work with the data they process is crucial. Typically, we can represent the input data for an ML algorithm (captured from various sources) as a set of sample values, and each sample can be a group of features. Let's take the example of a facial recognition algorithm that recognizes people when they upload an image to Facebook. Consider an image of 100×100 pixels where a single value from 0 to 255 represents each pixel. These pixels can be concatenated to form a feature vector. Each image can be represented to the ML algorithm as a vector of data, along with an associated label for that data. The ML algorithm would use multiple feature vectors and their associated labels during the training phase to produce an ML model. This model would then be used with fresh, unseen data (testing samples) to predict the result—in this case, to recognize a person.

Measuring the performance of ML models

The ability of an ML model to accurately predict the final result is a measure of how well the ML model generalizes to unseen data or to data introduced for the first time. This accuracy is usually measured empirically, and it varies depending on factors such as the number of training samples, the algorithm used to build the model, the quality of the training samples, and the selection of hyperparameters for the ML algorithm. It is equally important to preprocess the raw data before feeding it to the ML models in some applications that use different mechanisms to extract the essential features from raw data. These mechanisms may involve various techniques (such as principal component analysis) to project data to a lower dimension.

1.2.3 *Why privacy protection in ML is important*

When personal information is used for a wrong or unintended purpose, it can be manipulated to gain a competitive advantage. When massive volumes of personal records are coupled with ML algorithms, no one can predict what new results they may produce or how much private information those results may reveal. The Facebook–Cambridge Analytica scandal discussed earlier is a perfect example of the wrongful use of personal data.

Hence, when designing ML algorithms for an application, ensuring privacy protection is vital. First, it ensures that other parties (data users) cannot use the personal data for their own advantage. Second, everyone has things that they do not want others to know. For example, they may not want others to know the details of their medical history. But ML applications are data driven, and we need training samples to build a model. We want to use the private data to build a model, but we want to prevent the ML algorithm from learning anything sensitive. How can we do that?

Let's consider a scenario where we use two databases: a sanitized medical database that lists patients' histories of medication prescriptions, and another data source with user information and pharmacies visited. When these sources are linked together, the correlated database can have additional knowledge, such as which patient bought their medication from which pharmacy. Suppose we are using this correlated dataset with an ML application to extract relationships between the patients, medications, and pharmacies. While it will extract the obvious relations between different diseases and the medications prescribed, it may also learn roughly where the patient resides simply by referring to the zip codes of their most-visited pharmacies, even if the data does not contain patient addresses. This is a simple example, but you can imagine how severe the consequences could be if privacy is not protected.

1.2.4 *Regulatory requirements and the utility vs. privacy tradeoff*

Traditionally, data security and privacy requirements were set by the data owners (such as organizations) to safeguard the competitive advantage of the products and services they offered. However, in the big data era, data has become the most valuable asset in the digital economy, and governments imposed many privacy regulations to prevent the use of sensitive information beyond its intended purpose. Privacy standards such as

HIPAA (Health Insurance Portability and Accountability Act of 1996), PCI DSS (Payment Card Industry Data Security Standard), FERPA (Family Educational Rights and Privacy Act), and the European Union's GDPR (General Data Protection Regulation) are some of the privacy regulations that organizations commonly adhere to. For example, regardless of the size of practice, most healthcare providers transmit health information electronically, such as for claims, medication records, benefit eligibility inquiries, referral authorization requests, and the like. However, HIPAA regulations require that these healthcare providers protect sensitive patient health information from being disclosed without the patient's consent or knowledge.

Regardless of whether the data is labeled or not, or whether raw data is preprocessed, ML models are essentially very sophisticated statistics based on the training dataset, and ML algorithms are optimized to squeeze every bit of utility out of the data. Therefore, in most conditions, they are capable of learning sensitive attributes in the dataset, even when that is not the intended task. When we attempt to preserve privacy, we want to prevent these algorithms from learning sensitive attributes. Hence, as you can see, utility and privacy are on opposite ends of the spectrum. When you tighten privacy, it can affect the performance of the utility.

The real challenge is balancing privacy and performance in ML applications so that we can better utilize the data while ensuring the privacy of the individuals. Because of the regulatory and application-specific requirements, we cannot degrade privacy protection just to increase the utility of the application. On the other hand, privacy has to be implemented systematically without using arbitrary mechanisms, as many additional threats must be considered. ML applications are prone to different privacy and security attacks. We will explore these potential attacks in detail next and look at how we can mitigate them by designing privacy-preserving ML (PPML) algorithms.

1.3 Threats and attacks for ML systems

We discussed a few privacy leakage incidents in the previous section, but many other threats and attacks on ML systems are being proposed and discussed in the literature and could potentially be deployed in real-world scenarios. For instance, figure 1.2 is a timeline showing a list of threats and attacks for ML systems, including de-anonymization

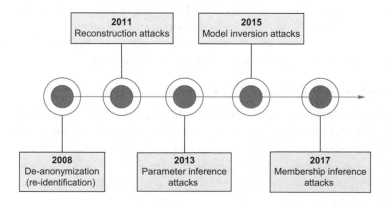

Figure 1.2 A timeline of threats and attacks identified for ML systems

(re-identification) attacks, reconstruction attacks, parameter inference attacks, model inversion attacks, and membership inference attacks. We will briefly explore the details of these threats or attacks in this section.

Although some leading companies, such as Google and Apple, started designing and utilizing their own privacy-preserving methodologies for ML tasks, it is still a challenge to improve public awareness of these privacy technologies, mainly due to the lack of well-organized tutorials and books that explain the concepts methodically and systematically.

1.3.1   The problem of private data in the clear

Figure 1.3 illustrates a typical client/server application scenario. As you can see, when an application collects private information, that information is often transferred, possibly through encrypted channels, to cloud-based servers where the learning happens. In the figure, a mobile application connects to a cloud server to perform an inference task.

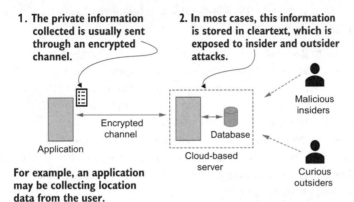

1. The private information collected is usually sent through an encrypted channel.

2. In most cases, this information is stored in cleartext, which is exposed to insider and outsider attacks.

Malicious insiders

Application

Encrypted channel

Database

Curious outsiders

Cloud-based server

For example, an application may be collecting location data from the user.

Figure 1.3   The problem of storing private data in cleartext format

For example, a parking app may send the user's location data to find a nearby available garage. Even though the communication channel is secured, the data most likely resides in the cloud in its original unencrypted form or as features extracted from the original record. This is one of the biggest challenges to privacy because that data is susceptible to various insider and outsider attacks.

1.3.2   Reconstruction attacks

As you've seen, it is essential to store private data on the server in encrypted form, and we should not send raw data directly to the server in its original form. However, reconstruction attacks pose another possible threat: the attacker could reconstruct data even without having access to the complete set of raw data on the server. In this case, the adversary gains an advantage by having external knowledge of feature vectors (the data used to build the ML model).

The adversary usually requires direct access to the ML models deployed on the server, which is referred to as white-box access (see table 1.1). They then try to reconstruct the raw private data by using their knowledge of the feature vectors in the model. These attacks are possible when the feature vectors used during the training phase to build the ML model are not flushed from the server after building the model.

Table 1.1   Difference between white-box, black-box, and grey-box access

White-box access	Black-box access	Grey-box access
Has full access to the internal details of the ML models, such as parameters and loss functions	Has no access to the internal details of the ML models	Has partial access to the internal details of the ML models

HOW RECONSTRUCTION WORKS: AN ATTACKER'S PERSPECTIVE

Now that you've had a high-level overview of how a reconstruction attack works, let's look into the details of how it is possible. The approach taken to reconstruct the data depends on what information (background knowledge) the attacker has available to reproduce the data accurately. We'll consider the following two use case examples of biometric-based authentication systems:

- *Reconstruction of fingerprint images from a minutiae template*—Nowadays, fingerprint-based authentication is prevalent in many organizations: users are authenticated by comparing a newly acquired fingerprint image with a fingerprint image already saved in the user authentication system. In general, these fingerprint-matching systems use one of four different representation schemes known as *grayscale*, *skeleton*, *phase*, and *minutiae* (figure 1.4). Minutiae-based representation is the most widely adopted due to the compactness of the representation. Because of this compactness, many people erroneously think that the minutiae template does not contain enough information for attackers to reconstruct the original fingerprint image.

  In 2011, a team of researchers successfully demonstrated an attack that could reconstruct fingerprint images directly from minutiae templates [1]. They reconstructed a phase image from minutiae, which was then converted into the original (grayscale) image. Next, they launched an attack against fingerprint recognition systems to infer private data.

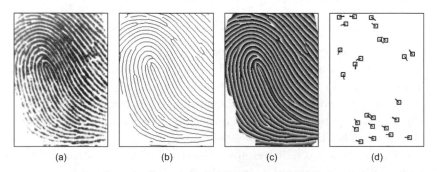

(a)   (b)   (c)   (d)

Figure 1.4   The four different types of representation schemes used in fingerprint matching systems: (a) grayscale image, (b) skeleton image, (c) phase image, and (d) minutiae

- *Reconstruction attacks against mobile-based continuous authentication systems*—Al-Rubaie et al. investigated the possibility of reconstruction attacks that used gestural raw data from users' authentication profiles in mobile-based continuous authentication systems [2]. Continuous authentication is a method of verifying the user not just once but continuously throughout an entire session (such as Face ID in iPhones). Without continuous authentication, organizations are more vulnerable to many attack vectors, such as a system being taken over when it is no longer being used but the session remains open. In such a scenario, a reconstruction attack could use available private information that is leaked to the adversary. At a high level, Al-Rubaie et al. used the feature vectors stored in user profiles to reconstruct the raw data and then used that information to hack into other systems.

In most of these cases, the privacy threat resulted from a security threat to the authentication system in which reconstructed raw data misguided the ML system by forcing it to think that the raw data belonged to a specific user. For example, in the case of mobile-based continuous authentication systems, an attacker gained access to the mobile device and its personal records; hence, the authentication mechanism failed to protect the user's privacy. Another class of reconstruction attack might reveal private information directly, as you'll see next.

A REAL-WORLD SCENARIO INVOLVING RECONSTRUCTION ATTACKS

In 2019, Simson Garfinkel and his team at the US Census Bureau presented a detailed example of how a reconstruction attack can be primed by an attacker, just utilizing data available to the public [3]. They further explained that publishing the frequency count, mean, and median age of a population, broken down by a few demographics, allows anyone with access to the statistics and a personal computer to accurately reconstruct the personal data of almost the entire survey population. This incident raised concerns about the privacy of census data. Based on this finding, the US Census Bureau conducted a series of experiments on 2010 census data. Among 8 billion statistics, 25 data points per person allowed successful reconstruction of confidential records for more than 40% of the US population.

Even though this is not directly related to ML algorithms, you can probably understand how scary the problem is. The vast amount of sensitive data published by statistical agencies each year may provide a determined attacker with more than enough information to reconstruct some or all of the target database and breach the privacy of millions of people. The US Census Bureau has identified this risk and implemented the correct measures to protect the 2020 US Census, but it is important to note that reconstruction is no longer a theoretical danger. It is real.

Now the question is, how can we prevent such attacks from succeeding? In terms of mitigating reconstruction attacks tailored for ML models, the best approach is to avoid storing explicit feature vectors inside the ML model. If the feature vectors are required to be stored (e.g., SVM requires feature vectors and metadata to be stored alongside the model), they should be inaccessible to the users of the ML model so that they are hard to reconstruct. Feature names can at least be anonymized. To mitigate reconstruction attacks targeting database or data mining operations (as in the US Census example), different and well-established data sanitization and disclosure-avoidance techniques can be used.

This discussion has just been a summary of how reconstruction attacks work. We will discuss these techniques and other mitigation strategies in more detail in the forthcoming chapters.

1.3.3 Model inversion attacks

While some ML models store explicit feature vectors, other ML algorithms (such as neural networks and ridge regression) do not keep feature vectors inside the model. In these circumstances, the adversary's knowledge is limited, but they may still have access to the ML model, as discussed in the white-box access scenario.

In another black-box access scenario, the adversary does not have direct access to the ML model: they can listen for incoming requests to an ML model when a user submits new testing samples and for responses generated by the model. In model inversion attacks, the adversary utilizes the responses generated by the ML model in a way that resembles the original feature vectors used to create the ML model [4]. Figure 1.5 illustrates how a model inversion attack works.

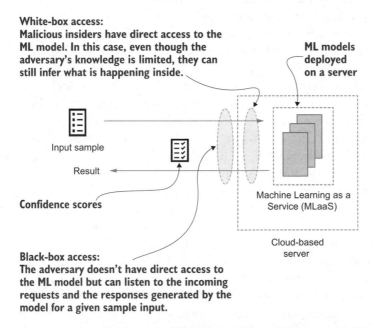

White-box access:
Malicious insiders have direct access to the ML model. In this case, even though the adversary's knowledge is limited, they can still infer what is happening inside.

ML models deployed on a server

Input sample

Result

Confidence scores

Machine Learning as a Service (MLaaS)

Cloud-based server

Black-box access:
The adversary doesn't have direct access to the ML model but can listen to the incoming requests and the responses generated by the model for a given sample input.

Figure 1.5   The difference between white-box access and black-box access. White-box access requires direct access and permission for the ML model to infer data; black-box access usually involves listening to the communication channel.

Typically, such attacks utilize the confidence values received from the ML model (such as the probability decision score) to generate feature vectors. For example, let's consider a facial recognition algorithm. When you submit a face image to the algorithm, the algorithm produces a result vector with the class and the corresponding confidence score based on the features it identifies in that image. For now, assume the result vector generated by the algorithm is

$$[John:.99, \ Simon:.73, \ Willey:.65]$$

What is the meaning of this result? The algorithm is 99% confident (the decision score) that this image belongs to John (the class) and 73% confident that it belongs to Simon, and so on.

What if the adversary can listen to all these communications? Even though they do not have the input image or know whose image it is, they can deduce that they will get a confidence score in this range if they input a similar image. By accumulating results over a certain period, the attacker can produce an average score representing a certain class in the ML model. If the class represents a single individual, as in a facial recognition algorithm, identifying the class could result in a threatening privacy breach. At the beginning of the attack, the adversary does not know who the person is, but by accumulating data over time, they will be able to identify the person, which is serious.

Therefore, the model inversion attack is a severe threat to ML-based systems. Note that in some cases, model inversion attacks can be classified as a subclass of reconstruction attacks, based on how well the features are arranged in raw data.

In mitigating model inversion attacks, limiting the adversary to black-box access is important, because it limits the adversary's knowledge. In our example of face recognition-based authentication, instead of providing the exact confidence value of a certain ML class, we could round it. Alternatively, only the final predicted class label may be returned, so that it is harder for an adversary to learn anything beyond the specific prediction.

1.3.4 *Membership inference attacks*

Whereas model inversion attacks do not try to reproduce an actual sample from the training dataset, membership inference attacks try to infer a sample based on the ML model output to identify whether it was in the original training dataset. The idea behind a membership inference attack is that given an ML model, a sample, and domain knowledge, the adversary can determine whether the sample is a member of the training dataset used to build the ML model, as shown in figure 1.6.

Let's consider an ML-based disease diagnosis system by analyzing the input medical information and conditions. For instance, suppose a patient participates in a study that diagnoses the correct difficulty level for a complex game designed to identify people who have Alzheimer's disease. If an attacker succeeds in carrying out membership inference, they will know whether this patient was in the original dataset used to build

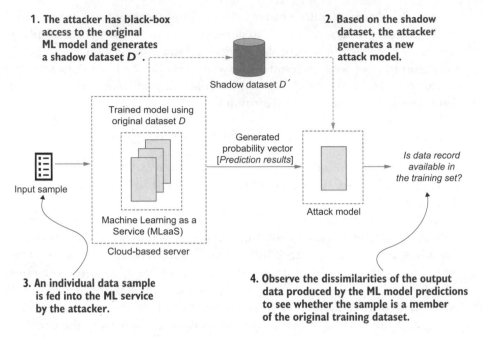

1. The attacker has black-box access to the original ML model and generates a shadow dataset D´.

2. Based on the shadow dataset, the attacker generates a new attack model.

Shadow dataset D´

Trained model using original dataset D

Generated probability vector [*Prediction results*]

Is data record available in the training set?

Input sample

Machine Learning as a Service (MLaaS)

Attack model

Cloud-based server

3. An individual data sample is fed into the ML service by the attacker.

4. Observe the dissimilarities of the output data produced by the ML model predictions to see whether the sample is a member of the original training dataset.

Figure 1.6 How membership inference attack works

the model. Not only that, by knowing the difficulty level of the game, the adversary can deduce whether this patient suffers from Alzheimer's disease. This scenario describes is a serious leakage of sensitive information that could be used later for targeted action against the patient.

How to infer the membership

In this kind of attack, the adversary intends to learn whether an individual's personal record was used to train the original ML model. To do so, the attacker first generates a secondary attack model by utilizing the model's domain knowledge. Typically, these attack models are trained using shadow models previously generated based on noisy versions of actual data, data extracted from model inversion attacks, or statistics-based synthesis. To train these shadow models, the adversary requires black- or white-box access to the original ML model and sample datasets.

With that, the attacker has access to both the ML service and the attack model. The attacker observes the dissimilarities between the output data produced by ML model predictions used during the training phase and the data not included in the training set [5], as depicted in figure 1.6. Membership inference attempts to learn whether a particular record is in the training dataset, not the dataset itself.

There are a couple of strategies for mitigating membership inference attacks, such as regularization or coarse precision of prediction values. We will discuss these regularization strategies in chapter 8. However, limiting the output of the ML model only to class labels is the most effective way of downgrading the threat. In addition, differential privacy (DP) is an effective resisting mechanism for membership inference attacks, as we'll discuss in chapter 2.

1.3.5   De-anonymization or re-identification attacks

Anonymizing datasets before releasing them to third-party users is a typical approach to protecting user privacy. In simple terms, anonymization protects private or sensitive information by erasing or changing identifiers that connect an individual to stored data. For example, you can anonymize personally identifiable information such as names, addresses, and social security numbers through a data anonymization process that retains the data but keeps the source anonymous. Some organizations employ various strategies to release only anonymized versions of their datasets for the general public's use (e.g., public voter databases, Netflix prize dataset, AOL search data, etc.). For example, Netflix published a large dataset of 500,000 Netflix subscribers with anonymized movie ratings by inviting different contestants to perform data mining and propose new algorithms to build better movie recommender systems.

However, even when data is cleared of identifiers, attacks are still possible through de-anonymization. De-anonymization techniques can easily cross-reference publicly available sources and reveal the original information. In 2008, Narayanan et al. demonstrated that even with data anonymization techniques such as k-anonymity, it is possible to infer the private information of individuals [6]. In their attack scenario, they utilized the Internet Movie Database (IMDb) as background knowledge to identify the Netflix records of known users, apparently uncovering users' political preferences. Thus, simple syntax-based anonymization cannot reliably protect data privacy against strong adversaries. We need to rely on something like differential privacy. We will discuss re-identification attacks in more detail in chapter 8.

1.3.6   Challenges of privacy protection in big data analytics

Apart from the threats and attacks tailored explicitly to ML models and frameworks, another privacy challenge arises at the opposite end of the ML and privacy spectrum. That is, how can we protect *data at rest*, such as data stored in a database system before it is fed to an ML task, and *data in transit*, where data flows through various elements in the underlying ML framework? The ongoing move toward larger and connected data reservoirs makes it more challenging for database systems and data analytics tools to protect data against privacy threats.

One of the significant privacy threats in database systems is linking different database instances to explore an individual's unique fingerprint. This type of attack can be categorized as a subclass of a re-identification attack and is most often an insider attack in terms of database applications. Based on the formation and identification of data, these attacks can be further classified into two types: correlation attacks and identification attacks.

CORRELATION ATTACKS

The ultimate purpose of a correlation attack is to find a correlation between two or more data fields in a database or set of database instances to create unique and informative data tuples. As you know, in some cases we can bring domain knowledge from external data sources into the identification process. For example, let's take a medical records database that lists user information with a history of medication prescriptions. Consider another data source with user information along with pharmacies visited. Once these sources are linked together, the correlated database can include some additional knowledge, such as which patient bought their medication from which pharmacy. Moreover, if it is smart enough to explore the frequently visited pharmacies, an adversary might obtain a rough estimate of where the patient resides. Thus, the final correlated dataset can have more private information per user than the original datasets.

IDENTIFICATION ATTACKS

While a correlation attack tries to extract more private information, an identification attack tries to identify a targeted individual by linking entries in a database instance. The idea is to explore more personal information about a particular individual for identification. We can consider this one of the most threatening types of data privacy attacks on a dataset as it affects an individual's privacy more. For example, suppose an employer looked into all the occurrences of its employees in a medical record or pharmacy customer database. That might reveal lots of additional information about the employees' medication records, medical treatments, and illnesses. Thus, this attack is an increasing threat to individual privacy.

At this point, it should be clear that we need to have sophisticated mechanisms in data analytics and ML applications to protect individuals' privacy from different targeted attacks. Using multiple layers of data anonymization and data pseudonymization techniques makes it possible to protect privacy in such a way that linking different datasets is still possible, but identifying an individual by analyzing the data records is challenging. Chapters 7 and 8 provide a comprehensive assessment of different privacy-preserving techniques, a detailed analysis of how they can be used in modern data-driven applications, and a demonstration of how you can implement them in Python.

1.4 Securing privacy while learning from data: Privacy-preserving machine learning

Many privacy-enhancing techniques concentrate on allowing multiple input parties to collaboratively train ML models without releasing the private data in its original form. This collaboration can be performed by utilizing cryptographic approaches (e.g., secure multiparty computation) or differential private data release (perturbation techniques). Differential privacy is especially effective in preventing membership inference attacks. Finally, as discussed previously, the success of model inversion and membership inference attacks can be decreased by limiting the model's prediction output (e.g., class labels only).

This section introduces several privacy-enhancing techniques at a high level to give you a general understanding of how they work. These techniques include differential privacy, local differential privacy (LDP), privacy-preserving synthetic data generation, privacy-preserving data mining techniques, and compressive privacy. Each will be expanded on later in this book.

1.4.1   Use of differential privacy

The data explosion has resulted in greatly increased amounts of data being held by individuals and entities, such as personal images, financial records, census data, and so on. However, the privacy concern is raised when this data leaves the hands of data owners and is used in some computations. The AOL search engine log attack [7] and Netflix prize contest attacks [8] demonstrate the existence of such threats and emphasize the importance of having privacy-aware ML algorithms.

Differential privacy (DP) is a promising solution for providing privacy protection for data. It attempts to protect an individual's sensitive information from any inference attacks targeting the statistics or aggregated data of the individual. Publishing only the statistics or aggregated data of multiple people in a dataset does not necessarily ensure privacy protection in many cases. Let's consider a simple retail use case with a loyalty card scenario. Suppose we have two aggregate statistics: the total amount spent by all customers on a particular day and a subgroup of that—the total amount spent by customers using a loyalty card on the same day. Suppose there is precisely one customer who purchases without a loyalty card. In that case, by simply comparing the difference between two such statistics, someone could easily infer this customer's total amount spent, based on only those aggregate statistics.

DP is based on the idea that statistics or aggregated data (including ML models) should not reveal whether an individual appears in the original dataset (the training data for the ML models). For example, given two identical datasets, one including an individual's information and the other without their information, DP ensures that the probability of generating specific statistics or aggregated values is nearly the same whether conducted on the first or the second dataset.

To be more specific, consider a trusted data curator that gathers data from multiple data owners and performs a computation on the data, such as calculating the mean value or finding the maximum or minimum value. To ensure no one can reliably infer any individual sample from the computation result, DP requires the curator to add random noise to the result, such that the released data will not change if any sample of the underlying data changes. Since no single sample can significantly affect the distribution, adversaries cannot confidently infer the information corresponding to any individual sample. Thus, a mechanism is differentially private if the computation result of the data is robust to any change in the individual samples.

Due to its underlying mechanisms, DP techniques resist membership inference attacks by adding random noise to the input data, to iterations of a particular ML algorithm, or to algorithm output. In chapters 2 and 3, we will thoroughly analyze how we can adopt differential privacy in privacy-preserving ML (PPML) applications.

1.4.2 *Local differential privacy*

When the input parties do not have enough information to train an ML model, it can be better to utilize approaches that rely on local differential privacy (LDP). For instance, multiple cancer research institutions want to build an ML model to diagnose skin lesions, but no single party has enough data to train a model. LDP is one of the solutions that they can use to train an ML model collaboratively without violating individual privacy.

In LDP, individuals send their data to the data aggregator after privatizing data by perturbation. Hence, these techniques provide plausible deniability (an adversary cannot prove that the original data exists) for individuals. The data aggregator collects all the perturbed values and estimates statistics such as the frequency of each value in the population. Compared with DP, LDP shifts the perturbation from the central site to the local data owner. It considers a scenario where there is no trusted third party and an untrustworthy data curator needs to collect data from data owners and perform certain computations. The data owners are still willing to contribute their data, but the privacy of the data must be enforced.

An old and well-known version of local privacy is a randomized response (RR), which provides plausible deniability for respondents to sensitive queries. For example, a respondent flips a fair coin:

1 If tails, the respondent answers truthfully.
2 If heads, they flip a second coin and respond "yes" if heads and "no" if tails.

An ML-oriented work, AnonML, utilized the ideas of RR to generate histograms from multiple input parties [9]. AnonML uses these histograms to create synthetic data on which an ML model can be trained. Like other LDP approaches, AnonML is a good option when no input party has enough data to build an ML model on their own (and when there is no trusted aggregator). In chapters 4 and 5, we will present a detailed analysis of how LDP differs from differential privacy and how it can be used in different ML applications.

1.4.3 *Privacy-preserving synthetic data generation*

Although many privacy-preserving techniques have been proposed and developed for all kinds of ML algorithms, sometimes data users may want to execute new ML algorithms and analysis procedures. When there is no predefined algorithm for the requested operation, data users may request data to utilize it locally. To that end, different privacy-preserving data-sharing techniques such as *k*-anonymity, *l*-diversity, *t*-closeness, and data perturbation have been proposed in the past. These techniques can be fine-tuned to generate a new anonymized dataset from the same original dataset.

However, in some cases, anonymization alone may hurt the utility of the underlying ML algorithms. Thus, a promising solution for data sharing is to generate synthetic yet representative data that can be safely shared with others.

Synthetic data is generated artificially rather than produced through real-world events at a high level. It is usually generated algorithmically and is often used as a stand-in for training and testing ML models. Nevertheless, in practice, sharing a synthetic dataset in the same format (preserving the same statistical characteristics) as the original dataset gives data users much more flexibility with minimal privacy concerns.

Different studies have investigated privacy-preserving synthetic data generation on different dimensions. For instance, *plausible deniability* is one such approach employing a privacy test after generating the synthetic data. In 2012, Hardt et al. proposed an algorithm that combines the multiplicative weights approach and an exponential mechanism for differentially private data release [10]. On the other hand, Bindschaedler et al. proposed a generative model, a probabilistic model that captures the joint distribution of features based on correlation-based feature selection [11]. In 2017, Domingo-Ferrer et al. proposed a micro-aggregation–based differential private data releasing approach, which reduces the noise required by differential privacy based on k-anonymity [12]. All in all, privacy-preserving synthetic data generation is gaining traction within the ML community.

The benefits of using synthetic data, such as reduced constraints when using sensitive data and the capability to tailor the data for certain conditions that cannot be obtained with authentic data, have already gained attention in many real-world practical use cases. In chapter 6, we will introduce different mechanisms for synthetic data generation with the goal of privacy-preserving ML.

1.4.4 Privacy-preserving data mining techniques

So far in this chapter, we have looked into different privacy protection approaches for ML algorithms. Now, let's focus on protecting privacy while engaging data mining operations. The evolving interest in advances in ML algorithms, storage, and the flow of sensitive information poses significant privacy concerns. As a result, different approaches to handling and publishing sensitive data have been proposed over the past decade.

Among privacy-preserving data mining (PPDM) techniques, the vast majority rely on either modifying data or removing some of the original content to protect privacy. The resulting quality degradation from this sanitization or transformation is the tradeoff between the quality of data and the level of privacy. Nevertheless, the basic idea behind all these PPDM techniques is to efficiently mine data while preserving the privacy of individuals. There are three main classes of techniques for dealing with PPDM, based on the different stages of data collection, publishing, and processing. Let's briefly look at these approaches.

TECHNIQUES FOR PRIVACY-PRESERVING DATA COLLECTION

The first class of PPDM techniques ensures privacy at the stage of data collection. It usually incorporates different randomization techniques at the data collection stage and generates privatized values, so original values are never stored. The most common randomization approach is to modify data by adding some noise with a known distribution. Whenever data mining algorithms are involved, the original data distribution, but not the individual values, can be reproduced. Additive and multiplicative noise approaches are two of the most common data randomization techniques in this category.

DIFFERENT APPROACHES TO DATA PUBLISHING AND PROCESSING

The second class of PPDM deals with techniques related to when data is released to third parties (published) without disclosing the ownership of sensitive information. Removing attributes that can explicitly identify an individual from a dataset is not sufficient, as users may still be identified by combining nonsensitive attributes or records. For example, consider a dataset of patient records from a hospital. We can remove the identifiable attributes, such as name and address, from this dataset before publishing it, but if someone else knows the age, gender, and zip code of a patient, they might be able to combine that information to trace the specific patient's record in the dataset, even without having access to the name attribute.

Hence, PPDM techniques usually incorporate one or more data sanitization operations, such as generalization, suppression, anatomization, and perturbation. Based on these sanitization operations, a set of privacy models can be proposed, which are now broadly used in different application domains for privacy protection. We will discuss these techniques and privacy models in chapter 7.

PROTECTING PRIVACY OF DATA MINING ALGORITHM OUTPUT

Even with only implicit access to the original dataset, outputs of data mining algorithms may reveal private information about the underlying dataset. An active adversary may access these algorithms and query data to infer some private information. Thus, different techniques have been proposed to preserve the privacy of the output of data mining algorithms:

- *Association rule hiding*—In data mining, association rule mining is a popular rule-based data mining approach to discover relationships between different variables in datasets. However, these rules sometimes may disclose an individual's private or sensitive information. The idea of association rule hiding is to mine only the nonsensitive rules, ensuring that no sensitive rule is discovered. The most straightforward approach is to perturb the entries so that all sensitive, but not nonsensitive, rules are hidden.

- *Downgrading classifier effectiveness*—As we discussed in the context of membership inference attacks, classifier applications may leak information such that an adversary can determine whether a particular record is in the training dataset. Going back to our example of an ML service for diagnosing diseases, an adversary can devise an attack to learn whether a record for a specific individual has been used to train the ML model. In such circumstances, downgrading the accuracy of the classifier is one way to preserve privacy.

- *Query auditing and restriction*—In some applications, users can query the original dataset but with limited query functionality, such as aggregate queries (SUM, AVERAGE, etc.). However, an adversary may still infer some private information by looking at the sequences of the queries and their corresponding results. Query auditing is commonly used to protect privacy in such scenarios by either perturbing the query results or denying one or more queries from a sequence of queries. On the downside, the computational complexity of this approach is much higher than that of the other approaches.

This discussion is just an overview of how PPDM works. In chapters 7 and 8, we will walk through a comprehensive analysis of PPDM techniques, as well as privacy-enhanced data management techniques in database systems.

1.4.5 Compressive privacy

Compressive privacy perturbs the data by projecting it to a lower-dimensional hyperplane via compression and dimensionality reduction techniques. Most of these transformation techniques are lossy. Liu et al. suggested that compressive privacy would strengthen the privacy protection of the sensitive data, since recovering the exact original data from a transformed version (i.e., compressed or dimensionality reduced data) would not be possible [13].

In figure 1.7, x^i is the original data, and $\tilde{x}^i$ is the corresponding transformed data—the projection of x^i on dimension U^1. We know that $\tilde{x}^i$ can be mapped back to an infinite number of points perpendicular to U^1. In other words, the possible solutions are infinite as the number of equations is less than the number of unknowns. Therefore, Liu et al. proposed applying a random matrix to reduce the dimensions of the input data. Since a random matrix might decrease the utility, other approaches used both unsupervised and supervised dimensionality reduction techniques, such as principal component analysis, discriminant component analysis, and multidimensional scaling. These techniques attempt to find the best projection matrix for utility purposes while relying on the reduced dimensionality to enhance privacy.

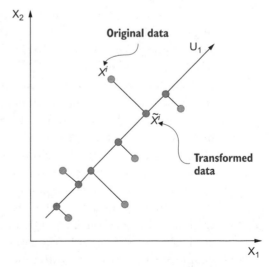

Figure 1.7 Compressive privacy works by projecting data to a lower-dimensional hyperplane.

DEFINITION   What is a lower dimensional hyperplane? In general, a hyperplane is a subspace whose dimension is one less than that of its original space. For example, in figure 1.7 the original ambient space is two-dimensional; hence, its hyperplanes are one-dimensional lines, as shown.

Compressive privacy guarantees that the original data can never be fully recovered. However, we can still obtain an approximation of the original data from the reduced dimensions. Therefore, some approaches, such as Jiang et al. [14], combine compressive privacy techniques (dimensionality reduction) with differential privacy techniques to publish differentially private data.

Although some entities may attempt to totally hide their data, compressive privacy has another benefit for privacy. For datasets that have samples with two labels—a utility label and a privacy label—Kung [15] proposes a dimensionality reduction method that enables the data owner to project their data in a way that maximizes the accuracy of learning the utility labels while decreasing the accuracy of learning the privacy labels. Although this method does not eliminate all data privacy risks, it controls the misuse of the data when the privacy target is known. Chapter 9 will walk through the different approaches to and applications of compressive privacy.

1.5   *How is this book structured?*

The forthcoming chapters of this book are structured as follows. Chapters 2 and 3 will discuss how differential privacy can be utilized in PPML, with different use case scenarios and applications. If you are interested in finding out how to use DP in practical applications, along with a set of real-world examples, these chapters have got you covered.

In chapters 4 and 5, we will walk through methods and applications of applying differential privacy in the local setup, with an added restriction so that even if an adversary has access to individual responses, they will still be unable to learn anything beyond those responses.

Chapter 6 will investigate how synthetic data generation techniques can be used in the PPML paradigm. As we already discussed, synthetic data generation is gaining traction within the ML community, especially as a stand-in for training and testing ML models. If you are interested in finding ways and means to generate synthetic data with the goal of PPML, this is your chapter.

In chapters 7 and 8, we will explore how privacy-enhancing technologies can be applied in data mining tasks and used and implemented in database systems. We know that, ultimately, everything has to be stored in a database somewhere, whether the data model is relational, NoSQL, or NewSQL. What if these databases or data mining applications are prone to privacy attacks while accessing or releasing data? These two chapters will investigate different techniques, methodologies, and well-established industry practices for mitigating such privacy leaks.

Next, we will look at another possible approach to PPML involving compressing or reducing the dimension of data by projecting it to another hyperplane. To that end, we will be discussing different compressive privacy approaches with their applications in chapter 9. If you are designing or developing privacy applications for constrained environments with compressed data, we suggest you invest more time in this chapter. We will employ practical examples of data compression techniques to achieve privacy preservation for different application scenarios.

Finally, in chapter 10 we will put everything together and design a platform for research data protection and sharing by emphasizing the design challenges and implementation considerations.

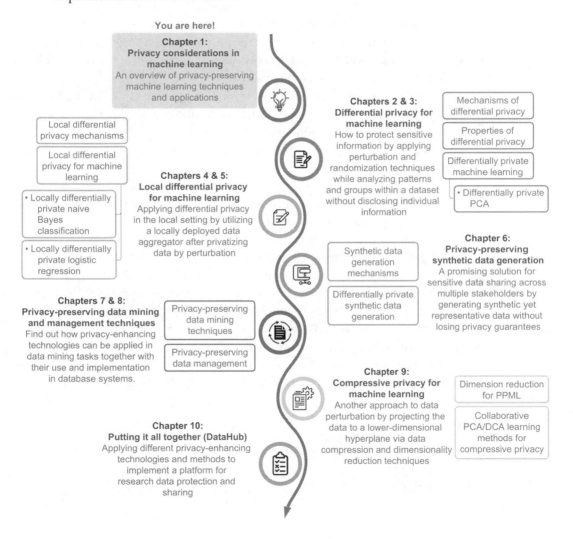

Summary

- In reconstruction attacks, the adversary gains the advantage by having external knowledge of feature vectors or the data used to build the ML model.
- Reconstruction attacks usually require direct access to the ML models deployed on the server; we call this *white-box access.*
- Sometimes an adversary can listen to both the incoming requests to an ML model, when a user submits new testing samples, and the responses generated by the model for a given sample. This can lead to model inversion attacks.
- A membership inference attack is an extended version of the model inversion attack where an adversary tries to infer a sample based on the ML model's output to identify whether the sample is in the training dataset.
- Even when datasets are anonymized, ensuring a system's ability to reliably protect data privacy is challenging because attackers can utilize background knowledge to infer data with de-anonymization or re-identification attacks.
- Linking different database instances together to explore an individual's unique fingerprint is a significant privacy threat to database systems.
- Differential privacy (DP) attempts to protect sensitive information from inference attacks targeting an individual's statistics or aggregated data by adding random noise.
- Local differential privacy (LDP) is the local setting of DP, where individuals send their data to the data aggregator after privatizing the data by perturbation, thus providing plausible deniability.
- Compressive privacy perturbs data by projecting it to a lower-dimensional hyperplane via compression and dimensionality reduction techniques.
- Synthetic data generation is a promising solution for data sharing that produces and shares a synthetic dataset in the same format as the original data, which gives much more flexibility in how data users can use the data, with no concerns about query-based budgets for privacy.
- Privacy-preserving data mining (PPDM) can be achieved using different techniques, which can be categorized into three main classes: privacy-preserving approaches to data collection, data publishing, and modifying data mining output.

Differential privacy for machine learning

This chapter covers

- What differential privacy is
- Using differential privacy mechanisms in algorithms and applications
- Implementing properties of differential privacy

In the previous chapter, we investigated various privacy-related threats and vulnerabilities in machine learning (ML) and concepts behind privacy-enhancing technologies. From now on, we will focus on the details of essential and popular privacy-enhancing technologies. The one we will discuss in this chapter and the next is *differential privacy* (DP).

Differential privacy is one of the most popular and influential privacy protection schemes used in applications today. It is based on the concept of making a dataset robust enough that any single substitution in the dataset will not reveal any private information. This is typically achieved by calculating the patterns of groups within the dataset, which we call *complex statistics*, while withholding information about individuals in the dataset.

For instance, we can consider an ML model to be complex statistics describing the distribution of its training data. Thus, differential privacy allows us to quantify the degree of privacy protection provided by an algorithm on the (private) dataset it operates on. In this chapter, we'll look at what differential privacy is and how it has been widely adopted in practical applications. You'll also learn about its various essential properties.

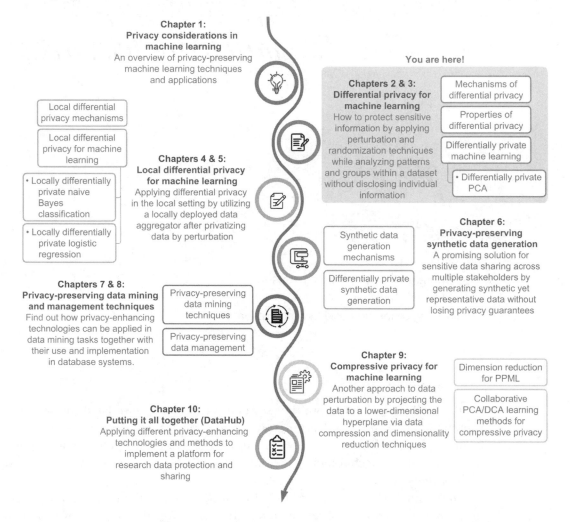

2.1   What is differential privacy?

Many modern applications generate a pile of personal data belonging to different individuals and organizations, and there are serious privacy concerns when this data leaves the hands of the data owners. For instance, the AOL search engine log data leak [1] and Netflix recommendation contest privacy lawsuit [2] show the threats and the need for rigorous privacy-enhancing techniques for ML algorithms. To address these challenges, differential privacy (DP) has evolved as a promising privacy-enhancing technique that provides a rigorous definition of privacy [3], [4].

2.1.1 The concept of differential privacy

Before introducing the definition of differential privacy, let's look at an example, which is illustrated in figure 2.1.

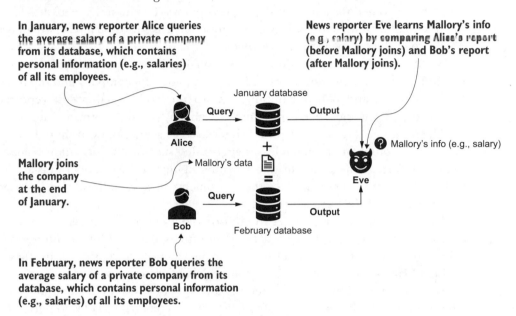

In January, news reporter Alice queries the average salary of a private company from its database, which contains personal information (e.g., salaries) of all its employees.

News reporter Eve learns Mallory's info (e.g., salary) by comparing Alice's report (before Mallory joins) and Bob's report (after Mallory joins).

Mallory joins the company at the end of January.

In February, news reporter Bob queries the average salary of a private company from its database, which contains personal information (e.g., salaries) of all its employees.

Figure 2.1   The problem of personal information leakage

Suppose Alice and Bob are news reporters from different news agencies who wanted to report on the average salary of a private company. This company has a database containing the personal information of all its employees (such as position, wages, and contacts). Since the database includes personal data subject to privacy concerns, direct access to the database is restricted. Alice and Bob were required to demonstrate that they planned to follow the company's protocols for handling personal data by undergoing confidentiality training and signing data use agreements proscribing the use and disclosure of personal information obtained from the database. The company granted Alice and Bob access to query certain aggregated statistics from the company's database, including the total number of employees and the average salaries, but not to access any personal information, such as name or age.

In January 2020, Alice wrote an article based on the information obtained from that database, reporting that the private company has 100 employees, and the average salary is $55,000. In February 2020, Bob wrote an article based on the information he obtained from the database in the same way, reporting that the private company has

101 employees, and the average salary is $56,000. The only difference is that Alice accessed the database in January, whereas Bob accessed it in February.

Eve is a news reporter working at a third news agency. After reading the articles by Alice and Bob, Eve concluded that one new employee joined the company between January and February, and that their salary is $156,000 (i.e., $56,000 × 101 − $55,000 × 100). Eve interviewed employees of the company incognito, and someone told Eve that Mallory joined the company during that period. Eve then wrote an article reporting that Mallory joined the private company and earns $156,000 a year, which is much higher than the company's average salary.

Mallory's private information (her salary) has been compromised, so she complained to the relevant authorities and planned to sue the company and the reporters. However, Alice and Bob did nothing against the policies—they just reported the aggregated information, which does not contain any personal information.

This example illustrates a typical privacy leakage scenario. Even though the study, analysis, or computation only releases aggregated statistical information from a dataset, that information can still lead to meaningful but sensitive conclusions about individuals. How can we take care of these problems in a straightforward but rigorous way? Here comes differential privacy.

Differential privacy quantifies the information leakage of an algorithm from the computation over an underlying dataset, and it has attracted lots of attention in the privacy research community. Let's consider the example in figure 2.2. In the general setting of DP, a trusted data curator gathers data from multiple data owners to form a dataset. In our previous example, the private company was the data curator, and the data owners were the employees of that company. The goal of DP is to perform some computation or analysis on this collected dataset, such as finding a mean value (e.g.,

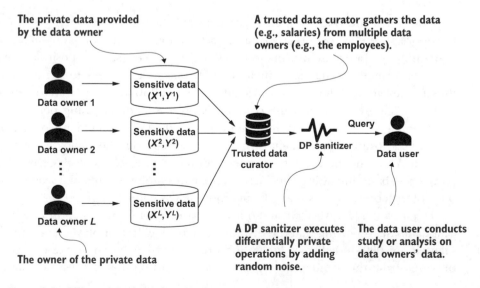

Figure 2.2   Differential privacy framework

the average salary) so that data users can access this information, without disclosing the private information of the data owners.

The beauty of DP is that it aims to strengthen the privacy protection by releasing aggregated or statistical information from a database or dataset without revealing the presence of any individual in that database. As discussed in the previous example, we can consider that the databases in January and February are identical to each other, except that the February database contains Mallory's information. DP ensures that no matter which database the analysis is conducted on, the probabilities of getting the same aggregated or statistical information or of reaching a specific conclusion are the same (as shown in figure 2.3).

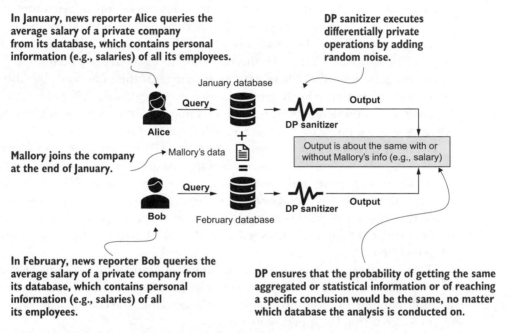

In January, news reporter Alice queries the average salary of a private company from its database, which contains personal information (e.g., salaries) of all its employees.

DP sanitizer executes differentially private operations by adding random noise.

Mallory joins the company at the end of January.

In February, news reporter Bob queries the average salary of a private company from its database, which contains personal information (e.g., salaries) of all its employees.

DP ensures that the probability of getting the same aggregated or statistical information or of reaching a specific conclusion would be the same, no matter which database the analysis is conducted on.

Figure 2.3 Using DP to protect personal data

If an individual data owner's private data won't significantly affect the calculation of certain aggregated statistical information, data owners should be less worried about sharing their data in the database, since the analysis results will not distinguish them. In a nutshell, differential privacy is about *differences*—a system is differentially private if it hardly makes any difference whether your data is in the system or not. This difference is why we use the word *differential* in the term *differential privacy*.

So far we've only discussed the general concepts of DP. Next, we'll look at how DP works in real-world scenarios.

2.1.2   *How differential privacy works*

As shown in figure 2.2, the data curator adds random noise (via a DP sanitizer) to the computation result so that the released results will not change if an individual's information in the underlying data changes. Since no single individual's information can significantly affect the distribution, adversaries cannot confidently infer that any information corresponds to any individual.

Let's look at what would have happened if our example private company had added random noise to the query results (i.e., to the total number of employees and the average salaries) before sending them to the news reporters Alice and Bob, as illustrated in figure 2.3.

In January, Alice would have written an article based on information obtained from the database (accessed in January), reporting that the private company has 103 employees (where 100 is the actual number and 3 is the added noise) and the average salary is $55,500 (where $55,000 is the real value and $500 is the added noise).

In February, Bob would have written an article in the same way (but using data accessed in February), reporting that the private company has 99 employees (where 101 is the actual number and –2 is the added noise) and the average salary is $55,600 (where $56,000 is the real value and –$400 is the added noise).

The noisy versions of the number of employees and average salary don't have much effect on the private company's information appearing in the news articles (the number of employees is around 100, and the average salary is around $55,000–$56,000). However, these results would prevent Eve from concluding that one new employee joined the private company between January and February (since 99 – 104 = –5) and from figuring out their salary, thus reducing the risk of Mallory's personal information being revealed.

This example shows how DP works by adding random noise to the aggregated data before publishing it. The next question is, how much noise should be added for each DP application? To answer this question, we'll introduce the concepts of *sensitivity* and *privacy budget* within DP applications.

THE SENSITIVITY OF DP APPLICATIONS

One of the core technical problems in DP is to determine the amount of random noise to be added to the aggregated data before publishing it. The random noise cannot come from an arbitrary random variable.

If the random noise is too small, it cannot provide enough protection for each individual's private information. For example, if Alice reported that the company has 100.1 employees (i.e., +0.1 noise) and the average salary is $55,000.10 (i.e., +$0.10 noise), while in February Bob reported that the private company has 101.2 employees (i.e., +0.2 noise) and the average salary is $55,999.90 (i.e., –$0.10 noise), Eve could still infer that one new employee had likely joined the company, and that their salary was around $155,979.90, which is virtually identical to $156,000.00, the actual value.

Similarly, the published aggregated data would be distorted and meaningless if the random noise were too large; it would provide no utility. For instance, if Alice reported that the private company has 200 employees (i.e., +100 noise) and the average salary is \$65,000 (i.e., +\$10,000 noise), while Bob reported that the company has 51 employees (i.e., −50 noise) and the average salary is \$50,000 (i.e., −\$6,000 noise), nearly none of the employees' private information would be revealed, but the reports would not provide any meaningful information about the real situation.

How can we possibly decide on the amount of random noise to be added to the aggregated data, in a meaningful and scientific way? Roughly speaking, if you have an application or analysis that needs to publish aggregated data from a dataset, the amount of random noise to be added should be proportional to the largest possible difference that one individual's private information (e.g., one row within a database table) could make to that aggregated data. In DP, we call "the largest possible difference that one individual's private information could make" the *sensitivity* of the DP application. The sensitivity usually measures the maximum possible effect that each individual's information can have on the output of the analysis.

For example, in our private company scenario, we have two aggregated datasets to be published: the total number of employees and the average salary. Since an old employee leaving or a new employee joining the company could at most make a +1 or −1 difference to the total number of employees, its sensitivity is 1. For the average salary, since different employees (having different salaries) leaving or joining the company could have different influences on the average salary, the largest possible difference would come from the employee who has the highest possible salary. Thus, the sensitivity of the average salary should be proportional to the highest salary.

It is usually difficult to calculate the exact sensitivity for an arbitrary application, and we need to estimate some sensitivities. We will discuss the mathematical definitions and sensitivity calculations for more complex scenarios in section 2.2.

THERE'S NO FREE LUNCH FOR DP: THE PRIVACY BUDGET OF DP

As you've seen, it is essential to determine the appropriate amount of random noise to add when applying DP. The random noise should be proportional to the sensitivity of the applications (mean estimation, frequency estimation, regression, classification, etc.). But "proportional" is a fuzzy word that could refer to a small proportion or a large proportion. What else should we consider when determining the amount of random noise to be added?

Let's first revisit our private company scenario, where random noise is added to the query results from the database (before and after Mallory joins the company). Ideally, when applying DP, the estimation of the average salary should remain the same regardless of whether an employee, like Mallory, leaves or joins the company. However, ensuring that the estimate is "exactly the same" would require the total salary to exclude Mallory's information for this study. However, we could continue with the same argument and exclude the personal information of every employee in the company's database. But if the estimated average salary cannot rely on any employee's information, it would be not very meaningful.

To avoid this dilemma, DP requires that the output of the analysis remain "approximately the same" but not "exactly the same" both with and without Mallory's information. In other words, DP permits a slight deviation between the output of the analyses with or without any individual's information. The permitted deviation is referred to as the *privacy budget* for DP. If you can tolerate more permitted deviation when you include or exclude an individual's data, you can tolerate more privacy leakage, and you thus have more privacy budget to spend.

The Greek letter ϵ (epsilon) is utilized to represent this privacy budget when quantifying the extent of the permitted deviation. The privacy budget ϵ is usually set by the data owners to tune the level of privacy protection required. A smaller value of ϵ results in a smaller permitted deviation (less privacy budget) and thus is associated with more robust privacy protection but less accuracy for utility. There is no free lunch with DP. For instance, we can set ϵ to 0, which permits zero privacy budget and provides perfect privacy protection meaning no privacy leakage under the definition of DP. The analysis output would always be the same no matter whose information has been added or removed. However, as we discussed previously, this also requires ignoring all the information available and thus would not provide any meaningful results. What if we set ϵ to 0.1, a small number but larger than zero? The permitted deviation with or without any individual's information would be slight, providing more robust privacy protection and enabling data users (such as news reporters) to learn something meaningful.

In practice, ϵ is usually a small number. For statistical analysis tasks such as mean or frequency estimation, ϵ is generally set between 0.001 and 1.0. For ML or deep learning tasks, ϵ is usually set somewhere between 0.1 and 10.0.

FORMULATING A DP SOLUTION FOR OUR PRIVATE COMPANY SCENARIO

You probably now have a general understanding of DP and how to derive the random noise based on the sensitivity of the application and the data owner's privacy budget. Let's see how we can apply these techniques to our previous private company example mathematically.

In figure 2.4, the private company's January database (before Mallory joined the company) is on the left, and that's what Alice queries. On the right side is the private company's February database (after Mallory joins the company), and it's what Bob queries. We want to derive differentially private solutions so the private company can share two aggregated values with the public (Alice and Bob): the total number of employees and the average salary.

Let's start with the easier task, publishing the total number of employees. First, we'll derive the sensitivity. As we've explained, it does not matter whether an employee is leaving or joining the company; the influence on the total number of employees is 1, so the sensitivity of this task is 1. Second, we need to design the random noise that will be added to the total number of employees before publishing it. As discussed previously, the amount of noise should be positively correlated to the sensitivity and negatively correlated to the privacy budget (since less privacy budget

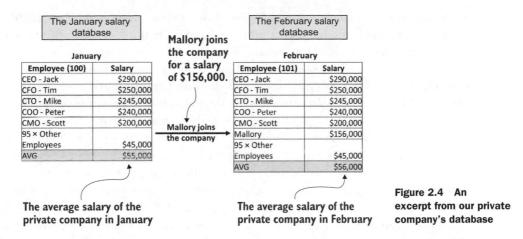

Figure 2.4 An excerpt from our private company's database

The average salary of the private company in January

The average salary of the private company in February

means stronger privacy protection, thus requiring more noise). The random noise should be proportional to $\Delta f/\epsilon$, where Δf is the sensitivity and ϵ is the privacy budget.

In this example, we could draw our random noise from the zero-mean Laplace distribution, which is a "double-sided" exponential distribution, illustrated in figure 2.5.

The Laplace distribution

The Laplace distribution (centered at μ; usually we use $\mu = 0$) with scale b is defined by the probability density function as

$$Lap(x|b) = \frac{1}{2b} \cdot e^{-\frac{|\mu - x|}{b}}$$

where the variance is $\sigma^2 = 2b^2$. We can also consider the Laplace distribution as a symmetric version of the exponential distribution.

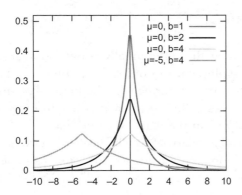

Figure 2.5 The Laplace distribution

With that, we can calculate $b = \Delta f / \epsilon$ and draw random noise from $Lap(x|\Delta f/\epsilon)$ to be added to the total number of employees. Figure 2.6 illustrates the published total number of employees for January and February while applying different privacy budgets (i.e., ϵ). Based on the definition of DP, better privacy protection usually means the numbers of employees published in January and February are closer to each other with a higher probability. In other words, the results have a lower probability of revealing Mallory's information to anyone seeing those two published values. The utility performance usually refers to the accuracy of the computations of certain aggregated data or statistics. In this case, it refers to the difference between the published perturbed value and its real value, with a lower difference meaning better utility performance. There is usually a tradeoff between privacy protection and utility performance for any data anonymization algorithm, including DP. For instance, as ϵ decreases, more noise will be added, and the difference between the two published values will be closer to each other, thus leading to stronger privacy protection. In contrast, specifying a larger value for ϵ could provide better utility but less privacy protection.

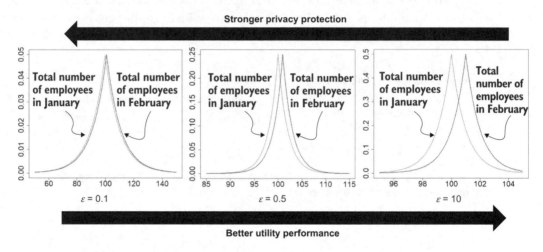

Figure 2.6   The tradeoff between privacy and utility

Now let's consider the case of publishing the differentially private average salary. Regardless of whether any individual employee leaves or joins the company, the largest possible difference should come from the employee with the highest possible salary (in this case the CEO, Jack, who makes \$290,000). For instance, in the extreme situation where there is only one employee in the database, and that happens to be the CEO, Jack, who has the highest possible salary, \$290,000, his leaving would result in the largest possible difference to the company's average salary. Hence, the sensitivity should be \$290,000. We can now follow the same procedure as we did for the total number of employees, adding random noise drawn from $Lap(x|\Delta f/\epsilon)$.

We'll look at the details of applying random noise drawn from the Laplace distribution in the next section. For more information regarding the mathematics and formal definition of DP, refer to section A.1 of the appendix.

2.2   Mechanisms of differential privacy

In the last section we introduced the definition and usage of DP. In this section we'll discuss some of the most popular mechanisms in DP, which will also become building blocks for many DP ML algorithms that we'll introduce in this book. You can also use these mechanisms in your own design and development.

We'll start with an old but simple DP mechanism—binary mechanism (randomized response).

2.2.1   Binary mechanism (randomized response)

Binary mechanism (randomized response) [5] is an approach that has long been utilized by social scientists in social science studies (since the 1970s), and it is much older than the formulation of DP. Although the randomized response is simple, it satisfies all the requirements of a DP mechanism.

Let's assume that we need to survey of a group of 100 people on whether they have used marijuana in the last 6 months. The answer collected from each individual will be either yes or no, which is considered a *binary response*. We can give the value 1 to each "yes" answer and 0 to each "no" answer. Thus, we can obtain the percentage of marijuana usage in the survey group by counting the number of 1s.

To protect the privacy of each individual, we could apply a small amount of noise to each real answer before the submitted answer is collected. Of course, we are also hoping that the added noise will not alter the final survey results. To design a differentially private solution to collect the survey data, we could use a balanced coin (i.e., $p = 0.5$) for the randomized response mechanism, which proceeds as follows and is depicted in figure 2.7:

1 Flip a balanced coin.
2 If it comes up heads, the submitted answer is the same as the real answer (0 or 1).
3 If the coin comes up tails, flip the balanced coin one more time, and answer 1 if it comes up heads and 0 if tails.

The randomization in this algorithm comes from the two coin flips. This randomization creates uncertainty about the true answer, which provides the source of privacy. In this case, each data owner has a 3/4 probability of submitting the real answer and 1/4 chance of submitting the wrong answer. For a single data owner, their privacy will be preserved, since we will never be sure whether they are telling the truth. But the data user that conducts the survey will still get the desired answers, since 3/4 of the participants are expected to tell the truth.

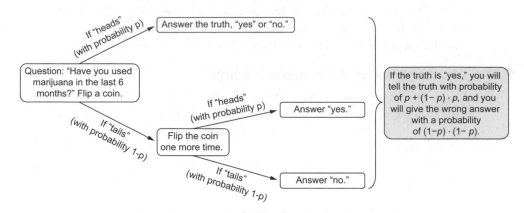

Figure 2.7   How the binary mechanism (randomized response) works

Let's revisit the definition of ϵ-DP (a more detailed and formal definition of DP can be found in section A.1). Let's say we have a simple randomized response mechanism, which we'll call M for now. This M satisfies ϵ-DP for every two neighboring databases or datasets, x, y, and for every subset $S \subseteq Range(M)$,

$$\frac{|\Pr[M(x) \in S]|}{|\Pr[M(y) \in S]|} \leq e^{\epsilon}$$

In our example with the two coin flips, the data is either 1 or 0, and the output of M is also either 1 or 0. Hence, we have the following:

$$\frac{\Pr[M(1) = 1]}{\Pr[M(0) = 1]} = \frac{\Pr[M(0) = 0]}{\Pr[M(1) = 0]} = \frac{\frac{3}{4}}{\frac{1}{4}} = 3 \leq e^{\epsilon}$$

We can deduce that our simple randomized response mechanism M satisfies $ln(3)$-DP, where $ln(3)$ is the privacy budget ($ln(3) \approx 1.099$).

The basic idea of randomized response is that, while answering a binary question, one can tell the truth with higher probability and give the false answer with lower probability. The utility can be maintained by the somewhat higher probability of telling the truth, while privacy is theoretically protected by randomizing one's response. In the previous example, we assumed that the coin is balanced. If we used an unbalanced coin, we could formulate a randomized response mechanism that satisfies other DP privacy budgets.

Based on the mechanism in figure 2.7, let's assume the coin will come up heads with probability p and come up tails with probability $(1 - p)$, where $p > 1/2$:

- Given an arbitrary survey participant, their answer will be either 0 or 1, depending on whether the participant answered truthfully with a "no" or "yes."
- The output of our randomized response mechanism M can also be either 0 or 1.

Based on the definition of DP, we have

$$\frac{\Pr[M(1)=1]}{\Pr[M(0)=1]} = \frac{p+(1-p)\cdot p}{(1-p)\cdot p} = 1 + \frac{1}{1-p} \le e^{\epsilon}$$

$$\frac{\Pr[M(0)=0]}{\Pr[M(1)=0]} = \frac{p+(1-p)\cdot(1-p)}{(1-p)\cdot(1-p)} = 1 + \frac{p}{(1-p)\cdot(1-p)} \le e^{\epsilon}$$

Then we have

$$max\left(\frac{\Pr[M(1)=1]}{\Pr[M(0)=1]}, \frac{\Pr[M(0)=0]}{\Pr[M(1)=0]}\right) = max\left(1 + \frac{1}{1-p}, 1 + \frac{p}{(1-p)\cdot(1-p)}\right) \le e^{\epsilon}$$

Since we assume $p > 1/2$, we have

$$max\left(1 + \frac{1}{1-p}, 1 + \frac{p}{(1-p)\cdot(1-p)}\right) = 1 + \frac{p}{(1-p)\cdot(1-p)} \le e^{\epsilon}$$

Therefore, the privacy budget of using an unbalanced coin is

$$ln\left[1 + \frac{p}{(1-p)\cdot(1-p)}\right] \le \epsilon$$

That is the general formulation for calculating the privacy budget for the randomized response mechanism.

Now let's try to formulate the concept with pseudocode, where x indicates the true value, and it can be either 0 or 1:

```
def randomized_response_mechanism(x, p):
    if random() < p:
        return x
    elif random() < p:
        return 1
    else:
        return 0
```

Let's take a closer look at the privacy budget of our binary mechanism while using different values for p (i.e., the probability of the coin coming up heads). Based on the preceding analysis, if $p = 0.8$, the privacy budget of our binary mechanism would be $ln(1 + 0.8/(0.2 \times 0.2))$, leading to $ln(21)$, which is 3.04. We can compare this to the earlier $p = 0.5$ example, whose privacy budget was $ln(3) = 1.099$.

As we discussed in the previous section, the privacy budget can be considered a measure of tolerance to privacy leakage. In this example, a higher p value means less noise is added (since it will generate the true answer with a higher probability), leading to more privacy leakage and a higher privacy budget. In essence, with this binary mechanism, the users can adjust the p value to accommodate their own privacy budget.

2.2.2   *Laplace mechanism*

In the binary mechanism, the privacy budget was determined by the probability of flipping a coin. In contrast, the Laplace mechanism achieves DP by adding random noise drawn from a Laplace distribution to the target queries or functions [6]. We already touched on the Laplace mechanism in the solution to our private company scenario. In this section we'll introduce the Laplace mechanism in a more systematic way and walk through some examples.

Let's go back to our private company scenario. To design a differentially private solution using the Laplace mechanism, we simply perturbed the output of the query function f (e.g., the total number of employees or the average salary) with random noise drawn from a Laplace distribution whose scale was correlated to the sensitivity of the query function f (divided by the privacy budget ϵ).

According to the design of the Laplace mechanism, given a query function $f(x)$ that returns a numerical value, the following perturbed function satisfies ϵ-DP,

$$M_L(x, f(\cdot), \epsilon) = f(x) + Lap(\tfrac{\Delta f}{\epsilon})$$

where Δf is the sensitivity of query function $f(x)$, and $Lap(\Delta f/\epsilon)$ denotes the random noise drawn from the Laplace distribution with center 0 and scale $\Delta f/\epsilon$.

We established the concept of *sensitivity* in the previous section, but let's do a refresh! Intuitively, the sensitivity of a function provides an upper bound on how much we have to perturb its output to preserve the individual's privacy. For instance, in our previous example, where the database contains all employees' salaries and the query function aims to calculate the average salary of all employees, the sensitivity of the query function should be determined by the highest salary in the database (e.g., the CEO's salary). That's because the higher the specific employee's salary, the more influence it will have on the query's output (i.e., the average salary) in the database. If we can protect the privacy of the employee with the highest salary, the privacy of the other employees is guaranteed. That's why it is important to identify the sensitivity when designing a differentially private algorithm.

Now let's explore some pseudocode that applies the Laplace mechanism:

```
def laplace_mechanism(data, f, sensitivity, epsilon):
    return f(data) + laplace(0, sensitivity/epsilon)
```

DP is typically designed and used in applications to answer specific queries. Before we go into any further detail, let's explore some query examples that could apply the Laplace mechanism.

EXAMPLE 1: DIFFERENTIALLY PRIVATE COUNTING QUERIES

Counting queries are queries of the form "How many elements in the database satisfy a given property P?" Many problems can be considered counting queries. Let's first consider a counting query regarding census data without applying DP.

In the following listing, we are calculating the number of individuals in the dataset who are more than 50 years old.

Listing 2.1 Counting query

```
import numpy as np
import matplotlib.pyplot as plt
ages_adult = np.loadtxt("https://archive.ics.uci.edu/ml/machine-learning-
  databases/adult/adult.data", usecols=0, delimiter=", ")

count = len([age for age in ages_adult if age > 50])   ⟵——— How many individuals in
print(count)                                                  the census dataset are
                                                              more than 50 years old?
```

The output will be 6,460.

Now let's look at ways to apply DP to this kind of counting query. To apply DP on this query, we first need to determine the sensitivity of the query task, which is querying the number of individuals more than 50 years old. Since any single individual leaving or joining the census dataset could change the count at most by 1, the sensitivity of this counting query task is 1. Based on our previous description of the Laplace mechanism, we can add noise drawn from $Lap(1/\epsilon)$ to each counting query before publishing it, where ϵ is the privacy specified by the data owners. We can implement the DP version of this counting query by using NumPy's `random.laplace`, as follows (using $\epsilon =$ 0.1, `loc=0` for center 0):

```
sensitivity = 1
epsilon = 0.1

count = len([i for i in ages_adult if i > 50]) + np.random.laplace
  (loc=0, scale=sensitivity/epsilon)

print(count)
```

The output is 6,472.024,453,709,334. As you can see, the result of the differentially private counting query is still close to the real value of 6,460 while using $\epsilon = 0.1$. Let's try it with a much smaller ϵ (which means it will add more noise), $\epsilon = 0.001$:

```
sensitivity = 1
epsilon = 0.001

count = len([i for i in ages_adult if i > 50]) + np.random.laplace
  (loc=0, scale=sensitivity/epsilon)

print(count)
```

The output is 7,142.911,556,855,243. As you can see, when we use $\epsilon = 0.001$, the result has more noise added to the real value (6,460).

EXAMPLE 2: DIFFERENTIALLY PRIVATE HISTOGRAM QUERIES

We can consider a histogram query to be a special case of a counting query, where the data is partitioned into disjoint cells and the query asks how many database elements lie in each of the cells. For example, suppose a data user would like to query the histogram of ages from the census data. How could we design a differentially private histogram query to study the distribution of ages without compromising the privacy of a single individual?

First, let's first explore a histogram query of ages on the census data without DP.

Listing 2.2 Histogram query without DP

```
import numpy as np
import matplotlib.pyplot as plt

ages_adult = np.loadtxt("https://archive.ics.uci.edu/ml/machine-learning-
➥ databases/adult/adult.data",
                        usecols=0, delimiter=", ")
hist, bins = np.histogram(ages_adult)
hist = hist / hist.sum()

plt.bar(bins[:-1], hist, width=(bins[1]-bins[0]) * 0.9)
plt.show()
```

We will get output similar to figure 2.8.

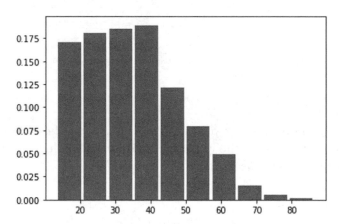

Figure 2.8   Output of the histogram query without DP

To apply DP on this histogram query, we first need to calculate the sensitivity. Since the sensitivity of a histogram query is 1 (adding or deleting the information of a single individual can change the number of elements in a cell by at most 1), the sensitivity of the histogram query task is 1. Next, we need to add noise drawn from $Lap(1/\epsilon)$ to each of the histogram cells before publishing it, where ϵ is the privacy budget specified by the data owners.

We could easily implement the DP version of this histogram query using NumPy's `random.laplace`, as in our previous example. Here we will explore an implementation using IBM's Differential Privacy Library, `diffprivlib`.

First, install `diffprivlib` and import `diffprivlib.mechanisms.Laplace`:

```
!pip install diffprivlib
from diffprivlib.mechanisms import Laplace
```

Now we can implement the DP version of the histogram query using `diffprivlib .mechanisms.Laplace`.

Listing 2.3   DP version of the histogram query

```
def histogram_laplace(sample, epsilon=1, bins=10, range=None, normed=None,
    weights=None, density=None):
  hist, bin_edges = np.histogram(sample, bins=bins, range=range,
    normed=None, weights=weights, density=None)
  dp_mech = Laplace(epsilon=1, sensitivity=1)
  dp_hist = np.zeros_like(hist)

  for i in np.arange(dp_hist.shape[0]):
    dp_hist[i] = dp_mech.randomise(int(hist[i]))

  if normed or density:
    bin_sizes = np.array(np.diff(bin_edges), float)
    return dp_hist / bin_sizes / dp_hist.sum(), bin_edges

  return dp_hist, bin_edges
```

Then the differentially private histogram query works as follows ($\epsilon = 0.01$):

```
dp_hist, dp_bins = histogram_laplace(ages_adult, epsilon=0.01)
dp_hist = dp_hist / dp_hist.sum()

plt.bar(dp_bins[:-1], dp_hist, width=(dp_bins[1] - dp_bins[0]) * 0.9)
plt.show()
```

The output will look like the right side of figure 2.9. Can you see the difference between the histogram queries before and after applying DP? Even after applying DP, the shape of the distribution is still essentially the same, isn't it?

The preceding two examples demonstrate that the most important step when applying the Laplace mechanism is to derive the appropriate sensitivity for a given application. Let's go through some exercises to learn how to determine the sensitivity of the Laplace mechanism in different situations.

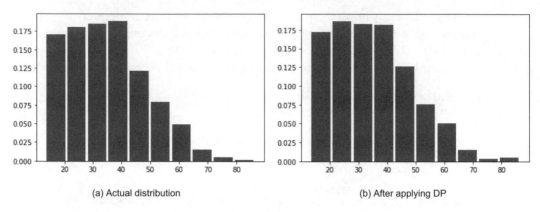

(a) Actual distribution   (b) After applying DP

Figure 2.9   Comparing the histogram queries before and after applying DP

EXERCISE 1: DIFFERENTIALLY PRIVATE FREQUENCY ESTIMATION

Suppose we have a class of students, some of whom like to play football, while others do not (see table 2.1). The teacher wants to know which of the two groups has the greatest number of students. This question can be considered a special case of the histogram query. What's the sensitivity of this application?

Table 2.1   Students who do and don't like football

Student name	Likes football
Alice	Yes
Bob	No
Eve	Yes
...	...

Hint: Every student in the class can either like football or not, so the sensitivity is 1. Based on our description of the Laplace mechanism, we can simultaneously calculate the frequency of students who like football or not by adding noise drawn from $Lap(1/\epsilon)$ to each frequency, where ϵ is the privacy budget specified by the students. You may base your solution on the following pseudocode implementation:

```
sensitivity = 1
epsilon = 0.1

frequency[0] is the number of students who like football
frequency[1] is the number of students do not like football

dp_frequency = frequency[i] + np.random.laplace(loc=0,
➡  scale=sensitivity/epsilon)
```

EXERCISE 2: MOST COMMON MEDICAL CONDITION FOR COVID-19

Suppose we wish to know which condition (among different symptoms) is approximately the most common for COVID-19 in the medical histories of a set of patients (table 2.2):

- What's the sensitivity of this application?
- If we want to generate a histogram of the medical conditions for COVID-19, what should the sensitivity be?

Table 2.2 Symptoms of COVID-19 patients

Patient	Fever	Cough	Shortness of breath	Fatigue	Headache	Sore throat	Diarrhea
Alice	X	X	X				
Bob	X	X	X		X		X
Eve	X	X		X		X	
Mallory	X		X	X		X	X
...	...	...	...	...	...	...	...

Hints:

- Since individuals can experience many conditions, the sensitivity of this set of questions can be high. However, if we only report the most common medical condition, each individual at most results in a 1 number difference. Thus, the sensitivity of the most common medical condition is still 1. We could get the ϵ-differentially private result by adding noise drawn from $Lap(1/\epsilon)$ to each output of the most common medical condition.

- What if we want to generate a histogram of the medical conditions for COVID-19? What should the sensitivity be? Since each individual could experience multiple conditions (and at most could have all the conditions), the sensitivity is much more than 1—it could be the total number of different medical conditions reported for COVID-19. Therefore, the sensitivity of the histogram of the medical conditions for COVID-19 should equal to the total number of medical conditions, which is 7, as shown in table 2.2.

2.2.3 *Exponential mechanism*

The Laplace mechanism works well for most query functions that result in numerical outputs and where adding noise to the outputs will not destroy the overall utility of the query functions. However, in certain scenarios, where the output of a query function is categorical or discrete, or where directly adding noise to the outputs would result in meaningless outcomes, the Laplace mechanism runs out of its magical power.

For example, given a query function that returns the gender of a passenger (male or female, which is categorical data), adding noise drawn from the Laplace mechanism would produce meaningless results. There are many such examples, such as the value of a bid in an auction [4], where the purpose is to optimize revenue. Even though the auction prices are real values, adding even a small amount of positive noise to the price (to protect the privacy of a bid) could destroy an evaluation of the resulting revenue.

The exponential mechanism [7] was designed for scenarios where the goal is to select the "best" response but where adding noise directly to the output of the query function would destroy the utility. As such, the exponential mechanism is the natural solution for selecting one element from a set (numerical or categorical) using DP.

Let's see how we can use the exponential mechanism to provide ϵ-DP for a query function f. Here are the steps:

1 The analyst should define a set A of all possible outputs of the query function f.
2 The analyst should design a *utility function* (a.k.a. a *score function*) H, whose input is data x and the potential output of $f(x)$, denoted as $a \in A$. The output of H is a real number. $\triangle H$ denotes the sensitivity of H.
3 Given data x, the exponential mechanism outputs the element $a \in A$ with probability proportional to $exp(\epsilon \cdot H(x, a)/(2\triangle H))$.

Let's explore some examples that could apply the exponential mechanism, so you can see how to define the utility functions and derive the sensitivities.

EXAMPLE 3: DIFFERENTIALLY PRIVATE MOST COMMON MARITAL STATUS

Suppose a data user wants to know the most common marital status in the census dataset. If you load the dataset and quickly go through the "marital-status" column, you will notice that the records include seven different categories (married-civ-spouse, divorced, never-married, separated, widowed, married-spouse-absent, married-AF-spouse).

Let's first take a look at the number of people in each category in the dataset. Before proceeding with listing 2.4, you will need to download the adult.csv file from the book's code repository found at https://github.com/nogrady/PPML/.

Listing 2.4 **Number of people in each marital status group**

```
import matplotlib.pyplot as plt
import pandas as pd
import numpy as np

adult = pd.read_csv("adult.csv")

print("Married-civ-spouse: "+ str(len([i for i in adult['marital-status']
    if i == 'Married-civ-spouse'])))
print("Never-married: "+ str(len([i for i in adult['marital-status']
    if i == 'Never-married'])))
print("Divorced: "+ str(len([i for i in adult['marital-status']
    if i == 'Divorced'])))
print("Separated: "+ str(len([i for i in adult['marital-status']
    if i == 'Separated'])))
print("Widowed: "+ str(len([i for i in adult['marital-status']
    if i == 'Widowed'])))
```

```
print("Married-spouse-absent: "+ str(len([i for i in adult['marital-
➥ status'] if i == 'Married-spouse-absent'])))
print("Married-AF-spouse: "+ str(len([i for i in adult['marital-status']
➥ if i == 'Married-AF-spouse'])))
```

The result will look like the following:

```
Married-civ-spouse: 22379
Never-married: 16117
Divorced: 6633
Separated: 1530
Widowed: 1518
Married-spouse-absent: 628
Married-AF-spouse: 37
```

As you can see, Married-civ-spouse is the most common marital status in this census dataset.

To use the exponential mechanism, we first need to design the utility function. We could design it as $H(x, a)$, which is proportional to the number of people of each marital status x, where x is one of the seven marital categories and a is the most common marital status. Thus, a marital status that includes a greater number of people should have better utility. We could implement this utility function as shown in the following code snippet:

```
adult = pd.read_csv("adult.csv")
sets = adult['marital-status'].unique()

def utility(data, sets):
    return data.value_counts()[sets]/1000
```

With that, we can move into designing a differentially private most common marital status query function using the exponential mechanism.

Listing 2.5   Number of people in each marital status group, with exponential mechanism

```
def most_common_marital_exponential(x, A, H, sensitivity, epsilon):
    utilities = [H(x, a) for a in A]          ◁──────┐ Calculate the utility for each element of A.

    probabilities = [np.exp(epsilon * utility / (2 * sensitivity))
    ➥ for utility in utilities]

    probabilities = probabilities / np.linalg.norm(probabilities, ord=1)  ◁──────┐

    return np.random.choice(A, 1, p=probabilities)[0]
```

Calculate the probability for each element, based on its utility.

Normalize the probabilities so they sum to 1.

Choose an element from A based on the probabilities.

Before using this query, we need to determine the sensitivity and the privacy budget. For the sensitivity, since adding or deleting the information of a single individual can change the utility score of any marital status by at most 1, the sensitivity should be 1. For the privacy budget, let's try ε = 1.0 first:

```
most_common_marital_exponential(adult['marital-status'], sets,
➡ utility, 1, 1)
```

As you can see, the output is Married-civ-spouse. To better illustrate the performance of most_common_marital_exponential, let's check the result after querying it 10,000 times:

```
res = [most_common_marital_exponential(adult['marital-status'], sets,
➡ utility, 1, 1) for i in range(10000)]
pd.Series(res).value_counts()
```

You will get output similar to the following:

```
Married-civ-spouse        9545
Never-married              450
Divorced                     4
Married-spouse-absent        1
```

According to these results, most_common_marital_exponential could randomize the output of the most common marital status to provide privacy protection. However, it also produces the actual result (Married-civ-spouse) with the highest probability of providing utility.

You can also check these results by using different privacy budgets. You'll observe that with a higher privacy budget, it is more likely to result in Married-civ-spouse, which is the true answer.

EXERCISE 3: DIFFERENTIALLY PRIVATE CHOICE FROM A FINITE SET

Suppose the people in a city want to vote to decide what kind of sports competition they want in the summer. Since the city's budget is limited, only one competition from four choices (football, volleyball, basketball, and swimming) is possible, as shown in table 2.3. The mayor wants to make the voting differentially private, and each person has one vote. How can we publish the voting results in a differentially private way by using the exponential mechanism?

Table 2.3 Votes for different sports

Sport	Number of votes
Football	49
Volleyball	25
Basketball	6
Swimming	2

Hint: To use the exponential mechanism, we should first decide on the utility function. We could design the utility function as $H(x, a)$, which is proportional to the number of votes for each category x, where x is one of the four sports, and a is the sport that has the highest vote. Thus, the sport that has a higher number of votes should have better utility. Then we could apply the exponential mechanism to the voting results to achieve ϵ-DP.

The pseudocode for the utility function could be defined as follows:

```
def utility(data, sets):
    return data.get(sets)
```

We can then implement the differentially private votes query function using the exponential mechanism with the following pseudocode.

Listing 2.6 Differentially private votes query

```
def votes_exponential(x, A, H, sensitivity, epsilon):
    utilities = [H(x, a) for a in A]          ◁──────┐ Calculate the utility for each element of A.

    probabilities = [np.exp(epsilon * utility / (2 * sensitivity))
        ➡ for utility in utilities]

    probabilities = probabilities / np.linalg.norm(probabilities, ord=1)  ◁──────┐

    return np.random.choice(A, 1, p=probabilities)[0]
```

Calculate the probability for each element, based on its utility.

Choose an element from A based on the probabilities.

Normalize the probabilities so they sum to 1.

As with any mechanism, we need to determine the sensitivity and the privacy budget before using this query. For the sensitivity, since each voter can only vote for one type of sport, each individual can change the utility score of any sport by at most 1. Hence, the sensitivity should be 1. For the privacy budget, let's try $\epsilon = 1.0$ first.

We could call the DP query function as shown in the following pseudocode:

```
A = ['Football', 'Volleyball', 'Basketball', 'Swimming']
X = {'Football': 49, 'Volleyball': 25, 'Basketball': 6, 'Swimming':2}
votes_exponential(X, A, utility, 1, 1)
```

Given this implementation, your results should be similar to example 3, with it outputting football (the sport with the highest votes) with a higher probability. When you use a higher privacy budget, it will be more likely to select football correctly.

In this section we've introduced the three most popular mechanisms in DP in use today, and they are the building blocks for many differentially private ML algorithms. Section A.2 of the appendix lists some more advanced mechanisms that can be utilized in special scenarios, some of which are variations on the Laplace and exponential mechanisms.

So far, with our private company example, we've designed solutions for tasks (the total number of employees, and the average salary) that will satisfy DP individually. However, these tasks are not independent of each other. Conducting both tasks at the same time (sharing both the total number of employees and the average salary) requires further analysis in terms of the DP properties. That's what we'll do next.

2.3   *Properties of differential privacy*

Thus far, you have learned the definition of DP and seen how to design a differentially private solution for a simple scenario. DP also has many valuable properties that make it a flexible and complete framework for enabling privacy-preserving data analysis on sensitive personal information. In this section we'll introduce three of the most important and commonly utilized properties for applying DP.

2.3.1   *Postprocessing property of differential privacy*

In most data analysis and ML tasks, it takes several processing steps (data collection, preprocessing, data compression, data analysis, etc.) to accomplish the whole task. When we want our data analysis and ML tasks to be differentially private, we can design our solutions within any of the processing steps. The steps that come after applying the DP mechanisms are called *postprocessing* steps.

Figure 2.10 illustrates a typical differentially private data analysis and ML scenario. First, the private data (D_1) is stored in a secure database controlled by the data owner. Before publishing any information (such as a sum, count, or model) regarding the private data, the data owner will apply the DP sanitizer (DP mechanisms that add random noise) to produce the differentially private data (D_2). The data owner could directly publish D_2 or conduct postprocessing steps to get D_3 and publish D_3 to the data user.

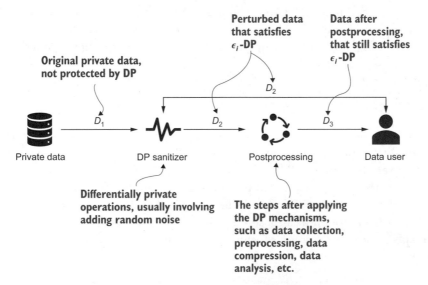

Figure 2.10   Postprocessing property of differential privacy

It is noteworthy that the postprocessing steps could actually reduce the amount of random noise added by the DP sanitizer to the private data. Let's continue to use our private company scenario as a concrete example.

As you saw earlier, the private company designed a differentially private solution for publishing its total number of employees and average salary by adding random noise drawn from Laplace distributions scaled to $\Delta f/\epsilon$, where Δf is the sensitivity and ϵ is the privacy budget. This solution perfectly satisfies the concept of DP. However, directly publishing the data after adding the random noise could lead to potential problems, since the noise drawn from the zero-mean Laplace distribution is a real number and could also be negative real numbers (with 50% probabilities). For instance, adding Laplace random noise to the total number of employees could result in non-integer numbers, such as 100 –> 100.5 (+0.5 noise), and negative numbers, such as 5 –> −1 (−6 noise), which is meaningless.

A simple and natural solution to this problem involves postprocessing by rounding negative values up to zero, and values that are larger than n can be rounded down to n (the next integer): 100.5 –> 100 (round down real value to the next integer), −1 –> 0 (round up negative value to zero).

As you can see, this postprocessing step solves the problem, but it could also reduce the amount of noise added to the private data as compared to when postprocessing was not being done. For instance, suppose y is the private data and $\bar{y}$ is the perturbed data, where $\bar{y} = y + Lap(\Delta f/\epsilon)$, and y' is the rounded up perturbed data. If y is positive due to the addition of Laplacian noise, $\bar{y}$ is negative. By rounding $\bar{y}$ up to zero (i.e., $\hat{y}' = 0$), we can clearly see that it becomes closer to the true answer so that the amount of noise added has been reduced. The same conclusion could also be reached for the case where $\bar{y}$ is a real number but greater than y.

At this point, a question could be raised: will this solution remain differentially private even after we perform the previously described postprocessing step? The short answer is yes. DP is immune to postprocessing [3], [4]. The postprocessing property guarantees that given the output of a differentially private algorithm (one that satisfies ϵ-DP), any other data analyst, without additional knowledge about the original private database or dataset, cannot come up with any postprocessing mechanism or algorithm to make the output less differentially private. To summarize: If an algorithm $M(x)$ satisfies ϵ-DP, then for any (deterministic or randomized) function $F(\cdot)$, $F(M(x))$ satisfies ϵ-DP.

Based on the postprocessing property of DP, once the sensitive data of an individual is claimed to be protected by a randomized algorithm, no other data analyst can increase its privacy loss. We can consider postprocessing techniques to be any de-noising, aggregation, data analysis, and even ML operations on the DP private data that do not directly involve the original private data.

2.3.2   *Group privacy property of differential privacy*

In our previous examples, we only discussed privacy protection or leakage for a single individual. Let's now look at an example of privacy protection or leakage that could involve a group of people.

Figure 2.11 shows a scenario where there are k scientists who collaboratively conduct a research study by sharing their results with each other. A real-world example would be the case of different cancer research institutions collaboratively working on a research study to discover a new drug. They cannot share patients' records or the formula due to privacy concerns, but they can share the sanitized results.

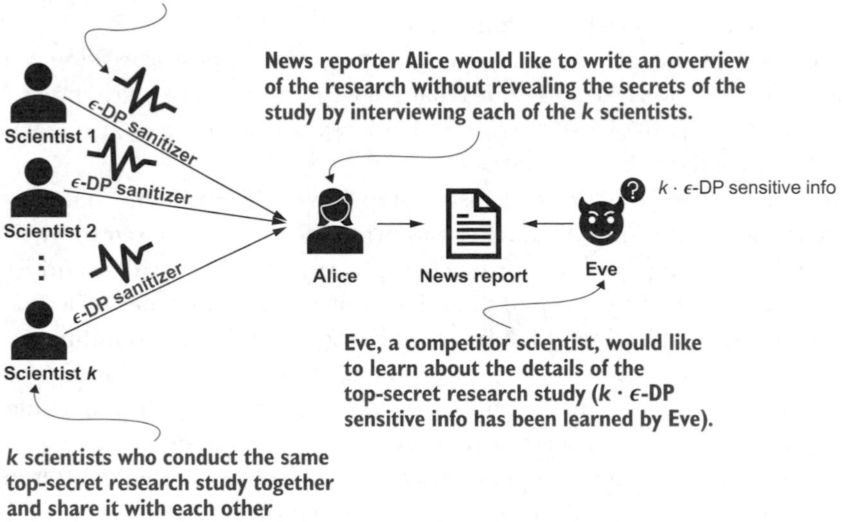

Differentially private operations, usually involving adding random noise

Scientist 1
ϵ-DP sanitizer

Scientist 2
ϵ-DP sanitizer

$\vdots$
ϵ-DP sanitizer

Scientist k

News reporter Alice would like to write an overview of the research without revealing the secrets of the study by interviewing each of the k scientists.

Alice   News report   Eve

$k \cdot \epsilon$-DP sensitive info

Eve, a competitor scientist, would like to learn about the details of the top-secret research study ($k \cdot \epsilon$-DP sensitive info has been learned by Eve).

k scientists who conduct the same top-secret research study together and share it with each other

Figure 2.11   The group privacy property of differential privacy

Now assume that news reporter Alice would like to report on the study's highlights without revealing the secrets of the study by interviewing each of the k scientists. To ensure none of the scientists reveal secrets about their research study, the scientists designed a protocol to follow while each of them is interviewed by the reporter, such that whatever information is exchanged about the research study should be sanitized by an ϵ-DP randomized mechanism.

Alice conducted the interviews with each of the k scientists and published her report. However, more recently, it was found that Eve, a competitor scientist, learned the details about the research study beyond what was exchanged with Alice just based on Alice's report. What could have happened?

Recall from the definition of DP that ϵ is the privacy budget that controls how much the output of a randomized mechanism can differ from the real-world scenario.

It can be shown that the difference between the output of the ϵ-differentially private randomized mechanism from the k scientists and the real-world scenario grows to at most a privacy budget of $k \cdot \epsilon$. Therefore, even though interviewing each scientist only cost a privacy budget of ϵ, since the k scientists share the same secret, interviewing all of them actually costs a privacy budget of $k \cdot \epsilon$. As such, the privacy guarantee degrades moderately as the size of the group increases. If k is large enough, Eve could learn everything about the research study, even though each of the k scientists follows an ϵ-differentially private randomized mechanism when answering during the interviews. A meaningful privacy guarantee can be provided to groups of individuals up to a size of about $k \approx 1/\epsilon$. However, almost no protection is guaranteed to groups of $k \approx 100/\epsilon$.

The k scientists example illustrates the group property of DP, where sometimes a group of members (such as families or employees of a company) would like to join an analytical study together, and the sensitive data might therefore have something to do with all the group members. To summarize: If algorithm $M(x)$ satisfies ϵ-DP, applying $M(x)$ to a group of k correlated individuals satisfies $k \cdot \epsilon$-DP.

The group privacy property of DP enables researchers and developers to design efficient and useful DP algorithms for a group of individuals. For instance, consider a scenario of federated learning (i.e., collaborative learning). In general, federated learning enables decentralized data owners to collaboratively learn a shared model while keeping all the training data local. In essence, the idea is to perform ML without the need to share training data. At this point, it is important to protect the privacy of each data owner who owns a group of data samples, but not each sample itself, where DP can play a big role.

2.3.3 *Composition properties of differential privacy*

Another very important and useful property of DP is its composition theorems. The rigorous mathematical design of DP enables the analysis and control of cumulative privacy loss over multiple differentially private computations. Understanding these composition properties will enable you to better design and analyze more complex DP algorithms based on simpler building blocks. There are two main composition properties, and we'll explore them next.

SEQUENTIAL COMPOSITION
In data analysis and ML, the same information (statistics, aggregated data, ML models, etc.) is usually queried multiple times. For instance, in our previous private company scenario, the total number of employees and the average salary could be queried by different people (such as Alice and Bob) multiple times. Even though random noise is added to the queried results each time, more queries will cost more privacy budget and potentially result in more privacy leakage. For instance, if Alice or Bob could gather enough noisy query results from the current (static) database, they could cancel the noise simply by calculating the average of those noisy query results, since the random noise is always drawn from the same zero mean Laplace distribution.

Therefore, we should be careful when designing a differentially private solution for private data that requires multiple sequential queries.

To illustrate the sequential composition property of DP, let's consider another scenario. Suppose Mallory's personal information (her salary) is contained in the private company's employee information database that is used by a potential business analyzer in two separate differentially private queries. The first query might be about the average salary of the company, while the second query might be about the number of people who have a salary higher than $50,000. Mallory is concerned about these two queries, because when the two results are compared (or combined), they could reveal the salaries of individuals.

The sequential composition property of DP confirms that the cumulative privacy leakage from multiple queries on data is always higher than the single query leakage. For example, if the first query's DP analysis is performed with a privacy budget of $\epsilon_1 = 0.1$, and the second has a privacy budget of $\epsilon_2 = 0.2$, the two analyses can be viewed as a single analysis with a privacy loss parameter that is potentially larger than ϵ_1 or ϵ_2 but at most $\epsilon_3 = \epsilon_1 + \epsilon_2 = 0.3$. To summarize: If algorithm $F_1(x)$ satisfies ϵ_1-DP, and $F_2(x)$ satisfies ϵ_2-DP, the sequential composition of $F_1(x)$ and $F_2(x)$ satisfies $(\epsilon_1 + \epsilon_2)$-DP.

Now let's explore an example that demonstrates the sequential composition property of DP.

EXAMPLE 4: SEQUENTIAL COMPOSITION OF DIFFERENTIALLY PRIVATE COUNTING QUERIES

Let's reconsider the scenario shown in example 1, where we wanted to determine how many individuals in the census dataset were more than 50 years old. The difference is that now we have two DP functions with different privacy budgets. Let's see what will happen after applying different DP functions sequentially.

In the following listing, we define four DP functions, where F_1 satisfies 0.1-DP ($\epsilon_1 = 0.1$), F_2 satisfies 0.2-DP ($\epsilon_2 = 0.2$), F_3 satisfies 0.3-DP ($\epsilon_3 = \epsilon_1 + \epsilon_2$), and F_{seq} is the sequential composition of F_1 and F_2.

Listing 2.7 Applying sequential composition

```
import numpy as np
import matplotlib.pyplot as plt
ages_adult = np.loadtxt("https://archive.ics.uci.edu/ml/machine-learning-
   databases/adult/adult.data", usecols=0, delimiter=", ")

sensitivity = 1
epsilon1 = 0.1
epsilon2 = 0.2
epsilon3 = epsilon1 + epsilon2

def F1(x):                                                          Satisfies
    return x+np.random.laplace(loc=0, scale=sensitivity/epsilon1)   0.1-DP

def F2(x):                                                          Satisfies
    return x+np.random.laplace(loc=0, scale=sensitivity/epsilon2)   0.2-DP
```

```
def F3(x):                                                              Satisfies
    return x+np.random.laplace(loc=0, scale=sensitivity/epsilon3)       0.3-DP

def F_seq(x):             The sequential composition
    return (F1(x)+F2(x))/2    of F1 and F2
```

Now, given that *x* is the real value of "how many individuals in the census dataset are more than 50 years old?" let's compare the output of F_1, F_2, and F_3:

```
x = len([i for i in ages_adult if i > 50])                        Plot F1            Plot F2
                                                                            (should look
plt.hist([F1(x) for i in range(1000)], bins=50, label='F1');  ⟵              the same)

plt.hist([F2(x) for i in range(1000)], bins=50, alpha=.7, label='F2');  ⟵

plt.hist([F3(x) for i in range(1000)], bins=50, alpha=.7, label='F3');  ⟵

plt.legend();                                                  Plot F3 (should look the same)
```

In figure 2.12 you can see that the distribution of outputs from F_3 looks "sharper" than that of F_1 and F_2 because F_3 has a higher privacy budget (ϵ) that indicates more privacy leakage and thus a higher probability of outputting results close to the true answer (6,460).

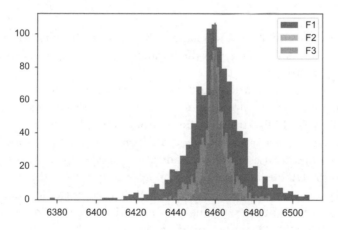

Figure 2.12   Output of sequential composition of differentially private counting queries

Now let's compare the output of F_3 and F_{seq}, as shown in the following code snippet:

```
plt.hist([F_seq(x) for i in range(1000)], bins=50, alpha=.7,
⇨ label='F_seq');          ⟵
                                 Plot F_seq                              Plot F3
plt.hist([F3(x) for i in range(1000)], bins=50, alpha=.7, label='F3');  ⟵

plt.legend();
```

As you can see in figure 2.13, the output of F_3 and F_{seq} are about the same, which demonstrates the sequential composition property of DP. But it is noteworthy that the sequential composition only defines an upper bound on the total ϵ of the sequential composition of several DP functions (i.e., the worst-case privacy leakage). The actual cumulative effect on the privacy might be lower. For more information regarding the mathematical theory of the sequential composition of DP, see section A.3.

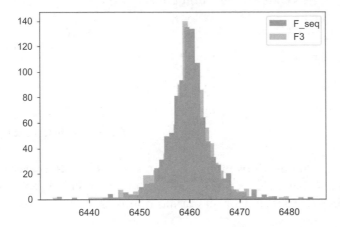

Figure 2.13   Comparing the distribution of outputs F_3 and F_{seq}

PARALLEL COMPOSITION

At this point, an obvious question is what will happen if someone combines several different DP algorithms in parallel. To illustrate the parallel composition property of DP, consider the following scenario.

Suppose company A maintains a database of its employees' salary information. Alice wants to learn the number of employees at company A whose salaries are higher than $150,000, while Bob would like to study the number of employees at company A whose salaries are less than $20,000. To meet the company's privacy protection requirements, Alice is asked to use ϵ_1-DP mechanisms to access the database, while Bob is required to apply ϵ_2-DP mechanisms to get the information from the same database. What's the total privacy leakage from Alice's and Bob's access to the database?

Since the employees whose salaries are higher than $150,000 and the employees whose salaries are less than $20,000 are two disjoint sets of individuals, releasing both sets of information will not cause any privacy leakage for the same employee twice. For instance, if $\epsilon_1 = 0.1$ and $\epsilon_2 = 0.2$, per the parallel composition property of DP, Alice's and Bob's accesses to the database utilize a total of $\epsilon_3 = max(\epsilon_1, \epsilon_2) = 0.2$ privacy budget.

To summarize: If algorithm $F_1(x_1)$ satisfies ϵ_1-DP, and $F_2(x_2)$ satisfies ϵ_2-DP, where (x_1, x_2) is a nonoverlapping partition of the whole dataset x, the parallel composition of $F_1(x_1)$ and $F_2(x_2)$ satisfies $max(\epsilon_1,\epsilon_2)$-DP. $max(\epsilon_1,\epsilon_2)$ defines an upper bound on the total ϵ of parallel composition of several DP functions (i.e., the worst-case privacy leakage); the actual cumulative effect on the privacy might be lower. For more information regarding the mathematical theory behind parallel composition of DP, see section A.4.

The sequential and parallel composition properties of DP are considered inherent properties of DP, where the data aggregator does not need to make any special effort to calculate the privacy bound while composing multiple DP algorithms. Such composition properties of DP enable researchers and developers to focus more on the design of simpler differentially private building blocks (i.e., mechanisms), and a combination of those simpler building blocks can be used directly to solve much more complex problems.

Summary

- DP is a promising and popular privacy-enhancing technique that provides a rigorous definition of privacy.
- DP aims to strengthen privacy protection by releasing the aggregated or statistical information of a database or dataset without revealing the presence of any individual in that database.
- The sensitivity usually measures the maximum possible effect of each individual's information on the output of the analysis.
- The privacy budget ϵ is usually set by the data owners to tune the level of privacy protection required.
- DP can be implemented by perturbing the aggregation or statistics of the sensitive information using different DP mechanisms.
- In the binary mechanism, randomization comes from the binary response (the coin flip), which helps to perturb the results.
- The Laplace mechanism achieves DP by adding random noise drawn from a Laplace distribution to the target queries or functions.
- The exponential mechanism helps cater for scenarios where the utility is to select the best response but where adding noise directly to the output of the query function would fully destroy the utility.
- DP is immune to postprocessing: once the sensitive data of an individual's DP is claimed to be protected by a randomized algorithm, no other data analyst can increase its privacy loss without involving information about the original sensitive data.
- DP can be applied to analyze and control the privacy loss coming from groups, such as families and organizations.
- DP also has sequential and parallel composition properties that enable the design and analysis of complex differentially private algorithms from simpler differentially private building blocks.

Advanced concepts of differential privacy for machine learning

This chapter covers

- Design principles of differentially private machine learning algorithms
- Designing and implementing differentially private supervised learning algorithms
- Designing and implementing differentially private unsupervised learning algorithms
- Walking through designing and analyzing a differentially private machine learning algorithm

In the previous chapter we investigated the definition and general use of differential privacy (DP) and the properties of differential privacy that work under different scenarios (the postprocessing property, group property, and composition properties). We also looked into common and widely adopted DP mechanisms that have served as essential building blocks in various privacy-preserving algorithms and applications. This chapter will walk through how you can use those building blocks to design and implement multiple differentially private ML algorithms and how you can apply such algorithms in real-world scenarios.

3.1 *Applying differential privacy in machine learning*

In chapter 2 we investigated different DP mechanisms and their properties. This chapter will showcase how you can use those DP mechanisms to design and implement various differentially private ML algorithms.

As shown in figure 3.1, we are considering a two-party ML training scenario with a data owner and a data user. The data owner provides the private data, which is the input or the training data. Usually, the training data will go through a data preprocessing stage to clean the data and remove any noise. The data user will then perform a specific ML algorithm (regression, classification, clustering, etc.) on this personal data to train and produce an ML model, which is the output.

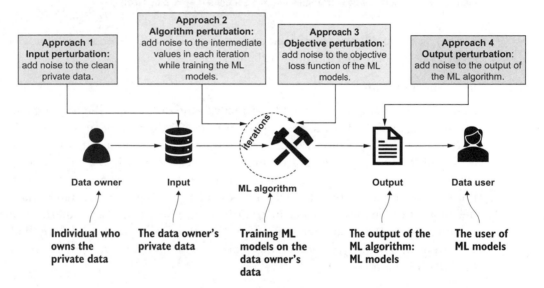

Figure 3.1 The design principles of differentially private ML

As we all know, DP has received growing attention over the last decade. As a result, various differentially private ML algorithms have been proposed, designed, and implemented by both industrial and academic researchers. DP can be applied to prevent data users from inferencing the private data by analyzing the ML model. As depicted in figure 3.1, the perturbation can be applied at different steps in the ML process to provide DP guarantees. For instance, the input perturbation approach adds noise directly to the clean private data or during the data preprocessing stage. The algorithm perturbation approach adds noise during the training of ML models. The objective perturbation approach adds noise to the objective loss functions of the ML model. Finally, output perturbation adds noise directly to the trained ML model that is the output of the ML algorithms.

Figure 3.2 identifies a set of popular perturbation strategies applied in ML algorithms as examples presented in this chapter. Of course, there are other possible examples out there, but we will stick to these methods, and we will discuss these perturbation approaches in detail in the next section.

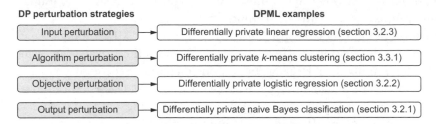

Figure 3.2   DP perturbation strategies and the sections they're discussed in

Let's walk through these four common design principles for differentially private ML algorithms, starting with input perturbation.

3.1.1   *Input perturbation*

In input perturbation, noise is added directly to the input data (the training data), as shown in figure 3.3. After the desired non-private ML algorithm computation (the ML training procedure) is performed on the sanitized data, the output (the ML model) will be differentially private. For example, consider the principal component analysis (PCA) ML algorithm. Its input is the covariance matrix of the private data, and its output is a projection matrix (the output model of PCA). Before performing the Eigen-decomposition on the covariance matrix (the input), we can add a symmetric Gaussian noise matrix to the covariance matrix [1]. Now the output will be a differentially private projection matrix (remember, the goal here is not releasing the projected data but the DP-projection matrix).

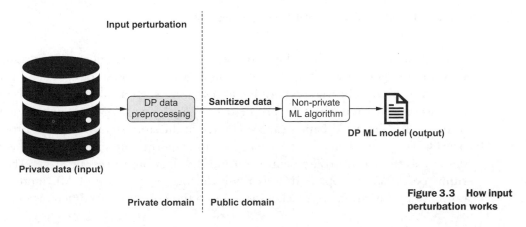

Figure 3.3   How input perturbation works

Input perturbation is easy to implement and can be used to produce a sanitized dataset that can be applied to different kinds of ML algorithms. Since this approach focuses on perturbing the input data to ML models, the same procedure can be generalized to many different ML algorithms. For instance, the perturbed covariance matrix can also be the input for many different component analysis algorithms, such as PCA, linear discriminant analysis (LDA), and multiple discriminant analysis (MDA). In addition, most DP mechanisms can be utilized in input perturbation approaches, depending on the properties of the input data.

However, input perturbation usually requires adding more noise to the ML input data, since the raw input data usually has a higher sensitivity. As discussed in chapter 2, sensitivity in DP is the largest possible difference that one individual's private information could make. Data with a higher sensitivity requires us to add more noise to provide the same level of privacy guarantee. In section 3.2.3, we'll discuss differentially private linear regression to show you how input perturbation can be utilized when designing DP ML algorithms.

3.1.2 Algorithm perturbation

With algorithm perturbation, the private data is input to the ML algorithm (possibly after non-private data preprocessing procedures), and then DP mechanisms are employed to generate the corresponding sanitized models (see figure 3.4). For ML algorithms that need several iterations or multiple steps, DP mechanisms can be used to perturb the intermediate values (i.e., the model parameters) in each iteration or step. For instance, Eigen-decomposition for PCA can be performed using the power iteration method, which is an iterative algorithm. In the noisy power method, Gaussian noise can be added in each iteration of the algorithm, which operates on the non-perturbed covariance matrix (i.e., the input), leading to DP PCA [2]. Similarly, Abadi proposed a DP deep learning system that modifies the stochastic gradient descent algorithm to have Gaussian noise added in each of its iterations [3].

As you can see, algorithm perturbation approaches are usually applied to ML models that need several iterations or multiple steps, such as linear regression, logistic

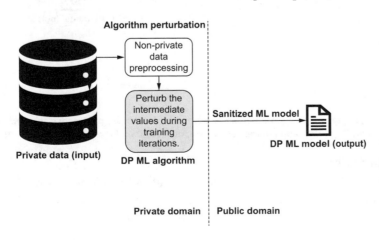

Figure 3.4 How algorithm perturbation works: Input is private data. Then we preprocess the data (non-private). Next, we perturb the intermediate values during training iterations inside the ML algorithm. Finally, we have a DP ML model.

regression, and deep neural networks. Compared with input perturbation, algorithm perturbation requires a specific design for different ML algorithms. However, it usually introduces less noise while using the same DP privacy budget, since the intermediate values in the training ML models generally have less sensitivity than the raw input data. Less noise usually leads to better utility of the DP ML models. In section 3.3.1 we'll introduce differentially private k-means clustering to discuss further how to utilize algorithm perturbation in the design of DP ML.

3.1.3 Output perturbation

With output perturbation we use a non-private learning algorithm and then add noise to the generated model, as depicted in figure 3.5. For instance, we could achieve DP PCA by sanitizing the projection matrix produced by the PCA algorithm by using an exponential mechanism (i.e., by sampling a random k-dimensional subspace that approximates the top k PCA subspace).

In general, output perturbation approaches are usually applied to ML algorithms that produce complex statistics as their ML models. For example, feature extraction and dimensionality reduction algorithms typically publish the extracted features. Thus, using a projection matrix for dimensionality reduction is a suitable scenario for using output perturbation. However, many supervised ML algorithms that require releasing the model and interacting with the testing data multiple times, such as linear regression, logistic regression, and support vector machines, are not suitable for output perturbation. In section 3.2.1 we'll walk through differentially private naive Bayes classification to discuss further how we can utilize output perturbation in DP ML.

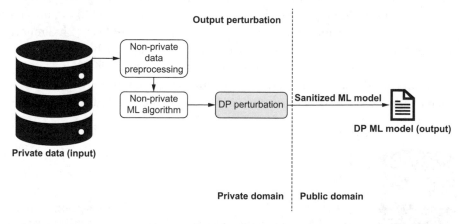

Figure 3.5   How output perturbation works: Input is private data. Then we preprocess the data (non-private). Next, we apply DP perturbation to the non-private ML algorithm. Finally, we have a DP ML model.

3.1.4 Objective perturbation

As shown in figure 3.6, objective perturbation entails adding noise to the objective function for learning algorithms, such as empirical risk minimization, that use the minimum/maximum of the noisy function as the output model. The core idea of

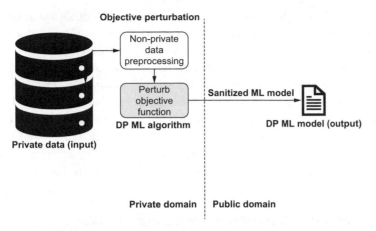

Figure 3.6 How objective perturbation works: The input is private data. Then we preprocess the data (non-private). Next, we perturb the objective function of the ML model during the training. Finally, we have a DP ML model.

empirical risk minimization is that we cannot know exactly how well an algorithm will work with actual data because we don't know the true distribution of the data that the algorithm will work on. However, we can measure its performance on a known set of training data, and we call this measurement the *empirical risk*. As such, in objective perturbation, a vector mechanism can be designed to accommodate noise addition. To learn more about exactly how to do that, refer to section A.2.

What is an objective function?

In mathematical optimization, an objective function attempts to maximize the cost (or minimize the losses) based on a set of constraints and the relationship between one or more decision variables. Typically, a loss function (or cost function) maps values of one or more variables to a real number (a numeric value) that then can be represented as the "cost" associated with the event. In practice, it could be the cost of a project, the profit margin, or even the quantity of a production line. With the objective function, we are trying to arrive at a target for output, profit, resource use, and the like.

In mathematical terms, the objective function can be represented like this.

$$Minimize\ or\ Maximize = \sum_{i=1}^{n} c_i X_i$$

Consider the example of maximizing the profit of a product where we have n number of variables that could directly affect the profit. In this formula, X_i is the ith variable among those variables, and c_i is the coefficient of the ith variable. What we want to achieve here is to determine the best setting for these variables in attempting to arrive at maximum profit.

As you'll know, a *sample space* is the set of all possible outcomes of an event or experiment. A real-world sample space can sometimes include both bounded values (values that lie within a specific range) and unbounded values covering an infinite set of possible outcomes. However, most perturbation mechanisms assume a bounded sample space. When the sample space is unbounded, it leads to unbounded sensitivity, resulting in unbounded noise addition. Hence, if the sample space is unbounded, we can assume that the value of each sample will be truncated in the preprocessing stage, and the truncation rule is independent of the private data. For instance, we could use common knowledge or extra domain knowledge to decide on the truncation rule. In section 3.2.2 we'll discuss differentially private logistic regression and objective perturbation in DP ML.

3.2   Differentially private supervised learning algorithms

Supervised learning employs labeled data where each feature vector is associated with an output value that might be a class label (classification) or a continuous value (regression). The labeled data is used to build models that can predict the labels of new feature vectors (during the testing phase). With classification, the samples usually belong to two or more classes, and the objective of the ML algorithm is to determine which class the new sample belongs to. Some algorithms might achieve that by finding a separating hyperplane between the different classes. An example application is face recognition, where a face image can be tested to ascertain that it belongs to a particular person.

Multiple classification algorithms can be used for each of the previously mentioned applications, such as support vector machines (SVMs), neural networks, or logistic regression. When a sample label is a continuous value (also referred to as a dependent or response variable) rather than a discrete one, the task is called regression. The samples are formed of features that are also called independent variables. The target of regression is fitting a predictive model (such as a line) to an observed dataset such that the distances between the observed data points and the line are minimized. An example of this would be estimating the price of a house based on its location, zip code, and number of rooms.

In the following subsections, we'll formulate the DP design of the three most common supervised learning algorithms: naive Bayes classification, logistic regression, and linear regression.

3.2.1   Differentially private naive Bayes classification

First, let's look into how differentially private naive Bayes classification works, along with some mathematical explanations.

NAIVE BAYES CLASSIFICATION

In probability theory, Bayes' theorem describes the probability of an event based on prior knowledge of conditions that might be related to the event. It is stated as follows:

$$P(A|B) = \frac{P(B|A) \times P(A)}{P(B)}$$

- *A* and *B* are the events.
- *P(A|B)* is the probability of *A*, given *B* is true.
- *P(B|A)* is the probability of *B*, given *A* is true.
- *P(A)* and *P(B)* are the independent probabilities of *A* and *B*.

The naive Bayes classification technique uses Bayes' theorem and the assumption of independence between every pair of features.

First, let the instance to be classified be the *n*-dimensional vector $X = [x_1, x_2,...,x_n]$, the names of the features be $[F_1, F_2,...,F_n]$, and the possible classes that can be assigned to the instance be $C = [c_1, c_2,...,c_n]$.

The naive Bayes classifier assigns the instance *X* to the class F_S if and only if $P(C_s|X) > P(C_j|X)$ for $1 \leq j \leq k$ and $j \neq s$. Hence, the classifier needs to compute $P(C_j | X)$ for all classes and compare these probabilities.

We know that when using Bayes' theorem, the probability $P(C_j|X)$ can be calculated as

$$P(C_j|X) = \frac{P(X|C_j) \times P(C_j)}{P(X)}$$

Since $P(X)$ is the same for all classes, it is sufficient to find the class with the maximum $P(X| C_j) \cdot P(C_j)$. Assuming the independence of features, that class is equal to $P(C_j) \cdot \prod_{i=1}^{n} P(F_i = x_i|C_j)$. Hence, the probability of assigning C_j to the given instance *X* is proportional to $P(C_1) \cdot \prod_{i=1}^{3} P(F_i = x_i|C_1)$.

That's the mathematical background of naive Bayes classification for now. Next, we'll demonstrate how to apply naive Bayes for discrete and continuous data with examples.

DISCRETE NAIVE BAYES

To demonstrate the concept of the naive Bayes classifier for discrete (categorical) data, let's use the dataset in table 3.1.

Table 3.1 **This is an extract from a dataset of mortgage payments. Age, income, and gender are the independent variables, whereas missed payment represents the dependent variable for the prediction task.**

Number	Age	Income	Gender	Missed payment (yes or no)
1	Young	Low	Male	Yes
2	Young	High	Female	Yes
3	Medium	High	Male	No
4	Old	Medium	Male	No

Table 3.1   This is an extract from a dataset of mortgage payments. Age, income, and gender are the independent variables, whereas missed payment represents the dependent variable for the prediction task. *(continued)*

Number	Age	Income	Gender	Missed payment (yes or no)
5	Old	High	Male	No
6	Old	Low	Female	Yes
7	Medium	Low	Female	No
8	Medium	Medium	Male	Yes
9	Young	Low	Male	No
10	Old	High	Female	No

In this example, the classification task is predicting whether a customer will miss a mortgage payment or not. Hence, there are two classes, C_1 and C_2, representing missing a payment or not, respectively. $P(C_1) = 4/10$ and $P(C_2) = 6/10$. In addition, conditional probabilities for the age feature are shown in figure 3.7. We can similarly calculate conditional probabilities for the other features.

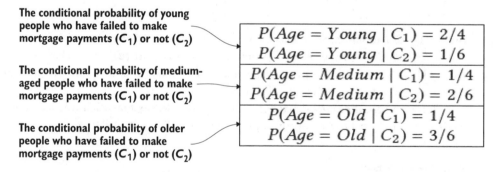

The conditional probability of young people who have failed to make mortgage payments (C_1) or not (C_2)

The conditional probability of medium-aged people who have failed to make mortgage payments (C_1) or not (C_2)

The conditional probability of older people who have failed to make mortgage payments (C_1) or not (C_2)

$$P(Age = Young \mid C_1) = 2/4$$
$$P(Age = Young \mid C_2) = 1/6$$
$$P(Age = Medium \mid C_1) = 1/4$$
$$P(Age = Medium \mid C_2) = 2/6$$
$$P(Age = Old \mid C_1) = 1/4$$
$$P(Age = Old \mid C_2) = 3/6$$

Figure 3.7   Conditional probabilities for F_1 (i.e., age) in the example dataset

To predict whether a young female with medium income will miss a payment or not, we can set $X = (Age = Young, Income = Medium, Gender = Female)$. Then, using the calculated results from the raw data in table 3.1, we will have $P(Age = Young|C_1) = 2/4$, $P(Income = Medium|C_1) = 1/4$, $P(Gender = Female|C_1) = 2/4$, $P(Age = Young|C_2) = 1/6$, $P(Income = Medium|C_2) = 1/6$, $P(Gender = Female|C_2) = 2/6$, $P(C_1) = 4/10$, and $P(C_2) = 6/10$.

To use the naive Bayes classifier, we need to compare $P(C_1) \cdot \prod_{i=1}^{3} P(F_i = x_i|C_1)$ and $P(C_2) \cdot \prod_{i=1}^{3} P(F_i = x_i|C_2)$. Since the first is equal to 0.025 (i.e., $4/10 \times 2/4 \times 1/4 \times 2/4 = 0.025$) and the second is equal to 0.0056 (i.e., $6/10 \times 1/6 \times 1/6 \times 2/6 = 0.0056$), it can be determined that is assigned for the instance X by the naive Bayes classifier. In other words, it can be predicted that a young female with medium income will miss her payments.

GAUSSIAN NAIVE BAYES

When it comes to continuous data (with infinite possible values between any two numerical data points), a common approach is to assume that the values are distributed according to Gaussian distribution. Then we can compute the conditional probabilities using the *mean* and the *variance* of the values.

Let's assume a feature F_i has a continuous domain. For each class $C_j \in C$, the mean $\mu_{i,j}$ and the variance $\sigma_{i,j}^2$ of the values of F_i in the training set are computed. Then, for the given instance X, the conditional probability $P(F_i = x_i \mid C_j)$ is computed using Gaussian distribution as follows:

$$P(F_i = x_i | C_j) = \frac{1}{\sqrt{2\pi\sigma_{i,j}^2}} e^{-\frac{(x_i - \mu_{i,j})^2}{2\sigma_{i,j}^2}}$$

You might have noticed that with discrete naive Bayes, the accuracy may reduce in large discrete domains because of the high number of values not seen in the training set. However, Gaussian naive Bayes can be used for features with large discrete domains as well.

IMPLEMENTING DIFFERENTIALLY PRIVATE NAIVE BAYES CLASSIFICATION

Now, let's look into how we can make naive Bayes classification differentially private. This design follows an output perturbation strategy [4], where the sensitivity of the naive Bayes model parameters is derived and the Laplace mechanism (i.e., adding Laplacian noise) is then directly applied to the model parameters (as described in section 2.2.2).

First, we need to formulate the sensitivity of the model parameters. Discrete and Gaussian naive Bayes model parameters have different sensitivities. In discrete naive Bayes, the model parameters are the probabilities

$$P(F_i = x_i | C_j) = \frac{n_{i,j}}{n}$$

where n is the total number of training samples where $C = C_j$, and $n_{i,j}$ is the number of such training samples that also have $F_i = x_i$.

Thus, the DP noise could be added to the number of training samples (i.e., $n_{i,j}$). We can see that whether we add or delete a new record, the difference of $n_{i,j}$ is always 1. Therefore, for discrete naive Bayes, the sensitivity of each model parameter $n_{i,j}$ is 1 (for all feature values $F_i = x_i$ and class values C_j).

For Gaussian naive Bayes, the model parameter $P(F_i = x_i \mid C_j)$ depends on the mean $\mu_{i,j}$ and the variance $\sigma_{i,j}^2$, so we need to figure out the sensitivity of these means and variances. Suppose the values of feature F_i are bounded by the range $[l_i, u_i]$. Then, as suggested by Vaidya et al. [4], the sensitivity of the mean $\mu_{i,j}$ is $(\mu_i - l_i)/(n + 1)$, and the sensitivity of the variance $\sigma_{i,j}^2$ is $n \cdot (\mu_i - l_i) / (n + 1)$, where n is the number of training samples where $C = C_j$.

To design our differentially private naive Bayes classification algorithm, we'll use the output perturbation strategy where the sensitivity of each feature is calculated according to whether it is discrete or numerical. Laplacian noise of the appropriate scale (as described in our discussion of the Laplace mechanism in section 2.2.2) is added to the parameters (the number of samples for discrete features and the means and variances for numerical features). Figure 3.8 illustrates the pseudocode of our algorithm, which is mostly self-explanatory.

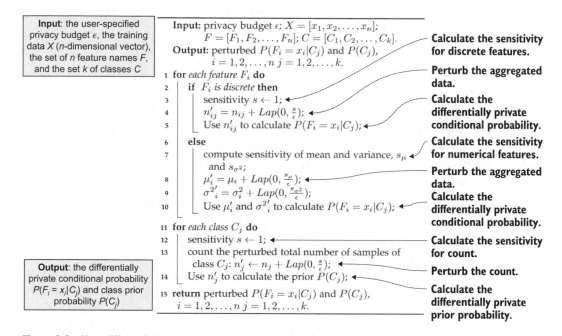

Figure 3.8 How differentially private naive Bayes classification works

Now we'll implement some of these concepts to get a little hands-on experience. Let's consider a scenario where we are training a naive Bayes classification model to predict whether a person makes over $50,000 a year based on the census dataset. You can find more details about the dataset at https://archive.ics.uci.edu/ml/datasets/adult.

First, we need to load the training and testing data from the adult dataset.

Listing 3.1 Loading the dataset

```
import numpy as np

X_train = np.loadtxt("https://archive.ics.uci.edu/ml/machine-learning-
    databases/adult/adult.data",
    usecols=(0, 4, 10, 11, 12), delimiter=", ")

y_train = np.loadtxt("https://archive.ics.uci.edu/ml/machine-learning-
    databases/adult/adult.data",
    usecols=14, dtype=str, delimiter=", ")
```

```
X_test = np.loadtxt("https://archive.ics.uci.edu/ml/machine-learning-
➥ databases/adult/adult.test",
➥ usecols=(0, 4, 10, 11, 12), delimiter=", ", skiprows=1)

y_test = np.loadtxt("https://archive.ics.uci.edu/ml/machine-learning-
➥ databases/adult/adult.test",
➥ usecols=14, dtype=str, delimiter=", ", skiprows=1)
y_test = np.array([a[:-1] for a in y_test])
```

Next, we'll train a regular (non-private) naive Bayes classifier and test its accuracy, as shown in the following listing.

Listing 3.2 Naive Bayes with no privacy

```
from sklearn.naive_bayes import GaussianNB
nonprivate_clf = GaussianNB()
nonprivate_clf.fit(X_train, y_train)

from sklearn.metrics import accuracy_score

print("Non-private test accuracy: %.2f%%" %
    (accuracy_score(y_test, nonprivate_clf.predict(X_test)) * 100))
```

The output will look like the following:

```
> Non-private test accuracy: 79.64%
```

To apply differentially private naive Bayes, we'll use the IBM Differential Privacy Library, `diffprivlib`:

```
!pip install diffprivlib
```

Using the `models.GaussianNB` module of `diffprivlib`, we can train a naive Bayes classifier while satisfying DP. If we don't specify any parameters, the model defaults to epsilon = 1.00.

```
import diffprivlib.models as dp
dp_clf = dp.GaussianNB()

dp_clf.fit(X_train, y_train)

print("Differentially private test accuracy (epsilon=%.2f): %.2f%%" %
➥ (dp_clf.epsilon, accuracy_score(y_test,
➥ dp_clf.predict(X_test)) * 100))
```

You will get something like the following as the output:

```
> Differentially private test accuracy (epsilon=1.00): 78.59%
```

As you can see from the preceding output accuracies, the regular (non-private) naive Bayes classifier produces an accuracy of 79.64%; by setting epsilon=1.00, the differentially private naive Bayes classifier achieves an accuracy of 78.59%. It is noteworthy that the training process of the (non-private) naive Bayes classifier and differentially private naive Bayes classifier is nondeterministic. Hence, you may obtain slightly different numbers than the accuracies we listed. Nevertheless, the result of DP-naive Bayes is slightly lower than its non-private version.

Using a smaller epsilon usually leads to better privacy protection with less accuracy. For instance, let's set epsilon=0.01:

```
import diffprivlib.models as dp
dp_clf = dp.GaussianNB(epsilon=float("0.01"))
dp_clf.fit(X_train, y_train)

print("Differentially private test accuracy (epsilon=%.2f): %.2f%%" %
➡ (dp_clf.epsilon, accuracy_score(y_test,
➡ dp_clf.predict(X_test)) * 100))
```

Now the output would look like this:

```
> Differentially private test accuracy (epsilon=0.01): 70.35%
```

3.2.2 *Differentially private logistic regression*

The previous subsection looked into the naive Bayes approach to differentially private supervised learning algorithms. Now let us look at how logistic regression can be applied under the deferential privacy setup.

LOGISTIC REGRESSION

Logistic regression (LR) is a model for binary classification. LR is usually formulated as training the parameters w by minimizing the negative log-likelihood over the training set (X, Y),

$$- \sum_{i=1}^{n} \log\left(1 + \exp(-y_i w^T x_i)\right)$$

where $X = [x_1, x_2, ..., x_n]$ and $Y = [y_1, y_2, ..., y_n]$.

Compared with standard LR, regularized LR has a regularization term in its loss function. It is thus formulated as training the parameters w by minimizing

$$- \sum \log\left(1 + \exp(-y_i w^T x_i)\right) + \lambda w^T w$$

over the training set (X, Y), where $X = [x_1, x_2, ..., x_n]$, $Y = [y_1, y_2, ..., y_n]$, and λ is a hyperparameter that sets the strength of regularization.

Why do we need regularization in logistic regression?

Overfitting is a common problem in ML tasks. Often, we'll train a model on one set of data, and it appears to work well on that data, but when we test it on a new set of unseen data, the performance deteriorates. One of the reasons for this problem is overfitting, where the model too closely conforms to the training set and hence misses the more generalizable trends.

Regularizations are known as shrinkage methods because they "shrink" the coefficients in the resulting regression. This shrinkage of coefficients reduces the variance in the model, which helps to avoid overfitting. In simpler terms, with regularization, the prediction of the model changes less than it would have without regularization when the input variables are changed.

IMPLEMENTING DIFFERENTIALLY PRIVATE LOGISTIC REGRESSION

We can adopt the objective perturbation strategy in designing differentially private logistic regression, where noise is added to the objective function for learning algorithms. We will use the empirical risk minimization–based vector mechanism to decide the minimum and maximum of the noisy function to produce the DP noisy output model.

Theorem 3.1 proposed by Chaudhuri et al. formulates the sensitivity for the regularized logistic regression [5]. The training data input $\{(x_i, y_i) \in X \times Y : i = 1, 2, \dots, n\}$ consists of n data-label pairs. In addition, we will use the notation $\|A\|_2$ to denote L_2 norm of A. We are training the parameters w, and λ is a hyperparameter that sets the strength of regularization.

THEOREM 3.1

If $\|x_i\| \leq 1$ and $\sum_{i=1}^{n} \log\left(1 + e^{-y_i w^T x_i}\right)$ is 1-Lipschitz,

then for any X, X' with dist$(X, X') = 1$, $\|f(X) - f(X')\|_2 \leq \frac{2}{\lambda \cdot n}$

where $f(X) = \arg max_w \frac{1}{n} \sum_{i=1}^{n} \log\left(1 + e^{-y_i w^T x_i}\right) + \frac{\lambda}{2} w^T$.

You can refer to the original article for the mathematical proof and the details of getting there. For now, what we are looking at here is the calculation of sensitivity, which is the difference of $\|f(X) - f(X')\|_2$, and it is less than or equal to $2/\lambda \cdot n$.

Now we'll use the objective perturbation strategy to design our differentially private logistic regression algorithm, where the sensitivity is calculated according to theorem 3.1. Figure 3.9 illustrates the pseudocode. For more details regarding the empirical risk minimization-based vector mechanism, refer to the original paper [5].

Based on the adult dataset we used earlier, let's continue with our previous scenario by training a logistic regression classification model to predict whether a person makes over $50,000 a year. First, let's load the training and testing data from the adult dataset.

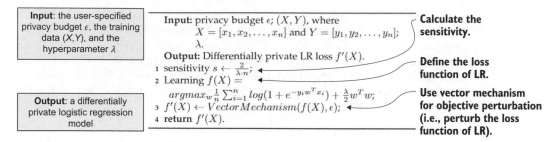

Figure 3.9   How differentially private logistic regression works

Listing 3.3   Loading testing and training data

```
import numpy as np

X_train = np.loadtxt("https://archive.ics.uci.edu/ml/machine-learning-
➥ databases/adult/adult.data",
➥ usecols=(0, 4, 10, 11, 12), delimiter=", ")

y_train = np.loadtxt("https://archive.ics.uci.edu/ml/machine-learning-
➥ databases/adult/adult.data",
➥ usecols=14, dtype=str, delimiter=", ")

X_test = np.loadtxt("https://archive.ics.uci.edu/ml/machine-learning-
➥ databases/adult/adult.test",
➥ usecols=(0, 4, 10, 11, 12), delimiter=", ", skiprows=1)

y_test = np.loadtxt("https://archive.ics.uci.edu/ml/machine-learning-
➥ databases/adult/adult.test",
➥ usecols=14, dtype=str, delimiter=", ", skiprows=1)

y_test = np.array([a[:-1] for a in y_test])
```

For `diffprivlib`, `LogisticRegression` works best when the features are scaled to control the norm of the data. To streamline this process, we'll create a `Pipeline` in sklearn:

```
from sklearn.linear_model import LogisticRegression
from sklearn.pipeline import Pipeline
from sklearn.preprocessing import MinMaxScaler

lr = Pipeline([
    ('scaler', MinMaxScaler()),
    ('clf', LogisticRegression(solver="lbfgs"))
])
```

Now let's first train a regular (non-private) logistic regression classifier and test its accuracy:

```
lr.fit(X_train, y_train)

from sklearn.metrics import accuracy_score

print("Non-private test accuracy: %.2f%%" % (accuracy_score(y_test,
➥  lr.predict(X_test)) * 100))
```

You will have output like the following:

```
> Non-private test accuracy: 81.04%
```

To apply differentially private logistic regression, we'll start by installing the IBM Differential Privacy Library:

```
!pip install diffprivlib
```

Using the `diffprivlib.models.LogisticRegression` module of `diffprivlib`, we can train a logistic regression classifier while satisfying DP.

If we don't specify any parameters, the model defaults to `epsilon = 1` and `data_norm = None`. If the norm of the data is not specified at initialization (as in this case), the norm will be calculated on the data when `.fit()` is first called, and a warning will be thrown because it causes a privacy leak. To ensure no additional privacy leakage, we should specify the data norm explicitly as an argument and choose the bounds independent of the data. For instance, we can use domain knowledge to do that.

Listing 3.4 Training a logistic regression classifier

```
import diffprivlib.models as dp
dp_lr = Pipeline([
    ('scaler', MinMaxScaler()),
    ('clf', dp.LogisticRegression())
])

dp_lr.fit(X_train, y_train)

print("Differentially private test accuracy (epsilon=%.2f): %.2f%%" %
➥  (dp_lr['clf'].epsilon, accuracy_score(y_test,
➥  dp_lr.predict(X_test)) * 100))
```

The output will look something like the following:

```
> Differentially private test accuracy (epsilon=1.00): 80.93%
```

As you can see from the preceding output accuracies, the regular (non-private) logistic regression classifier produces an accuracy of 81.04%; by setting `epsilon=1.00`, the differentially private logistic regression could achieve an accuracy of 80.93%. Using a smaller epsilon usually leads to better privacy protection but lesser accuracy. For instance, suppose we set `epsilon=0.01`:

```
import diffprivlib.models as dp
dp_lr = Pipeline([
    ('scaler', MinMaxScaler()),
    ('clf', dp.LogisticRegression(epsilon=0.01))
])

dp_lr.fit(X_train, y_train)

print("Differentially private test accuracy (epsilon=%.2f): %.2f%%" %
➥ (dp_lr['clf'].epsilon, accuracy_score(y_test,
➥ dp_lr.predict(X_test)) * 100))
```

As expected, the result will look something like this:

```
> Differentially private test accuracy (epsilon=0.01): 74.01%
```

3.2.3 *Differentially private linear regression*

Unlike logistic regression, a linear regression model defines a linear relationship between an observed target variable and multiple explanatory variables in a dataset. It is often used in regression analysis for trend prediction. The most common way to compute such a model is to minimize the residual sum of squares between the observed targets (of explanatory variables) in the dataset and the targets (of explanatory variables) predicted by linear approximation.

Let's dig into the theoretical foundations. We can formulate the standard problem of liner regression as finding $\beta = \arg\ min_\beta \|X\beta - y\|^2$, where X is the matrix of explanatory variables, y is the vector of the explained variable, and β is the vector of the unknown coefficients to be estimated.

Ridge regression, a regularized version of linear regression, can be formulated as $\beta^R = \arg\ min_\beta \|X\beta - y\|^2 + w^2\|\beta\|^2$, which has a closed form solution: $\beta^R = (X^T X + w^2 I_{p \times p})X^T y$, where w is set to minimize the risk of β^R.

The problem of designing a differentially private linear regression becomes designing a differentially private approximation of the second moment matrix. To achieve this, Sheffet [6] proposed an algorithm that adds noise to the second moment matrix using the Wishart mechanism. For more details, you can refer to the original paper, but this is enough for us to proceed.

Let's consider the scenario of training a linear regression on a diabetes dataset. This is another popular dataset among ML researchers, and you can find more information about it here: https://archive.ics.uci.edu/ml/datasets/diabetes. We will work with the example proposed by scikit-learn (https://scikit-learn.org/stable/auto_examples/linear_model/plot_ols.html), and we'll use the diabetes dataset to train and test a linear regressor.

We'll begin by loading the dataset and splitting it into training and testing samples (an 80/20 split):

```
from sklearn.model_selection import train_test_split
from sklearn import datasets

dataset = datasets.load_diabetes()
X_train, X_test, y_train, y_test = train_test_split(dataset.data,
➥ dataset.target, test_size=0.2)
print("Train examples: %d, Test examples: %d" % (X_train.shape[0],
➥ X_test.shape[0]))
```

You will get a result something like the following, showing the number of samples in the train and test sets:

```
> Train examples: 353, Test examples: 89
```

We'll now use scikit-learn's native LinearRegression function to establish a non-private baseline for our experiments. We'll use the r-squared score to evaluate the goodness-of-fit of the model. The r-squared score is a statistical measure that represents the proportion of the variance of a dependent variable that's explained by an independent variable or variables in a regression model. A higher r-squared score indicates a better linear regression model.

```
from sklearn.linear_model import LinearRegression as sk_LinearRegression
from sklearn.metrics import r2_score

regr = sk_LinearRegression()
regr.fit(X_train, y_train)
baseline = r2_score(y_test, regr.predict(X_test))
print("Non-private baseline: %.2f" % baseline)
```

The result will look like the following:

```
> Non-private baseline: 0.54
```

To apply differentially private linear regression, let's start by installing the IBM Differential Privacy Library, if you have not done so already:

```
!pip install diffprivlib
```

Now let's train a differentially private linear regressor (epsilon=1.00), where the trained model is differentially private with respect to the training data:

```
from diffprivlib.models import LinearRegression

regr = LinearRegression()
regr.fit(X_train, y_train)

print("R2 score for epsilon=%.2f: %.2f" % (regr.epsilon,
➥ r2_score(y_test, regr.predict(X_test))))
```

You will get an R2 score similar to the following:

```
> R2 score for epsilon=1.00: 0.48
```

3.3   *Differentially private unsupervised learning algorithms*

Unsupervised learning is a type of algorithm that learns patterns from unlabeled data. The feature vectors do not come with class labels or response variables in this type of learning. The target, in this case, is to find the structure of the data.

Clustering is probably the most common unsupervised learning technique, and it aims to group a set of samples into different clusters. Samples in the same cluster are supposed to be relatively similar and different from samples in other clusters (the similarity measure could be the Euclidean distance). k-means clustering is one of the most popular clustering methods, and it's used in many applications. This section will introduce the differentially private design of k-means clustering, and we'll walk you through the design process.

3.3.1   *Differentially private k-means clustering*

We will now moving on to differentially private unsupervised learning algorithms. We'll start by checking out k-means clustering and how it works.

WHAT IS K-MEANS CLUSTERING?

At a high level, k-means clustering tries to group similar items in clusters or groups. Suppose we have a set of data points that we want to assign to groups (or clusters) based on their similarity; the number of groups is represented by k.

There are multiple different implementations of k-means, including Lloyd's, MacQueen's, and Hartigan-Wong's k-means. We'll look at Lloyd's k-mean algorithm [7], as it is the most widely known implementation of k-means.

In the process of training a k-means model, the algorithm starts with k randomly selected centroid points that represent the k clusters. Then the algorithm iteratively clusters samples to the nearest centroid point and updates the centroid points by calculating the means of the samples that are clustered to the centroid points.

Let's look at an example. In the fresh produce section of your supermarket you'll see different kinds of fruits and vegetables. These items are arranged in groups by their types: all the apples are in one place, the oranges are kept together, and so on. You will quickly find that they form groups or clusters, where each of the items is within a group of their kind, forming the clusters.

IMPLEMENTING DIFFERENTIALLY PRIVATE K-MEANS CLUSTERING

Now that we've outlined k-means clustering, let's start walking through differentially private k-means clustering. This design follows an algorithm perturbation strategy called DPLloyd [8] (an extension of Lloyd's k-means), where the Laplace mechanism (i.e., adding Laplacian noise) is applied to the iterative update step in the Lloyd algorithm. In essence, it adds Laplace noise to the intermediate centroids and cluster sizes and produces differentially private k-means models.

Suppose each sample of the k-means clustering is a d-dimensional point, and assume the k-means algorithm has a predetermined number of running iterations, denoted as t. In each iteration of the k-means algorithm, two values are calculated:

- The total number of samples of each cluster C_i, denoted as n_i (i.e., the count queries)
- The sum of the samples of each cluster C_i (to recalculate the centroids), denoted as s_i (i.e., the sum queries)

Then, in k-means, each sample will involve $d \cdot t$ sum queries and t count queries. Adding or deleting a new sample will change n_i by 1, and this operation could happen in every iteration, so the sensitivity of n_i is t. Suppose the size of each dimension (i.e., feature) of each sample is bounded in the range $[-r,r]$. Then, by adding or deleting a new sample, the difference of x_i will be $d \cdot r \cdot t$.

As mentioned, we are going to use the algorithm perturbation strategy to design our differentially private k-means clustering algorithm, where the sensitivities of the count queries and the sum queries are calculated. The Laplace mechanism (i.e., adding Laplacian noise) is applied to the iterative update step in the Lloyd algorithm by adding noise to the intermediate centroids and cluster sizes. Figure 3.10 illustrates the pseudocode of the algorithm, which is mostly self-explanatory.

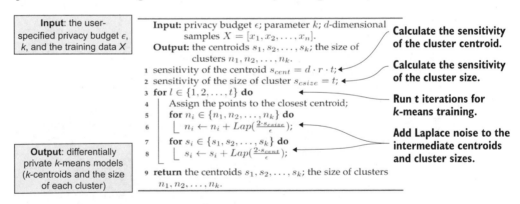

Figure 3.10 How differentially private k-means clustering works

Let's train a k-means clustering model on the scikit-learn load_digits dataset. We'll follow the example given by scikit-learn and use the load_digits dataset to train and test a k-means model. As you can see in listing 3.5, we'll use several different metrics for evaluating the clustering performance. Evaluating the performance of a clustering algorithm is not as trivial as counting the number of errors or the precision and recall of a supervised classification algorithm. As such, we will be looking at homogeneity, completeness, and V-measure scores, as well as adjusted rand index (ARI) and adjusted mutual information (AMI) score. Please refer to the scikit-learn documentation for detailed steps and the mathematical formulation: https://scikit-learn.org/stable/modules/clustering.html#clustering-evaluation.

> Listing 3.5   Training a *k*-means clustering model

```
import numpy as np
from time import time
from sklearn import metrics
from sklearn.cluster import KMeans
from sklearn.datasets import load_digits
from sklearn.preprocessing import scale

X_digits, y_digits = load_digits(return_X_y=True)
data = scale(X_digits)

n_samples, n_features = data.shape
n_digits = len(np.unique(y_digits))
labels = y_digits

sample_size = 1000

print("n_digits: %d, \t n_samples %d, \t n_features %d"
      % (n_digits, n_samples, n_features))
> n_digits: 10,   n_samples 1797,   n_features 64

print('init\t\ttime\tinertia\thomo\tcompl\tv-meas\tARI\tAMI\tsilhouette')
> nit time inertia homo compl v-meas ARI AMI silhouette

def bench_k_means(estimator, name, data):
    t0 = time()
    estimator.fit(data)
    print('%-9s\t%.2fs\t%i\t%.3f\t%.3f\t%.3f\t%.3f\t%.3f\t%.3f'
          % (name, (time() - t0), estimator.inertia_,
             metrics.homogeneity_score(labels, estimator.labels_),
             metrics.completeness_score(labels, estimator.labels_),
             metrics.v_measure_score(labels, estimator.labels_),
             metrics.adjusted_rand_score(labels, estimator.labels_),
             metrics.adjusted_mutual_info_score(labels,
             estimator.labels_),
             metrics.silhouette_score(data, estimator.labels_,
                                      metric='euclidean',
                                      sample_size=sample_size)))
```

We'll now use scikit-learn's native KMeans function to establish a non-private baseline for our experiments. We will use the k-means++ and random initializations:

```
bench_k_means(KMeans(init='k-means++', n_clusters=n_digits, n_init=100),
              name="k-means++", data=data)

bench_k_means(KMeans(init='random', n_clusters=n_digits, n_init=100),
              name="random", data=data)
```

The results may look like figure 3.11. As you can see, the preceding code covers different resulting score metrics such as homogeneity, completeness, and so on. Homogeneity, completeness, and V-measure scores are bounded below by 0.0 and above by 1.0, and the higher the value, the better. Intuitively, clustering with a bad V-measure can be qualitatively analyzed by using homogeneity and completeness scores to better determine what kinds of mistakes are being made by the assignment. For the ARI, AMI, and silhouette coefficient scores, the range is –1 to 1. Again, the higher the number, the better. On a final note, lower values generally indicate two largely independent labels, whereas values close to 1 indicate significant agreement.

```
init          time    inertia homo    compl   v-meas  ARI     AMI     silhouette
k-means++     3.57s   69404   0.605   0.653   0.628   0.467   0.624   0.149
random        2.03s   69408   0.600   0.648   0.623   0.464   0.619   0.152
```

Figure 3.11   Comparing results: `k-means++` vs. random initializations

Now let's apply differential privacy for k-means clustering:

```
!pip install diffprivlib
from diffprivlib.models import KMeans

bench_k_means(KMeans(epsilon=1.0, bounds=None, n_clusters=n_digits,
➥ init='k-means++', n_init=100), name="dp_k-means", data=data)
```

Once the differentially private *k*-means clustering is applied, you'll see results like those in figure 3.12. As you can see, dp_k-means provides much more varied results than k-means++ and random initializations, providing better privacy assurance. When you compare the numbers of the different score metrics, you will see how DP affects the final result.

```
init          time    inertia homo    compl   v-meas  ARI     AMI     silhouette
k-means++     3.59s   69418   0.604   0.653   0.628   0.467   0.624   0.139
random        2.20s   69406   0.605   0.653   0.628   0.469   0.623   0.146
dp_k-means    0.14s   97953   0.253   0.392   0.307   0.142   0.300   -0.005
```

Figure 3.12   Comparing results once the differentially private *k*-means clustering is applied

We've now investigated the design and use of several differentially private ML algorithms, and we've gone through some hands-on experiments. In the next section we'll use differentially private principal component analysis (PCA) as a case study application, and we'll walk you through the process of designing a differentially private ML algorithm.

3.4   *Case study: Differentially private principal component analysis*

In previous sections we discussed the DP mechanisms commonly used in today's applications and the design and usage of various differentially private ML algorithms. In this section we'll discuss how to design differentially private principal component analysis (PCA) as a case study, to walk you through the process of designing a differentially private ML algorithm. The content in this section is partially published in our paper [9], which you can refer to for further details. The implementation of this case study can be found in the book's GitHub repository: https://github.com/nogrady/PPML/blob/main/Ch3/distr_dp_pca-master.zip.

NOTE This section aims to walk you through all the mathematical formulations and empirical evaluations of our case study so that you can understand how to develop a differentially private application from scratch. If you do not need to know all these implementation details right now, you can skip to the next chapter and come back to this section later.

3.4.1 *The privacy of PCA over horizontally partitioned data*

PCA is a statistical procedure that computes a low-dimension subspace from the underlying data and generates a new set of variables that are linear combinations of the original ones. It is widely used in various data mining and ML applications, such as network intrusion detection, recommendation systems, text and image processing, and so on.

In 2016, Imtiaz et al. presented a first-of-its-kind privacy-preserving distributed PCA protocol [10]. Their main idea was to approximate the global PCA by aggregating the local PCA from each data owner, in which the data owner holds horizontally partitioned data. However, their work suffers from excessive running time and utility degradation, while the local principal components fail to provide a good representation of the data. More specifically, their solution requires all data owners to be online and to transfer the local PCA data one by one. This serialized computation made their protocol dependent on the number of data owners, which seriously degraded efficiency and scalability. Also, the local principal components cannot provide a good representation of the utility of the principal components when the amount of data is far less than its number of features.

The difference between horizontal and vertical partitioning of data

In many practical large-scale solutions, data is usually divided into partitions that can be managed and accessed separately. Partitioning can improve scalability and performance while reducing contention. Horizontal partitioning (often called sharding) partitions rows into multiple datastores with the same schema and columns. Vertical partitioning segments columns into multiple datastores containing the same rows.

In our case study, we will assume that the data is horizontally partitioned, which means all the data shares the same features. The number of data owners will be more than hundreds. We'll presume an untrustworthy data user would like to learn the principal components of the distributed data. An honest but curious intermediary party, named *proxy*, works between the data user and data owners.

Data owners simultaneously encrypt their own data share and send it to the proxy. The proxy runs a differentially private aggregation algorithm over the encrypted data and sends the output to the data user. The data user then computes the principal components from the output without learning the content of the underlying data.

In our experiments, we will study the running time, utility, and privacy tradeoff of the proposed protocol and compare it with previous work.

> ## What does "honest but curious" mean?
> Typically, in communication protocols, an honest-but-curious adversary is a legitimate participant or a user who will not deviate from the defined limits of the protocol but will attempt to learn all possible information from legitimately received messages.

Before moving forward with our protocol design, let's briefly go over the concepts of PCA and homomorphic encryption.

HOW PRINCIPAL COMPONENT ANALYSIS WORKS

Let's quickly walk through the mathematical formulation of PCA. Given a square matrix A, an eigenvector v of A is a nonzero vector that does not change the direction when A is applied to it, such that

$$Av = \lambda v$$

where λ is a real number scalar, referred to as the eigenvalue. Suppose $A \in \mathbb{R}^{(n \times n)}$, then it has at most n eigenvectors, and each eigenvector associates with a distinct eigenvalue.

Consider a dataset with N samples $x_1, x_2,...,x_N$, where each sample has M features ($x^i \in$). A center-adjusted scatter matrix $\bar{S} \in \mathbb{R}^{M \times M}$ is computed as follows,

$$\bar{S} = \sum_{i=1}^{N} (x_i - \mu)(x_i - \mu)^T = U\Lambda U^T$$

where μ is the mean vector, $\mu = 1/N \sum_{(i=1)}^{N} x_i$. By using eigenvalue decomposition (EVD) on $\bar{s}$, we will have Λ and U, where $\Lambda = \text{diag}(\lambda_1, \lambda_2,...,\lambda_M)$ is a diagonal matrix of eigenvalues.

This can be arranged to a non-increasing order in absolute value; in other words, $\|\lambda_1\| \geq \|\lambda_2\| \geq \cdots \geq \|\lambda_M\|$, $U = [u_1 \ u_2 \ ... u_M]$ is an $M \times M$ matrix where u_j denotes the jth eigenvector of $\bar{s}$.

In PCA, each eigenvector represents a principal component.

WHAT IS HOMOMORPHIC ENCRYPTION?

Homomorphic encryption is an essential building block of this work. In simple terms, it allows computations to be performed over the encrypted data, in which the decryption of the generated result matches the result of operations performed on the plaintext. In this section we will use the Paillier cryptosystem to implement the protocol.

To refresh your memory, the Paillier cryptosystem is a probabilistic asymmetric algorithm for public-key cryptography (a partially homomorphic encryption scheme) introduced by Pascal Paillier.

Let's consider the function $\varepsilon_{pk}[\cdot]$ to be the encryption scheme with public key *pk*, the function $D_{sk}[\cdot]$ to be the decryption scheme with private key *sk*. The additive homomorphic encryption can be defined as

$$a + b = D_{sk}\left[\varepsilon_{pk}[a] \otimes \varepsilon_{pk}[b]\right]$$

where $\otimes$ denotes the modulo multiplication operator in the encrypted domain and a and b are the plaintext messages. The multiplicative homomorphic encryption is defined as

$$a \cdot b = D_{sk}\left[\varepsilon_{pk}[a]^{b}\right]$$

Since the cryptosystem only accepts integers as input, real numbers should be discretized. In this example, we'll adopt the following formulation,

$$Discretize_{e,F}(x) = \left\lfloor \frac{(2^{e}-1)\cdot(x-min_{F})}{max_{F}-min_{F}} \right\rfloor$$

where e is the number of bits, and min_F, max_F are the minimal and maximal value of feature F, x is the real number to be discretized, and $Discretize_{(e,F)}(x)$ takes a value in $[0,2^{(e-1)}]$.

3.4.2 Designing differentially private PCA over horizontally partitioned data

Let's first revisit what we want to achieve here (see figure 3.13). Suppose there are L data owners, and each data owner l has a dataset $X^{l} \in \mathbb{R}^{N^{l} \times M}$, where M is the number of dimensions and N^{l} is the number of samples held by l. The horizontal aggregation of X^{l}, $i=1,2,\ldots,l$ generates a data matrix $X \in \mathbb{R}^{(N \times M)}$, where $N = \sum_{(i=1)}^{l} N^{i}$. Now assume a data user wants to perform PCA on X. To protect the privacy of the original data, data owners would not share the original data with the data user in cleartext form.

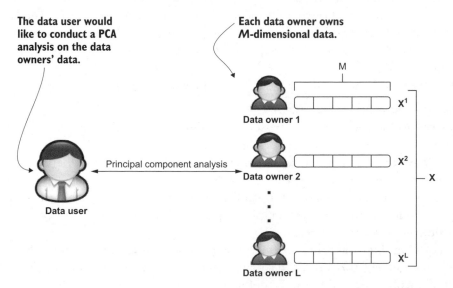

Figure 3.13 The high-level overview of distributed PCA

To accommodate this, we need to design a differentially private distributed PCA protocol that allows data users to perform PCA but to learn nothing except the principal components. Figure 3.14 illustrates one design for a differentially private distributed PCA protocol. In this scenario, data owners are assumed to be honest and not to collude with each other, but the data user is assumed to be untrustworthy and will want to learn more information than the principal components. The proxy works as an honest-but-curious intermediary party who does not collude with the data user or owners.

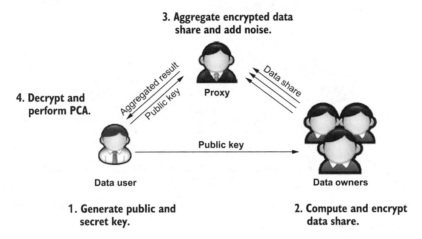

Figure 3.14   The design of the protocol and how it works

In order to learn the principal components of X, the scatter matrix of X needs to be computed. In the proposed protocol, each data owner l computes a data share of X^l. To prevent the proxy learning the data, each data share is encrypted before it is sent to the proxy. Once the proxy receives the encrypted data share from each data owner, the proxy runs the differentially private aggregation algorithm and sends the aggregated result to the data user. Then the data user constructs the scatter matrix from the result and computes the principal components. Figure 3.14 outlines these steps.

COMPUTING THE SCATTER MATRIX

Let's look at the computation of the distributed scatter matrix.

Suppose there are L data owners, and each data owner l has a dataset, $X^l \in \mathbb{R}^{N^l \times M}$, where M is the number of dimensions, and N^l is the number of samples held by l. Each data owner locally computes a data share that contains

$$R^l = \sum_{i=1}^{N^l} x_i x_i^T, \, v^l = \sum_{i=1}^{N^l} x_i$$

where $x_i = [x_{i1} \ x_{i2} \dots \ x_{iM}]^T e$. The scatter matrix $\bar{s}$ can be computed by summing the data share from each data owner:

$$
\begin{aligned}
\bar{S} &= \sum_{i=1}^{N} (x_i - \mu)(x_i - \mu)^T \\
&= \sum_{i=1}^{N} x_i x_i^T - N\mu\mu^T \\
&= \sum_{i=1}^{L} R^l - \frac{1}{N}vv^T \\
&= R - \frac{1}{N}vv^T
\end{aligned}
$$

where

$$
\mu = \frac{1}{N}\sum_{i=1}^{N} x_i, \ R = \sum_{l=1}^{L} R^l, \ v = \sum_{l=1}^{L} v^l, \ N = \sum_{l=1}^{L} R^l
$$

The distributed scatter matrix computation allows each data owner to compute a partial result simultaneously. Unlike other methods [10], this approach reduces the dependence between data owners and allows them to send the data shares simultaneously.

DESIGNING THE PROTOCOL

It is crucial to prevent any possible data leakage through the proxy, so each individual data share should be encrypted by the data owners. Then the proxy aggregates the received encrypted shares. To prevent the inference from PCA, the proxy adds a noise matrix to the aggregated result, which makes the approximation of the scatter matrix satisfy (ϵ, δ)-DP. The aggregated result is then sent to the data user.

What is (ϵ, δ)-DP? δ is another privacy budget parameter, where, when $\delta = 0$, the algorithm satisfies ϵ-DP, which is a stronger privacy guarantee than (ϵ, δ)-DP with $\delta > 0$. You can find more details about δ in section A.1

This can be seen as the most general relaxation of ϵ-DP, which weakens the definition by allowing an additional small δ density of probability on which the upper bound ε does not hold. If you think of the practicality of DP, this leads to the dilemma of data release. You cannot always be true to the data and protect the privacy of all individuals. There is a tradeoff between the utility of the output and privacy. Especially in the case of outliers, an ϵ private release will have very little utility (as the sensitivity is very large, leading to a lot of noise being added).

Alternatively, you can remove the outliers or clip their values to achieve a more sensible sensitivity. This way the output will have better utility, but it is no longer a true representation of the dataset.

This all leads to (ϵ, δ) privacy. The data user decrypts the result, constructs an approximation of the scatter matrix, and then calculates PCA, as you saw earlier. Let's walk through the steps:

1   The data user generates a public key pair (*pk* and *sk*) for the Paillier cryptosystem and sends *pk* to the proxy and data owners. In practice, secure distribution of keys is important, but we are not emphasizing it here.

   Thereafter, the data owners compute the share R^l, v^l, $l = 1,2,...,L$, and send $\varepsilon_{pk}[R^l]$, $\varepsilon_{pk}[v^l]$, $\varepsilon_{pk}[N^l]$ to the proxy.

2   After receiving the encrypted data share from each data owner, the proxy aggregates the shares and applies the symmetric matrix noise to satisfy DP. This process is shown in algorithm 1 in figure 3.15.

Let's look at algorithm 1 to understand what's happening here:

1   Lines 2–4: Aggregate the data shares from each data owner.

$$\varepsilon_{pk}[R] = \otimes_{l=1}^{L} \varepsilon_{pk}[R^l]$$
$$\varepsilon_{pk}[v] = \otimes_{l=1}^{L} \varepsilon_{pk}[v^l]$$
$$\varepsilon_{pk}[N] = \otimes_{l=1}^{L} \varepsilon_{pk}[N^l]$$

2   Lines 5–7: Construct the noisy $\varepsilon_{pk}[v']$. To prevent the data user learning information from v, the proxy generates a noisy $\varepsilon_{pk}[v']$ by summing a random vector $\varepsilon_{pk}[b]$ with $\varepsilon_{pk}[v]$, such that $\varepsilon_{pk}[v'] = \varepsilon_{pk}[v] \otimes \varepsilon_{pk}[b]$. It can be shown that the element v'_{ij} of $v'v'^T$ is

$$v'_{ij} = (v_i + b_i)(v_j + b_j)$$
$$= v_i v_j + v_i b_j + b_i v_j + b_i b_j$$

Both sides of the equation are divided by N, which yields

$$\frac{v'v'^T}{N} = \frac{vv^T}{N} + G$$

$$G_{ij} = \frac{v_i b_j + b_i v_j + b_i b_j}{N}$$

Thus, we have

$$\frac{v'_{ij}}{N} = \frac{v_i v_j}{N} + \frac{v_i b_j + b_i v_j + b_i b_j}{N}$$

Recall that, in the Paillier cryptosystem, the multiplicative homomorphic property is defined as

$$\varepsilon_{pk}[a \cdot b] = \varepsilon_{pk}[a]^b$$

Then, $\varepsilon_{pk}[G_{ij}]$ is

$$\varepsilon_{pk}[G_{ij}] = \varepsilon_{pk}[v_i]^{\frac{b_j}{N}} \otimes \varepsilon_{pk}[v_j]^{\frac{b_i}{N}} \otimes \varepsilon_{pk}\left[\frac{b_i b_j}{N}\right]$$

At this point we can make the exponent be an integer by multiplying b with N. It should be noted that during the encryption, the proxy has to learn N. To achieve this, the proxy sends $\varepsilon_{pk}[N]$ to the data user, and the data user returns N in cleartext once it's decrypted.

3 Lines 8–10: Apply symmetric matrix to satisfy (ϵ, δ)-DP. The proxy generates $G' \in \mathbb{R}^{M \times M}$, based on the DP parameter (ϵ, δ), and gets $\varepsilon_{pk}[R']$, $\varepsilon_{pk}[v']$, where

$$\varepsilon_{pk}[R'] = \varepsilon_{pk}[R] \otimes \varepsilon_{pk}[G] \otimes \varepsilon_{pk}[G']$$

$$\varepsilon_{pk}[v'] = \varepsilon_{pk}[v] \otimes \varepsilon_{pk}[b]$$

Then, $\varepsilon_{pk}[R']$, $\varepsilon_{pk}[v']$ are sent to the data user.

After receiving the aggregated result from the proxy, $\varepsilon_{pk}[N]$, $\varepsilon_{pk}[R']$, $\varepsilon_{pk}[v']$, the data user decrypts each and computes $\bar{S}'$.

$$\bar{S}' = R' - \frac{1}{N}v'{v'}^{T}$$

With $\bar{s}'$, the data user can proceed to compute the eigenvector and get the principal components.

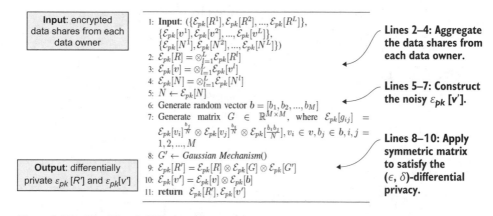

Figure 3.15 Algorithm 1: DPAggregate

ANALYZING THE SECURITY AND PRIVACY

Now let's determine whether the protocol is secure enough. In our example, the data user is assumed to be untrustworthy, and the proxy is assumed to be honest but curious. Furthermore, we are assuming that the proxy will not collude with the data user or data owners.

To protect the data against the proxy, R^l, v^l, and N^l are encrypted by the data owner. During the protocol execution, the proxy only learns N in plaintext, and it will not disclose the privacy of a single data owner. Without colluding with the data user, the proxy cannot learn the values of R^l, v^l, and N^l. On the other side, the proxy mixes R and v with random noise, to prevent the data user from gaining information other than the principal components.

Of the data received from the proxy, the data user decrypts $\varepsilon_{pk}[N]$, $\varepsilon_{pk}[R']$, $\varepsilon_{pk}[v']$ and then proceeds to construct an approximation of the scatter matrix, $\tilde{S} = \bar{S} + G'$, in which G' is the Gaussian symmetric matrix carried by R'. The (ϵ, δ)-DP is closed for the postprocessing algorithm of $\tilde{S}'$. Since the proxy is not colluding with the data user, the data user cannot learn the value of R and v. Therefore, the data user learns nothing but the computed principal components.

As a flexible design, this approach can cooperate with different symmetric noise matrices to satisfy (ϵ, δ)-DP. To demonstrate the protocol to you, we implemented the Gaussian mechanism as shown in algorithm 2 (figure 3.16).

1: **Input:** $\epsilon > 0, \delta > 0$
2: Set $\tau = \sqrt{2ln(1.25/\delta)}/\epsilon$
3: Let $E \in \mathcal{R}^{n \times n}$ be the symmetric matrix with the upper triangle (including the diagonal) entry is i.i.d samples from $\mathcal{N} \sim (0, \tau^2)$, and set $E_{ji} = E_{ij}, \forall i < j$.
4: **return** E

Figure 3.16   Algorithm 2: the Gaussian mechanism

It is noteworthy that once the data user learns the private principal components from the protocol, they could release the principal components to the public for further use, which would allow the proxy to access the components. In that case, the proxy would still not have enough information to recover the covariance matrix from a full set of principal components, which implies that the proxy cannot recover the approximation of the covariance matrix with the released private principal components. Moreover, the data user might release a subset (top K) of principal components rather than the full set of components, which would make it even harder for the proxy to recover the covariance matrix. Without knowing the approximation of the covariance matrix, the proxy could not infer the plain data by removing the added noise.

3.4.3   Experimentally evaluating the performance of the protocol

We've discussed the theoretical background of the proposed protocol, so now let's implement the differentially private distributed PCA (DPDPCA) protocol and evaluate it in terms of efficiency, utility, and privacy. For efficiency, we will measure the run-time efficiency of DPDPCA and compare it to similar work in the literature [10]; this will show that DPDPCA outperforms the previous work.

This experiment will be developed using Python and the Python Paillier homomorphic cryptosystem library published in https://github.com/mikeivanov/paillier.

THE DATASET AND THE EVALUATION METHODOLOGY

We will use six datasets for the experiments, as shown in table 3.2. The Aloi dataset is a collection of color images of small objects, the Facebook comment volume dataset contains features extracted from Facebook posts, and the Million Song dataset consists of audio features. The cardinalities of Aloi, Facebook, and Million Song are more than 100,000, and the dimensionality of each is less than 100. The CNAE dataset is a text dataset extracted from business documents, and the attributes are the term frequency. The GISETTE dataset contains grayscale images of the highly confusable digits 4 and 9, used in the NIPS 2003 feature selection challenge. ISOLET is a dataset of spoken letters, which records the 26 English letters from 150 subjects, and it has a combination of features like spectral coefficients and contour features. All the datasets, excluding Aloi, are from the UCI ML repository, whereas Aloi is from LIBSVM dataset repository. We'll evaluate the performance of DPDPCA in terms of SVM classification over the CNAE, GISETTE, and ISOLET datasets.

Table 3.2   A summary of the experimental datasets

Dataset	Feature	Cardinality
Aloi	29	108,000
Facebook	54	199,030
Million Song	90	515,345
CNAE	857	1,080
ISOLET	617	7,797
GISETTE	5,000	13,500

For the classification result, we'll measure the precision, recall, and F1 scores because the datasets are unbalanced. You can refer to the following mathematical formulations for the details of these measurements. In addition, all experiments will be run 10 times, and the mean and standard deviation of the result will be drawn in figures.

$$Precision = \frac{TruePositive(TP)}{TruePositive(TP) + FalsePositive(FP)}$$

$$Recall = \frac{TruePositive(TP)}{TruePositive(TP) + FalseNegative(FN)}$$

$$F1\ Score = 2 \cdot \frac{Precision \cdot Recall}{Precision + Recall}$$

THE EFFICIENCY OF THE PROPOSED APPROACH

As we've mentioned, the previous work suffered from two main problems: the excessive protocol running time and the utility degradation when the local principal components failed to provide good data representation. In this section we'll compare both protocols in these two aspects. For brevity, we'll refer to the proposed protocol as "DPDPCA" and the work done by Imtiaz and Sarwate [11] as "PrivateLocalPCA."

First, we'll look at the results of the running times of DPDPCA and Private-LocalPCA. The total running time of DPDPCA included the following:

- The average local computation time of the data owner
- The time of the private aggregation algorithm in the proxy
- The time of performing PCA by the data user
- The data transmission time among parties

For PrivateLocalPCA, the running time started with the first data owner and ended with the last data owner, including the local PCA computation and transmission time. We simulated the data transmission using I/O operations rather than the local network to make the communication consistent and stable. We measured the protocol running time for the different number of data owners, and all samples were distributed evenly to each data owner. The experiment ran on a desktop machine (i7-5820k, 64 GB memory).

The results are shown in figure 3.17. The horizontal axis specifies the number of data owners, and the vertical axis specifies the running time in seconds. You can see

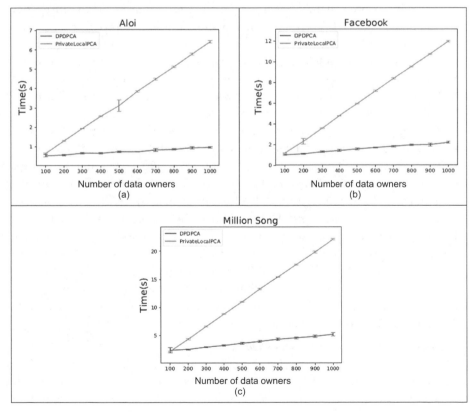

Figure 3.17   Running-time comparison between DPDPCA and PrivateLocalPCA, $\epsilon = 0.3$

that PrivateLocalPCA runs almost linearly upon the number of data owners. That's because PrivateLocalPCA requires that the local principal components are transmitted through data owners one by one, and the next data owner has to wait for the result from the previous one. Thus, it has a time complexity of $O(n)$, where n is the number of data owners. In contrast, DPDPCA costs far less time than PrivateLocalPCA, given the same number of data owners. The reason is, first, that the distributed scatter matrix computation allows each data owner to compute their local share simultaneously, and second, that the proxy can implement the aggregation of the local shares in parallel, which runs loglinearly upon the number of data owners. Overall, DPDPCA has better scalability than PrivateLocalPCA regarding the number of data owners.

THE EFFECT ON THE UTILITY OF THE APPLICATION

Next, we'll explore the utility degradation of PrivateLocalPCA and DPDPCA when the amount of data is far less than the number of features. We are considering a scenario where each data owner holds a dataset where the cardinality may be far smaller than the number of features, such as the images, ratings of music and movies, and personal activity data. To simulate this scenario, we distributed different sized samples to each data owner in the experiment. For PrivateLocalPCA, the variance is not fully preserved because only the first few principal components are used to represent the data.

In contrast, DPDPCA is not affected by the number of samples that each data owner holds, and the local descriptive statistics are aggregated to build the scatter matrix. Thus, the total variance is not lost. In this experiment, we measured the F1 score of the transformed data regarding the different number of private principal components. The number of principal components was determined by each data owner's rank of the data. Training and testing data were projected to a lower-dimensional space with components from each protocol. Then we used the transformed training data to train an SVM classifier with the RBF kernel and test the classifier with unseen data. To provide ground truth, the noiseless PCA was performed over the training data as well. Also, the same symmetric matrix noise mechanism [10] was applied to DPDPCA to make a fair comparison.

Figure 3.18 shows the results. The horizontal axis specifies the number of samples held by each data owner, and the vertical axis shows the F1 score. You can see that the F1 score of DPDPCA is invariant to the number of samples for the data owner, and the result is compatible with the noiseless PCA, which implies that high utility is maintained. In contrast, the F1 score of PrivateLocalPCA is heavily affected by the number of samples for each data owner, and it cannot maintain the utility with only a few samples. Overall, for the CNAE and GISETTE datasets, the F1 score of DPDPCA outperforms PrivateLocalPCA under all settings.

THE TRADEOFF BETWEEN UTILITY AND PRIVACY

The other important concern is the tradeoff between utility and privacy. Let's investigate the tradeoff for DPDPCA by measuring the captured variance of the private principal components using the Gaussian mechanism, where the standard deviation of the additive noise is inversely proportional to ϵ. The smaller ϵ is, the more noise is added

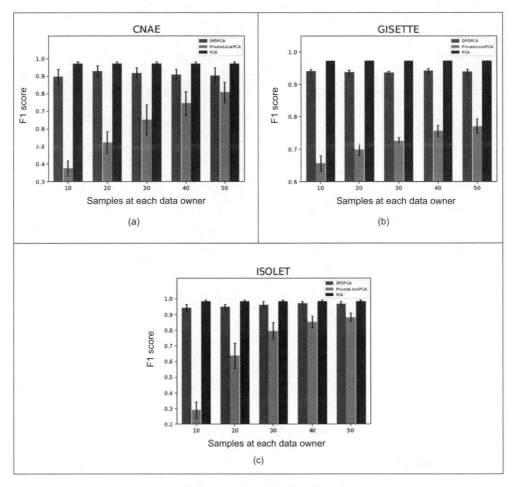

Figure 3.18   Principal components utility comparison between DPDPCA and PrivateLocalPCA, $\epsilon = 0.5$

and the more privacy is gained. The result is shown in figure 3.19, where the horizontal axis specifies ϵ, and the vertical axis shows the ratio of the captured variance. In the figure you can see that the variance captured by the Gaussian mechanism almost maintained the same level for the given ϵ range. Moreover, the value of the ratio implies that the Gaussian mechanism captures a large proportion of the variance.

In conclusion, this case study presents a highly efficient and largely scalable (ϵ, δ)-DP distributed PCA protocol, DPDPCA. As you can see, we considered the scenario where the data is horizontally partitioned and an untrustworthy data user wants to learn the principal components of the distributed data in a short time. We can think of practical applications, such as disaster management and emergency response. Compared to previous work, DPDPCA offers higher efficiency and better utility. Additionally, it can incorporate different symmetric matrix schemes to achieve (ϵ, δ)-DP.

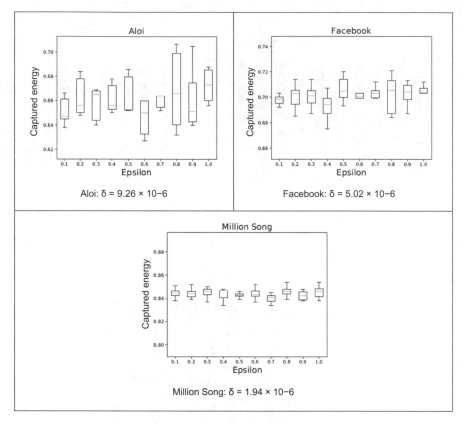

Figure 3.19 **Captured variance, δ = 1/N**

Summary

- DP techniques resist membership inference attacks by adding random noise to the input data, to iterations in the algorithm, or to algorithm output.
- For input perturbation–based DP approaches, noise is added to the data itself, and after the desired non-private computation has been performed on the noisy input, the output will be differentially private.
- For algorithm perturbation–based DP approaches, noise is added to the intermediate values in iterative ML algorithms.
- Output perturbation–based DP approaches involve running the non-private-learning algorithm and adding noise to the generated model.
- Objective perturbation DP approaches entail adding noise to the objective function for learning algorithms, such as empirical risk minimization.
- Differentially private naive Bayes classification is based on Bayes' theorem and the assumption of independence between every pair of features.

- We can adopt the objective perturbation strategy in designing differentially private logistic regression, where noise is added to the objective function for learning algorithms.
- In differentially private k-means clustering, the Laplace noise is added to the intermediate centroids and cluster sizes and finally produces differentially private k-means models.
- The concept of DP can be used in many distributed ML scenarios, such as PCA, to design highly efficient and largely scalable (ϵ, δ)-DP distributed protocols.

Part 2

Local differential privacy and synthetic data generation

Part 2 looks at another level of differential privacy, called local differential privacy, and at generating synthetic data to ensure privacy. Chapter 4 introduces the core concepts and definitions of local differential privacy. Chapter 5 looks at the more advanced mechanisms of local differential privacy, focusing on various data types and real-world applications, and then presents another case study. Chapter 6 focuses on generating synthetic data for machine learning tasks.

Local differential privacy
for machine learning

This chapter covers

- Local differential privacy (LDP)
- Implementing the randomized response mechanism for LDP
- LDP mechanisms for one-dimensional data frequency estimation
- Implementing and experimenting with different LDP mechanisms for one-dimensional data

In the previous two chapters we discussed centralized differential privacy (DP), where there is a trusted data curator who collects data from individuals and applies different techniques to obtain differentially private statistics about the population. Then the curator publishes privacy-preserving statistics about this population. However, these techniques are unsuitable when individuals do not completely trust the data curator. Hence, various techniques to satisfy DP in the local setting have been studied to eliminate the need for a trusted data curator. In this chapter we will walk through the concept, mechanisms, and applications of the local version of DP, local differential privacy (LDP).

This chapter will mainly look at how LDP can be implemented in ML algorithms by looking at different examples and implementation code. In the next chapter we'll also walk you through a case study of applying LDP naive Bayes classification for real-world datasets.

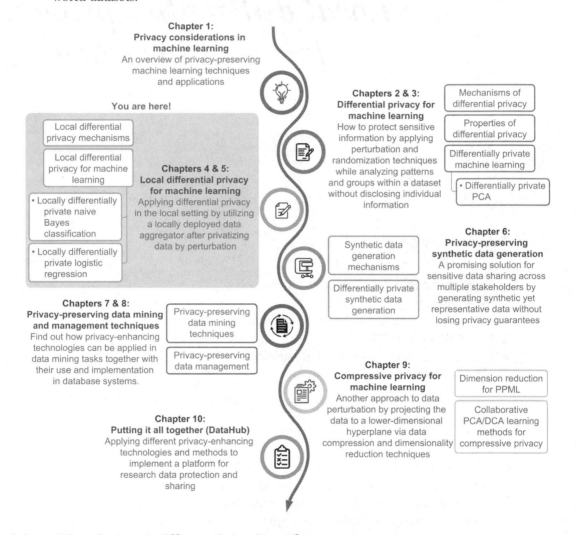

4.1   *What is local differential privacy?*

DP is a widely accepted standard for quantifying individual privacy. In the original definition of DP, there is a trusted data curator who collects data from individuals and applies techniques to obtain differentially private statistics. This data curator then publishes privacy-preserving statistics about the population. We looked at how to satisfy DP in the context of ML in chapters 2 and 3. However, those techniques cannot be applied when individuals do not completely trust the data curator.

Different techniques have been proposed to ensure DP in the local setting without a trusted data curator. In LDP, individuals send their data to the data aggregator after privatizing the data by perturbation (see figure 4.1). These techniques provide plausible deniability for individuals. The data aggregator collects all the perturbed values and makes an estimation of the statistics, such as the frequency of each value in the population.

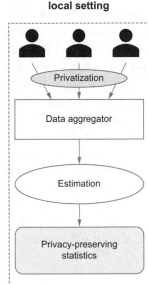

Figure 4.1   Centralized vs. local DP

4.1.1   The concept of local differential privacy

Many real-world applications, including those from Google and Apple, have adopted LDP. Before we discuss the concept of LDP and how it works, let's look at how it's applied to real-world products.

HOW GOOGLE AND APPLE USE LDP

In 2014 Google introduced Randomized Aggregatable Privacy-Preserving Ordinal Response (RAPPOR) [1], a technology for anonymously crowdsourcing statistics from end-user client software with strong privacy guarantees. This technology has lately been integrated with the Chrome web browser. Over the last five years, RAPPOR has processed up to billions of daily, randomized reports in a manner that guarantees LDP. The technology is designed to collect statistics on client-side values and strings over large numbers of clients, such as categories, frequencies, histograms, and other statistics. For any reported value, RAPPOR offers a strong deniability guarantee for the reporting client, which strictly limits the private information disclosed, as measured by DP, and it even holds for a single client that often reports on the same value.

In 2017 Apple also released a research paper on how it uses LDP to improve the user experience with their products by getting insight into what many of their users are doing. For example, what new words are trending and might make the most relevant suggestions? What websites have problems that could affect battery life? Which emojis are chosen most often? The DP technology used by Apple is rooted in the idea that slightly biased statistical noise can mask a user's data before it is shared with Apple. If many people submit the same data, the noise added can average out over large numbers of data points, and Apple can see meaningful information emerge. Apple details two techniques for collecting data while protecting users' privacy: the Count Mean Sketch and the Hadamard Count Mean Sketch. Both approaches insert random information into the data being collected. That random information effectively obfuscates any identifying aspects of the data so that it cannot be traced back to individuals.

As you can see in these examples, LDP is usually being applied for mean or frequency estimation. Frequency estimation in a survey (or in survey-like problems) is one of the most common approaches to utilizing LDP in day-to-day applications. For instance, companies, organizations, and researchers often use surveys to analyze behavior or assess thoughts and opinions, but collecting information from individuals for research purposes is challenging due to privacy reasons. Individuals may not trust the data collector to not share sensitive or private information. And although an individual may participate in a survey anonymously, it can sometimes still be possible to identify the person by using the information provided. On the other hand, even though the people conducting the surveys are more interested in the distribution of the survey answers, rather than the information about specific individuals, it is quite difficult for them to earn the trust of survey participants when it comes to sensitive information. This is where LDP comes in.

LDP IN DETAIL

Now that you have some background on how LDP is used, let's look at the details. LDP is a way of measuring individual privacy when the data collector is not trusted. LDP aims to guarantee that when an individual provides a value, it should be challenging to identify the original value, which provides the privacy protection. Many LDP mechanisms also aim to estimate the distribution of the population as accurately as possible based on the aggregation of the perturbed data collected from all individuals.

Figure 4.2 illustrates the typical use of LDP. First, each individual (data owner) generates or collects their own data, such as survey answers or personal data. Then, each individual perturbs their data locally using a specific LDP mechanism (which we'll discuss in section 4.2). After conducting the perturbation, each individual sends their data to a data collector, who will perform the data aggregation and statistics or models estimation. Finally, the estimated statistics or models will be published. It would be extremely hard for adversaries to infer an individual's data based on such published information (as guaranteed by the definition of LDP).

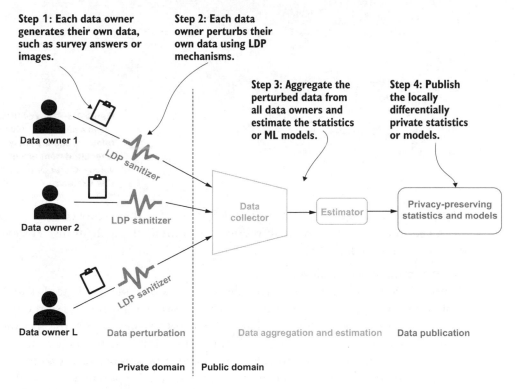

Figure 4.2 How local differential privacy works

LDP states that for any published estimated statistics or models using an ε-LDP mechanism, the probability of distinguishing two input values (i.e., an individual's data) by the data collector (or any other adversaries in the public domain) is at most $e^{-\epsilon}$.

A protocol P satisfies ε-LDP if for any two input values v_1 and v_2 and any output o in the output space of P, we have

$$\Pr[P(v_1) = o] \le \Pr[P(v_2) = o] \cdot e^\epsilon$$

where $\Pr[\cdot]$ means probabilities. $\Pr[P(v_1) = o]$ is the probability that given input v_1 to P, it outputs o. The ε parameter in the definition is the privacy parameter or the privacy budget. It helps to tune the amount of privacy the definition provides. Small values of ε require P to provide very similar outputs when given similar inputs and therefore provide higher levels of privacy; large values of ε allow less similarity in the outputs and therefore provide less privacy. For instance, as shown in figure 4.3, for a small value of ε, given a perturbed value o, it is (almost) equally likely that o resulted from any input value, that is, v_1 or v_2. In this way, just by observing an output, it is hard to infer back to its corresponding input; hence, the privacy of the data is ensured.

Input set   Output set

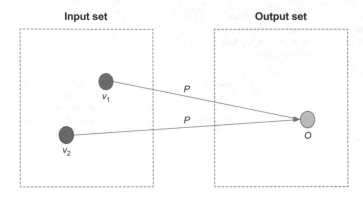

Figure 4.3   How ϵ-LDP works. Given a perturbed value o, it is (almost) equally likely that it resulted from any input value—either v_1 or v_2 in this example.

We have now discussed the concept and definition of LDP and looked at how it differs from centralized DP. Before we introduce any of the LDP mechanisms, let's look at a scenario where we'll apply LDP.

AN LDP SCENARIO WITH A SURVEY

Answering questions in online surveys or social network quizzes via tools like Survey-Monkey is a widespread practice today. LDP can protect the answers of these surveys before they leave the data owners. Throughout this chapter, we will use the following scenario to demonstrate the design and implementation of LDP mechanisms.

Let's say company A wants to determine the distribution of its customers (for a targeted advertising campaign). It conducts a survey, and sample survey questions might look like these:

- Are you married?
- What is your occupation?
- How old are you?
- What is your race category?

However, these questions are highly sensitive and private. To encourage its customers to participate in the survey, company A should provide privacy guarantees while still keeping the estimated distribution of its customers as accurate as possible when conducting the survey.

Not surprisingly, LDP is one technique that could help the company. There are several different LDP mechanisms that deal with different scenarios (i.e., data type, data dimensions, etc.). For instance, the answer to the question "Are you married?" is simply a categorical binary result: "yes" or "no." A randomized response mechanism would be suitable to solve such scenarios. On the other hand, the answers to the questions "What is your occupation?" and "What is your race category?" are still categorical but would be single items from a set of possible answers. For such scenarios, direct encoding and unary encoding mechanisms would work better. Moreover, for questions like "What is your age?" the answer is numerical, and the summary of all the answers looks like a histogram. We can use histogram encoding in such cases.

Given that simple outline of how LDP can be used in practice, we will introduce how LDP works in real-world scenarios by walking through how we could design and implement solutions that apply different LDP mechanisms for diverse survey questions. We will start with the most straightforward LDP mechanism, the randomized response.

4.1.2   Randomized response for local differential privacy

As discussed in chapter 2, randomized response (binary mechanism) is one of the oldest and simplest DP mechanisms, but it also satisfies LDP. In this section you will learn how to use the randomized response to design and implement an LDP solution for a privacy-preserving binary survey.

Let's assume we want to survey a group of people to determine the number of people more than 50 years old. Each individual will be asked, "Are you more than 50 years old?" The answer collected from each individual will be either "yes" or "no." The answer is considered a binary response to the survey question, where we give a binary value of 1 to each "yes" answer and a binary value of 0 to each "no" answer. Thus, the final goal is to determine the number of people who are more than 50 years old by counting the number of 1s sent by the individuals as their answers. How can we use the randomized response mechanism to design and implement a locally differentially private survey to gather the answers to this simple "yes" or "no" question?

Here comes the privacy protection. As shown in listing 4.1, each individual will either respond with the true answer or provide a randomized response according to the algorithm. Thus, the privacy of the individuals will be well protected. Also, since each individual will provide the actual answer with a probability of 0.75 (i.e., $1/2 + 1/4 = 0.75$) and give the wrong answer with a probability of 0.25, more individuals will provide true answers. Therefore, we will retain enough essential information to estimate the distribution of the population's statistics (i.e., the number of individuals more than 50 years old).

Listing 4.1   Randomized response-based algorithm

```
def random_response_ages_adult(response):
    true_ans = response > 50

    if np.random.randint(0, 2) == 0:            Flip the first coin.
        return true_ans
    else:
        return np.random.randint(0, 2) == 0     Flip the second coin and return
                                                 the randomized answer.
```

Return the true answer.

Let's implement and test our algorithm on the US Census dataset as shown in listing 4.2. In the next section, we will discuss more practical use cases, but for now we will use the census dataset to demonstrate how you can estimate the aggregated values.

Listing 4.2   Playing with the US Census dataset

```
import numpy as np
import matplotlib.pyplot as plt

ages_adult = np.loadtxt("https://archive.ics.uci.edu/ml/machine-
    learning-databases/adult/adult.data", usecols=0, delimiter=", ")

total_count = len([i for i in ages_adult])
age_over_50_count= len([i for i in ages_adult if i > 50])

print(total_count)
print(age_over_50_count)
print(total_count-age_over_50_count)
```

The output will be as follows:

```
32561
6460
26101
```

As you can see, there are 32,561 individuals in the US Census dataset: 6,460 individuals are more than 50 years old, and 26,101 individuals are younger than or equal to 50 years old.

Now let's see what will happen if we apply our randomized response-based algorithm to the same application.

Listing 4.3   Data perturbation

```
perturbed_age_over_50_count = len([i for i in ages_adult
    if random_response_ages_adult(i)])
print(perturbed_age_over_50_count)
print(total_count-perturbed_age_over_50_count)
```

The result will be as follows:

```
11424
21137
```

As you can see, after applying our randomized response algorithm, the perturbed number of individuals more than 50 years old becomes 11,424, and the perturbed number of individuals younger than or equal to 50 years old is 21,137. In this result, the number of people over 50 is still less than those below or equal to 50, which is in line with the trend of the original dataset. However, this result, 11,424, seems a bit away from the actual result that we want to estimate, 6,460.

Now the question is how to estimate the actual number of people over 50 years old based on our randomized response-based algorithm and the results we've got so far. Apparently, directly using the number of 1 or "yes" values is not a precise estimation of the actual values.

To precisely estimate the actual value of the number of people more than 50 years old, we should consider the source of the randomness in our randomized response-based algorithm and estimate the number of 1s that are from the people who are actually older than 50 years, and the number of 1s that are from the randomized response results. In our algorithm, each individual will tell the truth with a probability of 0.5 and make a random response again with a probability of 0.5. Each random response will result in a 1 or "yes" with a probability of 0.5. Thus, the probability that an individual replies 1 or "yes" solely based on randomness (rather than because they are actually older than 50 years) is $0.5 \times 0.5 = 0.25$. Therefore, as you can see, 25% of our total 1 or "yes" values are false yesses.

On the other hand, due to the first flip of the coin, we split the people who were telling the truth and those who were giving answers randomly. In other words, we can assume there are around the same number of people older than 50 in both groups. Therefore, the number of people over 50 years old is roughly twice the number of people over 50 years old in the group of people who were telling the truth.

Now that we know the problem, we can use the following implementation to estimate the total number of people over 50 years old.

Listing 4.4 Data aggregation and estimation

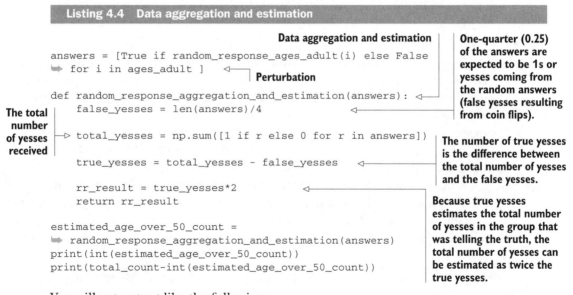

```
answers = [True if random_response_ages_adult(i) else False
    for i in ages_adult ]        Perturbation

def random_response_aggregation_and_estimation(answers):
    false_yesses = len(answers)/4

    total_yesses = np.sum([1 if r else 0 for r in answers])

    true_yesses = total_yesses - false_yesses

    rr_result = true_yesses*2
    return rr_result

estimated_age_over_50_count =
    random_response_aggregation_and_estimation(answers)
print(int(estimated_age_over_50_count))
print(total_count-int(estimated_age_over_50_count))
```

Data aggregation and estimation

One-quarter (0.25) of the answers are expected to be 1s or yesses coming from the random answers (false yesses resulting from coin flips).

The total number of yesses received

The number of true yesses is the difference between the total number of yesses and the false yesses.

Because true yesses estimates the total number of yesses in the group that was telling the truth, the total number of yesses can be estimated as twice the true yesses.

You will get output like the following:

```
6599
25962
```

Now we have a much more precise estimation of the number of people over 50 years old. How close is the estimate? The relative error is just $(6599 - 6460)/6460 = 2.15\%$. Our randomized response-based algorithm seems to have done a good job of estimating the number of people over 50 years old. Also, based on our analysis in chapter 2, the privacy budget of this algorithm is $ln(3)$ (i.e., $ln(3) \approx 1.099$). In other words, our algorithm satisfies $ln(3)$-LDP.

In this section we revisited the randomized response mechanism in the context of LDP by designing and implementing a privacy-preserving binary-question survey application. As you can see, the randomized response mechanism is only good at dealing with problems based on single binary questions, that is, "yes" or "no" questions.

In practice, most questions or tasks are not simply "yes" or "no" questions. They can involve choosing from a finite set of values (such as "What is your occupation?") or returning a histogram of a dataset (such as the distribution of the age of a group of people). We need more general and advanced mechanisms to tackle such problems. In the next section we will introduce more common LDP mechanisms that can be used in more widespread and complex situations.

4.2   The mechanisms of local differential privacy

We've discussed the concept and definition of LDP and how it works using the randomized response mechanism. In this section we'll discuss some commonly utilized LDP mechanisms that work in more general and complex scenarios. These mechanisms will also serve as the building blocks for LDP ML algorithms in the next chapter's case study.

4.2.1   Direct encoding

The randomized response mechanism works for binary (yes or no) questions with LDP. But how about questions that have more than just two answers? For instance, what if we want to determine the number of people with each occupation within the US Census dataset? The occupations could be sales, engineering, financial, technical support, etc. A decent number of different algorithms have been proposed for solving this problem in the local model of differential privacy [2], [3], [4]. Here we'll start with one of the simplest mechanisms, called *direct encoding*.

Given a problem where we need to utilize LDP, the first step is to define the domain of different answers. For example, if we want to learn how many people are in each occupation within the US Census dataset, the domain would be the set of professions available in the dataset. The following lists all the professions in the census dataset.

Listing 4.5   **Number of people in each occupation domain**

```
import pandas as pd
import numpy as np
import matplotlib.pyplot as plt
import sys
import io
import requests
import math

req = requests.get("https://archive.ics.uci.edu/ml/machine-learning-
➥ databases/adult/adult.data").content                    ⟵——————— Load data.
```

```
adult = pd.read_csv(io.StringIO(req.decode('utf-8')),
➥ header=None, na_values='?', delimiter=r", ")
adult.dropna()
adult.head()

domain = adult[6].dropna().unique()      ◁——— The domains
domain.sort()
domain
```

The result will look like the following:

```
array(['Adm-clerical', 'Armed-Forces', 'Craft-repair', 'Exec-managerial',
       'Farming-fishing', 'Handlers-cleaners', 'Machine-op-inspct',
       'Other-service', 'Priv-house-serv', 'Prof-specialty',
       'Protective-serv', 'Sales', 'Tech-support', 'Transport-moving'],
      dtype=object)
```

As we discussed in the previous section, LDP mechanisms usually contain three functions: encoding, which encodes each answer; perturbation, which perturbs the encoded answers; and aggregation and estimation, which aggregates the perturbed answers and estimates the final results. Let's define those three functions for the direct encoding mechanism.

In the direct encoding mechanism, there is usually no encoding of input values. We can use each input's index in the domain set as its encoded value. For example, "Armed-Forces" is the second element of the domain, so the encoded value of "Armed-Forces" is 1 (the index starts from 0).

Listing 4.6   Applying direct encoding

```
def encoding(answer):
    return int(np.where(domain == answer)[0])

print(encoding('Armed-Forces'))      ◁——— Test the encoding.
print(encoding('Craft-repair'))
print(encoding('Sales'))
print(encoding('Transport-moving'))
```

The output of the listing 4.6 will be as follows:

```
1
2
11
13
```

As mentioned, "Armed-Forces" is assigned the value 1, "Craft-repair" is assigned the value 2, and so on.

Our next step is the perturbation. Let's review the perturbation of direct encoding (illustrated in figure 4.4). Each person reports their value v correctly with a probability of the following:

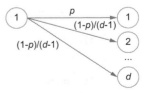

Figure 4.4   The perturbation of direct encoding

$$p = \frac{e^\epsilon}{(e^\epsilon + d - 1)}$$

Or they report one of the remaining $d - 1$ values with a probability of

$$q = \frac{(1 - p)}{(d - 1)} = \frac{1}{(e^\epsilon + d - 1)}$$

where d is the size of the domain set.

For instance, in our example, since there are 14 different professions listed in the US Census dataset, the size of the domain set is $d = 14$. As shown in listing 4.7, if we choose $\epsilon = 5.0$, we have $p = 0.92$ and $q = 0.0062$, which will output the actual value with a higher probability. If we choose $\epsilon = 0.1$, we have $p = 0.078$ and $q = 0.071$, which will generate the actual value with a much lower probability, thus providing more privacy guarantees.

Listing 4.7   Perturbation algorithm in direct encoding

```
def perturbation(encoded_ans, epsilon = 5.0):
    d = len(domain)                                          Size of the domain set
    p = pow(math.e, epsilon) / (d - 1 + pow(math.e, epsilon))
    q = (1.0 - p) / (d - 1.0)

    s1 = np.random.random()
    if s1 <= p:
        return domain[encoded_ans]      ←—— Return itself with probability p
    else:
        s2 = np.random.randint(0, d - 1)
        return domain[(encoded_ans + s2) % d]
print(perturbation(encoding('Armed-Forces')))      ←—  Test the perturbation,
print(perturbation(encoding('Craft-repair')))            epsilon = 5.0.
print(perturbation(encoding('Sales')))
print(perturbation(encoding('Transport-moving')))
print()                                                        Test the
                                                               perturbation,
print(perturbation(encoding('Armed-Forces'), epsilon = .1))  ←— epsilon = .1.
print(perturbation(encoding('Craft-repair'), epsilon = .1))
print(perturbation(encoding('Sales'), epsilon = .1))
print(perturbation(encoding('Transport-moving'), epsilon = .1))
```

The output will look like the following:

```
Armed-Forces
Craft-repair
Sales
Transport-moving

Other-service
Handlers-cleaners
Farming-fishing
Machine-op-inspct
```

Let's try to understand what is happening here. When you assign the epsilon value to be 5.0 (look at the first four results in the output), you get the actual values with a much higher probability. In this case, the accuracy is 100%. However, when you assign epsilon to be a much smaller number (in this case 0.1), the algorithm will generate actual values with a much lower probability; hence, the privacy assurance is better. As can be seen from the latter four results in the output, we are getting different occupations as a result. You can play with assigning different epsilon values in the code to see how it affects the final results.

Let's see what would happen after applying the perturbation to the answers to the survey question, "What is your occupation?" as follows.

Listing 4.8   Results of direct encoding after perturbation

```
perturbed_answers = pd.DataFrame([perturbation(encoding(i))
➥ for i in adult_occupation])
perturbed_answers.value_counts().sort_index()
```

The result after applying the direct encoding will look like this:

```
Adm-clerical        3637
Armed-Forces         157
Craft-repair        3911
Exec-managerial     3931
Farming-fishing     1106
Handlers-cleaners   1419
Machine-op-inspct   2030
Other-service       3259
Priv-house-serv      285
Prof-specialty      4011
Protective-serv      741
Sales               3559
Tech-support        1021
Transport-moving    1651
```

Now that we have the perturbed results, let's compare them with the actual results.

Listing 4.9   Comparison of actual results and perturbed values

```
adult_occupation = adult[6].dropna()          ◁──────┐  The number of people in
adult_occupation.value_counts().sort_index()          │  each occupation category
```

These are the actual results of the number of people in each occupation category:

```
Adm-clerical        3770
Armed-Forces           9
Craft-repair        4099
Exec-managerial     4066
Farming-fishing      994
Handlers-cleaners   1370
Machine-op-inspct   2002
```

```
Other-service       3295
Priv-house-serv      149
Prof-specialty      4140
Protective-serv      649
Sales               3650
Tech-support         928
Transport-moving    1597
```

For clarity, let's compare the results side by side, as shown in table 4.1. As can be seen, some of the aggregations of the perturbed answers have very high errors compared to the actual values. For instance, for the number of people with the occupation "Armed-Forces," the perturbed value is 157 but the true value is 9.

Table 4.1   Number of people in each profession, before and after perturbation

Number	Profession	Number of people	
		Original value	After perturbation
1	Adm-clerical	3770	3637
2	Armed-Forces	9	157
3	Craft-repair	4099	3911
4	Exec-managerial	4066	3931
5	Farming-fishing	994	1106
6	Handlers-cleaners	1370	1419
7	Machine-op-inspct	2002	2030
8	Other-service	3295	3259
9	Priv-house-serv	149	285
10	Prof-specialty	4140	4011
11	Protective-serv	649	741
12	Sales	3650	3559
13	Tech-support	928	1021
14	Transport-moving	1597	1651

To overcome such errors, we need to have an aggregation and estimation function along with the direct encoding mechanism. In the aggregation and estimation, when the aggregator collects the perturbed values from n individuals, it estimates the frequency of each occupation $I \in \{1,2,\ldots,d\}$ as follows: First, c_i is the number of times i is reported. The estimated number of occurrences of value i in the population is computed as $E_i = (c_i - n \cdot q)/(p - q)$. To ensure the estimated number is always a non-negative value, we set $E_i = \max(E_i, 1)$. You can try implementing listing 4.10 to see how it works.

Listing 4.10   Applying aggregation and estimation to direct encoding

```
def aggregation_and_estimation(answers, epsilon = 5.0):
    n = len(answers)
    d = len(domain)
    p = pow(math.e, epsilon) / (d - 1 + pow(math.e, epsilon))
    q = (1.0 - p) / (d - 1.0)

    aggregator = answers.value_counts().sort_index()

    return [max(int((i - n*q) / (p-q)), 1) for i in aggregator]

estimated_answers = aggregation_and_estimation(perturbed_answers)
list(zip(domain, estimated_answers))
```

Data aggregation and estimation

You will get something like the following as the output:

```
[('Adm-clerical', 3774),
 ('Armed-Forces', 1),
 ('Craft-repair', 4074),
 ('Exec-managerial', 4095),
 ('Farming-fishing', 1002),
 ('Handlers-cleaners', 1345),
 ('Machine-op-inspct', 2014),
 ('Other-service', 3360),
 ('Priv-house-serv', 103),
 ('Prof-specialty', 4183),
 ('Protective-serv', 602),
 ('Sales', 3688),
 ('Tech-support', 909),
 ('Transport-moving', 1599)]
```

With that result, let's compare the estimated results to the actual results as shown in table 4.2. As you can see, the estimated results of the direct encoding mechanism are much more precise than the perturbed results when using the privacy budget $x = 5.0$. You can try changing the privacy budget in this code or apply the code to other datasets to see how it works.

Table 4.2   Number of people in each profession, before and after aggregation and estimation

Number	Profession	Number of people	
		Original value	After aggregation and estimation
1	Adm-clerical	3770	3774
2	Armed-Forces	9	1
3	Craft-repair	4099	4074
4	Exec-managerial	4066	4095

Table 4.2   Number of people in each profession, before and after aggregation and estimation *(continued)*

Number	Profession	Number of people	
		Original value	After aggregation and estimation
5	Farming-fishing	994	1002
6	Handlers-cleaners	1370	1345
7	Machine-op-inspct	2002	2014
8	Other-service	3295	3360
9	Priv-house-serv	149	103
10	Prof-specialty	4140	4183
11	Protective-serv	649	602
12	Sales	3650	3688
13	Tech-support	928	909
14	Transport-moving	1597	1599

You've now seen one LDP mechanism that uses direct encoding. Those steps can be summarized in the following three components:

- Encoding: Direct encoding (generalization of binary randomized response)
- Perturbation: $p = \frac{e^{\varepsilon}}{d - 1 + e^{\varepsilon}}$ for ε-LDP
- Estimation: $E_i = \frac{\Sigma^i - nq}{p - q}$ where $q = (1 - p)/(d - 1)$

4.2.2 Histogram encoding

The direct encoding mechanism enables us to apply LDP to categorical and discrete problems. In contrast, histogram encoding enables us to apply LDP to numerical and continuous data.

Consider a survey question that has numerical and continuous answers. For example, suppose someone wants to know the distribution or histogram of people's ages within a group of people, which we cannot achieve with direct encoding. They could conduct a survey to ask each individual a survey question: "What is your age?" Let's take the US Census dataset as an example and plot the histogram of people's ages.

Listing 4.11   Plotting a histogram with people's ages

```
import pandas as pd
import numpy as np
import matplotlib.pyplot as plt
import sys
import io
import requests
```

```
import math

req = requests.get("https://archive.ics.uci.edu/ml/machine-learning-
➥   databases/adult/adult.data").content
adult = pd.read_csv(io.StringIO(req.decode('utf-8')),        Load data.
➥   header=None, na_values='?', delimiter=r", ")
adult.dropna()
adult.head()

adult_age = adult[0].dropna()              ◁──── The ages of the people
ax = adult_age.plot.hist(bins=100, alpha=1.0)
```

The output will look like the histogram in figure 4.5, indicating the number of people in each age category. As you can see, the largest number of people are in the age ranges of ~20 to 40, whereas a lesser number of people are reported in the other values. The histogram-encoding mechanism is designed to deal with such numerical and continuous data.

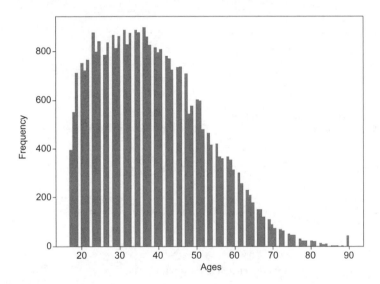

Figure 4.5   Histogram of people's ages from US Census dataset

We first need to define the input domain (i.e., the survey answers). Here, we assume all the people taking the survey will be from 10 to 100 years old.

Listing 4.12   Input domain of the survey people's ages

```
domain = np.arange(10, 101)       ◁───┐  The domain is in the
domain.sort()                         │  range of 10 to 100.
domain
```

Therefore, the domain will look like this:

```
array([ 10,  11,  12,  13,  14,  15,  16,  17,  18,  19,  20,  21,  22,
        23,  24,  25,  26,  27,  28,  29,  30,  31,  32,  33,  34,  35,
```

```
36,  37,  38,  39,  40,  41,  42,  43,  44,  45,  46,  47,  48,
49,  50,  51,  52,  53,  54,  55,  56,  57,  58,  59,  60,  61,
62,  63,  64,  65,  66,  67,  68,  69,  70,  71,  72,  73,  74,
75,  76,  77,  78,  79,  80,  81,  82,  83,  84,  85,  86,  87,
88,  89,  90,  91,  92,  93,  94,  95,  96,  97,  98,  99, 100])
```

In histogram encoding, an individual encodes their value v as a length-d vector $[0.0,0.0,\ldots,0.0,1.0,0.0,\ldots,0.0]$ where only the vth component is 1.0 and the remaining components are 0.0. For example, suppose there are 6 values in total ($\{1,2,3,4,5,6\}$), that is, $d = 6$, and the actual value to be encoded is 6. In that case, the histogram encoding will output the vector ($\{0.0,0.0,0.0,0.0,0.0,1.0\}$), where only the sixth position of the vector is 1.0 and all the other positions are 0.0 (see figure 4.6).

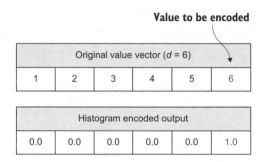

Value to be encoded

Only the sixth position of the vector is 1.0 and all the other positions are 0.0.   **Figure 4.6   How histogram encoding works**

The following listing shows the implementation of the encoding function.

Listing 4.13   Histogram encoding

```
def encoding(answer):
    return [1.0 if d == answer else 0.0 for d in domain]

print(encoding(11))   ◁─── Test the encoding for input age 11.

answers = np.sum([encoding(r) for r in adult_age], axis=0)   ◁──┐ Data
plt.bar(domain, answers)                                        │ encoding
                                                                │ plot
```

The output of listing 4.13 follows, and the histogram result is shown in figure 4.7:

```
[0.0, 1.0, 0.0, 0.0, 0.0, 0.0, 0.0, 0.0, 0.0, 0.0, 0.0, 0.0, 0.0, 0.0, 0.0,
    0.0, 0.0, 0.0, 0.0, 0.0, 0.0, 0.0, 0.0, 0.0, 0.0, 0.0, 0.0, 0.0, 0.0,
    0.0, 0.0, 0.0, 0.0, 0.0, 0.0, 0.0, 0.0, 0.0, 0.0, 0.0, 0.0, 0.0, 0.0,
    0.0, 0.0, 0.0, 0.0, 0.0, 0.0, 0.0, 0.0, 0.0, 0.0, 0.0, 0.0, 0.0, 0.0,
    0.0, 0.0, 0.0, 0.0, 0.0, 0.0, 0.0, 0.0, 0.0, 0.0, 0.0, 0.0, 0.0, 0.0,
    0.0, 0.0, 0.0, 0.0, 0.0, 0.0, 0.0, 0.0, 0.0, 0.0, 0.0, 0.0, 0.0, 0.0,
    0.0, 0.0, 0.0, 0.0, 0.0, 0.0]
```

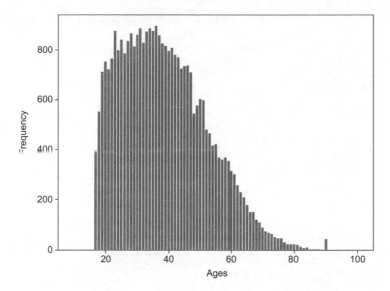

Figure 4.7 Histogram of encoded ages

The data owners perturb their value by adding $Lap(2/\epsilon)$ to each component in the encoded value, where $Lap(2/\epsilon)$ is a sample from the Laplace distribution with mean 0 and scale parameter $2/\epsilon$. If you need a refresher on the Laplace distribution and its properties, look back to section 2.1.2.

When the data aggregator collects all the perturbed values, the aggregator has two options for estimation methods:

- Summation with histogram encoding (SHE)
- Thresholding with histogram encoding (THE)

SUMMATION WITH HISTOGRAM ENCODING (SHE)

Summation with histogram encoding (SHE) calculates the sum of all values reported by individuals. To estimate the number of occurrences of value i in the population, the data aggregator sums the ith component of all reported values.

The following listing shows the implementation of the perturbation using SHE.

Listing 4.14 Summation with histogram encoding

```
def she_perturbation(encoded_ans, epsilon = 5.0):
    return [she_perturb_bit(b, epsilon) for b in encoded_ans]

def she_perturb_bit(bit, epsilon = 5.0):
    return bit + np.random.laplace(loc=0, scale = 2 / epsilon)

print(she_perturbation(encoding(11)))      ◁─── Test the perturbation, epsilon = 5.0.
print()

print(she_perturbation(encoding(11), epsilon = .1))   ◁─┤ Test the perturbation,
                                                        │ epsilon = .1.

she_estimated_answers = np.sum([she_perturbation(encoding(r))
 ➡ for r in adult_age], axis=0)     ◁───
plt.bar(domain, she_estimated_answers)  │ Data perturbation, aggregation, and estimation
```

The output of listing 4.14 follows, and figure 4.8 shows a histogram of the results.

```
[0.4962679135705772, 0.3802597925066964, -0.30259173228948666,
    -1.3184657393652501, ......, 0.2728526263450592,
    0.6818717669557512, 0.5099963270758622,
    -0.3750514505079954, 0.3577214398174087]
```

```
[14.199378030914811, 51.55958531259166, -3.168607913723072,
    -14.592805035271969, ......, -18.342283098694853,
    -33.37135136829752, 39.56097740265926,
    15.187624540264636, -6.307239922495188,
    -18.130661553271608, -5.199234599011756]
```

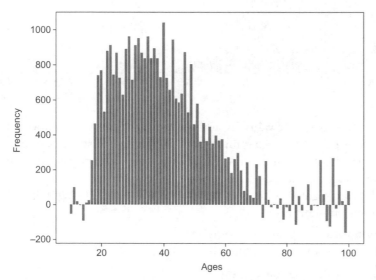

Figure 4.8 Summation of estimated ages using SHE

As you can see from figure 4.8, estimated values using SHE have a shape similar to the original encoded histogram in figure 4.7. However, the histogram in figure 4.8 is generated using an estimation function. Those estimated values have noise in them, so they are not real, and they can result in negative values. A negative age frequency is invalid for this example, so we can discard those values.

THRESHOLDING WITH HISTOGRAM ENCODING (THE)

In the case of thresholding with histogram encoding (THE), the data aggregator sets all values greater than a threshold θ to 1, and the remaining values to 0. Then it estimates the number of is in the population as $E_i = (c_i - n \cdot q)/(p - q)$, where $p = 1 - 1/2\,e^{(\epsilon \cdot (1-\theta)/2)}$, $q = e^{(\epsilon \cdot (0-\theta)/2)}$, and c_i is the number of 1s in the ith components of all reported values after applying thresholding.

The following listing shows the implementation of the perturbation using THE.

Listing 4.15   Thresholding with histogram encoding

```
def the_perturbation(encoded_ans, epsilon = 5.0, theta = 1.0):
    return [the_perturb_bit(b, epsilon, theta) for b in encoded_ans]

def the_perturb_bit(bit, epsilon = 5.0, theta = 1.0):
    val = bit + np.random.laplace(loc=0, scale = 2 / epsilon)

    if val > theta:
        return 1.0
    else:
        return 0.0

print(the_perturbation(encoding(11)))          ◁——— Test the perturbation, epsilon = 5.0.
print()
                                                       Test the perturbation,
print(the_perturbation(encoding(11), epsilon = .1))  ◁——┘ epsilon = .1.

the_perturbed_answers = np.sum([the_perturbation(encoding(r))
➥  for r in adult_age], axis=0)             ◁——┐
plt.bar(domain, the_perturbed_answers)             Total perturbation
plt.ylabel('Frequency')
plt.xlabel('Ages')

def the_aggregation_and_estimation(answers, epsilon = 5.0, theta = 1.0):  ◁—┐
    p = 1 - 0.5 * pow(math.e, epsilon / 2 * (1.0 - theta))
    q = 0.5 * pow(math.e, epsilon / 2 * (0.0 - theta))       THE—aggregation
                                                              and estimation
    sums = np.sum(answers, axis=0)
    n = len(answers)

    return [int((i - n * q) / (p-q)) for i in sums]
```

The output will look like the following for different epsilon values. Figure 4.9 shows the total perturbation before the THE estimation function.

```
[0.0, 1.0, 0.0, 0.0, 0.0, 0.0, 0.0, 0.0, 1.0, 0.0, 0.0, 0.0, 0.0, 0.0, 0.0,
    0.0, 0.0, 0.0, 1.0, 0.0, 0.0, 0.0, 0.0, 0.0, 0.0, 1.0, 0.0, 0.0, 0.0,
    0.0, 0.0, 0.0, 0.0, 0.0, 0.0, 0.0, 0.0, 0.0, 0.0, 0.0, 0.0, 0.0, 0.0,
    0.0, 0.0, 0.0, 0.0, 0.0, 0.0, 0.0, 0.0, 0.0, 0.0, 0.0, 0.0, 0.0, 0.0,
    0.0, 0.0, 0.0, 0.0, 0.0, 0.0, 0.0, 0.0, 0.0, 0.0, 0.0, 0.0, 0.0, 0.0,
    0.0, 0.0, 0.0, 0.0, 0.0, 0.0, 0.0, 0.0, 0.0, 0.0, 0.0, 0.0, 0.0, 0.0,
    0.0, 0.0, 0.0, 0.0, 0.0, 0.0]

[1.0, 1.0, 1.0, 0.0, 0.0, 0.0, 0.0, 0.0, 1.0, 0.0, 0.0, 0.0, 0.0, 0.0, 1.0,
    1.0, 0.0, 1.0, 0.0, 1.0, 1.0, 0.0, 1.0, 1.0, 0.0, 0.0, 0.0, 1.0, 0.0,
    0.0, 0.0, 1.0, 0.0, 0.0, 1.0, 1.0, 1.0, 0.0, 0.0, 1.0, 0.0, 0.0, 0.0,
    1.0, 1.0, 1.0, 0.0, 0.0, 0.0, 1.0, 1.0, 0.0, 0.0, 0.0, 0.0, 0.0, 1.0,
    0.0, 1.0, 1.0, 0.0, 1.0, 0.0, 1.0, 0.0, 0.0, 0.0, 1.0, 1.0, 1.0, 1.0,
    0.0, 0.0, 0.0, 1.0, 0.0, 0.0, 0.0, 0.0, 0.0, 1.0, 1.0, 0.0, 1.0, 0.0,
    1.0, 0.0, 0.0, 0.0, 0.0, 1.0]
```

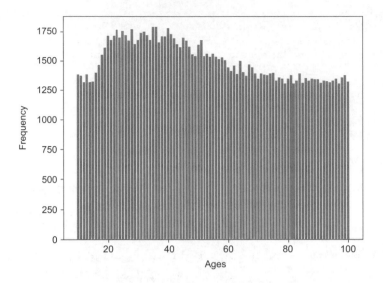

Figure 4.9   Histogram of perturbed answers using THE

The estimated values can be obtained as shown in the following code snippet:

```
# Data aggregation and estimation
the_perturbed_answers = [the_perturbation(encoding(r)) for r in adult_age]
estimated_answers = the_aggregation_and_estimation(the_perturbed_answers)
plt.bar(domain, estimated_answers)
plt.ylabel('Frequency')
plt.xlabel('Ages')
```

The output histogram is shown in figure 4.10. The estimated values of THE follow a shape similar to the original encoded histogram in figure 4.7.

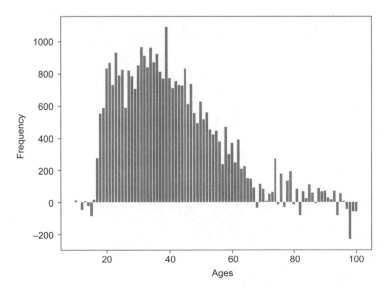

Figure 4.10 Thresholding estimated ages

In summary, histogram encoding enables us to apply LDP for numerical and continuous data, and we discussed two estimation mechanisms for LDP under histogram encoding: SHE and THE. SHE sums up the reported noisy histograms from all users, whereas THE interprets each noisy count above a threshold as 1 and each count below the threshold as 0. When you compare histogram encoding with direct encoding, you'll realize that direct encoding has a more significant variance when the size of the domain set d becomes larger. With THE, by fixing ε, you can choose a θ value to minimize the variance. This means THE can improve the estimation over SHE because thresholding limits the effects of large amounts of noise:

- Summation with histogram encoding (SHE):
    - Encoding: Encode(v) = [0.0, 0.0,...,1.0,...,0.0] where only the vth component is 1.0.
    - Perturbation: Add $Lap(2/\varepsilon)$ to each component.
    - Estimation: Sums up the reported noisy histograms from all individuals.
- Thresholding with histogram encoding (THE):
    - Encoding: Encode(v) = [0.0, 0.0,...,1.0,...,0.0] where only the vth component is 1.0.
    - Perturbation: Add $Lap(2/\varepsilon)$ to each component. Set the values $> \theta$ to 1, and the remaining values to 0.
    - Estimation: $E_i = \frac{\Sigma^i - nq}{p - q}$ where $p = 1 - \frac{1}{2}e^{\frac{\varepsilon}{2}(1-\theta)}$ and $q = 1 - \frac{1}{2}e^{-\frac{\varepsilon}{2}(\theta)}$.

4.2.3 Unary encoding

The unary encoding mechanism is a more general and efficient LDP mechanism for categorical and discrete problems. In this method, an individual encodes their value v as a length-d binary vector [0, ..., 1, ..., 0] where only the vth bit is 1 and the remaining bits are 0. Then, for each bit in the encoded vector, they report the value correctly with probability p and incorrectly with probability $1 - p$ if the input bit is 1. Otherwise, they can report correctly with probability $1 - q$ and incorrectly with probability q.

In unary encoding, we again have two different options to proceed with:

- Symmetric unary encoding (SUE)
- Optimal unary encoding (OUE)

In the case of symmetric unary encoding, p is selected as $\frac{e^{\frac{\varepsilon}{2}}}{e^{\frac{\varepsilon}{2}}+1}$ and q is selected as $1 - p$. In optimal unary encoding, p is selected as $1/2$ and q is selected as $1/(e^{\varepsilon} + 1)$. Then the data aggregator estimates the number of 1s in the population as $E_i = (c_i - m \cdot q)/(p - q)$, where c_i denotes the number of 1s in the ith bit of all reported values.

As an example of the unary encoding mechanism, suppose someone wants to determine how many people there are of different races. They would need to ask each individual the question, "What is your race?" Let's try to implement SUE on the US Census dataset. The OUE implementation would be an extension of the SUE implementation, with changes to the definitions of p and q in the implementation. (You can also refer to the sample implementation of OUE in our code repository.)

First, let's load the data and check the domains.

Listing 4.16   Retrieving different race categories in the dataset

```
import pandas as pd
import numpy as np
import matplotlib.pyplot as plt
import sys
import io
import requests
import math

req = requests.get("https://archive.ics.uci.edu/ml/machine-learning-
➥ databases/adult/adult.data").content             ◄─┐  Load the data.
adult = pd.read_csv(io.StringIO(req.decode('utf-8')), │
➥ header=None, na_values='?', delimiter=r", ")
adult.dropna()
adult.head()

domain = adult[8].dropna().unique()      ◄──── The domains
domain.sort()
domain
```

The output of listing 4.16 will look like the following

```
array(['Amer-Indian-Eskimo', 'Asian-Pac-Islander', 'Black', 'Other',
       'White'], dtype=object)
```

As you can see, there are five different races in the dataset.

Now let's look at the actual numbers of people of different races in the US Census dataset.

Listing 4.17   Number of people of each race

```
adult_race = adult[8].dropna()
adult_race.value_counts().sort_index()
```

Here is the output with the actual numbers in the dataset:

```
Amer-Indian-Eskimo       311
Asian-Pac-Islander      1039
Black                   3124
Other                    271
White                  27816
```

As you can see, we have 311 people in the category of "Amer-Indian-Eskimo," 1,039 people in "Asian-Pac-Islander," and so on.

Now let's look into the implementation of the SUE mechanism.

Listing 4.18   Symmetric unary encoding

```
def encoding(answer):
    return [1 if d == answer else 0 for d in domain]

print(encoding('Amer-Indian-Eskimo'))     ◄──── Test the encoding.
```

```
print(encoding('Asian-Pac-Islander'))
print(encoding('Black'))
print(encoding('Other'))
print(encoding('White'))
```

You should get an output similar to the following:

```
[1, 0, 0, 0, 0]
[0, 1, 0, 0, 0]
[0, 0, 1, 0, 0]
[0, 0, 0, 1, 0]
[0, 0, 0, 0, 1]
```

As we discussed at the beginning of this section, the idea is that each individual encodes their value v as a length-d binary vector [0,....,1,...,0] where only the vth bit is 1 and the remaining bits are 0.

The following listing shows how you could implement the perturbation of the SUE mechanism. It is mostly self-explanatory.

Listing 4.19   Perturbation of the symmetric unary encoding

```
def sym_perturbation(encoded_ans, epsilon = 5.0):
    return [sym_perturb_bit(b, epsilon) for b in encoded_ans]

def sym_perturb_bit(bit, epsilon = 5.0):
    p = pow(math.e, epsilon / 2) / (1 + pow(math.e, epsilon / 2))
    q = 1 - p

    s = np.random.random()
    if bit == 1:
        if s <= p:
            return 1
        else:
            return 0
    elif bit == 0:
        if s <= q:
            return 1
        else:
            return 0

print(sym_perturbation(encoding('Amer-Indian-Eskimo')))
print(sym_perturbation(encoding('Asian-Pac-Islander')))
print(sym_perturbation(encoding('Black')))
print(sym_perturbation(encoding('Other')))
print(sym_perturbation(encoding('White')))
print()

print(sym_perturbation(encoding('Amer-Indian-Eskimo'), epsilon = .1))
print(sym_perturbation(encoding('Asian-Pac-Islander'), epsilon = .1))
print(sym_perturbation(encoding('Black'), epsilon = .1))
print(sym_perturbation(encoding('Other'), epsilon = .1))
print(sym_perturbation(encoding('White'), epsilon = .1))
```

Symmetric unary encoding—perturbation

Test the perturbation, epsilon = 5.0.

Test the perturbation, epsilon = .1.

The output of listing 4.19 will look like the following:

```
[1, 0, 0, 0, 0]
[0, 1, 0, 0, 0]
[0, 0, 1, 0, 0]
[0, 0, 0, 1, 0]
[0, 0, 0, 0, 1]

[1, 1, 0, 0, 1]
[0, 1, 1, 0, 1]
[1, 0, 1, 0, 0]
[1, 0, 0, 0, 1]
[1, 0, 0, 0, 1]
```

This shows two sets of vectors, similar to what we had in earlier mechanisms. The first set is with epsilon assigned 5.0, and the other is with epsilon assigned 0.1.

Now we can test it to see the perturbed answers:

```
sym_perturbed_answers = np.sum([sym_perturbation(encoding(r))
➥ for r in adult_race], axis=0)
list(zip(domain, sym_perturbed_answers))
```

You will have results similar to these:

```
[('Amer-Indian-Eskimo', 2851),
 ('Asian-Pac-Islander', 3269),
 ('Black', 5129),
 ('Other', 2590),
 ('White', 26063)]
```

Remember, these are only the values after the perturbation. We are not done yet!

Next comes the aggregation and estimation of the SUE mechanism.

Listing 4.20   Estimation of the symmetric unary encoding

```
def sym_aggregation_and_estimation(answers, epsilon = 5.0):    ◁──┐
    p = pow(math.e, epsilon / 2) / (1 + pow(math.e, epsilon / 2))  │
    q = 1 - p                                                      │
                                          Symmetric unary encoding—│
    sums = np.sum(answers, axis=0)        aggregation and estimation│
    n = len(answers)                                               │

    return [int((i - n * q) / (p-q)) for i in sums]

sym_perturbed_answers = [sym_perturbation(encoding(r)) for r in adult_race]  ◁──┐
estimated_answers = sym_aggregation_and_estimation(sym_perturbed_answers)        │
list(zip(domain, estimated_answers))                                             │
                                                                  Data aggregation│
                                                                   and estimation │
```

The final values of the estimation will look like these:

```
[('Amer-Indian-Eskimo', 215),
 ('Asian-Pac-Islander', 1082),
 ('Black', 3180),
 ('Other', 196),
 ('White', 27791)]
```

Now you know how SUE works. Let's compare the actual and estimated values side by side to see what the difference looks like. If you pay close attention to table 4.3, you will understand that SUE works better with this kind of categorical data.

Table 4.3 Number of people in each race, before and after applying SUE

Number	Race	Number of people	
		Original value	After applying SUE
1	Amer-Indian-Eskimo	311	215
2	Asian-Pac-Islander	1039	1082
3	Black	3124	3180
4	Other	271	196
5	White	27816	27791

In this section we introduced two LDP mechanisms with unary encoding:

- Symmetric unary encoding (SUE):
  - Encoding: Encode(v) = [0, 0, ..., 1, ..., 0] where only the vth bit is 1.
  - Perturbation: Each bit is perturbed as in the binary randomized response mechanism. $p = \frac{e^{\frac{\varepsilon}{2}}}{e^{\frac{\varepsilon}{2}}+1}$ for ε-LDP.
  - Estimation: For each value, use the estimation formula in the binary randomized response mechanism.
- Optimized unary encoding (OUE):
  - Encoding: Encode(v) = [0, 0, ..., 1, ..., 0] where only the vth bit is 1.
  - Perturbation: $p = 1/2$, $q = 1/(e^{\varepsilon} + 1)$ (as shown in figure 4.11).
  - Estimation: $E_i = \frac{\Sigma^i - nq}{p - q}$.

This chapter mainly focused on how different LDP mechanisms work, particularly for one-dimensional data. In chapter 5, we will extend our discussion and look at how we can work with multidimensional data using more advanced mechanisms.

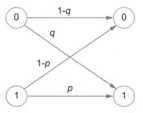

Figure 4.11 The perturbation of optimized unary encoding

Summary

- Unlike centralized DP, LDP eliminates the need for a trusted data curator; thus, individuals can send their data to the data aggregator after privatizing it using perturbation techniques.
- In many practical use cases, LDP is applied for mean or frequency estimation.
- The randomized response mechanism can also be used with LDP through the design and implementation of privacy-preserving algorithms.
- While direct encoding helps us apply LDP for categorical and discreet data, histogram encoding can be used to apply LDP for numerical and continuous variables.
- When the data aggregator collects the perturbed values, the aggregator has two options for estimation methods: summation with histogram encoding (SHE) and thresholding with histogram encoding (THE).
- Summation with histogram encoding (SHE) calculates the sum of all values reported by individuals.
- In the case of thresholding with histogram encoding (THE), the data aggregator sets all values greater than a threshold θ to 1, and the remaining values to 0.
- The unary encoding mechanism is a more general and efficient LDP mechanism for categorical and discrete problems.

5
Advanced LDP mechanisms for machine learning

This chapter covers

- Advanced LDP mechanisms
- Working with naive Bayes for ML classification
- Using LDP naive Bayes for discrete features
- Using LDP naive Bayes for continuous features and multidimensional data
- Designing and analyzing an LDP ML algorithm

In the previous chapter we looked into the basic concepts and definition of local differential privacy (LDP), along with its underlying mechanisms and some examples. However, most of those mechanisms are explicitly designed for one-dimensional data and frequency estimation techniques, with direct encoding, histogram encoding, unary encoding, and so on. In this chapter we will extend our discussion further and look at how we can work with multidimensional data.

First, we'll introduce an example machine learning (ML) use case with naive Bayes classification. Then, we'll look at a case study implementation of LDP naive Bayes by designing and analyzing an LDP ML algorithm.

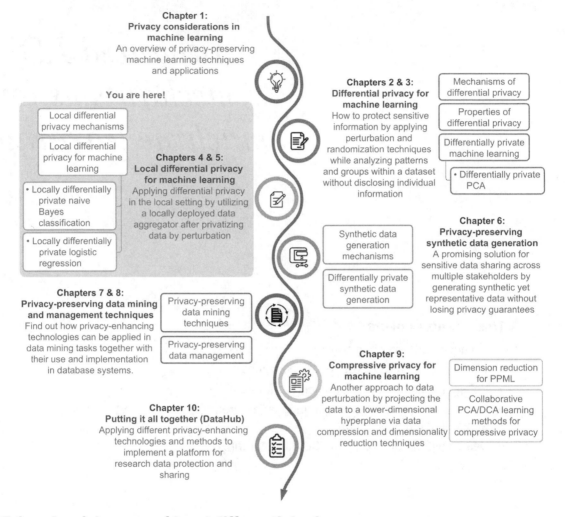

5.1   *A quick recap of local differential privacy*

As we discussed in the previous chapter, LDP is a way of measuring individual privacy when the data collector is not trusted. LDP aims to guarantee that when an individual provides a particular value, it should be difficult to identify the individual, thus providing privacy protection. Many LDP mechanisms also aim to estimate the distribution of the population as accurately as possible, based on an aggregation of perturbed data collected from multiple individuals.

Figure 5.1 summarizes the steps of applying LDP in different application scenarios. For more about how LDP works, see chapter 4.

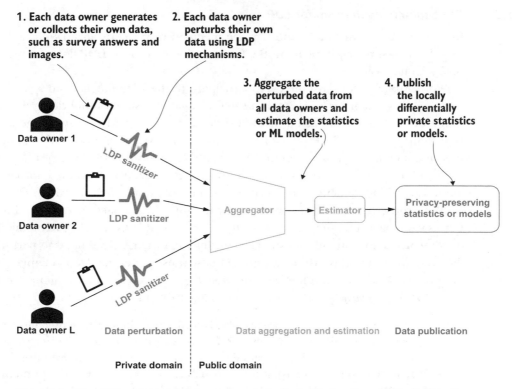

1. Each data owner generates or collects their own data, such as survey answers and images.

2. Each data owner perturbs their own data using **LDP** mechanisms.

3. Aggregate the perturbed data from all data owners and estimate the statistics or ML models.

4. Publish the locally differentially private statistics or models.

Data owner 1

Data owner 2

Data owner L

LDP sanitizer

Aggregator

Estimator

Privacy-preserving statistics or models

Data perturbation

Data aggregation and estimation

Data publication

Private domain | Public domain

Figure 5.1 How LDP works: each data owner perturbs their data locally and submits it to the aggregator.

Now that we've reviewed the basics of how LDP works, let's look at some more advanced LDP mechanisms.

5.2 *Advanced LDP mechanisms*

In chapter 4 we looked at the direct encoding, histogram encoding, and unary encoding LDP mechanisms. Those algorithms all work for one-dimensional categorical data or discrete numerical data. For example, the answer to the survey question "What is your occupation?" will be one occupation category, which is one-dimensional categorical data. The answer to the survey question "What is your age?" will be a one-dimensional discrete numerical value. However, many other datasets, especially when working with ML tasks, are more complex and contain multidimensional continuous numerical data. For instance, pixel-based images are usually high-dimensional, and mobile-device sensor data (such as gyroscope or accelerometer sensors) is multidimensional, usually continuous, numerical data. Therefore, learning about the LDP mechanisms that deal with such scenarios in ML tasks is essential.

In this section we'll focus on three different mechanisms that are designed for multidimensional continuous numerical data: the Laplace mechanism, Duchi's mechanism, and the Piecewise mechanism.

5.2.1 *The Laplace mechanism for LDP*

In chapter 2 we introduced the Laplace mechanism for centralized differential privacy. We can similarly implement the Laplace mechanism for LDP. First, though, let's review some basics.

For simplicity, let's assume each participant in the LDP mechanism is u_i and that each u_i's data record is t_i. This t_i is a usually one-dimensional numerical value in the range of −1 to 1 (as discussed in the previous chapter), and we can mathematically represent it as $t_i \in [-1,1]^d$. However, in this section we are going to discuss multidimensional data, so t_i can be defined as a d-dimensional numerical vector in the range of −1 to 1 as $t_i \in [-1, 1]^d$. In addition, we are going to perturb t_i with the Laplace mechanism, so we'll let t_i^* denote the perturbed data record of t_i after applying LDP.

With those basics covered, we can now dig into the Laplace mechanism for LDP. Let's say we have a participant u_i, and their data record is $t_i \in [-1,1]^d$. Remember, this data record is now multidimensional. In order to satisfy LDP, we need to perturb this data record, and in this case we are going to use noise generated from a Laplace distribution. We'll define a randomized function $t_i^* = t_i + Lap(2 * d/\epsilon)$ to generate a perturbed value t_i^*, *where Lap(λ) is* a random variable from a Laplace distribution of scale λ.

> **TIP** Are you wondering why we are always looking at the Laplace mechanism when it comes to differential privacy? The reason is that Gaussian perturbations are not always satisfactory, since they cannot be used to achieve pure DP (ε-DP), which requires heavier-tailed distributions. Thus, the most popular distribution is the Laplace mechanism, whose tails are "just right" for achieving pure DP.

The following listing shows the Python code that implements the Laplace mechanism for LDP.

Listing 5.1 The Laplace mechanism for LDP

```
def getNoisyAns_Lap(t_i, epsilon):
    loc = 0
    d = t_i.shape[0]
    scale = 2 * d / epsilon
    s = np.random.laplace(loc, scale, t_i.shape)
    t_star = t_i + s
    return t_star
```

The Laplace mechanism provides the basic functionality to perturb multidimensional continuous numerical data for LDP. However, as studied by Wang et al. [1], when using a smaller privacy budget ϵ (i.e., $\epsilon < 2.3$), the Laplace mechanism tends to result in more variance in the perturbed data, thus providing bad utility performance. In the next section we'll look into the Duchi's mechanism, which performs better when using a smaller privacy budget.

5.2.2 *Duchi's mechanism for LDP*

While the Laplace mechanism is one way to generate noise for the perturbation that is used with LDP, Duchi et al. [2] introduced another approach, known as Duchi's mechanism, to perturb multidimensional continuous numerical data for LDP. The concept is similar to the Laplace mechanism, but the data perturbation is handled differently.

Let's first look at how Duchi's mechanism handles perturbation for one-dimensional numerical data. Given a participant u_i, their one-dimensional data record $t_i \in [-1,1]$, and a privacy budget ϵ, Duchi's mechanism performs as follows:

1. A Bernoulli variable u is sampled such that $\Pr[u = 1] = \frac{e^\epsilon - 1}{2e^\epsilon + 2} \cdot t_i + \frac{1}{2}$.
2. Then, if $u = 1$, the perturbed data will be $t_i^* = \frac{e^\epsilon + 1}{e^\epsilon - 1}$; otherwise, it is $t_i^* = -\frac{e^\epsilon + 1}{e^\epsilon - 1}$.
3. The perturbed data $t_i^* \in \left\{ -\frac{e^\epsilon + 1}{e^\epsilon - 1}, \frac{e^\epsilon + 1}{e^\epsilon - 1} \right\}$ will be the output of Duchi's mechanism.

The Python implementation of this algorithm is shown in the following listing.

Listing 5.2 Duchi's mechanism for one-dimensional data

```python
def Duchi_1d(t_i, eps, t_star):
    p = (math.exp(eps) - 1) / (2 * math.exp(eps) + 2) * t_i + 0.5
    coin = np.random.binomial(1, p)
    if coin == 1:
        return t_star[1]
    else:
        return t_star[0]
```

What is the Bernoulli distribution?

In probability theory, the Bernoulli distribution is one of the simplest distributions to understand, and it is often used as a building block for more complex distributions. At a high level, the Bernoulli distribution is a discrete probability distribution with only two possible values for the random variable, where it takes the value 1 with probability p and the value 0 with probability $q = 1 - p$.

In simpler terms, if an experiment has only two possible outcomes, "success" and "failure," and if p is the probability of success, then

$$P(n) = \begin{cases} 1 - p & for\ n = 0 \\ p & for\ n = 1 \end{cases}$$

In this context, we usually consider "success" to be the outcome that we want to keep track of.

Now that you know how Duchi's mechanism works for one-dimensional data, let's extend it for multidimensional data. Given a d-dimensional data record $t_i \in [-1,1]^d$ and the privacy budget ϵ, Duchi's mechanism for multidimensional data performs as follows:

1 Generate a random d-dimensional data record $v \in [-1,1]^d$ by sampling each $v[A_j]$ independently from the following distribution,

$$\Pr[v[A_j] = x] = \begin{cases} \frac{1}{2} + \frac{1}{2}t_i[A_j], & if\ x = 1 \\ \frac{1}{2} - \frac{1}{2}t_i[A_j], & if\ x = -1 \end{cases}$$

where $v[A_j]$ is the jth value of v.

2 Define T^+ (resp. T^-) as the set of all data records $t^* \in \{-B,B\}^d$ such that $t^* \cdot v \geq 0$ (resp. $t^* \cdot v \leq 0$), where we have

$$B = \frac{\exp(\epsilon) + 1}{\exp(\epsilon) - 1} \cdot C_d$$

$$C_d = \begin{cases} \dfrac{2^{d-1}}{\binom{d-1}{\frac{d-1}{2}}} & if\ d\ is\ odd \\[2ex] \dfrac{2^{d-1} + \frac{1}{2}\binom{d}{\frac{d}{2}}}{\binom{d-1}{\frac{d}{2}}} & otherwise \end{cases}$$

3 A Bernoulli variable u is sampled such that $\Pr[u = 1] = \frac{e^\epsilon}{e^\epsilon+1}$.

4 Finally, if $u = 1$, output a data record uniformly selected from T^+; otherwise, output a data record uniformly selected from T^-.

The following listing shows the Python implementation of this algorithm. If you carefully follow the steps we just discussed, you will quickly understand what we are doing in the code.

Listing 5.3   Duchi's mechanism for multidimensional data

```
def Duchi_md(t_i, eps):
    d = len(t_i)
    if d % 2 != 0:
        C_d = pow(2, d - 1) / comb(d - 1, (d - 1) / 2)
    else:
        C_d = (pow(2, d - 1) + 0.5 * comb(d, d / 2)) / comb(d - 1, d / 2)

    B = C_d * (math.exp(eps) + 1) / (math.exp(eps) - 1)
    v = []
    for tmp in t_i:
        tmp_p = 0.5 + 0.5 * tmp
        tmp_q = 0.5 - 0.5 * tmp
        v.append(np.random.choice([1, -1], p=[tmp_p, tmp_q]))
    bernoulli_p = math.exp(eps) / (math.exp(eps) + 1)
    coin = np.random.binomial(1, bernoulli_p)

    t_star = np.random.choice([-B, B], len(t_i), p=[0.5, 0.5])
    v_times_t_star = np.multiply(v, t_star)
    sum_v_times_t_star = np.sum(v_times_t_star)
```

```
    if coin == 1:
        while sum_v_times_t_star <= 0:
            t_star = np.random.choice([-B, B], len(t_i), p=[0.5, 0.5])
            v_times_t_star = np.multiply(v, t_star)
            sum_v_times_t_star = np.sum(v_times_t_star)
    else:
        while sum_v_times_t_star > 0:
            t_star = np.random.choice([-B, B], len(t_i), p=[0.5, 0.5])
            v_times_t_star = np.multiply(v, t_star)
            sum_v_times_t_star = np.sum(v_times_t_star)
return t_star.reshape(-1)
```

Duchi's mechanism performs well with a smaller privacy budget (i.e., $\epsilon < 2.3$). However, it performs worse than the Laplace mechanism in terms of the utility when you are using a larger privacy budget. Could there be a more general algorithm that works well regardless of whether the privacy budget is small or large? We'll look at the Piecewise mechanism in the next section.

5.2.3   *The Piecewise mechanism for LDP*

So far in this chapter you've learned about mechanisms that can be used for LDP. A third mechanism, called the Piecewise mechanism [1], had been proposed to deal with multidimensional continuous numerical data when using LDP, and it can overcome the disadvantages of the Laplace and Duchi's mechanisms. The idea is to perturb multidimensional numerical values with an asymptotic optimal error bound. Hence, it requires only one bit for each individual to be reported to the data aggregator.

First, let's look at the Piecewise mechanism for one-dimensional data. Given the participant u_i's one-dimensional data record $t_i \in [-1,1]$ and privacy budget ϵ, the Piecewise mechanism performs as follows:

1 A value x is selected in the range of 0 to 1, uniformly at random.
2 If $x < \frac{e^{\frac{\epsilon}{2}}}{e^{\frac{\epsilon}{2}}+1}$, we sample t_i^* uniformly at random from $[l(t_i),\ r(t_i)]$; otherwise, we sample t_i^* uniformly at random from $[-C, l(t_i) \cup r(t_i), C]$, where

$$C = \frac{\exp\left(\frac{\epsilon}{2}\right) + 1}{\exp\left(\frac{\epsilon}{2}\right) - 1}$$

$$l(t_i) = \frac{C+1}{2} \cdot t_i - \frac{C-1}{2}$$

and

$$r(t_i) = l(t_i) + C - 1$$

3 Perturbed data $t_i^* \in \{-C, C\}$ will be the output of the Piecewise mechanism.

The Piecewise mechanism consists of three pieces: the center piece, the right piece $r()$, and the left piece $l()$. The centerpiece is calculated as $t_i^* \in [l(t_i), r(t_i)]$, the rightmost piece as $t_i^* \in [r(t_i), C]$, and the leftmost piece as $t_i^* \in [-C, l(t_i)]$. You can see a Python implementation of this algorithm in the following listing.

Listing 5.4 Piecewise mechanism for one-dimensional data

```python
def PM_1d(t_i, eps):
    C = (math.exp(eps / 2) + 1) / (math.exp(eps / 2) - 1)
    l_t_i = (C + 1) * t_i / 2 - (C - 1) / 2
    r_t_i = l_t_i + C - 1

    x = np.random.uniform(0, 1)
    threshold = math.exp(eps / 2) / (math.exp(eps / 2) + 1)
    if x < threshold:
        t_star = np.random.uniform(l_t_i, r_t_i)
    else:
        tmp_l = np.random.uniform(-C, l_t_i)
        tmp_r = np.random.uniform(r_t_i, C)
        w = np.random.randint(2)
        t_star = (1 - w) * tmp_l + w * tmp_r

    return t_star
```

> **Providing the size parameter in uniform() would result in an ndarray.**

How can we deal with multidimensional data? We can simply extend the Piecewise mechanism from its one-dimensional version to work with multidimensional data. Given a d-dimensional data record $t_i \in [-1,1]^d$ and a privacy budget ϵ, the Piecewise mechanism for multidimensional data performs as follows:

1 Sample k values uniformly without replacement from $\{1, 2, \ldots, d\}$, where

$$k = \max\left\{1, \min\left\{d, \left\lfloor \frac{\epsilon}{2.5} \right\rfloor\right\}\right\}$$

2 For each sampled value j, feed $t_i[A_j]$ and $\frac{\epsilon}{k}$ as the input to the one-dimensional version of the Piecewise mechanism and obtain a noisy value $x_{i,j}$.
3 Output t_i^*, where $t_i^*[A_j] = \frac{d}{k}x_{i,j}$.

The following listing shows a Python implementation of this algorithm.

Listing 5.5 Piecewise mechanism for multidimensional data

```python
def PM_md(t_i, eps):
    d = len(t_i)
    k = max(1, min(d, int(eps / 2.5)))
    rand_features = np.random.randint(0, d, size=k)
    res = np.zeros(t_i.shape)
    for j in rand_features:
        res[j] = (d * 1.0 / k) * PM_1d(t_i[j], eps / k)
    return res
```

Now that we have studied three advanced LDP mechanisms for multidimensional numerical data, let's look at a case study showing how LDP can be implemented with real-world datasets.

5.3 A case study implementing LDP naive Bayes classification

In the previous chapter we introduced a set of mechanisms that can be used to implement LDP protocols. In this section we'll use the LDP naive Bayes classification design as a case study to walk through the process of designing an LDP ML algorithm. The content in this section has been partially published in one of our research papers [3]. The implementation and the complete code for this case study can be found at https://github.com/nogrady/PPML/tree/main/Ch5.

> **NOTE** This section will walk you through the mathematical formulations and empirical evaluations for this case study so that you can learn how to develop an LDP application from scratch. If you do not need to know these implementation details right now, you can skip ahead to the next chapter.

5.3.1 Using naive Bayes with ML classification

In section 3.2.1 you learned how differentially private naive Bayes classification works and its mathematical formulations. In this section we will broaden the discussion and explore how we can use naive Bayes with LDP. As discussed in the previous chapter, LDP involves individuals sending their data to the data aggregator after privatizing the data by perturbation. These techniques provide plausible deniability for individuals. The data aggregator then collects all the perturbed values and estimates statistics such as the frequency of each value in the population.

To guarantee the privacy of the individuals who provide training data in a classification task, LDP techniques can be used at the data collection stage. In this chapter we'll apply LDP techniques to naive Bayes classifiers, which are a set of simple probabilistic classifiers based on Bayes' theorem. To quickly recap, naive Bayes classifiers assume independence between every pair of features. Most importantly, these classifiers are highly scalable and particularly suitable when the number of features is high or when the training data is small. Naive Bayes can often perform better than or close to more sophisticated classification methods, despite its simplicity.

Let's get into the details now. Given a new instance (a known class value), naive Bayes computes the conditional probability of each class label and then assigns the class label with maximum likelihood to the given instance. The idea is that, using Bayes' theorem and the assumption of independence of features, each conditional probability can be decomposed as the multiplication of several probabilities. We need to compute each of these probabilities using training data to achieve naive Bayes classification. Since the training data must be collected from individuals by preserving privacy, we can utilize LDP frequency and statistical estimation methods to collect perturbed data from individuals and then estimate conditional probabilities with the naive Bayes classification.

In this case study, we'll first look into how we can work with discrete features using an LDP naive Bayes classifier by preserving the relationships between the class labels and the features. Second, we'll walk through the case of continuous features. We'll discuss how we can discretize data and apply Gaussian naive Bayes after adding Laplace noise to the data to satisfy LDP. We will also show you how to work with continuous data perturbation methods. Finally, we'll explore and implement these techniques with a set of experimental scenarios and real datasets, showing you how LDP guarantees are satisfied while maintaining the accuracy of the classifier.

> ### Discrete versus continuous features
>
> *Discrete variables* are numeric variables with a countable number of values between any two values. A discrete variable is always numeric. For example, the number of defective parts or the number of missed payments can be treated as discrete values.
>
> In contrast, *continuous variables* are numeric variables with infinite values between any two values. A continuous variable can be numeric or it can be a date/time, such as the length of a part or the date/time a payment is received.
>
> Nevertheless, we sometimes treat discrete data as continuous and continuous data as discrete, depending on the application.

5.3.2   *Using LDP naive Bayes with discrete features*

Before digging into the theory, let's first look at an example. An independent analyst wants to train an ML classifier to predict "how likely a person is to miss a mortgage payment." The idea is to use data from different mortgage and financial companies, train a model, and use this model to predict the behavior of future customers. The problem is that none of the financial companies want to participate because they do not want to share their customers' private or sensitive information. The best option for them is to share a perturbed version of their data so that their customers' privacy is preserved. But how can we perturb the data so that it can be used to train a naive Bayes classifier while protecting privacy? That's what we are going to find out.

We discussed how naive Bayes classification works in section 3.2.1, so we'll only recap the essential points here. Refer back to chapter 3 for more details.

In probability theory, Bayes' theorem describes the probability of an event, based on prior knowledge of conditions that might be related to the event. It is stated as follows:

$$P(A|B) = \frac{P(B|A) \cdot P(A)}{P(B)}$$

The naive Bayes classification technique uses Bayes' theorem and the assumption of independence between every pair of features. Suppose the instance to be classified is the n-dimensional vector $X = \{x_1, x_2, ..., x_n\}$, the names of the features are $F_1, F_2, ..., F_n$, and the possible classes that can be assigned to the instance are $C = \{C_1, C_2, ..., C_k\}$. A naive

Bayes classifier assigns the instance X to the class C_s if and only if $P(C_s \mid X) > P(C_j \mid X)$ for $1 \leq j \leq k$ and $j \neq s$. Hence, the classifier needs to compute $P(C_j \mid X)$ for all classes and compare these probabilities. Using Bayes' theorem, the probability $P(C_j \mid X)$ can be calculated as

$$P(C_j \mid X) = \frac{P(X \mid C_j) \cdot P(C_j)}{P(X)}$$

Since $P(X)$ is same for all classes, it is sufficient to find the class with the maximum $P(X \mid C_j) \cdot P(C_j)$.

Let's first consider the case where all the features are numerical and discrete. Suppose there are m different records or individuals (among these financial companies) that can be used to train this classifier. Table 5.1 shows an extract from a mortgage payment dataset that we discussed in chapter 3.

Table 5.1 An extract from a dataset of mortgage payments. Age, income, and gender are the independent variables, whereas missed payment represents the dependent variable for the prediction task.

Number	Age	Income	Gender	Missed payment (yes or no)
1	Young	Low	Male	Yes
2	Young	High	Female	Yes
3	Medium	High	Male	No
4	Old	Medium	Male	No
5	Old	High	Male	No
6	Old	Low	Female	Yes
7	Medium	Low	Female	No
8	Medium	Medium	Male	Yes
9	Young	Low	Male	No
10	Old	High	Female	No

Our objective is to use this data to train a classifier that can be used to predict future customers and to determine whether a particular customer is likely to miss a mortgage payment or not. Thus, in this case, the classification task is the prediction of the customer's behavior (whether they will miss a mortgage payment or not), which makes it a binary classification—we only have two possible classes.

Much as we did in chapter 3, let's define these two classes as C_1 and C_2 where C_1 represents missing a previous payment and C_2 represents otherwise. Based on the data reported in table 5.1, the probabilities of these classes can be computed as follows:

$$P(C_1) = \frac{4}{10} \qquad P(C_2) = \frac{6}{10}$$

Similarly, we can compute the conditional probabilities. Table 5.2 summarizes the conditional probabilities we already calculated in chapter 3 for the age feature.

Table 5.2   A summary of conditional probabilities computed for the age feature

Conditional probability	Result
$P(Age = Young \mid C_1)$	2/4
$P(Age = Young \mid C_2)$	1/6
$P(Age = Medium \mid C_1)$	1/4
$P(Age = Medium \mid C_2)$	2/6
$P(Age = Old \mid C_1)$	1/4
$P(Age = Old \mid C_2)$	3/6

Once we have all the conditional probabilities, we can predict whether, for example, a young female with medium income will miss a payment or not. To do that, first we need to set X as $X = (Age = Young, Income = Medium, Gender = Female)$. Chapter 3 presents the remaining steps and computations for using the naive Bayes classifier, and you can refer back if necessary.

Based on the results of these computations, the naive Bayes classifier will assign C_2 for the instance X. In other words, a young female with medium income will not miss a payment.

$$P(C_1) \cdot \prod_{i=1}^{3} P(F_i = x_i | C_1) = 0.025$$

and

$$P(C_2) \cdot \prod_{i=1}^{3} P(F_i = x_i | C_2) = 0.055$$

With this basic understanding of how the naive Bayes classifier works, let's see how we can use the LDP frequency estimation methods discussed earlier to compute the necessary probabilities for a naive Bayes classifier. Remember, in LDP, the data aggregator is the one that computes the class probabilities $P(C_j)$ for all classes in $C = \{C_1, C_2, ..., C_k\}$ and conditional probabilities $P(F_i = x_i \mid C_j)$ for all possible x_i values.

Suppose an individual's data, Alice's data, is $(a_1, a_2, ..., a_n)$ and her class label is C_v. In order to satisfy LDP, she needs to prepare her input and perturb it. Let's look at the details of how Alice's data can be prepared and perturbed and how the class probabilities and the conditional probabilities can be estimated by the data aggregator.

COMPUTING CLASS PROBABILITIES
For the computation of class probabilities, Alice's input becomes $v \in \{1, 2, ..., k\}$ since her class label is C_v. Then Alice encodes and perturbs her value v and reports to the data

aggregator. Any LDP frequency estimation method we discussed earlier can be used. Similarly, other individuals report their perturbed class labels to the data aggregator.

The data aggregator collects all the perturbed data and estimates the frequency of each value $j \in \{1, 2, ..., k\}$ as E_j. Now the probability $P(C_j)$ is estimated as

$$\frac{E_j}{\sum_{i=1}^{k} E_i}$$

Let's consider an example to make it clearer. There are only two options for the class label in the example dataset in table 5.1: missing a payment or not. Let's say Alice has a missing payment. Then Alice's input v becomes 1 and she reports it to the data aggregator. Similarly, if she does not have a missing payment, she would report 2 as her input to the data aggregator. Figure 5.2 shows three people submitting their perturbed values to the data aggregator. The data aggregator then estimates the frequency of each value and calculates the class probabilities.

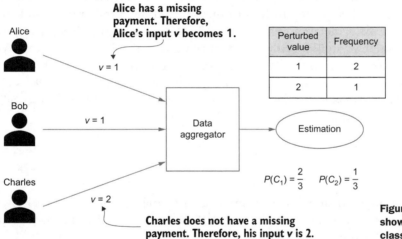

Figure 5.2   An example showing how to compute class probabilities

COMPUTING CONDITIONAL PROBABILITIES

In order to estimate the conditional probabilities $P(F_i = x_i \mid C_j)$, it is not sufficient to report the feature values directly. To compute these probabilities, the relationship between class labels and features must be preserved, which means individuals need to prepare their inputs using a combination of feature values and class labels.

We'll let the total number of possible values for F_i be n_i. If Alice's value in ith dimension is $a_i \in \{1, 2, ..., n_i\}$ and her class label value is $v \in \{1, 2, ..., k\}$, then Alice's input for feature F_i becomes $v_i = (a_i - 1) \cdot k + v$. Therefore, each individual calculates her input for the ith feature in the range of $[1, k \cdot n_i]$.

It's a bit hard to follow, isn't it? But don't worry. Let's look at this through an example. For instance, suppose the age values in table 5.1 are enumerated as (*Young* = 1), (*Medium* = 2), (*Old* = 3). For this age feature, an individual's input can be a value from

1 to 6, as shown in table 5.3, where 1 represents that the age is young and there is a missing payment, and 6 represents that the age is old and there is no missing payment.

Table 5.3 **Preparing input as a combination of feature values and class labels**

Relationship between class label and feature	Enumerated value
$(Age = Young \mid C_1)$	1
$(Age = Young \mid C_2)$	2
$(Age = Medium \mid C_1)$	3
$(Age = Medium \mid C_2)$	4
$(Age = Old \mid C_1)$	5
$(Age = Old \mid C_2)$	6

You may have noticed that there is one input value for each line in table 5.2. Similarly, the number of possible inputs for income is 6, and the number of possible inputs for gender is 4. After determining her input in the ith feature, Alice encodes and perturbs her value v_i, and reports the perturbed value to the data aggregator. To estimate the conditional probabilities for F_i, the data aggregator estimates the frequency of individuals having the value $y \in \{1, 2, ..., n_i\}$ and class label $z \in \{1, 2, ..., k\}$ as $E_{y,z}$ by estimating the frequency of input $(y-1) \cdot k + z$. Hence, the conditional probability $P(F_i = x_i \mid C_j)$ is estimated as

$$\frac{E_{x_i,j}}{\sum_{h=1}^{n_i} E_{h,j}}$$

For the example in table 5.3, to estimate the probability $P(Age = Medium \mid C_2)$, the data aggregator estimates the frequency of 2, 4, and 6 as $E_{1,2}$, $E_{2,2}$, and $E_{3,2}$, respectively. Then $P(Age = Medium \mid C_2)$ can be estimated as

$$\frac{E_{2,2}}{E_{1,2} + E_{2,2} + E_{3,2}}$$

It is noteworthy that in order to contribute to the computation of class probabilities and conditional probabilities, each individual can prepare $n + 1$ inputs (i.e., $\{v, v_1, v_2, ..., v_n\}$ for Alice) that can be reported after perturbation. However, reporting multiple values that are dependent on each other usually decreases the privacy level. Hence, each individual reports only one input value.

Finally, when the data aggregator estimates a value such as E_j or $E_{(y,z)}$, the estimate may be negative. We can set all negative estimates to 1 to obtain a valid and reasonable probability.

USING LDP WITH MULTIDIMENSIONAL DATA

The aforementioned frequency and mean estimation methods only work for one-dimensional data. But what if we have higher-dimensional data? If the data owned by individuals is multidimensional, reporting each value with these methods may cause privacy leaks due to the dependence on features.

To that end, three common approaches can be used with n-dimensional data:

- *Approach 1*—The Laplace mechanism (discussed in chapter 3) could be used with LDP if the noise is scaled with the number of dimensions n. Hence, if an individual's input is $V = (v_1, ..., v_n)$ such that $v_i \in [-1,1]$ for all $i \in \{1, ..., n\}$, individuals can report each v_i after adding $Lap(2n/\varepsilon)$. However, this approach is not suitable if the number of dimensions n is high, because a large amount of noise reduces the accuracy.

- *Approach 2*—We could utilize the Piecewise mechanism that we described in section 5.2.3. The Piecewise mechanism can be used to perturb multidimensional numerical values with LDP protocols.

- *Approach 3*—The data aggregator can request only one perturbed input from each individual to satisfy ϵ-LDP. Each individual can select the input to be reported uniformly at random, or the data aggregator can divide the individuals into n groups and request different input values from each group. As a result, each feature is approximately reported by m/n individuals. This approach is suitable when the number of individuals m is high, relative to the number of features n. Otherwise, the accuracy decreases, since the number of reported values is low for each feature.

Now that we've looked at how multidimensional data works with LDP, let's look at the details of LDP in naive Bayes classification for continuous data.

5.3.3 Using LDP naive Bayes with continuous features

So far, we've seen how to apply LDP for discrete features. Now we're going to explore how we can use the same concept for continuous features. LDP in naive Bayes classification for continuous data can be approached in two different ways:

- We can discretize the continuous data and apply the discrete naive Bayes solution outlined in the previous section. In that case, continuous numerical data is divided into buckets to make it finite and discrete. Each individual perturbs their input after discretization.

- The data aggregator can use Gaussian naive Bayes to estimate the probabilities.

Let's start with the first approach, discrete naive Bayes.

DISCRETE NAIVE BAYES

For discrete naive Bayes, we need to discretize the continuous data and use LDP frequency estimation techniques to estimate the frequency. Based on known features within a continuous domain, the data aggregator determines the intervals for the buckets in order to discretize the domain—Equal-Width Discretization (EWD) or

Equal-Width Binning (EWB) can be used to equally partition the domain. EWD computes the width of each bin as $(max - min)/n_b$ where *max* and *min* are the maximum and minimum feature values and n_b is the number of desired bins. In section 5.3.4, we'll use the EWD method in some experiments for discretization.

What is equal-width binning?

In general, binning is a data preprocessing method used to minimize the effects of small observation errors by dividing the original data values into small intervals known as *bins*. The original values are then replaced by a general value calculated for that bin. Basically, binning methods transform numerical variables into categorical counterparts but do not use the target (or class) information. This has a better chance of reducing overfitting in the case of smaller datasets.

There are two basic methods of dividing data into bins:

- *Equal Frequency Binning (EFB)*—In this case, all the bins have equal frequency.
  - Example input data: [0,4,12,16,16,18,24,26,28]
  - Bin 1: [0,4,12]
  - Bin 2: [16,16,18]
  - Bin 3: [24,26,28]

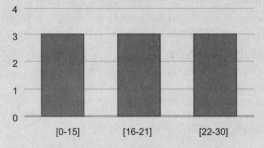

- *Equal Width Binning (EWB)*—In this case, the data is divided into intervals of equal size where the interval (or width) is defined as $w = (max - min)/(number\ of\ bins)$.
  - Example input data: [0,4,12,16,16,18,24,26,28]
  - Bin 1: [0,4]
  - Bin 2: [12,16,16,18]
  - Bin 3: [24,26,28]

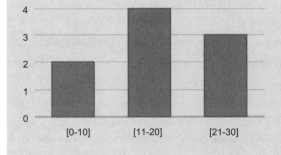

When the data aggregator shares the intervals with individuals, each individual discretizes their continuous feature values and applies a procedure similar to what we discussed for LDP naive Bayes with discrete features. The data aggregator also estimates the probabilities using the same procedure as for LDP naive Bayes for discrete data. Each individual should report just one perturbed value to guarantee ϵ-LDP. As you can see, discretization through binning is a kind of data preprocessing approach. The actual privacy protection is achieved through discrete naive Bayes.

GAUSSIAN NAIVE BAYES

The second approach for continuous data is using Gaussian naive Bayes. In this case, the most common practice is to assume the data is normally distributed. For LDP Gaussian naive Bayes, computing class probabilities is the same as for discrete features. To compute conditional probabilities, the data aggregator needs to have the mean and the variance of the training values for each feature given a class label. In other words, to compute $P(F_i = x_i \mid C_j)$, the data aggregator needs to estimate the mean $\mu_{(i,j)}$ and the variance σ_{ij}^2 using the F_i values of individuals with class label C_j. That means the association between features and class labels has to be maintained (similar to the discrete naive Bayes classifier).

We already discussed the mean estimation process, but to compute the mean $\mu_{(i,j)}$ and the variance σ_{ij}^2 together, the data aggregator can divide the individuals into two groups. One group contributes to the estimation of the mean (i.e., $\mu_{(i,j)}$) by perturbing their inputs and sharing them with the data aggregator. The other group contributes to estimating the mean of squares (i.e., μ_{ij}^s) by perturbing the squares of their inputs and sharing them with the data aggregator.

Let's consider another example. Suppose Bob has class label C_j and a feature F_i with a value b_i. Let's also assume that the domain of each feature is normalized to have a value between $[-1,1]$. If Bob is in the first group, he would add the Laplace noise to his value b_i and obtain the perturbed feature value b_i'. When the data aggregator collects all perturbed feature values from individuals in the first group having class label C_j, it computes the mean of the perturbed feature values, which gives an estimate of the mean $\mu_{(i,j)}$ because the mean of the noise added by individuals is 0. A similar approach could be followed by the second group. If Bob is in the second group, he would add noise to his squared value b_i^2 to obtain $b_i^{2'}$ and would share it with the data aggregator. Again, the data aggregator computes the estimate of the mean of squares (μ_{ij}^s). Finally, the variance σ_{ij}^2 can be computed as $\mu_{ij}^s - (\mu_{ij})^2$. Once again, each individual reports only one of their values or squares of their values after perturbation because they are dependent.

Thus far, the calculation of probabilities is clear and straightforward. But did you notice that when we calculate the mean and the variance, the class labels of individuals are not hidden from the data aggregator? How can we hide the original class labels?

To overcome this problem and hide the class labels, we can adopt the following approach: let's say Bob is reporting a feature value $F_i = b_i$ associated with class C_j where $j \in \{1, 2, ..., k\}$. First he constructs a vector of length k where k is the number of class labels. The vector is initialized to zeros except for the *j*th element corresponding to the *j*th class label, which is set to the feature value b_i. After that, each element of the vector is perturbed as usual (i.e., by adding the Laplace noise) and contributed to the data aggregator. Since noise is added even to the zero elements of the vector, the data aggregator will not be able to deduce the actual class label, or the actual values.

As for estimating the actual mean value (and the mean of the squared values) for each class, the data aggregator only needs to compute the mean of the perturbed values as usual and then divide by the probability of that class. To understand why we need to do that, assume that a class *j* has probability $P(C_j)$. Thus, for a feature F_i, only $P(C_j)$ of the individuals have their actual values in the *j*th element of the input vector, while the remaining proportion $(1 - P(C_j))$ have zeros. Hence, after the noise clustered around the actual mean cancels each other, and the noise clustered around zero cancels each other, we will have $P(C_j) \times \mu_{(i,j)} = observed\ (shifted)\ mean$. Thereafter, we can divide the observed mean by $P(C_j)$ to obtain the estimated mean. The same applies to the mean of the squared values and hence for computing the variance.

5.3.4   *Evaluating the performance of different LDP protocols*

Now that we have gone through the theory, it's time to discuss the implementation strategies and the results of the experimental evaluation of different LDP protocols. These experiments are based on datasets obtained from the UCI Machine Learning Repository [4]. Table 5.4 summarizes the datasets used in the experiments.

Table 5.4   A summary of datasets used in the experiments

Name of the dataset	Number of instances	Number of features	Number of class labels
Car evaluation	1,728	6	4
Chess	3,196	36	2
Mushroom	8,124	22	2
Connect-4	67,557	42	3
Australian credit approval	690	14	2
Diabetes	768	8	2

To evaluate the accuracy of naive Bayes classification under LDP, we implemented the methods discussed in the previous sections in Python utilizing the pandas and NumPy libraries. We implemented five different LDP protocols for frequency estimation—direct encoding (DE), summation with histogram encoding (SHE), thresholding with histogram encoding (THE), symmetric unary encoding (SUE), and optimal unary encoding (OUE)—and the experiments were performed with different θ values in THE. With these experiments, we found that the best accuracy can be achieved whenever θ = 0.25, so we'll give the experimental results of SHE for θ = 0.25. In a nutshell, we will compare the results of these different implementations to show you which algorithm works best for each of these datasets.

EVALUATING LDP NAIVE BAYES WITH DISCRETE FEATURES

To evaluate the accuracy of using LDP naive Bayes for classifying data with discrete features, four different datasets from the UCI ML repository (Car evaluation, Chess, Mushroom, and Connect-4) were used. Initially, naive Bayes classification without LDP was performed as the baseline for comparing the accuracy of different encoding mechanisms under LDP.

Let's look at the experimental results for varying ϵ values up to 5, as shown in figure 5.3. The dotted lines show accuracy without privacy. As expected, when the number of instances in the training set increases, the accuracy is better for smaller ϵ values. For instance, in the Connect-4 dataset, all protocols except SHE provide more than 65% accuracy even for very small ϵ values. Since the accuracy without privacy is approximately 75%, the accuracy of all of these protocols for ϵ values smaller than 1 is noticeable. The results are also similar for the Mushroom dataset. When it comes to $\epsilon = 0.5$, all protocols except SHE provide nearly 90% classification accuracy.

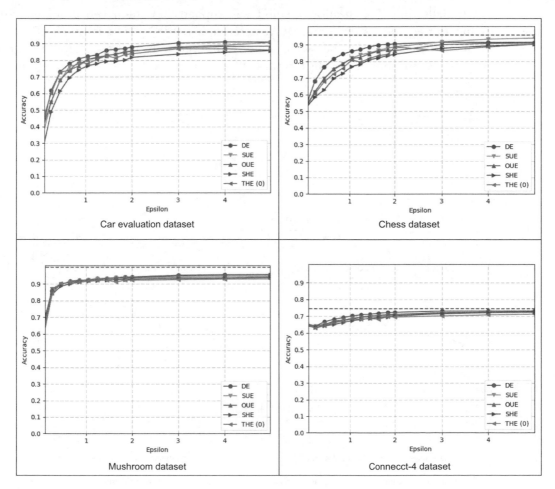

Figure 5.3   LDP naive Bayes classification accuracy for datasets with discrete features

In all of the datasets, you can see that the protocol with the worst accuracy is SHE. Since this protocol simply sums the noisy values, its variance is higher than the other protocols. In addition, DE achieves the best accuracy for small ϵ values in the Car Evaluation and Chess datasets because the input domains are small. On the other hand, the variance of DE is proportional to the size of the input domain. Therefore, its accuracy is better when the input domain is small. We can also see that SUE and OUE provide similar accuracy in all of the experiments. They perform better than DE when the size of the input domain is large. Although OUE is proposed to decrease the variance, a considerable utility difference between SUE and OUE was not observed in this set of experiments.

EVALUATING LDP NAIVE BAYES WITH CONTINUOUS FEATURES

Now let's discuss the results of LDP naive Bayes with continuous data. In this case, the experiments were conducted on two different datasets: Australian credit approval and Diabetes. The Australian dataset has 14 original features, and the Diabetes dataset has 8 features.

Initially, the discretization method was applied, and then two dimensionality reduction techniques (PCA and DCA) were implemented to observe their effect on accuracy. The results for the two datasets for different values of ϵ are given in figure 5.4. We also present the results for two LDP schemes, direct encoding and optimized

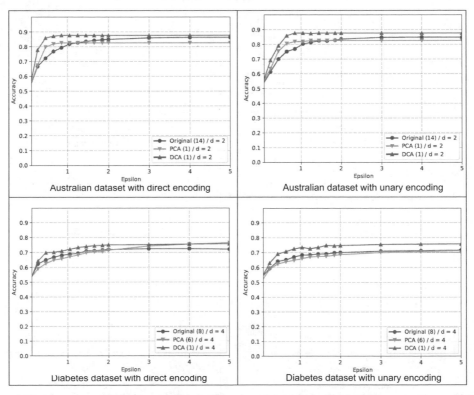

Figure 5.4   LDP naive Bayes classification accuracy for datasets with continuous features using discretization

unary encoding, which provide the best accuracy for different domain sizes. The input domain is divided into $d = 2$ buckets for the Australian dataset and $d = 4$ buckets for the Diabetes dataset.

As you can see, for the Australian dataset, the best results for principal component analysis (PCA) and discriminant component analysis (DCA) are obtained when the number of features is reduced to 1. On the other hand, for the Diabetes dataset, the best accuracy is achieved when PCA reduces the number of features to 6 and when DCA reduces the number of features to 1. As is evident in figure 5.4, DCA provides the best classification accuracy, which shows the advantage of using dimensionality reduction before discretization. You can also see that DCA's accuracy is better than PCA's, since DCA is mainly designed for classification.

> ### What are PCA and DCA?
> Principal component analysis (PCA) and discriminant component analysis (DCA) are two well-known dimensionality reduction methods that are often used to reduce the dimensionality of large datasets. Both PCA and DCA work by projecting data to a lower-dimensional hyperplane. However, the critical difference between them is that PCA assumes a linear relationship to the gradients, while DCA assumes a unimodal relationship. We will discuss different dimensionality reduction approaches in more detail in chapter 9.

In addition, we applied LDP Gaussian naive Bayes (LDP-GNB) on the same two datasets. All three perturbation approaches that we discussed for multidimensional data (in the subsection titled "Using LDP with multidimensional data") were implemented. Figure 5.5 shows the results of performing LDP-GNB on these two datasets.

As you can see, the first of the three approaches (using the Laplace mechanism) results in the lowest utility, since individuals report all the features by adding more noise, proportional to the number of dimensions. In each figure, three curves are shown, corresponding to using the original data (with 14 or 8 features for the Australian and Diabetes datasets, respectively) or projecting the data using PCA or DCA before applying the LDP noise. All the graphs show the positive effect of reducing the dimensions. In both datasets, and for PCA and DCA, the number of reduced dimensions was 1. DCA or PCA always performs better than the original data and for all perturbation approaches.

Finally, when you compare the results of discretization and Gaussian naive Bayes for continuous data, you'll see that discretization provides better accuracy. Especially for smaller ϵ values, the superiority of discretization is apparent. Although it is impossible to compare the amount of noise for randomized response and the Laplace mechanism, discretization possibly causes less noise due to the smaller input domain.

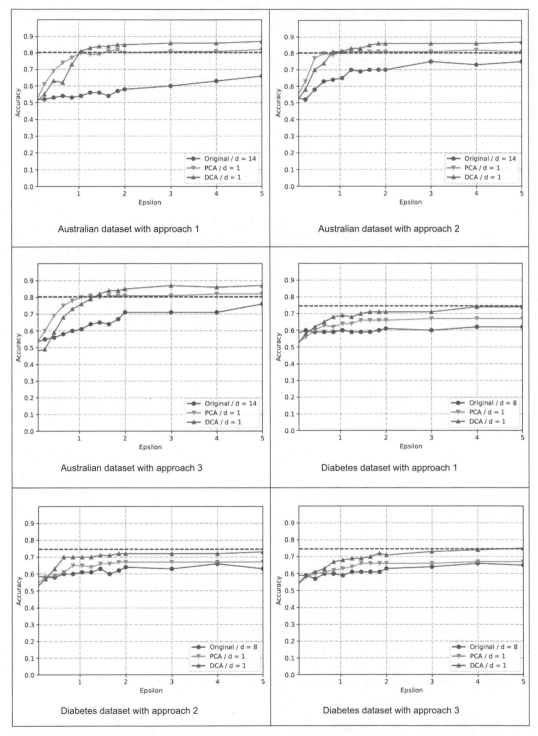

Figure 5.5   LDP Gaussian naive Bayes classification accuracy for datasets with continuous features

Summary

- There are different advanced LDP mechanisms that work for both one-dimensional and multidimensional data.
- As we did with the centralized setting of DP, we can implement the Laplace mechanism for LDP as well.
- While the Laplace mechanism is one way to generate noise for the perturbation, Duchi's mechanism can also be used to perturb multidimensional continuous numerical data for LDP.
- The Piecewise mechanism can be used to deal with multidimensional continuous numerical data for LDP while overcoming the disadvantages of the Laplace and Duchi's mechanisms.
- Naive Bayes is a simple yet powerful ML classifier that can be used with LDP frequency estimation techniques.
- LDP naive Bayes can be used with both discrete and continuous features.
- When it comes to LDP naive Bayes with continuous features, there are two main approaches, namely, discrete naive Bayes and Gaussian naive Bayes.

Privacy-preserving synthetic data generation

This chapter covers

- Synthetic data generation
- Generating synthetic data for anonymization
- Using differential privacy mechanisms to generate privacy-preserving synthetic data
- Designing a privacy-preserving synthetic data generation scheme for machine learning tasks

So far we've looked into the concepts of differential privacy (including the centralized, DP, and the local, LDP, versions) and their applications in developing privacy-preserving query-processing and machine learning (ML) algorithms. As you saw, the idea of DP is to add noise to the query results (without disturbing their original properties) such that the results can assure the privacy of the individuals while satisfying the utility of the application.

But sometimes data users may request the original data to utilize it locally and directly, perhaps to develop new queries and analysis procedures. Privacy-preserving data-sharing methods can be used for such purposes. This chapter will look into synthetic data generation—a promising solution for data sharing—which generates synthetic yet representative data that can be shared among multiple parties safely and securely. The idea of synthetic data generation is to artificially generate data that has distribution and properties similar to the original data. And because it is artificially produced, we do not have to worry about privacy concerns.

We'll start this chapter by introducing the concepts and basics of synthetic data generation. Subsequent sections will present implementations of synthetic data generation approaches using different data anonymization techniques or DP. Toward the end of this chapter, we'll walk you through a case study that implements a novel privacy-preserving synthetic data generation approach using data anonymization and DP for ML purposes.

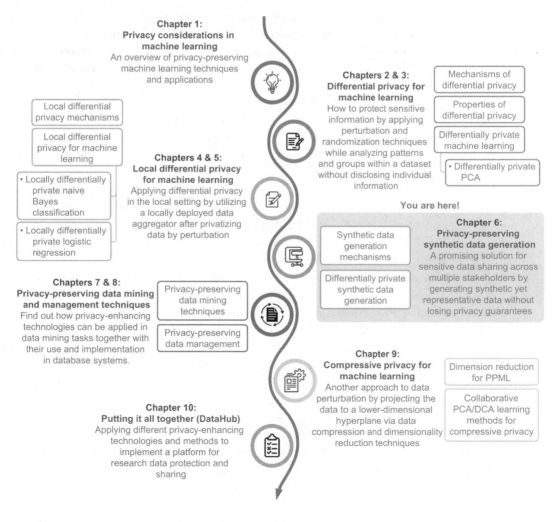

6.1   *Overview of synthetic data generation*

In essence, data is a collection of facts that can be translated into a form that a computer can understand and process. With today's modern applications, data collection happens almost everywhere, such as in business analytics, engineering optimization, social science analysis, scientific research, and so on. Typically, different characteristics or patterns of data can be used to achieve various objectives. For instance, in healthcare applications, diverse image data such as x-rays, CT scans, and dermoscopic images can be used by ML applications to diagnose particular diseases or aid treatments.

However, in practice, it is very challenging to obtain real (and sensitive) data for many reasons, including privacy concerns, and even when you can collect the data, you are usually not permitted to share it with other parties. When it comes to ML applications, most algorithms require a large amount of training data to achieve their best performance, but it is not always feasible to collect such an amount of real data. Thus, there is a need for synthetic (yet representative) data, and due to the aforementioned concerns, synthetic data has become an increasingly important and popular topic.

6.1.1   *What is synthetic data? Why is it important?*

The performance of an ML model largely depends on the amount and quality of data accumulated to train the model. When an organization does not have sufficient data for the training, data sharing often happens between organizations that have similar research interests. This enables the research to scale, but the privacy problem remains the same. The data usually includes sensitive personal information that can cause privacy leakage for the individuals. Hence, it is imperative to enable privacy-preserving mechanisms when data sharing. To that end, generating privacy-preserving synthetic data is one of the best alternatives—it is a flexible and viable next-step solution for sharing sensitive data across multiple stakeholders.

Synthetic data is a kind of artificially formulated data, usually generated with artificial algorithms rather than being collected by real-world direct measurement techniques. But it still carries some critical features of the actual data (e.g., statistical properties, functionalities, or conclusions). Analyzing the synthetic data can produce results similar to analyzing the actual data itself. Another advantage of synthetic data is that it can be generated for the specific characteristics of rare testing scenarios that are extremely hard to observe in reality (i.e., scenarios where it is challenging to obtain actual data). This enables the engineers and researchers to generate different datasets to validate various models, evaluate ML algorithms, and test new products, pipelines, and tools under different scenarios.

Moreover, synthetic data helps us ensure privacy protection. Synthetic data can have statistical characteristics similar to the original data without disclosing the original data, which paves a safer way of protecting privacy and confidentiality. For instance, primary care providers (such as hospitals) collect and share their patients' information for research purposes with the consent of those patients. However, most patients will not agree to share their private information with other parties. Instead of sharing the original data, we can generate artificial or synthetic data based on the properties of the original dataset. Then we can share the synthetically produced data with other data users. That retains the utility of the application and preserves the privacy of the original data.

6.1.2   *Application aspects of using synthetic data for privacy preservation*

Synthetic data does not contain any personal information; it is an artificially produced dataset with a distribution similar to the original data. Hence, engineering, business, and scientific research applications can benefit from using synthetic data for privacy-preserving purposes.

   For instance, let's consider an example of sharing clinical and medical data between different healthcare entities (e.g., hospitals and research institutions). Let's assume that two hospitals, A and B, plan to conduct a research program to learn the relationship between an individual's specific personal information (age, BMI, glucose, etc.) and their probability of getting breast cancer. Both hospitals can collect valuable data from their patients, but because of the patient-hospital agreements, the two hospitals cannot share their data with each other. Furthermore, because the number of samples is limited, one hospital's data is not sufficient to support such research. Hence, the two hospitals have to work together to conduct the research without compromising their patients' personal information.

   In this situation, we can use synthetic data generation techniques to produce synthetic yet representative data that can be safely shared. Typically, the generated synthetic data has the same format, statistics, and distribution as the original data (as shown in figure 6.1), without leaking any information from a single individual. Sharing a synthetic dataset in the same form as the original data gives much more flexibility in how data users can use it with no privacy concerns.

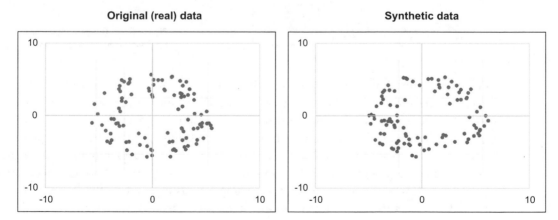

Figure 6.1   The synthetic data retains the structure of the original data, but they are not the same.

Synthetic data can also be utilized in business scenarios. For instance, suppose a company wants to conduct a business analysis to improve its marketing spend. To conduct this analysis, the company's marketing units are usually required to have their customers' consent to use their data. However, customers will likely not consent to share their data, since the data might contain sensitive information, such as transactions, locations, and shopping information. In this scenario, using synthetic data generated from the customers' data will enable the company to run an accurate simulation for the business analysis without requiring the consent of the customers. Since the synthetic data is generated based on the statistical properties of the actual data, it can be reliably used in such studies.

6.1.3   *Generating synthetic data*

Before we look at specific generation techniques, let's go through the general process of generating synthetic data, illustrated in figure 6.2.

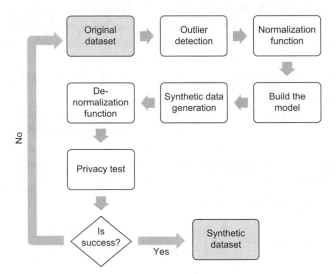

Figure 6.2   **General pipeline for generating synthetic data**

Before extracting any statistical characteristics from the original dataset, the first step is to preprocess the original dataset by removing the outliers and normalizing the feature values. Outliers are data points distant from other observations. They may result from variability and measurement error in the experiments, which sometimes provide incorrect information to data users. In most cases, outliers are likely to mislead the synthetic data generator to generate more outliers, making the ML model inaccurate. One common way of detecting outliers is using a density-based method: observing if the probability of the presence of specific points in a certain area is much lower than the expected value in that area.

The next step is feature normalization. Each dataset has a different number of features, and each feature has a different range of values. Feature normalization usually scales all the features to the same range, which helps us extract the statistical characteristics while giving equal consideration to the different features. After normalizing the dataset, we can build the distribution extraction model, which keeps the statistical characteristics of the original data.

Finally, the privacy test is designed to ensure that the generated synthetic data satisfies certain predefined privacy guarantees (*k*-anonymity, DP, etc.). If the generated synthetic data cannot provide the predefined privacy guarantees, the privacy test will be failed. We can generate synthetic datasets repeatedly until one passes the privacy test.

Now that we have covered the basic concepts, the application scenarios, and the general synthetic data generation process, let's look into some of the most popular synthetic generation techniques based on data anonymization and DP. We'll start with the data anonymization approaches.

6.2 Assuring privacy via data anonymization

The previous chapters discussed different techniques for privatizing sensitive information by adding noise and using perturbation techniques. And as we discussed at the beginning of this chapter, synthetic data is artificially produced data. Hence, different data anonymization techniques can also be used to create a synthetic dataset.

In this section we'll discuss historical non-DP approaches that use data anonymization techniques to share private and sensitive information without betraying the individual's privacy. In section 6.3 we'll discuss using DP for synthetic data generation.

6.2.1 Private information sharing vs. privacy concerns

Before we look at how anonymization techniques work, let's consider the scenario where individuals' medical records are released to the public for research purposes. Sharing such information has many benefits for research, including assisting the research community in confirming published results and facilitating them to do more qualitative in-depth analyses of the data. Thus, anonymizing the data is common before releasing data to the public.

But can we anonymize a dataset arbitrarily? In 1997, the Group Insurance Commission from Massachusetts wanted to release a dataset of hospital visits by state employees, which was to be used for research purposes [1]. Of course, there were privacy considerations, so they removed all the columns that could be used to identify who the patient was, such as name, phone number, SSN, and address. Do you think this data release went well?

Unfortunately, it did not. A researcher from MIT, Latanya Sweeney [2], found that even though the main identifiers were removed, some demographic information was left in the dataset, such as zip code, date of birth, and gender. Sweeney realized that the claims of the Massachusetts governor, who insisted that the privacy of the individuals was respected, were actually not correct. She decided to re-identify which records of the published (or anonymized) dataset were the governor's, so she investigated the public voter records from Massachusetts, which had full identifiers, such as name, address, and demographic data, including zip code and date of birth. She was able to identify records of prescriptions and visits in the dataset that belonged to the governor.

> **NOTE** In data security, a *re-identification attack* is when someone tries to link external data sources to identify a particular individual or a sensitive record.

As you can see, data anonymization techniques can be used to synthesize a dataset, but we need to make sure sensitive values in the dataset are no longer unique. How can we create an anonymized dataset such that none of the sensitive values in the dataset are unique? Here comes *k*-anonymity, a popular data anonymization approach.

6.2.2 *Using k-anonymity against re-identification attacks*

K-anonymity is a key security concept used to alleviate the risk of someone re-identifying anonymized data by linking it to external datasets [3]. The idea is simple. It uses techniques called *generalization* and *suppression* to hide an individual's identity in a group of similar people. In technical terms, a dataset is said to be *k*-anonymous when every possible combination of values for sensitive columns appears at least for *k* different records, where *k* represents the number of records in that group. If, for any individual in a particular dataset, there are at least *k*-1 other individuals who have the same properties, we can say that dataset is *k*-anonymized.

For example, suppose we have the same Group Insurance Commission dataset, we are looking at the zip code in that dataset, and we set *k* to 20. If we look at any person in that dataset, we should always find 19 other individuals who share the same zip code. The bottom line is that we will not be able to specifically identify an individual just by referring to their zip code. The same concept can be extended further to combining multiple attributes. For example, we could consider both zip code and age as the attributes. In that case, the anonymized dataset should always have 19 other individuals sharing the same age and zip code, which makes re-identification much harder than in the previous case.

The dataset in table 6.1 is 2-anonymous, where every combination of values (in this case, zip code and age) appears at least *k* = 2 times.

Table 6.1 An example 2-anonymous dataset where every combination of zip code and age appears at least twice

Zip code	Age
33617	24
33620	35
33620	35
33617	24
33620	35

HOW TO MAKE A SYNTHETIC DATASET K-ANONYMOUS

There are two different techniques that can be used to make an original dataset *k*-anonymous: generalization and suppression.

In generalization, the main idea is to make a value less precise so that records with different values are generalized into records that share the same values. Let's consider the original dataset shown in table 6.2 and the 2-anonymous version shown in table 6.3.

Table 6.2 The original dataset

Zip code	Age
33617	24
23620	41
23622	43
33617	29

Table 6.3 The 2-anonymous version of the dataset in table 6.2

Zip code	Age
33617	20–29
33617	20–29
236**	40–49
236**	40–49

Suppose table 6.2 represents the original dataset we are interested in, and we need to transform it to its 2-anonymous version. In this case, we can transform the numerical values in the dataset into numerical ranges so that the resulting table verifies 2-anonymity, as shown in table 6.3.

As you can see, even after the anonymization process, the resultant values are still relatively close to the original values in the dataset. For example, age 24 became the range of 20 to 29, but it is still close to the original.

Now let's consider table 6.4. Here the first four records can simply be converted to their 2-anonymous versions. But the last record is an outlier. If we try to group it with one of the pairs, the result would have a very large range of values. For instance, age would range from 10 to 49, while the zip code would be completely removed. Hence, the simplest solution is to remove the outlier from the dataset and keep the rest of the records. That process is called *suppression*.

At a high level, this is how we can apply *k*-anonymity for a dataset to produce an anonymized (or synthetic) dataset. We will be discussing more detailed examples and techniques in chapter 7, along with hands-on exercises.

Table 6.4   An example dataset with an outlier. As you can see, age 12 in the last row is an outlier.

Zip code	Age
33617	24
23620	41
23622	43
33617	29
19352	12

As you can see, by generalizing and suppressing the data, *k*-anonymity makes privacy leakage difficult. However, it has some drawbacks, which we will discuss next.

6.2.3   *Anonymization beyond k-anonymity*

While *k*-anonymity makes it harder to re-identify records, it also has some drawbacks. For example, suppose all individuals in a dataset share the same value for the attributes in consideration. In such a case, that information may be revealed simply by knowing that these individuals are part of the dataset.

Let's consider the dataset in table 6.5. As you can see, it is already 2-anonymized, but what if Bob lives in the 33620 zip code and knows that his neighbor recently went for a medical appointment? Bob might deduce that his neighbor has heart disease. Therefore, even though Bob cannot distinguish which record belongs to his neighbor (thanks to *k*-anonymity), he can still infer which disease his neighbor has.

Table 6.5   Even with a *k*-anonymized dataset, it is possible to leak some information.

Zip code	Age	Disease
33617	20–29	Cancer
33617	20–29	Viral infection
33620	40–49	Heart disease
33620	40–49	Heart disease

This problem can usually be solved by increasing the diversity of the sensitive values within the equivalence group. Here comes *l*-diversity, an extension of *k*-anonymity to provide privacy protection. The basic approach of *l*-diversity is to ensure that each group has at least *l* distinct sensitive values so that it is hard to identify an individual or the sensitive attribute. The same dataset can be *l*-diversified by increasing the diversity of the records, as shown in table 6.6.

As you can see, compared to table 6.5, table 6.6 is now 2-diverse ($l = 2$), and Bob cannot distinguish whether his neighbor has cancer, a viral infection, or heart disease.

Table 6.6 The diversity of records can be increased to protect against situations where *k*-anonymity does not work.

Zip code	Age	Disease
33***	20–29	Cancer
33***	20–29	Viral infection
33***	40–49	Heart disease
33***	40–49	Heart disease

However, *l*-diversity may still not work in some situations. What if Bob knows that his neighbor is in his early 40s? Now he might be able to reduce his search space to the last two rows of table 6.6, and he will know that the neighbor has heart disease. If we need to mitigate that, we can generalize the age column again so that it ranges from 20 to 49. However, that would significantly reduce the utility of the resulting data. We will discuss how *l*-diversity can be used in different scenarios with hands-on exercises in chapter 8.

The fundamental tradeoff between utility and privacy (an inverse relationship) is always a concern for data anonymization. To that end, synthetic data generation using other approaches is a viable next-step solution to this problem. In essence, we will use the original dataset to train an ML model, and then use that model to produce more realistic yet synthetic data with the same statistical properties as the underlying real data. In the next section we'll look at what techniques we can use to generate the synthetic data.

6.3 *DP for privacy-preserving synthetic data generation*

In the previous section we discussed generating synthetic data by using data anonymization techniques. In this section we'll look at applying DP for synthetic data generation.

Let's consider the following data-sharing scenario. Suppose company A has collected a lot of data about its customers (age, occupation, marital status, etc.), and they want to conduct a business analysis on that data to optimize the company's spending and sales. However, company A does not have the ability to do this analysis. They would like to outsource this task to a third-party operator, company B. However, company A cannot share the original data with company B due to critical privacy reasons. Hence, company A wants to generate a synthetic dataset that retains the statistical properties of the original dataset without leaking any private information. They can then share the synthetic dataset with company B for further analysis.

In such scenarios, company A has two synthetic data generation and sharing options. First, they can generate synthetic data representations of the original dataset, such as histograms, probability distributions, mean/median values, or standard deviations. Although such synthetic data representations can reflect certain properties of the original data, they do not have the same "shape" (i.e., the number of features and number of samples) as the original data. If the data analysis process requires specific or more complex and customizable algorithms (such as ML or deep learning algorithms), just providing synthetic data representations of the original data cannot fulfill those data requirements. For instance, most ML or deep learning algorithms are required to run directly on the feature vectors of the datasets rather than on statistics (such as mean or standard deviation) of the datasets. Thus, the second option, which is more general and flexible, is to provide a synthetic dataset that maintains the same statistical properties as the original dataset and has the same shape.

In the rest of this section we'll use a histogram as an example data representation to demonstrate how you can generate a synthetic data representation that satisfies DP. We will also examine how to use the DP synthetic data representation to generate differentially private synthetic data.

6.3.1 DP synthetic histogram representation generation

Let's continue with our previous data-sharing scenario. Suppose our outsourced company B wants to know how many company A customers are within a given age range. A straightforward solution would be to provide company B with a count query function that could directly query the original data of company A.

Let's use the US Census dataset as an example and load it as shown in the following listing.

Listing 6.1   Loading the US Census dataset

```
import pandas as pd
import numpy as np
import matplotlib.pyplot as plt
import sys
import io
import requests
import math

req = requests.get("https://archive.ics.uci.edu/ml/machine-learning-
    databases/adult/adult.data").content                              ⟵—— Load data.
adult = pd.read_csv(io.StringIO(req.decode('utf-8')), header=None,
    na_values='?', delimiter=r", ")
adult.dropna()
adult.head()
```

You will get results like those in figure 6.3.

	0	1	2	3	4	5	6	7	8	9	10	11	12	13	14
0	39	State-gov	77516	Bachelors	13	Never-married	Adm-clerical	Not-in-family	White	Male	2174	0	40	United-States	<=50K
1	50	Self-emp-not-inc	83311	Bachelors	13	Married-civ-spouse	Exec-managerial	Husband	White	Male	0	0	13	United-States	<=50K
2	38	Private	215646	HS-grad	9	Divorced	Handlers-cleaners	Not-in-family	White	Male	0	0	40	United-States	<=50K
3	53	Private	234721	11th	7	Married-civ-spouse	Handlers-cleaners	Husband	Black	Male	0	0	40	United-States	<=50K
4	28	Private	338409	Bachelors	13	Married-civ-spouse	Prof-specialty	Wife	Black	Female	0	0	40	Cuba	<=50K

Figure 6.3   A snapshot of the US Census dataset

Now let's implement a count query to count the number of people within a given age range. In this example, we'll look for the number of people within the age range 44 to 55.

Listing 6.2 Implementing a count query

The ages of people →
```
adult_age = adult[0].dropna()

def age_count_query(lo, hi):
    return sum(1 for age in adult_age if age >= lo and age < hi)

age_count_query(44, 55)
```
Count the number of people within certain age ranges [lo, hi).

You will find that there are 6,577 people in this dataset within the age range of 44 to 55. At this point, we could add the DP perturbation mechanisms to the output of the count query to fulfill the requirement of company B. However, such an implementation can only satisfy the requirement of company B for a one-time count query on the original data of company A. In reality, company B will not use this count query only once. As we discussed in chapter 2, increasing the number of differentially private queries on the same dataset means we need to either increase the overall privacy budget, which means tolerating more privacy leakage from the original dataset, or add more noise to the output of the queries, which results in downgrading the accuracy.

How can we improve this solution to cater to the requirements? The answer is to provide a differentially private synthetic data representation of the original data rather than a differentially private query function. Here we can use a synthetic histogram to represent the original data and provide enough information for a count query. First, let's implement a synthetic histogram generator using our previously defined count query.

Listing 6.3 Synthetic histogram generator

```
age_domain = list(range(0, 100))    ←——— The domain of ages

age_histogram = [age_count_query(age, age + 1) for age in age_domain]    ←—

plt.bar(age_domain, age_histogram)
plt.ylabel('The number of people (Frequency)')
plt.xlabel('Ages')
```
Create the histogram of ages using the age count query.

You will get a histogram like the one in figure 6.4. The output shown here is the histogram generated using the age count query in listing 6.2. As you can see, it shows how many people are in this dataset for each age.

Let's call this a synthetic histogram or synthetic data representation. Remember, we have not generated any synthetic data yet—this is the "representation" that we will use to generate synthetic data.

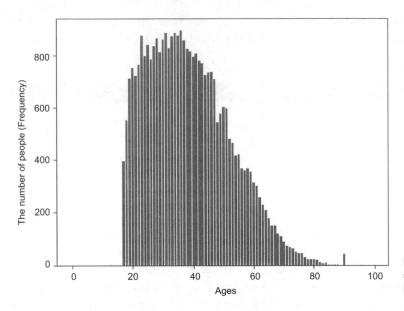

Figure 6.4   Histogram showing the number of people for each age

Let's now use this histogram to create the count query.

Listing 6.4   Implementing a count query using a synthetic histogram generator

```
def synthetic_age_count_query(syn_age_hist_rep, lo, hi):
    return sum(syn_age_hist_rep[age] for age in range(lo, hi))

synthetic_age_count_query(age_histogram, 44, 55)
```

> Generate synthetic count query results from the synthetic histogram of ages.

The output from the synthetically produced data will be 6,577. As you can see, the result generated by the synthetic histogram data representation is the same as the result produced using the previous count query on the original data. The point here is that we don't always need the original data to query or infer some information. If we can get a synthetic data representation of the original data, that is sufficient for us to answer some of the queries.

In listing 6.3 we used the original data to generate the histogram. Now let's implement a differentially private synthetic histogram generator using the Laplace mechanism (with sensitivity and epsilon both equal to 1.0).

Listing 6.5   Adding the Laplace mechanism

```
def laplace_mechanism(data, sensitivity, epsilon):
    return data + np.random.laplace(loc=0, scale = sensitivity / epsilon)

sensitivity = 1.0
epsilon = 1.0
dp_age_histogram = [laplace_mechanism(age_count_query(age, age + 1),
⇢ sensitivity, epsilon) for age in age_domain]
```

> Generate a differentially private synthetic histogram.

> The Laplace mechanism for DP

```
plt.bar(age_domain, dp_age_histogram)
plt.ylabel('The number of people (Frequency)')
plt.xlabel('Ages')
```

The result is shown in figure 6.5. Let's call this a differentially private synthetic histogram data representation. Observe the pattern of this histogram and the one in figure 6.4. Do you see any difference? The two look very similar, but this one was not generated using the original dataset. Instead, we used the Laplace mechanism (DP) to generate the data.

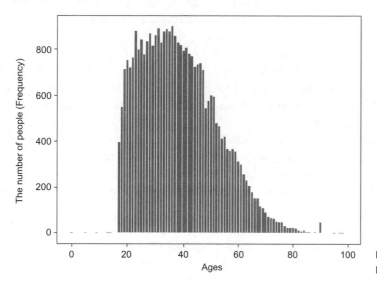

Figure 6.5   A differentially private synthetic histogram

Now the question is, "If we run the count query, will this give us the same result?" Let's generate a count query result with the differentially private synthetic histogram, given the same inputs.

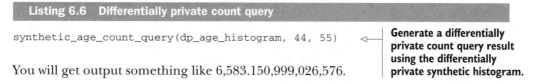

Listing 6.6   Differentially private count query

```
synthetic_age_count_query(dp_age_histogram, 44, 55)
```

Generate a differentially private count query result using the differentially private synthetic histogram.

You will get output something like 6,583.150,999,026,576.

> **NOTE**   Since this is a random function, you will get a different result, but it should be close to this value.

As you can see, the result is still very similar to the previous ground truth result. In other words, the differentially private synthetic histogram data representation can fulfill the data-sharing requirements of company B while still protecting the privacy requirements of company A because we are using synthetically produced data rather than the original data.

6.3.2 DP synthetic tabular data generation

In the previous section we saw how to enable privacy-preserving data sharing using differentially private synthetic data representations. But what if company B wants to conduct even more complex data analytics approaches, such as ML or deep learning algorithms, that require using a dataset with the same shape as the original one? In this case, we need to generate synthetic data with the same shape as the original data, again from the synthetic data representation.

In our example, the US Census dataset contains tabular data. To generate synthetic tabular data with the same shape, we could use the synthetic histogram as a probability distribution representing the underlying distribution of the original data. We could then use this synthetic histogram to generate synthetic tabular data.

Simply put, given a histogram, we can treat the sum of the counts of all the histogram bins as the total. For each histogram bin, we can use its count divided by the total to represent the probability that a sample fell into that histogram bin. Once we have those probabilities, we can easily sample a synthetic dataset using the histogram and the domain of its bins.

Suppose we already have a differentially private synthetic histogram. We then need to preprocess the synthetic histogram to ensure that all the counts are non-negative and normalized. That means the count of each bin should be a probability (they should sum to 1.0). The following listing shows the preprocessing and normalization operation.

Listing 6.7   Preprocessing and normalization operation

```
dp_age_histogram_preprocessed = np.clip(dp_age_histogram, 0, None)
dp_age_histogram_normalized = dp_age_histogram_preprocessed /
➥ np.sum(dp_age_histogram_preprocessed)

plt.bar(age_domain, dp_age_histogram_normalized)
plt.ylabel('Frequency Rates (probabilities)')
plt.xlabel('Ages')
```

The probability histogram may look like figure 6.6.

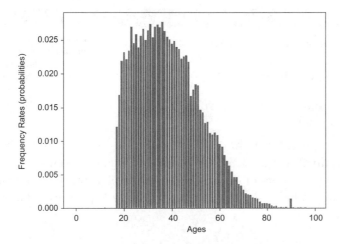

Figure 6.6   A normalized differentially private synthetic histogram

As you can see, the y-axis of this histogram is now normalized, but it still has the same shape as the input differentially private synthetic histogram in figure 6.5.

Now let's generate the differentially private synthetic tabular data.

Listing 6.8 Generating the differentially private synthetic tabular data

```
def syn_tabular_data_gen(cnt):
    return np.random.choice(age_domain, cnt, p = dp_age_histogram_normalized)

syn_tabular_data = pd.DataFrame(syn_tabular_data_gen(10), columns=['Age'])
syn_tabular_data
```

	Age
0	65
1	43
2	18
3	34
4	24
5	58
6	48
7	39
8	42
9	39

The results are shown in figure 6.7. Remember, this is a random function, so your results will be different.

What are we doing in listing 6.8? We generated ten different synthetic data records using the normalized synthetic histogram that we produced in listing 6.7. That means we generated completely new synthetic data records using the properties of the normalized synthetic histogram. Now we have two different datasets: the original dataset and the synthetically produced dataset.

Now let's compare the statistical properties of the synthetic data and the original data using histograms, as shown in listings 6.9 and 6.10.

Figure 6.7 A sample set of differentially private synthetic tabular data

---
Listing 6.9 The histogram of the synthetic data

```
syn_tabular_data = pd.DataFrame(syn_tabular_data_gen(len(adult_age)),
➥ columns=['Age'])
plt.hist(syn_tabular_data['Age'], bins=age_domain)
plt.ylabel('The number of people (Frequency) - Synthetic')
plt.xlabel('Ages')
```

This code produces a histogram of the synthetic data as shown in figure 6.8.

To make a comparison, let's generate a histogram of the original data.

Listing 6.10 The histogram of the original data

```
plt.bar(age_domain, age_histogram)
plt.ylabel('The number of people (Frequency) - True Value')
plt.xlabel('Ages')
```

The result may look like figure 6.9.

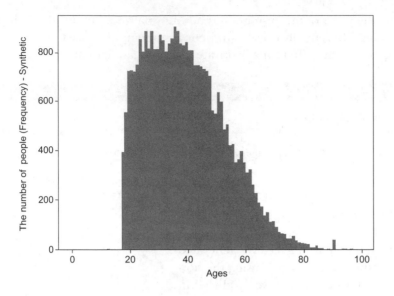

Figure 6.8   A histogram produced using synthetic tabular data generation

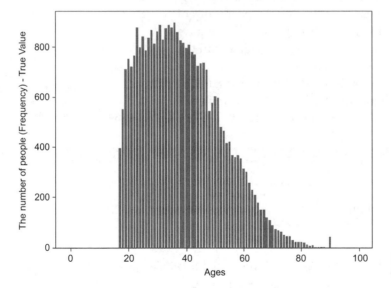

Figure 6.9   A histogram of the original data

If you compare the shapes of the histograms in figures 6.8 and 6.9, you'll see that they are extremely similar. In other words, the synthetic data that we produced has the same statistical properties as the original data. Interesting, isn't it?

6.3.3   *DP synthetic multi-marginal data generation*

The last section introduced an approach for generating privacy-preserving single-column synthetic tabular data from a synthetic histogram data representation using DP. But most real-world datasets consist of multiple-column tabular data. How can we tackle this problem?

A straightforward solution is to generate synthetic data for each column of a multiple-column tabular data using our previously described approach and then combine all the synthetic single-column tabular data together. This solution looks easy, but it does not reflect the correlations between those columns. For instance, in the US Census dataset, age and marital status are intuitively highly correlated to each other. What should we do in such cases?

We could consider multiple columns altogether. For instance, we could count how many people are 18 years old and never married, how many are 45 years old and divorced, how many are 90 years old and become widows, and so forth. Then we could calculate the probability of each case using the previous approach and sample the synthetic data from the simulated probability distribution. We'll call this result *synthetic multi-marginal data*.

Let's implement this idea on the US Census dataset containing age and marital status.

Listing 6.11 The 2-way marginal representation

```
two_way_marginal_rep = adult.groupby([0, 5]).size().
⮕   reset_index(name = 'count')
two_way_marginal_rep
```

The 2-way marginal representation of the original dataset is shown in figure 6.10. Remember, column 0 is the age, and column 5 is the marital status. As you can see in the second row (index 1), 393 people are never married and age 17.

	0	5	count
0	17	Married-civ-spouse	2
1	17	Never-married	393
2	18	Divorced	1
3	18	Married-civ-spouse	7
4	18	Married-spouse-absent	1
...	...	...	...
391	90	Divorced	1
392	90	Married-civ-spouse	20
393	90	Never-married	14
394	90	Separated	2
395	90	Widowed	6

396 rows × 3 columns

Figure 6.10 A snapshot of a 2-way marginal representation of the original dataset

We have 396 categories like this for each marital status and age combination. Once we generate a 2-way marginal dataset like this, we can use the Laplace mechanism to make it differentially private.

Listing 6.12   The differentially private 2-way marginal representation

```
dp_two_way_marginal_rep = laplace_mechanism(two_way_marginal_rep["count"],
➥ 1, 1)
dp_two_way_marginal_rep
```

The result of the 2-way marginal representation is shown in figure 6.11. As you can see, we have generated a differentially private value for all 396 categories.

```
0         1.790936
1       392.790936
2         0.790936
3         6.790936
4         0.790936
           ...
391       0.790936
392      19.790936
393      13.790936
394       1.790936
395       5.790936
Name: count, Length: 396, dtype: float64
```

Figure 6.11   A snapshot of a differentially private 2-way marginal representation

Now we can use our proposed approach to generate synthetic multi-marginal data that includes age and marital status. The following listing uses the 2-way marginal representation produced in listing 6.12 to generate a synthetic dataset.

Listing 6.13   Generating synthetic multi-marginal data

```
dp_two_way_marginal_rep_preprocessed = np.clip(dp_two_way_marginal_rep,
➥ 0, None)
dp_two_way_marginal_rep_normalized = dp_two_way_marginal_rep_preprocessed /
➥ np.sum(dp_two_way_marginal_rep_preprocessed)
dp_two_way_marginal_rep_normalized

age_marital_pairs = [(a,b) for a,b,_ in
➥ two_way_marginal_rep.values.tolist()]
list(zip(age_marital_pairs, dp_two_way_marginal_rep_normalized))

set_of_potential_samples = range(0, len(age_marital_pairs))

n = laplace_mechanism(len(adult), 1.0, 1.0)

generating_synthetic_data_samples = np.random.choice(
➥ set_of_potential_samples, int(max(n, 0)),
➥ p=dp_two_way_marginal_rep_normalized)
synthetic_data_set = [age_marital_pairs[i] for i in
➥ generating_synthetic_data_samples]

synthetic_data = pd.DataFrame(synthetic_data_set,
➥ columns=['Age', 'Marital status'])
synthetic_data
```

The resulting synthetically produced 2-way marginal dataset is shown in figure 6.12.

	Age	Marital status
0	30	Married-civ-spouse
1	29	Married-civ-spouse
2	68	Married-civ-spouse
3	42	Divorced
4	46	Married-civ-spouse
...	...	...
32556	27	Never-married
32557	50	Divorced
32558	90	Never-married
32559	49	Divorced
32560	49	Married-civ-spouse

32561 rows × 2 columns

Figure 6.12   A snapshot of a synthetically produced 2-way marginal dataset

Let's compare the statistical properties of the synthetic data and the original data. First, let's compare the histograms of the age data.

Listing 6.14   The histogram produced using synthetic multi-marginal data

```
plt.hist(synthetic_data['Age'], bins=age_domain)
plt.ylabel('The number of people (Frequency) - Synthetic')
plt.xlabel('Ages')
```

The histogram of the synthetic data is shown in figure 6.13.

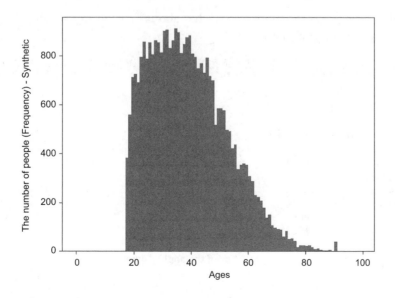

Figure 6.13 A histogram produced using synthetically generated multi-marginal data

To compare the results, we'll use the following code (the same as in listing 6.10) to generate a histogram of the original data.

Listing 6.15   The histogram of the original data

```
plt.bar(age_domain, age_histogram)
plt.ylabel('The number of people (Frequency) - True Value')
plt.xlabel('Ages')
```

The histogram of the original data is shown in figure 6.14. By simply looking at their shapes and how data points are distributed, we can quickly conclude that the two histograms in figures 6.13 and 6.14 are similar.

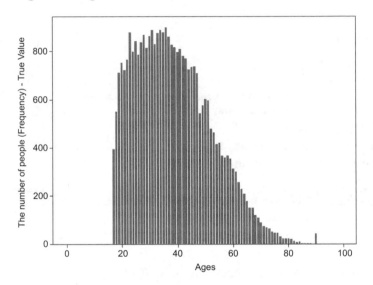

Figure 6.14   A histogram of the original data

We've looked at how age is distributed, but what about marital status? Let's compare the distribution of the marital status data.

Listing 6.16   The statistics of the original data

```
adult_marital_status = adult[5].dropna()
adult_marital_status.value_counts().sort_index()
```

The results are shown in figure 6.15.

```
Divorced                 4443
Married-AF-spouse          23
Married-civ-spouse       14976
Married-spouse-absent     418
Never-married            10683
Separated                1025
Widowed                   993
Name: 5, dtype: int64
```

Figure 6.15   Summary of statistics of the original data

The next listing will summarize marital status data in the original dataset.

> **Listing 6.17   The statistics of the synthetic data**

```
syn_adult_marital_status = synthetic_data['Marital status'].dropna()
syn_adult_marital_status.value_counts().sort_index()
```

Figure 6.16 shows the summary of synthetically produced data. As you can see, the marital status of the differentially private synthetic multi-marginal data looks similar to the original data (but is not the same).

```
Divorced                4476
Married-AF-spouse         22
Married-civ-spouse     15001
Married-spouse-absent    404
Never-married          10623
Separated               1032
Widowed                 1003
Name: Marital status, dtype: int64
```

Figure 6.16   Summary of statistics of the synthetically produced marital status data

Once again, we can conclude that instead of using the original data, we can use synthetically produced data to do the same tasks while preserving the privacy of the original data.

We have looked at generating synthetic histogram data representations that satisfy DP, and we have walked through using the differentially private synthetic histogram representations to generate privacy-preserving synthetic single-column tabular data and multi-marginal data. But wait! How can we deal with a large dataset with more than two or three columns and tons of records? We'll find out the answers to that next. The next section will look at a more complex case study to demonstrate how we can apply data anonymization and DP for privacy-preserving synthetic data generation for ML.

EXERCISE 1: TRY IT YOURSELF

In listing 6.11 we looked at a the 2-way marginal representation with age and marital status. As discussed, age and marital status are highly correlated, and we wanted to see whether the synthetically produced data also followed a similar distribution. Now try following the same steps for the education and occupation columns to see whether you have similar results.

Hint: In the original dataset, education is in column 3, and column 6 is the occupation. Start by changing the columns in listing 6.11 as follows:

```
adult.groupby([3, 6]).size().reset_index(name = 'count')
```

Then follow all the steps.

EXERCISE 2: TRY IT YOURSELF

Repeat the same process but for 3-way marginal representation with 3-column data. For example, you might consider age, occupation, and marital status as the 3-way representation.

6.4   Case study on private synthetic data release via feature-level micro-aggregation

Now that we have discussed different approaches to generating synthetic data, let's walk through a case study on designing a private synthetic data-release mechanism via a feature-level micro-aggregation method. Sound too technical? Don't worry, we'll go through the details step by step.

First, though, recall that DP is a mechanism that provides a strong privacy guarantee to protect individual data records (as we discussed in chapter 2). In this case study, we will discuss a privacy-preserving synthetic data generation method under DP guarantee that will work with multiple ML tasks. It was developed on differentially private generative models of clustered data to generate synthetic datasets. In the latter part of this section, we will show you how effective this method is compared to some existing approaches, and how it improved the utility compared to other methods.

Before we look at the details of the case study, let's first recap some of the basics. Usually, designing a powerful privacy-preserving synthetic data generation method for ML comes with many challenges. First, a privacy-preserving method usually introduces perturbation to data samples that hurts the utility of the data. Mitigating the perturbation so that you reach a certain level of utility is not an easy task. Second, ML can be represented in many different tasks, like classification, regression, and clustering. An effective synthetic data generation method should be applicable to all these various tasks. Third, some data can come in the form of very complex distributions. In that case, it is hard to form an accurate generator based on the whole data distribution.

In the past, people have proposed several private synthetic data-release algorithms [4], [5]. One of the common approaches is to utilize noisy histograms to release synthetic data, but most of them are designed to work with categorical feature variables. On the other hand, some algorithms are designed to generate synthetic data under a statistical model with some preprocessing on the original dataset. However, they usually only generate synthetic data based on the whole data distribution.

In this study, we will focus on how we can generate synthetic data while maintaining statistical characteristics similar to the original dataset while ensuring data owners have no privacy concerns.

Now that you have a basic understanding of what we're going to do, let's dig into the details.

6.4.1   Using hierarchical clustering and micro-aggregation

An essential part of our methodology that we'll build on is *hierarchical clustering*. In essence, hierarchical clustering is an algorithm that clusters input samples into different clusters based on the *proximity matrix* of samples. This proximity matrix represents the distance between each cluster. In this case, we'll use *agglomerative hierarchical clustering* [6], a bottom-up approach, which starts by assigning each data sample to its own group and merging the pairs of clusters that have the smallest distance, until there is only a single cluster left.

As discussed in section 6.2, *k*-anonymity can be used to anonymize data. Here, we will use a data anonymization algorithm called *micro-aggregation* that can achieve *k*-anonymity. The micro-aggregation approach we are referring to here is a simple heuristic method called *maximum distance to average record* (MDAV) proposed by Domingo-Ferrer et al. [7]. The idea is to separate samples into clusters, and each cluster contains exactly *k* records except the last one. Records in the same cluster are supposed to be as similar as possible in terms of distance. In addition, each record in the cluster will be replaced by a representative record for the cluster to complete the data anonymization.

6.4.2 Generating synthetic data

In this synthetic data generation mechanism, four main components operate collectively to generate synthetic data that satisfies DP:

- *Data preprocessing*—Combines independent feature sets and feature-level micro-aggregation to produce data clusters that describe the data more generally.
- *Statistic extraction*—Extracts the representative statistical information of each data cluster.
- *DP sanitizer*—Adds differential private noise on extracted statistical information.
- *Data generator*—Generates synthetic data sample by sample from the perturbed generative model.

These four components are shown in figure 6.17.

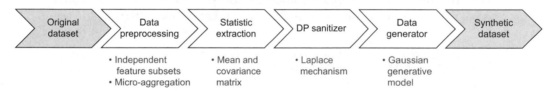

Figure 6.17 Different components of the synthetic data generation algorithm

HOW DATA PREPROCESSING WORKS

In data preprocessing, we use micro-aggregation as the clustering method for samples in full feature dimension (samples that cover all the features we are interested in). Instead of replacing records with a representative record, we will use a differentially private generative model to model each cluster. However, there are a few challenges here.

When modeling the output clusters from MDAV, some clusters may carry correlations that may not exist in the actual data distribution. This false feature correlation may apply unnecessary constraints when modeling the data clusters, and this may lead the synthetic data into a different shape. On the other hand, we know that a noise variance is usually introduced by DP. Intuitively, the less the noise introduced by DP, the higher the utility. Hence, reducing the DP mechanism's noise also helps us improve the data's utility. To address these adverse effects, we can sample data not only at the sample level but also at the feature level.

Here is how feature-level and sample-level clustering work:

- *Feature-level clustering*—Whenever we have a numerical dataset $D^{(n \times d)}$, we can divide these d data features into m independent feature sets using agglomerative hierarchical clustering. Here, a distance function that converts Pearson correlation to distance can be used to form the proximity matrix in hierarchical clustering. Features with higher correlation should have lower distance, and lower correlation corresponds to a higher distance. This approach will help us to ensure the features in the same set are more correlated to each other and less correlated to features in the other feature sets.

- *Sample-level clustering*—Once we have the output of feature-level clustering, we split data on the feature level and then apply micro-aggregation to each data segment. The idea is to assign the homogeneous samples to the same cluster, which will help us preserve more information from the original data. The sensitivity of each sample cluster can also be potentially reduced compared to the global sensitivity. This reduction will involve less noise in the DP mechanism. In other words, it enhances the data's utility under the same level of privacy guarantee.

THE CONCEPTS BEHIND GENERATING SYNTHETIC DATA

The micro-aggregation process outputs several clusters having at least k records each. Assuming each cluster forms a multivariate Gaussian distribution, the mean (μ) and covariance matrix (Σ) are computed for each cluster c. Then the privacy sanitizer adds the noise on μ and Σ to ensure that the model is satisfied with DP. Finally, the generative model is built. The complete process of generating synthetic data is illustrated in figure 6.18.

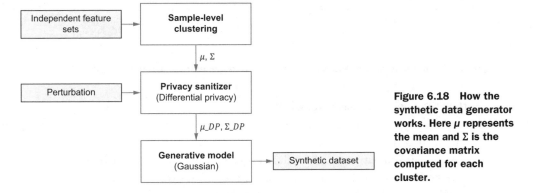

Figure 6.18 How the synthetic data generator works. Here μ represents the mean and Σ is the covariance matrix computed for each cluster.

In figure 6.18, the original multivariate Gaussian model is parameterized by the mean (μ) and covariance matrix (Σ). It is noteworthy that the privacy sanitizer outputs two parameters, μ_DP and Σ_DP, that are protected by DP. Hence, the multivariate Gaussian model that is parameterized by μ_DP and Σ_DP is also protected by DP. In addition, depending on the postprocessing invariance of DP, all the synthetic data derived from DP multivariate Gaussian models is also protected by DP.

Variance, covariance, and covariance matrix

In statistics, *variance* usually measures the variation of a single random variable (for instance, the height of a person in a population), whereas *covariance* is a measure of how much two random variables vary together. For example, we can consider the height of a person and the weight of a person in a population to calculate the covariance.

The formula for the covariance of two random variables *x* and *y* is given by

$$\sigma(x, y) = \frac{1}{n-1} \sum_{i=1}^{n} (x_i - \bar{x})(y_i - \bar{y})$$

where *n* is the number of samples. A covariance matrix is a square matrix given by $C_{(i,j)} = \sigma(x_i, x_j)$ where $C \in \mathbb{R}^{(n \times n)}$ and *n* is the number of random variables. The diagonal entries of the covariance matrix are the variances, while the other entries are the covariances. For the case of two random variables, the covariance matrix can be computed as follows:

$$C = \begin{bmatrix} \sigma(x, x) & \sigma(x, y) \\ \sigma(y, x) & \sigma(y, y) \end{bmatrix}$$

6.4.3 *Evaluating the performance of the generated synthetic data*

To evaluate the performance of the proposed method, we have implemented it in Java. Yes, this time it's Java. The complete source code, dataset, and evaluation tasks are available in the book's GitHub repository: https://github.com/nogrady/PPML/blob/main/Ch6/PrivSyn_Demo.zip.

We generated different synthetic datasets and performed experiments under different cluster sizes (*k*) and privacy budgets (ε). The setting of ε varies from 0.1 to 1 and cluster size varies: *k* = 25, 50, 75, 100. For each synthetic dataset, we looked at the performance on three general ML tasks: classification, regression, and clustering. To accomplish these tasks, we have two different experiment scenarios using different synthetic and original data combinations.

- *Experiment scenario 1*—Original data is used for training, and synthetic data is used for testing.

  The ML model trains on the original datasets and tests the generated synthetic datasets. For each experimental dataset, 30% of the samples are used as the seed dataset to generate the synthetic dataset, and 70% is used as original data to train the model. Generated synthetic data is used for testing.

- *Experiment scenario 2*—Synthetic data is used for training, and original data is used for testing.

  The ML model trains on the synthetic datasets and tests on the original datasets. For each experimental dataset, 80% of the samples are used as a seed dataset to generate the synthetic dataset, and 20% is used as original data to test the model.

DATASETS USED FOR THE EXPERIMENTS

For this performance evaluation, we used three datasets from the UCI Machine Learning Repository [8] and LIBSVM data repository to examine the performance of the different algorithms. All the features in the dataset were scaled to [−1,1]:

- *Diabetes dataset*—This dataset contains diagnostic measurements of patient records with 768 samples and 9 features, including patient information such as blood pressure, BMI, insulin level, and age. The objective is to identify whether a patient has diabetes.
- *Breast cancer dataset*—This dataset was collected from clinical cases for breast cancer diagnosis. It has 699 samples and 10 features. All the samples are labeled as benign or malignant.
- *Australian dataset*—This is the Australian credit approval dataset from the Stat-Log project. Each sample is a credit card application, and the dataset contains 690 samples and 14 features. The samples are labeled by whether the application is approved or not.

PERFORMANCE EVALUATION AND THE RESULTS

As discussed, we are interested in three main ML tasks for the evaluation of synthetic data: classification, regression, and clustering.

A support vector machine (SVM) was used for the classification task. In each training phase, we used grid search and cross-validation to choose the best parameter combination for the SVM model. In terms of selecting the best performing SVM model, the F1 score was utilized. The model with the highest F1 score was used to test classification accuracy.

For the regression task, linear regression was used as the regressor. The evaluation metric of regression is mean squared error (MSE).

Finally, k-means clustering was used as the clustering task. As you learned in the previous chapters, clustering is an unsupervised ML task that groups similar data. Unlike the preceding classification and regression tasks, all data in the original dataset is considered the seed for synthetic data in clustering. The k-means algorithm is applied on both the original and synthetic datasets, and both result in two clusters that present the binary class in experimental datasets. In each experiment, k-means runs 50 times with different centroid seeds, and it outputs the best case of 50 consecutive runs.

The results of the three ML tasks are shown in figures 6.19, 6.20, and 6.21. You can see that when ε ranges from 0.1 to 0.4, the performance of each k increases rapidly, but the peak performance is not always coming from a fixed k value. For example figure 6.19 (e) has a local optimal point when $k = 50$, and figures 6.21 (a) and figure 6.21 (c) have a local optimal point when $k = 75$.

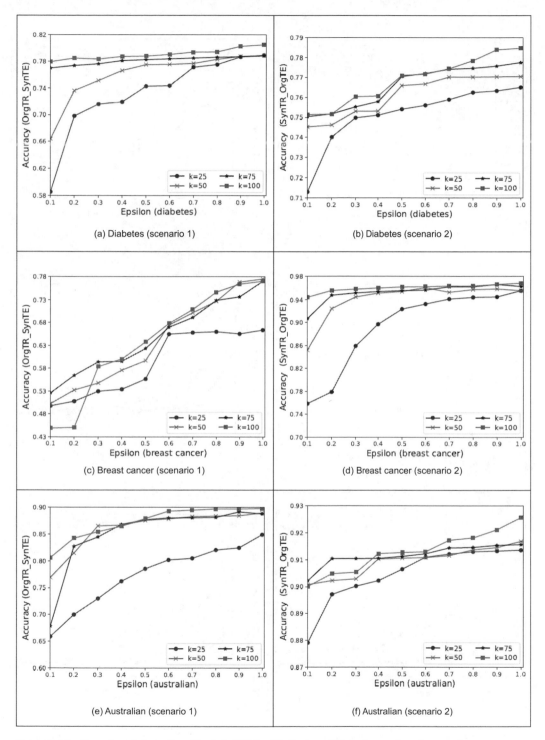

Figure 6.19 Experimental results of task 1 (SVM) with the two different experiment scenarios

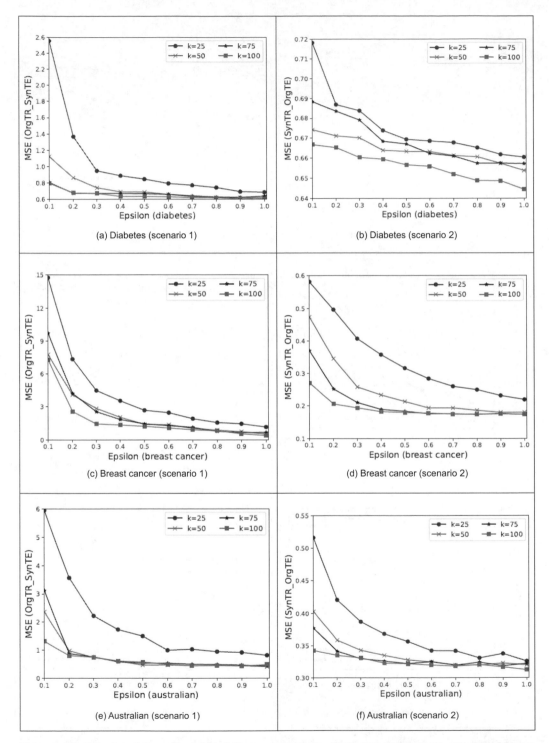

Figure 6.20   Experimental results of task 2 (linear regression) with the two different experiment scenarios

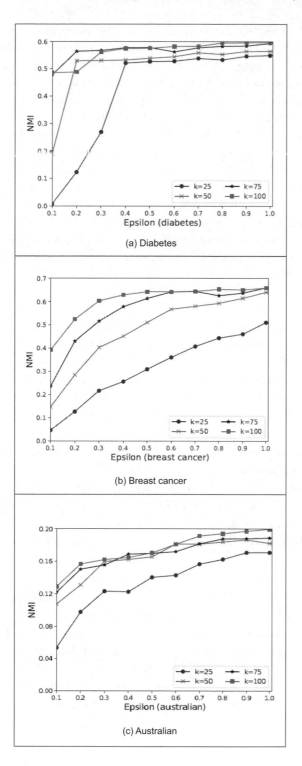

(a) Diabetes

(b) Breast cancer

(c) Australian

Figure 6.21   Experimental results of task 3 (*k*-means clustering)

Theoretically speaking, a small ε value usually introduces more noise to the synthetic data than a greater ε value, which brings more randomness. Comparing the two scenarios in the case of regression (figure 6.20), the randomness reflected in scenario 2 has much less MSE than in scenario 1, when the privacy budget was small. This is due to the testing data in scenario 1 having differentially private noise, and the testing data in scenario 2 not having the noise in it. Whenever $\varepsilon > 0.4$, the performance increase is somewhat steady, and when $k = 100$, the clustering method always outperforms the other k values under the same privacy budget. It is also noteworthy that when $k = 25$, the overall performance is much lower than for the other k values. That's because when we form a multivariate Gaussian generative model on a cluster that only contains a few data samples, the calculated mean and the covariance matrix can be biased. The cluster cannot reflect the data distribution very well. Thus, k should be a moderate value to form the multivariate Gaussian generative model. A greater k value can also make the model converge faster than a smaller k, as in figures 6.19 (a), 6.19 (d), 6.20 (a), and 6.21 (a).

Summary

- Synthetic data is artificial data that is generated from the original data and that keeps the original data's statistical properties and protects the original data's private information.
- The synthetic data generation process involves various steps, including outlier detection, a normalization function, and building the model.
- A privacy test is used to ensure that the generated synthetic data satisfies certain predefined privacy guarantees.
- *K*-anonymity is a good approach for generating anonymized synthetic data to mitigate re-identification attacks.
- While *k*-anonymity makes it harder to re-identify individuals, it also has some drawbacks, which leads to other anonymization mechanisms such as *l*-diversity.
- A synthetic representation of a dataset can capture statistical properties of the original dataset, but most of the time it will not have the same shape as the original dataset.
- We can use a synthetic histogram to generate synthetic tabular data.
- A synthetic representation can be used to generate a synthetic dataset with the same statistical properties and shape as the original dataset.
- We can generate differentially private synthetic data by applying the Laplace mechanism to the synthetic representation generator and then use the differentially private synthetic representation generator.
- We can generate differentially private synthetic data that satisfies *k*-anonymity by applying micro-aggregation techniques to synthetic data generation.

Part 3

Building privacy-assured machine learning applications

Part 3 covers the next-level core concepts required to build privacy-assured machine learning applications. Chapter 7 introduces the importance of privacy preservation in data mining applications, looking at privacy protection mechanisms widely used in data mining for processing and publishing data. Chapter 8 discusses widely used privacy models in data mining and their threats and vulnerabilities. Chapter 9 focuses on compressive privacy for machine learning, discussing its design and implementation. Finally, chapter 10 puts the concepts from all the previous chapters together to design a privacy-enhanced platform for protecting and sharing research data.

Privacy-preserving data mining techniques

This chapter covers

- The importance of privacy preservation in data mining
- Privacy protection mechanisms for processing and publishing data
- Exploring privacy-enhancing techniques for data mining
- Implementing privacy techniques in data mining with Python

So far we have discussed different privacy-enhancing technologies that the research community and the industry have partnered together on. This chapter focuses on how these privacy techniques can be utilized for data mining and management operations. In essence, *data mining* is the process of discovering new relationships and patterns in data to achieve further meaningful analysis. This usually involves machine learning, statistical operations, and data management systems. In this chapter we will explore how various privacy-enhancing technologies can be bundled with data mining operations to achieve privacy-preserving data mining.

First, we will look at the importance of privacy preservation in data mining and how private information can be disclosed to the outside world. Then we will walk through the different approaches that can be utilized to ensure privacy guarantees in data mining operations, along with some examples. Toward the end of this chapter, we will discuss the recent evolution of data management techniques and how these privacy mechanisms can be instrumented in database systems to design a tailor-made privacy-enriched database management system.

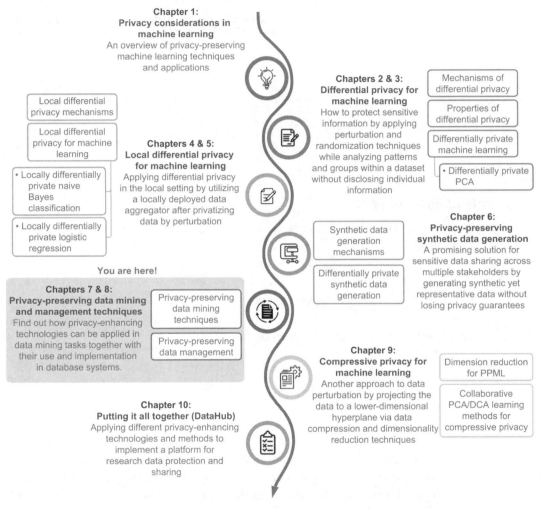

7.1   *The importance of privacy preservation in data mining and management*

Today's applications are continually generating large amounts of information, and we all know the importance of privacy protection in this deep learning era. It is similarly important to process, manage, and store the collected information in a time-efficient, secure data processing framework.

Let's consider a typical deployment of a cloud-based e-commerce application where the users' private information is stored and processed by the database application (figure 7.1).

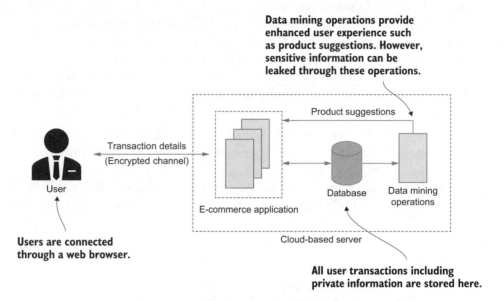

Figure 7.1   A typical deployment of an e-commerce web application. All user data, including private information, is stored in a database, and that data will be used by data mining operations.

In e-commerce applications, users connect through web browsers, choose the products or services they want, and make their payments online. All this is recorded on the backend database, including private information such as the customer's name, address, gender, product preferences, and product types. This information is further processed by data mining and ML operations to provide a better customer experience. For example, the customer's product preferences can be linked with the choices of other customers to suggest additional products. Similarly, customer addresses can be used to provide location-based services and suggestions. While this approach has numerous benefits for the customers, such as enhanced service quality, it also comes with many privacy concerns.

Let's take a simple example of a customer who regularly purchases clothes online. In this case, even though the gender may not specifically be mentioned, data mining algorithms might deduce the customer's gender simply by looking at what type of clothes the customer has purchased in the past. This becomes a privacy concern and is generally termed an *inference attack*. We will be looking at these attacks in more detail in the next chapter.

Now that most tech giants (such as Google, Amazon, and Microsoft) offer Machine Learning as a Service (MLaaS), small and medium-sized enterprises (SMEs) tend to launch their products based on these services. However, these services are vulnerable to various insider and outsider attacks, as we will discuss toward the end of this chapter. Thus, by linking two or more databases or services together, it is possible to infer more sensitive or private information. For example, an attacker who has access to the zip code and gender of a customer on an e-commerce website can combine that data with the publicly available Group Insurance Commission (GIC) dataset [1], and they might be able to extract the medical records of the individual. Therefore, privacy preservation is of utmost importance in data mining operations.

To that end, in this chapter and the next, we'll elaborate on the importance of privacy preservation for data mining and management, their applications and techniques, and the challenges in two particular aspects (as depicted in figure 7.2):

- *Data processing and mining*—Tools and techniques that can be used whenever the collected information is processed and analyzed through various data mining and analytical tools
- *Data management*—Methods and technologies that can be used to hold, store, and serve collected information for different data processing applications

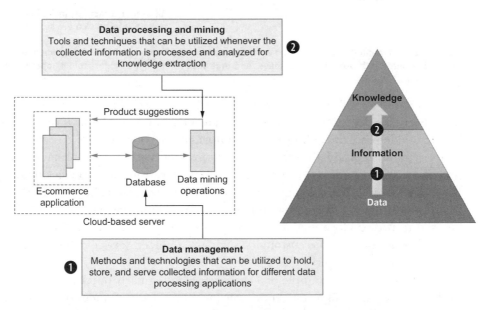

Figure 7.2   In essence, there are two aspects of privacy preservation when it comes to data mining and management.

Accordingly, we will look at how privacy preservation can be ensured by modifying or perturbing the input data and how we can protect privacy when data is released to other parties.

7.2   Privacy protection in data processing and mining

Data analysis and mining tools are intended to extract meaningful features and patterns from collected datasets, but direct use of data in data mining may result in unwanted data privacy violations. Thus, privacy protection methods utilizing data modification and noise addition techniques (sometimes called data perturbation) have been developed to protect sensitive information from privacy leakage.

However, modifying data may reduce the accuracy of the utility or even make it infeasible to extract essential features. The utility here refers to the data mining task; for example, in the previously mentioned e-commerce application, the mechanism that suggests products to the customer is the utility, and privacy protection methods can be used to protect this data. However, any data transformation should maintain the balance between privacy and the utility of the intended application so that data mining can still be performed on the transformed data.

Let's briefly look at what data mining is and how privacy regulations come into the picture.

7.2.1   What is data mining and how is it used?

Data mining is the process of extracting knowledge from a collected dataset or set of information. Information systems regularly collect and store valuable information, and the goal of storing information in a datastore is to extract information such as relationships or patterns. To that end, data mining is helpful in discovering new patterns from these datasets. Hence, data mining can be considered the process of learning new patterns or relationships. For instance, in our e-commerce example, a data mining algorithm could be used to determine how likely it is for a customer who purchased baby diapers to also purchase baby wipes. Based on such relationships, service providers can make timely decisions.

Generally, these relationships or patterns can be described with mathematical models that apply to a subset of the original data in the collection. In fact, the identified model can be used in two different ways. First, the model can be used in a descriptive way, where identified relationships between the data in a collection can be turned into human-recognizable descriptions. For example, a company's current financial situation (whether they are making profits or not) can be described based on the past financial data stored in a dataset. These are called *descriptive models*, and they usually provide accurate information based on historical data. *Predictive models* are the second way. Their accuracy may not be very precise, but they can be used to forecast the future based on past data. For example, a question like "If the company invests in this new project, will they will increase their profit margin five years down the line?" can be answered using predictive models.

As shown in figure 7.3, data mining can produce descriptive models and predictive models, and we can apply them for decision making based on the requirements of the underlying application. For example, in e-commerce applications, predictive models can be used to forecast the price fluctuations of a product.

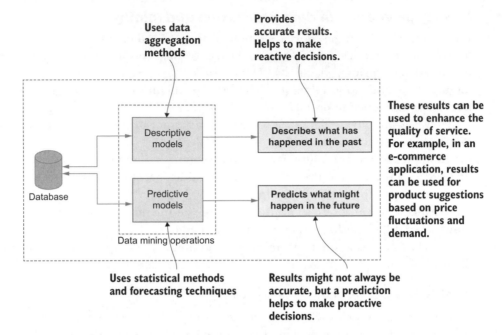

Figure 7.3   Relationships and patterns in data mining can be realized in two different ways.

7.2.2   *Consequences of privacy regulatory requirements*

Traditionally, data security and privacy requirements were set by the data owners (such as organizations on their own) to safeguard the competitive advantage of the products and services they offer. However, data has become the most valuable asset in the digital economy, and many privacy regulations have been imposed by governments to prevent the use of sensitive information beyond its intended purpose. Privacy standards such as HIPAA (Health Insurance Portability and Accountability Act of 1996), PCI-DSS (Payment Card Industry Data Security Standard), FERPA (Family Educational Rights and Privacy Act), and the European Union's GDPR (General Data Protection Regulation) are commonly adhered to by different organizations.

For instance, regardless of the size of the practice, almost every healthcare provider transmits health information electronically in connection with certain transactions, such as claims, medication records, benefit eligibility inquiries, referral authorization requests, and so on. However, the HIPAA regulations require all these healthcare providers to protect sensitive patient health information from being disclosed without the patient's consent or knowledge.

In the next section we'll look at different privacy-preserving data management technologies in detail and discuss their applications and flaws in ensuring these privacy requirements.

7.3   *Protecting privacy by modifying the input*

Now that you know the basics, let's get into the details. The well-established privacy-preserving data management (PPDM) technologies can be grouped into several different classes based on how privacy assurance is implemented. We will discuss the first two classes in this chapter; the others will be covered in the next chapter.

The first class of PPDM techniques ensures privacy when data is collected and before it is moved to the datastore. These techniques usually incorporate different randomization techniques at the data collection stage and generate privatized values individually for each record, so original values are never stored. The two most common randomization techniques are modifying data by adding noise with a known statistical distribution and modifying data by multiplying noise with a known statistical distribution.

Figure 7.4 illustrates the first of these two techniques. During the data collection stage, a publicly known noise distribution is added to produce a randomized result. Then, when data mining is involved, we can simply estimate the noise distribution based on the samples, and the original data distribution can be reconstructed. However, it's important to note that, while the original data distribution may be reconstructed, the original values are not.

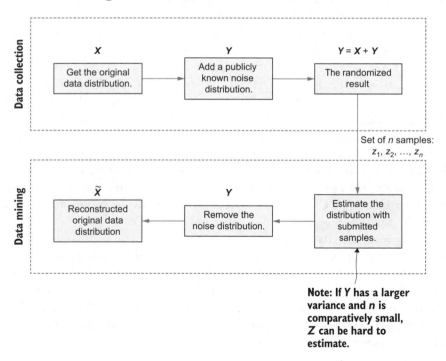

Figure 7.4   Using randomization techniques in data input modification

7.3.1   *Applications and limitations*

Now that we have looked at how input can be modified to preserve privacy, let's look at the merits and demerits of these randomization techniques.

Most importantly, those methods can preserve the statistical properties of the original data distribution even after randomization. This is why they have been used in different privacy-preserving applications, including differential privacy (which we discussed in chapters 2 and 3).

However, since the original data is perturbed and only the data distribution is available (not the individual data), these methods require special data mining algorithms that can extract the necessary information by looking at the distribution. Thus, depending on the application, this method might have a greater effect on the utility.

Tasks like classification and clustering can work well with these input randomization techniques, as they only require access to the data distribution. For example, consider employing such a technique on a medical diagnosis dataset for a disease identification task that is based on specific features or parameters. In such a case, access to the individual records is unnecessary, and the classification can be done based on the data distribution.

7.4   *Protecting privacy when publishing data*

The next class of PPDM deals with techniques for when data is released to third parties without disclosing the ownership of sensitive information. In this case, data privacy is achieved by applying data anonymization techniques for individual data records before they are released to the outside parties.

As discussed in the previous chapter, removing attributes that can explicitly identify an individual in a dataset is insufficient at this stage. Users in the anonymized data may still be identified by linking them to external data by combining nonsensitive attributes or records. These attributes are called quasi-identifiers.

Let's consider a scenario we discussed in chapter 6 of combining two publicly available datasets. It is quite straightforward to combine different values in the US Census dataset, such as zip code, gender, and date of birth, with an anonymized dataset from the Group Insurance Commission (GIC). By doing so, someone might be able to extract the medical records of a particular individual. For instance, if Bob knows the zip code, gender, and date of birth of his neighbor Alice, he could combine those two datasets using these three attributes, and he might be able to determine which medical records in the GIC dataset are Alice's. This is a privacy threat called a *linkage* or *correlation attack*, where values in a particular dataset are linked with other sources of information to create more informative and unique entries. PPDM techniques that are used when publishing data usually incorporate one or more data sanitization operations to preserve privacy.

> **NOTE**   If you are not familiar with the GIC dataset, it is an "anonymized" dataset of state employees that shows their every hospital visit in the USA. The goal was to help researchers, and the state spent time removing all key identifiers such as name, address, and social security number.

You may have already noticed that many data sanitization operations are used in practice, but most of these operations can be generalized as one of the following types of operations:

- *Generalization*—This operation replaces a particular value in a dataset with a more general attribute. For example, the numerical value of a person's salary, such as $56,000, can be replaced by a range of $50,000–$100,000. In this case, once the value is sanitized, we don't know the exact value, but we know it is between $50,000 and $100,000.

  This approach can be applied to categorical values as well. Consider the previously mentioned US Census dataset, which has employment details. As shown in figure 7.5, instead of categorizing people into different occupations, we can simply group them as "employed" or "unemployed" without exposing the individual occupations.

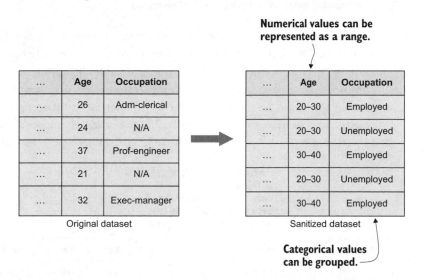

Figure 7.5   Generalization works by grouping the data.

- *Suppression*—Whereas generalization replaces the original record with a more general representation, the idea of suppression is to remove the record entirely from the dataset. Consider a dataset of hospital medical records. In such a medical database, it is possible to identify an individual based on their name (a sensitive attribute), so we can remove the name attribute from the dataset before publishing it to third parties (see figure 7.6).

Column suppressed

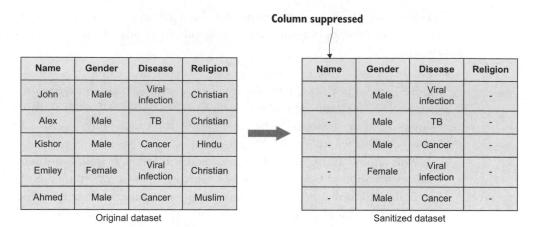

Figure 7.6   **Suppression works by removing the original record.**

- *Perturbation*—The other possible data sanitization operation is to replace the individual records with perturbed data that has the same statistical properties, and which can be generated using randomization techniques.

    One possible approach is adding noise to the original values using the techniques we discussed in the previous section, such as additive or multiplicative noise addition. In the example in figure 7.7, the original dataset's records in the first column are replaced with entirely different values based on random noise.

Perturbed data column. In this case, random noise has been added to each record such that the original value is perturbed.

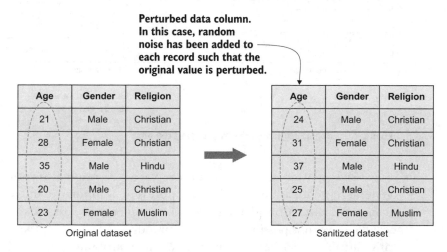

Figure 7.7   **Perturbation works by adding random noise.**

Another approach is to use synthetic data generation techniques as discussed in chapter 6. In that case, a statistical model is built using the original data, and that model can be used to generate synthetic data, which can then replace the original records in the dataset.

Another possible approach is to use data swapping techniques to accomplish the perturbation. The idea is to swap multiple sensitive attributes in a dataset in order to prevent records from being linked to individuals. Data swapping usually begins by randomly selecting a set of targeted records and then finding a suitable partner for each record with similar characteristics. Once a partner is found, the values are swapped for each other. In practice, data swapping is comparatively time consuming (as it has to loop through many records to find a suitable match), and it requires additional effort to perturb the data.

- *Anatomization*—Another possible sanitization approach is to separate the sensitive attributes and quasi-identifiers into two separate datasets. In this case, the original values remain the same, but the idea is to make it harder to link them together and identify an individual. Consider the medical dataset we discussed earlier in this list. As shown in figure 7.8, the original dataset can be separated into two distinct datasets: sensitive attributes (e.g., name, religion) and quasi-identifiers (e.g., gender, disease).

Name	Gender	Disease	Religion
John	Male	Viral infection	Christian
Alex	Male	TB	Christian
Kishor	Male	Cancer	Hindu
Emiley	Female	Viral infection	Christian
Ahmed	Male	Cancer	Muslim

Original dataset

Name	Religion
John	Christian
Alex	Christian
Kishor	Hindu
Emiley	Christian
Ahmed	Muslim

Sanitized dataset 1

Gender	Disease
Male	Viral infection
Male	TB
Male	Cancer
Female	Viral infection

Sanitized dataset 2

Figure 7.8 Using the anatomization approach

7.4.1 *Implementing data sanitization operations in Python*

In this section we'll implement these different data sanitization techniques in Python. For this example, we'll use a real-world dataset [2] that Barry Becker originally extracted from the 1994 US Census database. The dataset contains 15 different attributes, and we'll first look at how the dataset is arranged. Then we'll apply different sanitization operations, as depicted in figure 7.9.

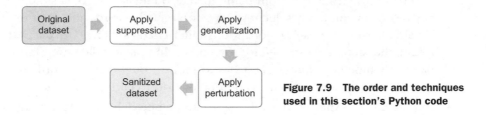

Figure 7.9   The order and techniques used in this section's Python code

First, we need to import the necessary libraries. If you are already familiar with the following packages, you probably have everything installed.

We'll install these libraries using the `pip` command:

```
pip install sklearn-pandas
```

Once everything is installed, import the following packages to the environment:

```
import pandas as pd
import numpy as np
import scipy.stats
import matplotlib.pyplot as plt
from sklearn_pandas import DataFrameMapper
from sklearn.preprocessing import LabelEncoder
```

Now let's load the dataset and see what it looks like. You can directly download the dataset from the book's code repository (http://mng.bz/eJYw).

```
df = pd.read_csv('./Data/all.data.csv')
df.shape
df.head()
```

With the `df.shape()` command, you can obtain the dimensionality (number of rows and columns) of the data frame. As you'll see, this dataset contains 48,842 records categorized in 15 different attributes. You can use the `df.head()` command to list the first five rows of the dataset, as shown in figure 7.10.

	age	workclass	fnlwgt	education	education-num	marital-status	occupation	relationship	race	sex	capital-gain	capital-loss	hours-per-week	native-country	salary
0	39	State-gov	77516	Bachelors	13	Never-married	Adm-clerical	Not-in-family	White	Male	2174	0	40	United-States	<=50k
1	50	Self-emp-not-inc	83311	Bachelors	13	Married-civ-spouse	Exec-managerial	Husband	White	Male	0	0	13	United-States	<=50k
2	38	Private	215646	HS-grad	9	Divorced	Handlers-cleaners	Not-in-family	White	Male	0	0	40	United-States	<=50k
3	53	Private	234721	11th	7	Married-civ-spouse	Handlers-cleaners	Husband	Black	Male	0	0	40	United-States	<=50k
4	28	Private	338409	Bachelors	13	Married-civ-spouse	Prof-specialty	Wife	Black	Female	0	0	40	Cuba	<=50k

Figure 7.10   First five records of the US Census dataset

You may have noticed that there are some sensitive attributes, such as relationship, race, sex, native-country, and the like, that need to be anonymized. Let's first apply *suppression* to some of the attributes so that they can be removed:

```
df.drop(columns=["fnlwgt", "relationship"], inplace=True)
```

Try `df.head()` again and see what has been changed.

WORKING WITH CATEGORICAL VALUES

If you look closely at the race column, you'll see categorical values such as White, Black, Asian-Pac-Islander, Amer-Indian-Eskimo, and so on. Thus, in terms of privacy preservation, we need to *generalize* these columns. For that, we will use `DataFrameMapper()` in `sklearn_pandas`, which allows us to transform the tuples into encoded values. In this example, we are using `LabelEncoder()`:

```
encoders = [(["sex"], LabelEncoder()), (["race"], LabelEncoder())]
mapper = DataFrameMapper(encoders, df_out=True)
new_cols = mapper.fit_transform(df.copy())
df = pd.concat([df.drop(columns=["sex", "race"]), new_cols], axis="columns")
```

Now check the results with `df.head()` again. It will list the first five rows of the dataset, as shown in figure 7.11.

	age	workclass	education	education-num	marital-status	occupation	capital-gain	capital-loss	hours-per-week	native-country	salary	sex	race
0	39	State-gov	Bachelors	13	Never-married	Adm-clerical	2174	0	40	United-States	<=50k	1	4
1	50	Self-emp-not-inc	Bachelors	13	Married-civ-spouse	Exec-managerial	0	0	13	United-States	<=50k	1	4
2	38	Private	HS-grad	9	Divorced	Handlers-cleaners	0	0	40	United-States	<=50k	1	4
3	53	Private	11th	7	Married-civ-spouse	Handlers-cleaners	0	0	40	United-States	<=50k	1	2
4	28	Private	Bachelors	13	Married-civ-spouse	Prof-specialty	0	0	40	Cuba	<=50k	0	2

Figure 7.11   Resultant dataset with encoded values

We generalized both the sex and race columns so that no one can have any idea what the gender and race of an individual are.

WORKING WITH CONTINUOUS VALUES

Continuous values such as age can still leak some information about the individuals, as we've already discussed. And even though the race is encoded (remember, race is a categorical value), someone could combine a couple of records to obtain more informed results. So let's apply the perturbation technique to anonymize age and race, as shown in the following listing.

Listing 7.1   Perturbing age and race

```
categorical = ['race']
continuous = ['age']
```

```
unchanged = []

for col in list(df):
    if (col not in categorical) and (col not in continuous):
        unchanged.append(col)

best_distributions = []
for col in continuous:
    data = df[col]
    best_dist_name, best_dist_params = best_fit_distribution(data, 500)
    best_distributions.append((best_fit_name, best_fit_params))
```

For the continuous variable age, we are using a function called `best_fit_distribution()`, which loops through a list of continuous functions to find the best fit function that has the smallest error. Once the best fit distribution is found, we can use it to approximate a new value for the age variable.

For the categorical variable race, we first determine how often a unique value appears in the distribution using `value_counts()`, and then we use `np.random.choice()` to generate a random value that has the same probability distribution.

All of this can be wrapped up in a function, as in the following listing.

Listing 7.2 **Perturbation for both numerical and categorical values**

```
def perturb_data(df, unchanged_cols, categorical_cols,
    ➥ continuous_cols, best_distributions, n, seed=0):
    np.random.seed(seed)
    data = {}

    for col in categorical_cols:
        counts = df[col].value_counts()
        data[col] = np.random.choice(list(counts.index),
            ➥ p=(counts/len(df)).values, size=n)

    for col, bd in zip(continuous_cols, best_distributions):
        dist = getattr(scipy.stats, bd[0])
        data[col] = np.round(dist.rvs(size=n, *bd[1]))


    for col in unchanged_cols:
        data[col] = df[col]

    return pd.DataFrame(data,
      columns=unchanged_cols+categorical_cols+continuous_cols)

gendf = perturb_data(df, unchanged, categorical, continuous,
➥ best_distributions, n=48842)
```

The result of using the `gendf.head()` command is shown in figure 7.12.

Look closely at the last two columns. The age and race values have been replaced with randomly generated data following the same probability distribution as in the original data. Thus, this dataset can now be treated as privacy preserved.

	workclass	education	education-num	marital-status	occupation	capital-gain	capital-loss	hours-per-week	native-country	salary	sex	race	age
0	State-gov	Bachelors	13	Never-married	Adm-clerical	2174	0	40	United-States	<=50k	1	4	65.0
1	Self-emp-not-inc	Bachelors	13	Married-civ-spouse	Exec-managerial	0	0	13	United-States	<=50k	1	4	35.0
2	Private	HS-grad	9	Divorced	Handlers-cleaners	0	0	40	United-States	<=50k	1	4	80.0
3	Private	11th	7	Married-civ-spouse	Handlers-cleaners	0	0	40	United-States	<=50k	1	4	47.0
4	Private	Bachelors	13	Married-civ-spouse	Prof-specialty	0	0	40	Cuba	<=50k	0	4	56.0

Figure 7.12 Resultant dataset after perturbing both numerical and categorical values

We have now discussed data sanitization operations that are commonly used in various privacy-preserving applications. Next, we'll look into how we can apply those operations in practice. We already covered the basics of *k*-anonymity in section 6.2.2; now, we'll extend the discussion. The next section covers the *k*-anonymity privacy model in detail, along with its code implementation in Python.

First, though, let's recap this section's sanitization operations in an exercise.

EXERCISE 1

Consider a scenario where a data mining application is linked with an organization's employee database. For brevity, we will consider the attributes in table 7.1.

Table 7.1 Employee database of an organization

Number	Name	Gender	Zip code	Salary (*k*)
1	John	Male	33617	78
2	Alex	Male	32113	90
3	Kishor	Male	33613	65
4	Emily	Female	33617	68
5	Ahmed	Male	33620	75

Now try to answer the following questions to make this dataset privacy-preserved:

- Which attributes can be sanitized using generalization operation? How?
- Which attributes can be sanitized using suppression operation? How?
- Which attributes can be sanitized using perturbation operation? How?
- Does anatomization work in this example? Why?

7.4.2 *k*-anonymity

One of the most common and widely adopted privacy models that can be used to anonymize a dataset is *k*-anonymity. Latanya Sweeney and Pierangela Samarati initially proposed it in the late 1990s in their seminal work, "Protecting privacy when disclosing information" [3]. It is a simple yet powerful tool that emphasizes that for a record in a dataset to be indistinguishable, there have to be at least k individual records sharing the same set of attributes that could be used to identify the record (quasi-identifiers) uniquely. In simple terms, a dataset is said to be k-anonymous if it has at least k similar records sharing the same sensitive attributes. We will look into this with an example to better understand how it works.

WHAT IS K AND HOW IT CAN BE APPLIED?

The value k is typically used to measure privacy, and it is harder to de-anonymize records when the value of k is higher. However, when the k value increases, the utility usually decreases, because the data becomes more generalized.

Many different algorithms have been proposed to achieve k-anonymity, but the vast majority of them apply sanitization operations such as suppression and generalization to achieve the required level of privacy. Figure 7.13 illustrates how to define sensitive and non-sensitive attributes in a dataset, which can be sanitized with k-anonymity in practice.

Sensitive attributes

Name	Zip code	Age	Gender	Disease	Religion
Alex	33620	17	Male	TB	Christian
Emily	33617	45	Female	Viral infection	Christian
Fathima	33620	28	Female	Cancer	Muslim
Jeremy	32005	29	Male	Viral infection	Christian
John	33617	24	Male	Viral infection	Christian
Kishor	33613	31	Male	Cancer	Hindu
Nataliya	32102	46	Male	TB	Christian
Ryan	32026	32	Male	Cancer	Buddhist
Samantha	33625	56	Female	Heart disease	Hindu

Original dataset

Figure 7.13 Sample dataset defining the sensitive and non-sensitive attributes

There are a couple of important and sensitive attributes and quasi-identifiers in this case. Thus, when we apply k-anonymity, it is vital to make sure that all the records are anonymized enough to make it hard for data users to de-anonymize the records.

NOTE The sensitivity of an attribute typically depends on the application's requirements. Attributes that are very sensitive in some cases might be non-sensitive in other application domains.

Let's consider the dataset shown in figure 7.14. As you can see, the name and religion attributes are sanitized with suppression, while zip code and age are generalized. If you look into that closer, you may realize that it is 2-anonymized ($k = 2$), meaning there are at least two records in each group. Let's take the first two records in the table as an example. As you can see, those records are in the same group, making the zip code, age, and gender the same for both; the only difference is the disease.

Generalized attribute

Name	Zip code	Age	Gender	Disease	Religion
*	32***	<35	Male	Viral infection	*
*	32***	<35	Male	Cancer	*
*	32***	>40	*	TB	*
*	32***	>40	*	Viral infection	*
*	336**	>30	Male	Cancer	*
*	336**	<30	Male	Viral infection	*
*	336**	<30	Male	TB	*
*	336**	<30	Female	Cancer	*
*	336**	>30	Female	Heart disease	*

Sanitized dataset

Suppressed attribute

Level of suppression and generalization has a direct effect on the accuracy of utility.

Figure 7.14 Using generalization and suppression

Now let's consider a scenario where Bob knows his friend resides in the 32314 zip code, and he is 34 years old. Just by looking at the dataset, Bob cannot distinguish whether his friend has a viral infection or cancer. That is how k-anonymity works. The original information is sanitized and hard to reproduce, but the results can still be used in data mining operations. In the previous example, $k = 2$, but when we increase the k, it's even harder to reproduce the original records.

K-ANONYMITY DOES NOT ALWAYS WORK

While k-anonymity is a powerful technique, it has some direct and indirect drawbacks. Let's try to understand these flaws to see how k-anonymity is vulnerable to different types of attacks:

- *Importance of wisely selecting sensitive attributes*—In k-anonymity, the selection of sensitive attributes has to be performed carefully. Still, those selected attributes must not reveal the information of already anonymized attributes. For example, certain diseases can be widespread in certain areas and age groups, so someone might be able to identify the disease by referring to the area or age group. To avoid such scenarios, it is essential to tune the level of suppression and generalization on those attributes of interest. For example, instead of changing the zip code to 32***, you might be able to suppress it to 3****, making the original value harder to guess.

- *Importance of having profoundly diversified data in the group*—The diversity of the data has major consequences for k-anonymity. Broadly speaking, there are two significant concerns in k-anonymity in terms of having well-represented diversified data. The first is that each represented individual has one and only one record in the group or equivalence classes. The second arises when the values of the sensitive attributes are the same for all the other k–1 records in the group or equivalence class, which could lead to identifying any individual in the group. Regardless of whether the sensitive attributes are the same, these concerns can make k-anonymity vulnerable to different types of attacks.

- *Importance of managing data at a low dimension*—When the data dimension is high, it is hard for k-anonymity to maintain the required level of privacy within practical limits. For example, stringing multiple data records together can sometimes uniquely identify an individual for data types such as location data. On the other hand, when the data records are sparsely distributed, a lot of noise must be added to group them in order to achieve k-anonymity.

Now let's look at the attacks we mentioned and how these attacks work. As shown in figure 7.15, there are a set of prerequisites for these attacks to work. For instance, for

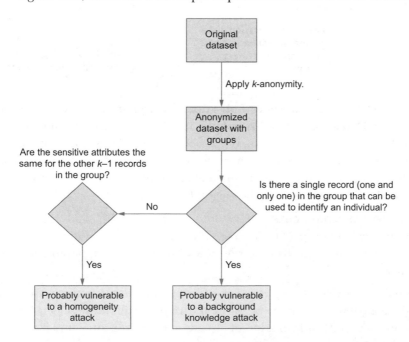

Figure 7.15   A flow diagram explaining possible flaws in k-anonymity leading to different attacks

some attacks, such as the homogeneity attack, to work, the value of the sensitive attributes has to be the same for other records within the group of a *k*-anonymized dataset. Let's look at the example depicted in figure 7.16. Suppose Alice knows her neighbor Bob has been admitted to the hospital, and they both live in the 33718 zip code. In addition, Bob is 36 years old. With that available information, Alice can infer that Bob probably has cancer. This is called a *homogeneity attack*, where the attacker uses already available information to find a group of records that an individual belongs to.

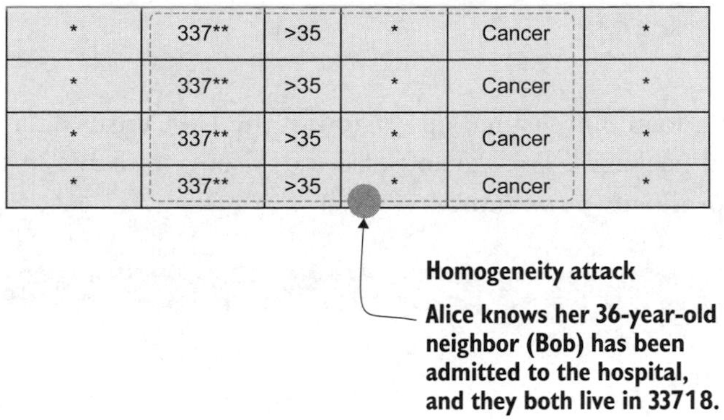

*	337**	>35	*	Cancer	*
*	337**	>35	*	Cancer	*
*	337**	>35	*	Cancer	*
*	337**	>35	*	Cancer	*

Homogeneity attack

Alice knows her 36-year-old neighbor (Bob) has been admitted to the hospital, and they both live in 33718.

Figure 7.16   Homogeneity attack

Alternatively, this could lead to a *background knowledge attack*, where an attacker uses external background information to identify an individual in a dataset (see figure 7.17). Suppose Alice has a Japanese friend, Sara, who is 26 years old and currently resides in the 33613 zip code. She also knows that Japanese people have a very low heart disease mortality rate. Given this, she could conclude that her friend is probably suffering from a viral infection.

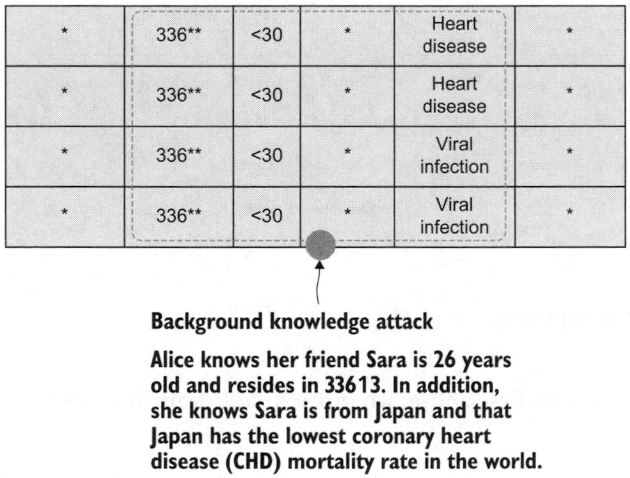

*	336**	<30	*	Heart disease	*
*	336**	<30	*	Heart disease	*
*	336**	<30	*	Viral infection	*
*	336**	<30	*	Viral infection	*

Background knowledge attack

Alice knows her friend Sara is 26 years old and resides in 33613. In addition, she knows Sara is from Japan and that Japan has the lowest coronary heart disease (CHD) mortality rate in the world.

Figure 7.17   Background knowledge attack

As you can see, we can prevent attacks resulting from attribute disclosure problems by increasing the diversity of the sensitive values within the equivalence group.

7.4.3   *Implementing k-anonymity in Python*

Now let's implement *k*-anonymity in code. For this, we'll use the `cn-protect` [4] package in Python. (At the time of publishing, the CN-Protect library has been acquired by Snowflake, and the library is no longer publicly accessible.) You can install it using the following `pip` code:

```
pip install cn-protect
```

Once it is ready, you can load our cleaned-up version of the US Census dataset along with the following listed packages. This version of the dataset is available in the code repository for you to download (http://mng.bz/eJYw).

Listing 7.3   Importing the dataset and applying *k*-anonymity

```
import pandas as pd
import matplotlib.pyplot as plt
import seaborn as sns
from cn.protect import Protect
sns.set(style="darkgrid")

df = pd.read_csv('./Data/all.data.csv')

df.shape
df.head()
```

The results will look like figure 7.18.

	age	workclass	fnlwgt	education	education-num	marital-status	occupation	relationship	race	sex	capital-gain	capital-loss	hours-per-week	native-country	salary
0	39	State-gov	77516	Bachelors	13	Never-married	Adm-clerical	Not-in-family	White	Male	2174	0	40	United-States	<=50k
1	50	Self-emp-not-inc	83311	Bachelors	13	Married-civ-spouse	Exec-managerial	Husband	White	Male	0	0	13	United-States	<=50k
2	38	Private	215646	HS-grad	9	Divorced	Handlers-cleaners	Not-in-family	White	Male	0	0	40	United-States	<=50k
3	53	Private	234721	11th	7	Married-civ-spouse	Handlers-cleaners	Husband	Black	Male	0	0	40	United-States	<=50k
4	28	Private	338409	Bachelors	13	Married-civ-spouse	Prof-specialty	Wife	Black	Female	0	0	40	Cuba	<=50k

Figure 7.18   The first few records of the imported dataset

Using the `Protect` class, we can first define what the quasi-identifiers are:

```
prot = Protect(df)
prot.itypes.age = 'quasi'
prot.itypes.sex = 'quasi'
```

You can look at the types of the attributes using the `prot` `.itypes` command, as shown in figure 7.19.

Now it's time to set the privacy parameters. In this example, we are using *k*-anonymity, so let's set the *k* value to be 5:

```
prot.privacy_model.k = 5
```

Once it is set, you can see the results by using the `prot.privacy_` `model` command. The result should be something like the following:

```
<KAnonymity: {'k': 5}>
```

You can observe the resultant dataset with the following code snippet (see figure 7.20):

```
prot_df = prot.protect()
prot_df
```

```
age             QUASI
workclass       INSENTIVE
fnlwgt          INSENTIVE
education       INSENTIVE
education-num   INSENTIVE
marital-status  INSENTIVE
occupation      INSENTIVE
relationship    INSENTIVE
race            INSENTIVE
sex             QUASI
capital-gain    INSENTIVE
capital-loss    INSENTIVE
hours-per-week  INSENTIVE
native-country  INSENTIVE
salary          INSENTIVE
dtype: object
```

Figure 7.19 Dataset attributes defining quasi-identifiers

	age	workclass	fnlwgt	education	education-num	marital-status	occupation	relationship	race	sex	capital-gain	capital-loss	hours-per-week	native-country	salary
0	*	State-gov	77516	Bachelors	13	Never-married	Adm-clerical	Not-in-family	White	Male	2174	0	40	United-States	<=50k
1	*	Self-emp-not-inc	83311	Bachelors	13	Married-civ-spouse	Exec-managerial	Husband	White	Male	0	0	13	United-States	<=50k
2	*	Private	215646	HS-grad	9	Divorced	Handlers-cleaners	Not-in-family	White	Male	0	0	40	United-States	<=50k
3	*	Private	234721	11th	7	Married-civ-spouse	Handlers-cleaners	Husband	Black	Male	0	0	40	United-States	<=50k
4	*	Private	338409	Bachelors	13	Married-civ-spouse	Prof-specialty	Wife	Black	Female	0	0	40	Cuba	<=50k
...	...	...	...	...	...	...	...	...	...	...	...	...	...	...	...
48837	*	Private	215419	Bachelors	13	Divorced	Prof-specialty	Not-in-family	White	Female	0	0	36	United-States	<=50k
48838	*	?	321403	HS-grad	9	Widowed	?	Other-relative	Black	Male	0	0	40	United-States	<=50k
48839	*	Private	374983	Bachelors	13	Married-civ-spouse	Prof-specialty	Husband	White	Male	0	0	50	United-States	<=50k
48840	*	Private	83891	Bachelors	13	Divorced	Adm-clerical	Own-child	Asian-Pac-Islander	Male	5455	0	40	United-States	<=50k
48841	*	Self-emp-inc	182148	Bachelors	13	Married-civ-spouse	Exec-managerial	Husband	White	Male	0	0	60	United-States	>50k

48842 rows × 15 columns

Figure 7.20 A 5-anonymized US Census dataset

Closely look at the resultant age and sex attributes. The dataset is now 5-anonymized. Try it yourself by changing the parameters.

EXERCISE 2

Consider a scenario where a data mining application involves the following loan information database from a mortgage company. Assume the dataset shown in table 7.2 has many attributes (including mortgage history, loan risk factors, and so on) and records, even though the table only shows a few of them. In addition, the dataset is already 2-anonymized ($k = 2$).

Table 7.2　Simplified employee database

Number	Name	Age	Zip code	Borrower race	Borrower income
1	*	21-40	336**	Black or African American	65k
2	*	31-40	34***	Asian	80k
3	*	31-40	34***	White	85k
4	*	21-40	336**	Black or African American	130k

Now try to answer the following questions to see whether this anonymized dataset still leaks some important information:

- Suppose John knows his neighbor Alice applied for a mortgage and they both live in the 33617 zip code? What information can John deduce?
- If Alice is an African American woman, what additional information can John learn?
- How can you protect this dataset such that John cannot learn anything beyond Alice's zip code and race?

Summary

- Adopting privacy preservation techniques in data mining and management operations is not a choice. More than ever, it's a necessity for today's data-driven applications.
- Privacy preservation in data mining can be achieved by modifying the input data with different noise addition techniques.
- Different data sanitization operations (generalization, suppression, perturbation, anatomization) can be used when publishing data to protect privacy in data mining applications.
- Data sanitization operations can be implemented in different ways depending on the application's requirements.
- *K*-anonymity is a widely used privacy model that can be implemented in data mining operations. It allows us to apply various sanitization operations while providing flexibility.
- Although *k*-anonymity is a powerful technique, it has some direct and indirect drawbacks.

- In a homogeneity attack, the attacker uses already available information to find a group of records that an individual belongs to.
- In a background knowledge attack, the attacker uses external background information to identify an individual in a dataset.

Privacy-preserving data management and operations

In the previous chapter we discussed different privacy-enhancing techniques that can be utilized in data mining operations and how to implement the k-anonymity privacy model. In this chapter we'll explore another set of privacy models that the research community has proposed to mitigate the flaws in the k-anonymity model. Toward the end of this chapter, we'll discuss the recent evolution of data management techniques, how these privacy mechanisms can be instrumented in database systems, and what to consider when designing a privacy-enriched database management system.

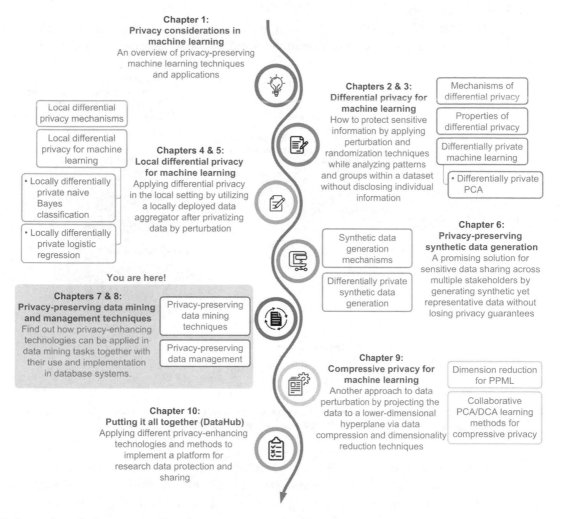

8.1   A quick recap of privacy protection in data processing and mining

You've seen that data analysis and mining tools are intended to extract meaningful features and patterns from collected datasets, and that direct use of original data in data mining may result in unwanted data privacy violations. Hence, we use different data sanitization operations to minimize private information disclosure. To that end, our discussion in chapter 7 and this chapter covers two particular aspects, which are summarized in figure 8.1:

- *Data processing and mining*—Tools and techniques that can be utilized whenever the collected information is processed and analyzed by data mining and analytical tools.
- *Data management*—Methods and technologies that can be utilized to hold, store, and serve collected information for different data processing applications.

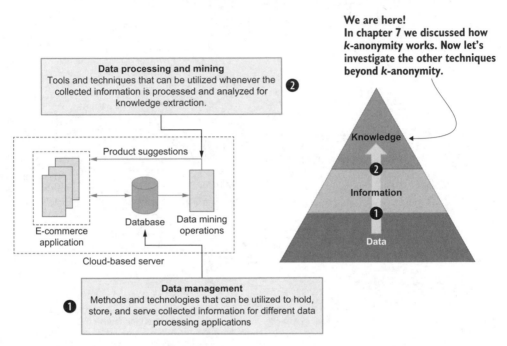

Figure 8.1   There are two main aspects of privacy preservation when it comes to data mining and management. In this chapter, we'll elaborate on these two different aspects.

So far we have discussed different sanitization operations, their implementation in Python, and their use in the *k*-anonymity privacy model. In the next section we will move on to discuss other popular privacy models that go beyond *k*-anonymity.

8.2   *Privacy protection beyond k-anonymity*

K-anonymity is a very powerful yet simple technique that can be utilized in many different scenarios to protect privacy in data mining operations. However, as we discussed in the previous chapter, *k*-anonymity does not work in all situations, as illustrated in the flow diagram in figure 8.2. It is susceptible to different attacks, such as homogeneity and background knowledge attacks (refer to section 7.4.2 for the details). Let's extend our discussion of privacy protection to see how we can mitigate these flaws.

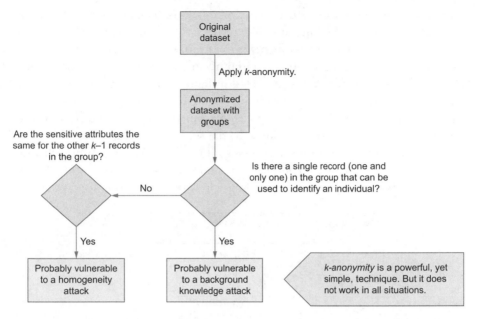

Figure 8.2 A flow diagram explaining possible flaws in k-anonymity leading to different attacks. As you can see, even after anonymization, if a single record can be used to identify an individual, it may lead to a background knowledge attack or a homogeneity attack.

8.2.1 *l-diversity*

Due to the limitations of *k*-anonymity, Machanavajjhala et al., in 2007, introduced a new technique called *l*-diversity [1] (with an "*l*" as in *l*ight). It is an extension of *k*-anonymity, where *l*-diversity states that each group must have at least *l* distinct sensitive records. Similar to the *k*-anonymity model, increasing the *l* value increases the variability of sensitive values in the same group, making it more robust against possible privacy leakages.

Let's consider the same hospital dataset scenario we discussed in the last chapter and take a *k*-anonymized example, as shown in figure 8.3.

Name	Zip code	Age	Gender	Disease	Religion
*	336**	31-40	*	Seasonal flu	*
*	336**	31-40	*	Cancer	*
*	34***	21-40	*	Viral infection	*
*	34***	21-40	*	Viral infection	*

Figure 8.3 An example of k-anonymity (k=2)

These data records are already 2-anonymous (*k* = 2). However, if an attacker knows that Alice lives in zip code 34317, they can easily reduce the search space to the last two rows. In addition, even though the attacker cannot distinguish which record belongs to Alice, they can easily deduce that Alice has a viral infection. The problem is that all the patients in that group share the same quasi-identifiers; thus, it leaks private information.

The basic approach of *l*-diversity is to ensure that each group has at least *l* distinct sensitive values so that it is hard to identify any individual. Let's make the dataset in figure 8.3 2-diverse ($l = 2$). As depicted in figure 8.4, each group now has at least two distinct sensitive values. For example, the first and fourth records are in the same group with zip code 3**** and age 21–40, but they have two different diseases (seasonal flu and viral infection). Similarly, the second and third records are in the same group, but with two different diseases, so it is impossible to distinguish which record belongs to which patient. Therefore, it is hard for an attacker to know which record corresponds to Alice and what the disease is, with the information available.

*	3****	21-40	*	Seasonal flu	*
*	3****	36	*	Cancer	*
*	3****	36	*	Viral infection	*
*	3****	21-40	*	Viral infection	*

Now the dataset is 2-diverse. Not only is the attacker unable to know which record belongs to Alice, they also cannot know which disease it is.

Figure 8.4   A 2-diverse (*l*=2) version of the example in figure 8.3

DOES IT LEAK ANY SORT OF INFORMATION?

Besides the privacy guarantees beyond *k*-anonymity, *l*-diversity also suffers from a couple of limitations:

- *Diversified data can still leak some sensitive information*—Even with the *l*-diversified data, sensitive information might still be leaked in some situations. Let's consider the same hospital dataset scenario with the example in figure 8.5, which serves 2-diversity.

*	33***	21-30	*	Seasonal flu	*
*	33***	21-30	*	Viral infection	*
*	32***	31-40	*	Melanoma	*
*	32***	31-40	*	Basal cell carcinoma	*

Figure 8.5   How *l*-diversity can leak sensitive information

Let's assume that the attacker knows that Bob lives in the 32317 zip code and is 35 years old. The attacker can reduce the search space such that Bob has either melanoma or basal cell carcinoma. Given this information, the attacker can infer that Bob has a skin disease that could be cancerous. Thus, it is still leaking some private information.

- *Probability distribution may also leak some information*—In some situations, even with *l*-diversified datasets, the probability distribution may leak some information, making datasets vulnerable to attackers. This privacy breach is called a *skewness attack.*

Consider the set of data depicted in figure 8.6. As you can see, it is already a 2-diverse dataset, but let's consider an attacker who knows that Bob lives in the 33617 zip code and is 27 years old. At this point, the attacker doesn't know whether Bob has a viral infection or heart disease, but based on the data distribution, the attacker knows that there is a higher chance of Bob having heart disease.

*	345**	21-30	*	Heart disease	*
*	345**	21-30	*	Viral infection	*
*	33***	21-30	*	Heart disease	*
*	33***	21-30	*	Viral infection	*
*	33***	21-30	*	Heart disease	*
*	33***	21-30	*	Heart disease	*
*	33***	21-30	*	Heart disease	*
*	33***	21-30	*	Heart disease	*
*	33***	21-30	*	Heart disease	*
*	33***	21-30	*	Heart disease	*
*	33***	21-30	*	Heart disease	*

Group one

Group two

Skewness attack

Attacker knows his friend Bob lives in 33617 and is 27 years old. There is a high possibility that Bob is suffering from heart disease.

Figure 8.6 Probability distribution may also leak some information.

You can see that having a diverse set of attributes in a dataset is not enough. We also need to balance the data distribution within the class.

> ## What does "within-class" mean?
> An equivalence class is a set of records belonging to the same group. For example, all nine records in group two in figure 8.6 belong to the same zip code and age category. Similarly, the records in group one also carry similar properties. These different groups can be called *classes*, and we use the within-class data distribution to find out their statistical properties.

8.2.2   t-closeness

Having learned from the flaws in the *l*-diversity approach, Li et al. presented another privacy model called *t*-closeness [2] to prevent attribute disclosure from distribution skewness. The idea behind *t*-closeness is to keep the distribution of sensitive records in each group (equivalence class) close enough to the corresponding distribution in the original dataset. In other words, the distance between the distribution of an attribute in the original dataset and the distribution of the same attribute within a group should be less than or equal to *t*, according to the *t*-closeness principle.

We can let $X = (x_1, x_2, …, x_n)$ be the distribution of values for the sensitive attributes in the original dataset and $Y = (y_1, y_2, …, y_n)$ be the values of the same attribute in the selected group. In order for these two distributions to satisfy *t*-closeness, the following equation has to be true:

$$Dist(X, Y) \leq t$$

Let's consider our previous hospital data mining scenario with another example of a 3-diverse dataset, shown in figure 8.7.

No	Name	Zip code	Age	Gender	Disease	Religion	
1	*	336**	2*	*	Gastric ulcer	*	
2	*	336**	2*	*	Gastritis	*	**Group one**
3	*	336**	2*	*	Stomach cancer	*	
4	*	3390*	>40	*	Gastritis	*	
5	*	3390*	>40	*	Viral flu	*	**Group two**
6	*	3390*	>40	*	Bronchitis	*	
7	*	336**	3*	*	Bronchitis	*	
8	*	336**	3*	*	Pneumonia	*	**Group three**
9	*	336**	3*	*	Stomach cancer	*	

Figure 8.7   An example of a 3-diverse dataset vulnerable to a skewness attack

As you can see, the dataset has three different groups having three distinct records in each. However, it is still vulnerable to the skewness attack that we discussed in the previous section. Suppose an attacker already knows that his friend Bob's record belongs to group one. The attacker can infer that Bob has some stomach-related disease, as all the diseases in group one are stomach-related. Therefore, a particular level of diversity may provide different levels of privacy—we need to consider the overall distribution of the data.

Let's try to convert this dataset to a *t*-closeness version. As we mentioned at the beginning of this section, *t*-closeness relies on the distance between the probability distributions. There are different ways of measuring the distance between two probability distributions, but, in practice, *t*-closeness uses distance metrics such as earth mover distance (also known as the Wasserstein metric), Kullback Leibler distance, or variational distance.

What is the earth mover distance?

The earth mover distance (EMD) is a technique for evaluating the similarity between two mathematical distributions. Suppose you have a distribution called "holes" and another distribution called "earth elements." The idea of EMD is to fill the holes with earth elements by moving earth elements toward the holes. EMD measures the least amount of work required to fill the holes by transporting a unit of earth by a unit of ground distance.

Let's say $P = (p_1, p_2, ..., p_m)$ is the weight of earth elements, and $Q = (q_1, q_2, ..., q_m)$ represents the holes. The ground distance between element i of P and element j of Q can be represented as d_{ij}.

The flow $F = [f_{ij}]$ (where f_{ij} is the flow of weight between p_i and q_j) that minimizes the overall cost can be defined as [2]

$$WORK(P, Q, F) = \sum_{i=1}^{m} \sum_{j=1}^{m} f_{ij} d_{ij}$$

subject to the following constraints:

$$f_{ij} \geq 0 \quad 1 \leq i \leq m, 1 \leq j \leq m$$

$$p_i - \sum_{j=1}^{m} f_{ij} + \sum_{j=1}^{m} f_{ji} = q_i \quad 1 \leq i \leq m$$

$$\sum_{i=1}^{m} \sum_{j=1}^{m} f_{ij} = \sum_{i=1}^{m} p_i = \sum_{j=1}^{m} q_i = 1$$

Once the transportation problem is solved and the optimal flow F is found, the EMD is defined as the work normalized by the total flow as follows:

$$EMD(P, Q) = \frac{\sum_{i=1}^{m} \sum_{j=1}^{m} f_{ij} d_{ij}}{\sum_{i=1}^{m} \sum_{j=1}^{m} f_{ij}}$$

(continued)
Let's consider an example to see how EMD works.

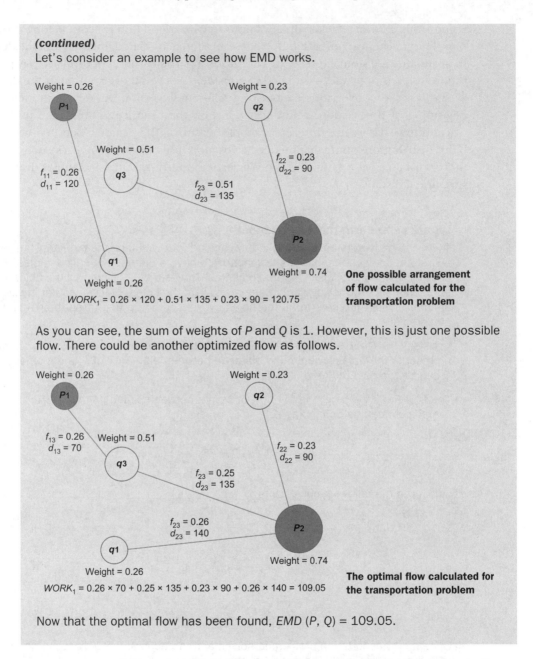

WORK$_1$ = 0.26 × 120 + 0.51 × 135 + 0.23 × 90 = 120.75

One possible arrangement of flow calculated for the transportation problem

As you can see, the sum of weights of *P* and *Q* is 1. However, this is just one possible flow. There could be another optimized flow as follows.

WORK$_1$ = 0.26 × 70 + 0.25 × 135 + 0.23 × 90 + 0.26 × 140 = 109.05

The optimal flow calculated for the transportation problem

Now that the optimal flow has been found, *EMD* (*P*, *Q*) = 109.05.

Consider the anonymized *t*-closeness version of the same dataset, as shown in figure 8.8. The skewness attack has been prevented because the attacker cannot clearly distinguish whether Bob has a stomach-related disease or not.

**To make records within a group dissimilar,
some attributes are rearranged and anonymized.**

1	*	3361*	<40	*	Gastric ulcer	*
8	*	3361*	<40	*	Pneumonia	*
3	*	3361*	<40	*	Stomach cancer	*
4	*	3390*	>40	*	Gastritis	*
5	*	3390*	>40	*	Viral flu	*
6	*	3390*	>40	*	Bronchitis	*
7	*	3363*	<40	*	Bronchitis	*
2	*	3363*	<40	*	Gastritis	*
9	*	3363*	<40	*	Stomach cancer	*

Group one (rows 1, 8, 3); Group two (rows 4, 5, 6); Group three (rows 7, 2, 9)

**Records 2 and 8 have been swapped
to prevent skewness attacks.**

Figure 8.8 How to prevent a skewness attack using *t*-closeness

The most important point here is that we have changed (generalized and suppressed) the zip code and age attributes, allowing us to switch records 2 and 8, making it hard to identify the disease in each group.

8.2.3 Implementing privacy models with Python

Now let's try out these privacy models in Python. For this example, we'll use the adult dataset that Barry Becker originally extracted from the 1994 US Census database [3]. The dataset contains 15 different attributes, and we'll look at how it can be privatized using *k*-anonymity, *l*-diversity, and *t*-closeness. (This example code is inspired by N. Prabhu's implementation on GitHub [4]).

First, we need to import the necessary libraries. If you are already familiar with the following packages, you probably have everything installed. If not, start installing them using the `pip` command.

Listing 8.1 Preparing the dataset

```
pip install sklearn-pandas          Once everything is installed,
                                     import the following packages
import pandas as pd          ◁───┘  to the environment.
import matplotlib.pylab as pl
import matplotlib.patches as patches
                                                        Enable the shell to
                                                        show all outputs.
from IPython.core.interactiveshell import InteractiveShell  ◁───┘
InteractiveShell.ast_node_interactivity = "all"
```

```
names = ('age', 'workclass', 'fnlwgt', 'education', 'education-num',  ◁────────┐
         'marital-status', 'occupation', 'relationship',
         'race', 'sex', 'capital-gain', 'capital-loss',
         'hours-per-week', 'native-country', 'income',)

categorical = set(('workclass', 'education', 'marital-status',
                   'occupation', 'relationship', 'sex',
                   'native-country', 'race', 'income',))

df = pd.read_csv("./Data/adult.all.txt",
                 sep=", ", header=None, names=names,
                 index_col=False, engine='python')

df.head()    ◁──── Print the header.
df.nunique()
```

Define the header names and categorical attributes.

The dataset contains 48,842 records categorized with 15 different attributes, as shown in figure 8.9.

	age	workclass	fnlwgt	education	education-num	marital-status	occupation	relationship	race	sex	capital-gain	capital-loss	hours-per-week	native-country	income
0	39	State-gov	77516	Bachelors	13	Never-married	Adm-clerical	Not-in-family	White	Male	2174	0	40	United-States	<=50k
1	50	Self-emp-not-inc	83311	Bachelors	13	Married-civ-spouse	Exec-managerial	Husband	White	Male	0	0	13	United-States	<=50k
2	38	Private	215646	HS-grad	9	Divorced	Handlers-cleaners	Not-in-family	White	Male	0	0	40	United-States	<=50k
3	53	Private	234721	11th	7	Married-civ-spouse	Handlers-cleaners	Husband	Black	Male	0	0	40	United-States	<=50k
4	28	Private	338409	Bachelors	13	Married-civ-spouse	Prof-specialty	Wife	Black	Female	0	0	40	Cuba	<=50k

Figure 8.9   The first few records of the US Census dataset

Let's find the value span by looking at each column, as shown in the following listing.

Listing 8.2   Finding the value span

```
for name in categorical:                    ◁──── Make these categorical.
    df[name] = df[name].astype('category')

def get_spans(df, partition, scale=None):   ◁──── Get the value span.

    spans = {}
    for column in df.columns:
        if column in categorical:
            span = len(df[column][partition].unique())
        else:
            span = df[column][partition].max()-df[column][partition].min()
        if scale is not None:
            span = span/scale[column]
        spans[column] = span
        print("Column:", column, "Span:", span)
    return spans

full_spans = get_spans(df, df.index)
```

Now let's partition the dataset. Our example is k-anonymized with $k = 3$, and we are using the age and education-num attributes as the quasi-identifiers.

Listing 8.3   Partitioning the dataset

```
def split(df, partition, column):           Split the data frame based
    dfp = df[column][partition]              on categorical or not.
    if column in categorical:
        values = dfp.unique()
        lv = set(values[:len(values)//2])
        rv = set(values[len(values)//2:])
        return dfp.index[dfp.isin(lv)], dfp.index[dfp.isin(rv)]
    else:
        median = dfp.median()
        dfl = dfp.index[dfp < median]
        dfr = dfp.index[dfp >= median]
        return (dfl, dfr)

def is_k_anonymous(df, partition, sensitive_column, k=3):     Check whether it's
    if len(partition) < k:                                    k-anonymous (k=3).
        return False
    return True

def partition_dataset(df, feature_columns, sensitive_column,
    ➥ scale, is_valid):
    finished_partitions = []          Partition the dataset.
    partitions = [df.index]
    while partitions:
        partition = partitions.pop(0)
        spans = get_spans(df[feature_columns], partition, scale)
        for column, span in sorted(spans.items(), key=lambda x:-x[1]):
            lp, rp = split(df, partition, column)
            if not is_valid(df, lp, sensitive_column) or
            ➥ not is_valid(df, rp, sensitive_column):
                continue
            partitions.extend((lp, rp))
            break
        else:
            finished_partitions.append(partition)
    return finished_partitions

feature_columns = ['age', 'education-num']
sensitive_column = 'income'
finished_partitions = partition_dataset(df,
➥ feature_columns, sensitive_column, full_spans,
➥ is_k_anonymous)
```

Now that the dataset is partitioned, let's build the anonymized dataset based on the partitions, as shown in the following listing.

Listing 8.4   Building the anonymized dataset

```
def agg_categorical_column(series):
    return [','.join(set(series))]

def agg_numerical_column(series):
    return [series.mean()]

def build_anonymized_dataset(df, partitions,
    ➥ feature_columns, sensitive_column, max_partitions=None):    ⊲──┐ Build
    aggregations = {}                                                    anonymized
    for column in feature_columns:                                       dataset.
        if column in categorical:
            aggregations[column] = agg_categorical_column
        else:
            aggregations[column] = agg_numerical_column
    rows = []
    for i, partition in enumerate(partitions):
        if i % 100 == 1:
            print("Finished {} partitions...".format(i))
        if max_partitions is not None and i > max_partitions:
            break
        grouped_columns = df.loc[partition].agg(aggregations,
        ➥ squeeze=False)

        sensitive_counts = df.loc[partition].groupby(
        ➥ sensitive_column).agg({
        ➥ sensitive_column : 'count'})
        values = grouped_columns.iloc[0].to_dict()
        for sensitive_value, count in
        ➥ sensitive_counts[sensitive_column].items():
            if count == 0:
                continue
            values.update({
                sensitive_column : sensitive_value,
                'count' : count,
            })
            rows.append(values.copy())
    return pd.DataFrame(rows)

dfn = build_anonymized_dataset(df, finished_partitions,
➥ feature_columns, sensitive_column)

dfn.head()    ⊲────  Print the header.
```

The resultant dataset will look like figure 8.10.

We've anonymized the dataset with *k*-anonymity. Now let's anonymize it with *l*-diversity. In the following listing, we'll use a value of $l = 2$.

	age	education-num	income	count
0	17.000000	7.200599	<=50k	334
1	18.227876	7.283186	<=50k	451
2	18.227876	7.283186	>50k	1
3	21.000000	10.000000	<=50k	568
4	21.000000	10.000000	>50k	2

Figure 8.10   An anonymized dataset with *k*-anonymity

Listing 8.5 Anonymizing the dataset with *l*-diversity

```
def diversity(df, partition, column):
    return len(df[column][partition].unique())

def is_l_diverse(df, partition, sensitive_column, l=2):
    return diversity(df, partition, sensitive_column) >= l

finished_l_diverse_partitions = partition_dataset(df,
➥ feature_columns, sensitive_column, full_spans,
➥ lambda *args: is_k_anonymous(*args) and is_l_diverse('args))

column_x, column_y = feature_columns[:2]
dfl = build_anonymized_dataset(df, finished_l_diverse_partitions,
➥    feature_columns, sensitive_column)

print(dfl.sort_values([column_x, column_y, sensitive_column]))
dfl.head()
```

Check whether it's
l-diverse (*l*=2).

Print the
l-diversified
output.

The resultant dataset is shown in figure 8.11.

	age	education-num	income	count
0	17.706107	7.248092	<=50k	785
1	17.706107	7.248092	>50k	1
2	20.080607	9.000000	<=50k	1707
3	20.080607	9.000000	>50k	5
4	19.320276	10.000000	<=50k	1301

Figure 8.11 An anonymized dataset with *l*-diversity

Now let's anonymize the same dataset with *t*-closeness. First, though, let's check the frequencies.

Listing 8.6 Checking the frequencies

```
global_freqs = {}
total_count = float(len(df))
group_counts = df.groupby(sensitive_column)[sensitive_column].agg('count')
for value, count in group_counts.to_dict().items():
    p = count/total_count
    global_freqs[value] = p

print(global_freqs)    ◁——— Print the frequencies.
```

You may notice that the overall probability of income <=50k is 0.76, whereas the probability of income >50k is 0.24. Now let's anonymize this dataset with *t*-closeness based on that probability.

Listing 8.7 Anonymizing the dataset with *t*-closeness

```
def t_closeness(df, partition, column, global_freqs):    ◁——— Calculate t-closeness.
    total_count = float(len(partition))
```

```
        d_max = None
        group_counts = df.loc[partition].groupby(column)[column].agg('count')
        for value, count in group_counts.to_dict().items():
            p = count/total_count
            d = abs(p-global_freqs[value])
            if d_max is None or d > d_max:
                d_max = d
        return d_max

def is_t_close(df, partition, sensitive_column, global_freqs, p=0.2):
        if not sensitive_column in categorical:
            raise ValueError("this method only works for categorical values")
        return t_closeness(df, partition, sensitive_column, global_freqs) <= p

finished_t_close_partitions = partition_dataset(df,
➥ feature_columns, sensitive_column, full_spans,
➥ lambda *args: is_k_anonymous(*args)
➥ and is_t_close(*args, global_freqs))

dft = build_anonymized_dataset(df, finished_t_close_partitions,
➥ feature_columns, sensitive_column)

#print the header
print(dft.sort_values([column_x, column_y, sensitive_column]))
dft.head()
```

**Check whether the
sensitive column is
categorical.**

Build the anonymized dataset.

The resultant dataset will look like figure 8.12.

	age	education-num	income	count
0	26.697666	8.124394	<=50k	10248
1	26.697666	8.124394	>50k	677
2	25.747108	10.000000	<=50k	5617
3	25.747108	10.000000	>50k	520
4	29.434809	13.299485	<=50k	3385

Figure 8.12   An anonymized
dataset with *t*-closeness

8.3   *Protecting privacy by modifying the data mining output*

So far we've discussed two main privacy-preserving data mining techniques: the first when we are collecting the information and the second when we are publishing the data (see figure 8.13). In this section now we are looking at the other important class of PPDM, which is associated with the techniques on how data mining output can be regulated to preserve data privacy.

The general idea is to ensure that no sensitive information is revealed by the results (the output values) of the mining process. The problem is that sometimes the output of a data mining algorithm can reveal sensitive information when a query is submitted repeatedly, even without direct access to the original dataset.

Let's consider a scenario where an organization's employee database is already anonymized (using techniques such as *k*-anonymity). Different applications use that dataset for data mining operations to make predictive decisions.

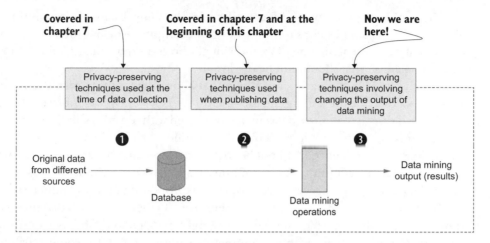

Figure 8.13 A high-level overview of different PPDM techniques

Suppose a data mining algorithm for a given query returns all the records corresponding to employees whose income is greater than $100,000 and whose age group is 25–35. Since the dataset is already anonymized, we don't know the names of those employees, but based on the data mining output, someone could deduce that these employees probably have their own cars, considering their age and wage. This is a simple example, but it can emphasize the importance of protecting data mining output to ensure individuals' privacy.

Now we'll investigate the different privacy techniques that have been developed to protect such leakages from the output of data mining algorithms.

8.3.1 Association rule hiding

Association rule data mining is a popular data mining approach for finding patterns and correlations of data. Generally, association rule mining can be used to explore the data's features (dimensions of the attributes), such as which features are correlated to each other and which features occur together.

For example, consider a scenario where we are data mining a patient record database. This dataset can be mined to find out whether patients who already have disease A are also likely to have disease B. This is called an association rule; if disease A occurs, the patients might also have disease B. Another classic example in a different context is whether people who have income greater than $100,000 and are aged 25–35 are likely to own a house. This is how association rule data mining works. We match the association between two or more attributes to find new discoveries.

Once the association rule is established, the rule's effectiveness can be evaluated using two important parameters called *support* and *confidence*. Support refers to how much historical data supports the mining rule, while confidence refers to how confident you are about the established rule.

The problem is that some of these rules may explicitly disclose private information about individuals. Let's consider the previous example involving income and age. It can reveal the annual income of an individual who owns a house, which might be private information that should not be disclosed.

Association rule hiding is a technique that allows data mining operations on non-sensitive rules while preventing the use of sensitive rules. A typical approach for association rule hiding is to remove data entries associated with sensitive rules by utilizing data suppression operations. For example, the income attribute in the aforementioned example would be sanitized and not be included in the data mining output. However, this could hide a significant number of nonsensitive rules as well, degrading the utility of the data mining operation. Thus, people have proposed different optimal solutions.

Instead of completely suppressing sensitive attributes, those attributes can be replaced with other (noisy) values to reduce the support and confidence of the association rule. For example, without completely suppressing the income attribute, we could add some noise to it when producing the results so that the original value is never exposed. As we discussed in chapters 2 and 3 of this book, differential privacy is a popular approach to producing noisy results.

8.3.2 *Reducing the accuracy of data mining operations*

There can be situations where adversaries can mislead data mining operations to reveal sensitive information about other individuals. Typically, these adversary users try to fool or mislead a system with malicious input. For instance, consider a scenario where an adversary provides someone else's medical to a disease-diagnosis machine learning service to examine whether that person has cancer or not. This is called a *membership inference attack*, and it is a threatening situation in data mining operations.

In membership inference attacks, the adversary seeks to infer the original record of an individual used in the training process of an ML model to which the adversary has black-box access. For instance, suppose the attacker uses Alice's personal information to determine whether the record is in the original dataset (the training set) or not. To achieve this, the attacker will typically use a secondary ML model built using the prediction results of the primary model.

As shown in figure 8.14, given an ML model, an input sample, and the adversary's domain knowledge, a membership inference attack tries to determine whether the sample was a member of the original training dataset used to build the ML model. This attack utilizes the dissimilarities of the output data produced by model predictions during the training phase and the data not included in the training set. Typically these attack models are trained using shadow (attack) models generated from either noisy versions of real data or data extracted from other approaches such as model inversion attacks (which we discussed in section 1.3).

To prevent such attacks while still supporting data mining operations, accuracy reduction approaches (downgrading the accuracy to some level) are often used. However, whenever the accuracy is downgraded, the results of the data mining operations

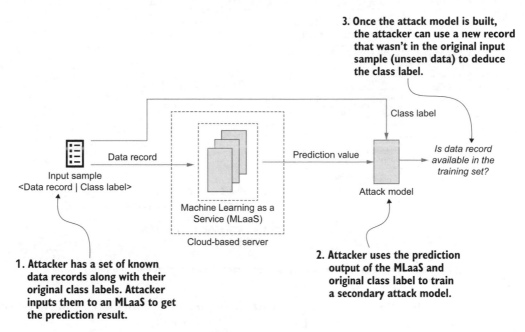

3. Once the attack model is built, the attacker can use a new record that wasn't in the original input sample (unseen data) to deduce the class label.

Class label

Data record

Input sample
<Data record | Class label>

Prediction value

Is data record available in the training set?

Attack model

Machine Learning as a Service (MLaaS)

Cloud-based server

1. Attacker has a set of known data records along with their original class labels. Attacker inputs them to an MLaaS to get the prediction result.

2. Attacker uses the prediction output of the MLaaS and original class label to train a secondary attack model.

Figure 8.14   How a membership inference attack works

become less accurate. Hence, the idea is to ensure that although the attacker can infer additional information, the attacker cannot deduce precise conclusions.

8.3.3   Inference control in statistical databases

The other important aspect of regulating data mining output to preserve privacy is employing inference control mechanisms. When data records in a database are updated frequently, it is challenging to generate a separate sanitized dataset for each data mining operation. Hence, organizations sometimes provide access to the original dataset with restricted controls, allowing statistical queries such as aggregations.

Let's go back to the e-commerce example we discussed in chapter 7. Typically, back-end databases for such applications are updated very frequently. This makes it challenging to maintain a sanitized current version of the dataset. In practice, we usually allow data mining operations to execute a limited set of statistical queries (such as COUNT, MAX, SUM, etc.) on original unsanitized data. However, some queries may still leak sensitive information, so different inference control mechanisms are typically implemented.

As you can see in figure 8.15, a query in the employee details database such as "What is Alex's age?" is not allowed, but a query like "What is the highest salary?" can be answered. The concern here is that someone could assume that the CEO is the highest-paid employee in the company, so their salary is $85,000. How can we mitigate this concern? The most straightforward answer is that we don't have to return the exact values; instead, we could return a range as the answer. For example, we could return $50,000–100,000 instead of $85,000 as the answer. There are also a few other approaches. We'll

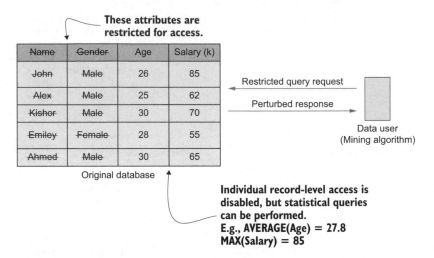

Figure 8.15   An example of how inference control works for aggregate queries

discuss the most common approaches to implementing inference control on statistical databases in section 8.4.4.

8.4   *Privacy protection in data management systems*

Thus far, we have discussed different approaches to enhance privacy, particularly in data mining operations. But what if data is leaking at the source? Let's look at how privacy can be handled at the database level.

Let's go back to our e-commerce application example. Typically, a database attached to an e-commerce application (such as Amazon) can have thousands of transactions or records within a couple of minutes. A database is obviously required to manage this information. In addition to managing the high volume of transactions, the application also needs to provide additional features, such as product suggestions, that involve data mining. Hence, beyond the simple storage functions, modern database systems need to facilitate powerful data mining capabilities.

As organizations have increased their use of database systems, especially for big data, the security of the information managed by these systems has become more vital. Confidentiality, integrity, and availability are considered the foundation of data security and privacy, but achieving these properties in modern database systems is still a significant concern. The movement of database infrastructure from on-premises to distributed cloud-based architectures has also increased the risk of security and privacy breaches, and most organizations do not store mission-critical data in the cloud, as there is higher confidence in security when the data is stored on-site. Thus, the new challenge for database systems is utilizing the state-of-the-art performance benefits they provide for big data applications without compromising security. This section will discuss what you'll need to consider when designing a database management system that can be tailored to meet modern-day data privacy requirements.

8.4.1 Database security and privacy: Threats and vulnerabilities

Before we look at how we can integrate privacy-enhancing technologies in database systems, let's quickly go through some general techniques for protecting data.

DATA PROTECTION SCHEMES CURRENTLY EMPLOYED BY THE INDUSTRY

Let's look at the existing solutions for providing security in database systems. Most relational database systems available today are equipped with encryption mechanisms to protect data both at rest and in transit. Some of these encryption technologies are specific to a given database system, and some are applied by many vendors.

Transparent Data Encryption (TDE) is a technology employed by many vendors to protect data at rest. Oracle Database and Microsoft SQL Server are two popular relational database systems that use TDE as their primary data encryption mechanism. They implement protection at the file level by encrypting the database on both the hard drive and backup media. However, many NoSQL solutions, such as Riak, Redis, Memcached, and CouchDB, are designed to work in secure and trusted environments, so they do not provide encryption mechanisms. Nevertheless, NoSQL datastores such as Cassandra and HBase now include TDE with their enterprise versions to provide encryption for data at rest.

While the protection for data at rest is implemented in the database engine, it is equally important to ensure data is protected when it is being exchanged, or during communication between the database server and client applications or other nodes within the same cluster. Traditionally, most database systems have employed firewall policies, operating system configuration, or organization-level virtual private networks (VPNs) to ensure the security of inter-node communications because they have usually been deployed in on-premises trusted environments. However, datastores are now more and more distributed, and their deployment architecture has changed from on-premises to cloud infrastructure, so special mechanisms are required to ensure protection for data in transit. Most database systems, including NoSQL and NewSQL, now support encryption for data in transit by using Transport Layer Security (TLS).

What is TLS?

Transport Layer Security (TLS) is a widely adopted cryptographic security protocol that facilitates privacy and data security between two or more communicating computer applications. In today's world, a primary use case for TLS is encrypting communications between web applications and servers, such as web browsers loading a website. Apart from that, TLS is used in many other applications to encrypt communications such as email, messaging, and voice over IP (VoIP).

PRIVACY ASSURANCE IS VERY CHALLENGING!

Even with all these security mechanisms, ensuring data privacy in practical deployments is challenging. You may have already noticed that most recent database engines do not provide any sort of integrated mechanisms to protect data against security or privacy attacks [5]. Large-scale compromises in database systems that manage sensitive information have influenced active research into the design of new technologies for securing information beyond the typical security and privacy mechanisms now available in database systems.

As a result of the requirements of modern big data applications, various protocols have also been proposed for securely outsourcing data to third-party database servers, using strong cryptographic primitives such as fully homomorphic encryption, oblivious RAM, order-preserving encryption, and so on [6]. However, some recent studies have demonstrated successful attacks, especially on encrypted databases, and found that these systems are still vulnerable [7], [8], [9]. Hence, if you plan to deploy a new data-driven application, it is essential to formally understand the performance and privacy tradeoffs in database systems, including the different attack strategies.

8.4.2   *How likely is a modern database system to leak private information?*

Now that you have some background on existing security mechanisms, let's look in detail at how database systems leak private information.

The most severe threat in database systems is usually the active attacker who fully compromises the database server and performs arbitrary malicious database operations. For example, database and system administrators or cloud service providers usually have unrestricted access to production databases. They can perform malicious operations and infer sensitive information from databases. Such attacks are pretty difficult to defend against.

Besides those active attackers, there can be passive attackers who do not interfere with the functionality of the database but instead passively observe all its operations. We can generally categorize them as honest but curious. They usually observe and analyze queries issued by data users and see how the queries access the data.

Most of these threat models are theoretical abstractions. However, there are many other types of data breaches, such as compromises through database log files, virtual machine (VM) snapshot leaks, application core dumps, etc. The following section discusses various possible attacks targeting database systems [5].

8.4.3   *Attacks on database systems*

We can categorize attacks on database systems into two main classes:

- *Attacks on the confidentiality of data*—For most attacks that violate the confidentiality of data, the adversary is honest but curious—a person who has some means of access to the database server or sniffs the communications on the server side. However, for query hijack attacks, such as injection attacks, the attacker can be on the client side, injecting malicious code into a remote web access request (through an API) when the web request is processed by the database client or protocol wrapper.

- *Attacks on data privacy*—For most attacks focused on privacy breaches, adversaries can be legitimate data users with unrestricted access to the database, such as data analysts.

At a high level, confidentiality controls protect against the unauthorized use of information already in the hands of an institution. In contrast, privacy protects the rights of an individual to control the information that the institution collects, maintains, and shares with others.

Toward the end of this chapter, we'll look at design considerations for a tailor-made privacy-preserving database system that can be customized for the user's privacy requirements. To achieve that, it is essential to study the effects of these attack vectors.

Figure 8.16 illustrates a typical database server deployment and summarizes possible database attacks. As you can see, there are many possible ways data can leak, even before it's processed at the database level: at the client-side drivers or wrappers, at the communication channel, or at the operating system level on the server side. Let's look at these in detail.

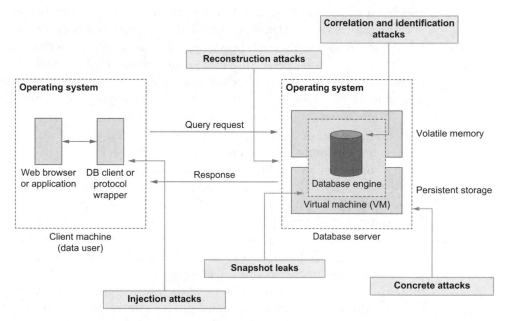

Figure 8.16 A typical database server deployment. Data leakage through attacks can occur on the client side, on the network interface itself, or even on server-side components.

ATTACKS TARGETING DATA CONFIDENTIALITY

The first category of database attacks is based on the attacker's ability to breach data confidentiality. Let's look at how these attacks can be deployed in day-to-day applications:

- *Injection attacks*—SQL injection is a common attack that works by inserting malicious code into SQL-based query statements, which the application passes to the database client (on the client machine). Most databases collect and store performance statistics in system-level diagnostic tables that can be used for database tune-ups and to resolve diagnosed problems. Sometimes, these tables keep a timestamped list of currently executing queries (e.g., the information schema and performance schema databases in MySQL). With a list of currently executing queries, an attacker can easily obtain a list of queries made by other users. This is even possible with NoSQL databases, and some studies have shown how an attacker can bypass authentication mechanisms to extract data illegally by injecting a malicious code.

- *Reconstruction (leakage-abuse) attacks*—This is an attack strategy where the adversary exploits some leakage to recover query information. This attack can be based on query access patterns and communication volume.

   Basically, a reconstruction attack using query access patterns involves a server learning *which records* are returned for a particular query. In contrast, a reconstruction attack using communication volume involves the server learning *how many records* are returned for a query. Moreover, these attacks are even possible with encrypted databases (EDBs). As you learned at the beginning of this section, encrypted databases are secure database systems where the data is stored in an encrypted form (not in cleartext) such that querying is still possible. Most EDBs rely on some kind of property-preserving encryption (PPE) mechanisms (e.g., deterministic or order-preserving encryption), which enables them to execute various database operations. However, these solutions still leak some amount of information due to weaknesses in the underlying encryption algorithms.

- *Concrete attacks*—Another possible attack scenario is the theft of persistent storage (disk theft). Most ACID-compliant databases use on-disk log files to facilitate rollback operations for the most recent transactions. By using standard forensic techniques, these log files can be used to reconstruct past query transactions issued on the database. In addition, the timing of SQL queries may carry sensitive information that can be extracted from log files that support replicated transactions. These attacks can be mitigated using data-at-rest encryption mechanisms.

- *Snapshot leaks*—Modern database systems are increasingly deployed on virtual machines (VMs), so they are exposed to a threat called *VM image leakage* attacks. In this case, an attacker obtains a snapshot image of a virtual machine and thereby reveals the point-in-time state of the entire persistent or volatile memory. In addition, by accessing individual pages in the cache memory, an attacker can disclose information about past executed queries.

- *Full system compromise*—Full system compromise is an attack strategy that involves rooting the database system and gaining full access to the database and the OS state. This can be a persistent passive or an active attack; passive attacks are more common.

ATTACKS TARGETING DATA PRIVACY

We have discussed a few attacks targeting the confidentiality of data. However, another major concern we are facing today is the linking of different types of datasets together to reveal unique fingerprints of an individual or sensitive information (also known as re-identification). Generally, these are insider attacks, and they can be categorized into two subclasses:

■ *Correlation attacks*—In correlation attacks, values in a dataset are linked with other sources of information to create unique and informative entries. Consider the scenario of a hospital database and a pharmacy database. If one published database lists user information with medication prescriptions, and another lists user information with the pharmacies visited, linking them could provide information such as which patient bought their medication from which pharmacy. Hence, the final correlated dataset could have more information about each user.

■ *Identification attacks*—While a correlation attack tries to link two datasets arbitrarily, an identification attack tries to find more information about a particular individual by linking entries in a database. This can be considered the most threatening type of data privacy attack, as it affects an individual's privacy more. For instance, if an employer searches for occurrences of its employees in a pharmacy customer database, this may reveal some information about medical treatments and illnesses of its employees.

Data anonymization or data pseudonymization techniques can play a big role in mitigating these attacks. Linking datasets is still feasible, but identifying individuals from the resulting dataset is difficult. The following section discusses how privacy-enhancing technologies can be used in database systems (particularly in statistical databases) to overcome the preceding threats and vulnerabilities.

8.4.4   Privacy-preserving techniques in statistical database systems

You now have a general understanding of the attack vectors. It's time to look at how privacy preservation can be applied in database systems.

Typically, statistical database (SDB) systems enable their users to retrieve aggregate statistics (e.g., count, average, sample mean, etc.) for a subset of entities presented in the database. For example, finding the average salary of employees in a company database is an aggregate statistical query performed within the database as a SQL query. Most of today's data-driven applications use data analytics (usually called *online analytical processing*, or OLAP) for decision-making purposes. However, as we already saw, current data security approaches cannot guarantee individuals' privacy when providing general-purpose access (for internal users), especially for OLAP queries in a database system. Common mechanisms like access control policies can limit access to a particular database, but once an inside analyst has access to the data, these policies cannot control how the data is used. As has been revealed by many insider attacks over the past, allowing unrestricted access to data is a significant cause of privacy breaches [10], [11], [12]. Providing security on statistical databases is already a public concern.

The research community has proposed several techniques to prevent statistical database compromises. These can be mainly categorized into two classes: noise addition and data or query restriction:

- *Noise addition techniques*—The most common approach to privacy protection in statistical databases is adding noise to the output query results. In this method, all data in the database is available for use, but only approximate values will be returned. The primary focus of the noise addition techniques is to mask the actual values of sensitive data by adding some level of noise to it. This is usually done in a controlled way to balance the competing needs of privacy and information loss. Based on how noise is added, these techniques can be further classified:

  - *Data perturbation approach*—In this approach, the original content of the database is replaced by a perturbed database where the statistical queries are performed, as shown in figure 8.17.

Name	Gender	Disease	Religion
John	Male	Viral infection	Christian
Alex	Male	TB	Christian
Kishor	Male	Cancer	Hindu
Emiley	Female	Viral infection	Christian
Ahmed	Male	Cancer	Muslim

Original database

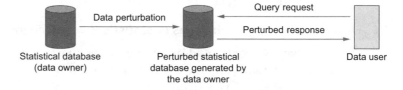

Statistical database (data owner) — Data perturbation → Perturbed statistical database generated by the data owner — Query request / Perturbed response — Data user

Name	Gender	Disease	Religion
Patient 1	Male	Viral infection	Rel A
Patient 2	Male	TB	Rel A
Patient 3	Male	Cancer	Rel C
Patient 4	Female	Viral infection	Rel A
Patient 5	Male	Cancer	Rel E

Perturbed database

Figure 8.17   The data perturbation approach

  - *Output perturbation approach*—With the output perturbation approach (shown in figure 8.18), queries are evaluated on the original data. However, noise is added (by the database) to the individual results before they are released to the querying party, so that the original values are never disclosed.

This can be achieved by using the data anonymizing noise addition techniques that we discussed at the beginning of this chapter. However, it is noteworthy that the final accuracy of the query depends on how much noise we add. Obviously, when the noise is high, the privacy is better, but it can affect the accuracy of the final result.

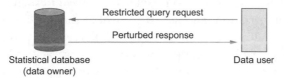

Statistical database
(data owner)

Data user

Figure 8.18   The output perturbation approach

- *Query (or data) restriction technique*—The query or data restriction technique applies data sanitization operations to the query results (see figure 8.19). These techniques can be further subdivided into three different approaches:
  - The *global recording* approach transforms an attribute into another domain to ensure privacy. For instance, instead of returning someone's age as 26, it transforms the age to a range value and returns it as something like a range of 20–30.
  - The *application of suppression* approach replaces the value of an attribute with a value that did not appear in the original dataset. This is similar to the suppression technique discussed in section 7.4, but instead of removing the record entirely, we replace it with another value. In order to find a replacement value, we first need to identify a value that was not available in the attribute we are looking at. For instance, let's say we have an attribute defined as Age = [20, 23, 35,…, 42, 26], and let's assume the list does not contain the value 33. Thus, 33 is a candidate for use as a replacement value.
  - With the *query restriction* technique, users' queries are either answered exactly or are rejected. The decision of which queries should be answered correctly is based on different parameters, such as query set size, query set overlap, and so on.

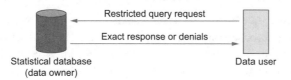

Statistical database
(data owner)

Data user

Figure 8.19   The query restriction approach

Now that we have discussed different privacy-enhancing techniques that can be implemented on database systems, and their limitations, let's look at how we can customize these privacy techniques. Different applications have different privacy requirements, so it is important to have a customizable set of privacy components in database systems, allowing users to configure privacy based on their needs. The following section will discuss how to design a privacy-preserving database system, emphasizing the main architectural requirements.

8.4.5   *What to consider when designing a customizable privacy-preserving database system*

Many modern database systems do not have the aforementioned privacy-enhancing technologies for various reasons. Most of today's database architectures were designed with high availability and performance in mind, but not privacy considerations. As a result, it is hard for these systems to cover data privacy, beyond such security primitives as authentication, authorization, and access control at the architectural design level. Privacy comes with an additional cost to utility. Implementing privacy techniques in database systems always involves a tradeoff between data privacy and performance.

Database management systems specially tailored to support privacy policies and standards have been investigated; the World Wide Web Consortium's (W3C's) Platform for Privacy Preferences Project (P3P) initiative was such an investigation. However, none of the leading database providers are capable of providing a practical privacy-guaranteed database system, which would require a combined approach of privacy-enhancing technologies and privacy-preserving data mining. In this section we'll briefly discusses the solid database architectural changes and requirements needed to design a privacy-preserving database system.

At a high level, it is crucial that privacy promises be enforced by the information systems once data is collected. Thus, designing such a system requires utilizing a wide range of security policies and other sanitization techniques. Let's look at them briefly.

KEEP A RICH SET OF PRIVACY-RELATED METADATA

Mechanisms such as P3P often require data users to specify the intended purpose of the data they retrieved, to ensure privacy guarantees. Thus, to facilitate access to such metadata, privacy-preserving DBMSs should implement mechanisms to store privacy-specific metadata with the data. For example, a set of data attributes in a database can have related metadata specifying their intended purpose, such as whether the data is to be used internally, whether it can be combined with other attributes, and so on. Moreover, this metadata should be associated with the data for a range of possible granularities with adequate flexibility and without degrading the overall performance of the datastore.

SUPPORT ATTRIBUTE-LEVEL ACCESS CONTROL MECHANISMS

A privacy-preserving database system should support access control up to the level of data attributes. Most database systems (whether relational, NoSQL, or NewSQL) are equipped with role-based access control (RBAC) mechanisms, where each user profile is assigned predefined roles, such as an administrator, end user, or special user. For example, an administrator can have the privileges to delete records, while end users may only be able to add or view records. Similarly, all users assigned an HR role may be granted access to payroll information, while others are not. However, RBAC does not provide application-dependent user profiles for use in privacy enforcement. These policies are usually defined for each data table (or collection) but not on an attribute basis. Therefore, it is necessary to have mechanisms to extend support for attribute-based or purpose-based access control mechanisms in privacy-preserving DBMSs.

What is attribute-based access control?

Unlike RBAC, attribute-based access control (ABAC) has a large number of possible control variables called "attributes" that enable access control on a more fine-grained basis than RBAC. These attributes can take different forms, such as user attributes (user_name, user_id, role, etc.), resource attributes (resource_owner, creation_date, privacy_level, etc.), or environmental attributes (access_date_time, data_location, risk_level, etc.). These different attributes allow ABAC to provide a more granular level of access control.

For example, suppose we have an RBAC where all the HR role users can access employee and payroll information in the database. With ABAC this could be further filtered such that only specific branches or offices could access payroll information, while others could be restricted.

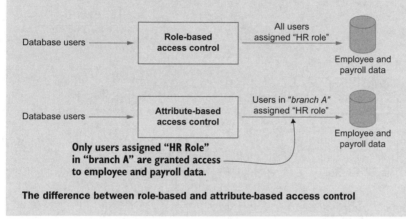

The difference between role-based and attribute-based access control

IMPLEMENT FINE-GRAINED ACCESS CONTROL TO DATA

In addition to ABAC mechanisms, fine-grained access control to data is of utmost importance.

In conventional relational database systems, fine granularity of access control is achieved through database views. A *view* is a virtual table that doesn't store data but can be queried like a table. Views generally combine a few tables or collections in a database and then grant access to a set of users to query that data. However, views are limited to a controlled group of attributes. Users cannot modify data at this level, but the data can be used for mining tasks.

To implement a privacy-enhanced DBMS solution, these view mechanisms should be extended to the level of each tuple or set of tuples that are being protected, and they should be implemented on a per-user basis. For example, HR managers could have access to all attributes in the HR view, while other HR users might only get access to a limited set of attributes in the view. The most straightforward approach to implementing this is to create new or additional views for each user or user group, but this is resource consuming. Therefore, the database system itself has to be equipped with mechanisms to provide this fine granularity in access control to data.

What is a view and how does it work?

A *view* is the result of a stored aggregation on a table, which database users can query as if it were a persistent collection object such as a table. Let's walk through a quick example of creating a view in MongoDB by joining two tables (called *collections* in MongoDB).

In this example, `viewName` is the name of the view we are going to create, and `table1` and `table2` are the tables we are joining. For the `$lookup`, the condition for the join is that `table2.col1=table1.col1`, and with parameter 0 in `$project` we are emphasizing that `col3` and `col4` of `table1` and `col1` and `col3` of `table2` should be removed from the final view.

```
Db.createView("viewName", "table1",
    [{$lookup: {from: "table2", localField: "col1",
foreignField: "col1", as: "t2"}},
    {$project: {"col3": 0, "col4": 0, "t2.col1": 0, "t2.col3": 0}}])
```

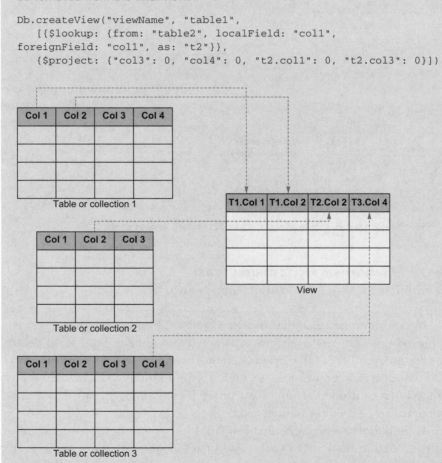

Generating a view in MongoDB

How could we join all three tables shown in the figure? You can try that yourself.

MAINTAIN A PRIVACY-PRESERVING INFORMATION FLOW

Another important consideration is maintaining a privacy-preserving data flow within the database system. In most distributed database systems, data flows across different domains, so it is vital that all privacy policies associated with the data also travel with the data, both within an organization and across organizations. It is also important that if sensitive data has been collected under a given privacy promise, those restrictions should be enforced when data is passed to different parties. For example, one of an organization's distributed database systems could be located globally with personal data being collected worldwide. Whenever data is collected from one region and passes through another, the same set of privacy enforcements should be guaranteed.

PROTECT AGAINST INSIDER ATTACKS

The misuse of privileges by legitimate high-privileged users is one of the most threatening attacks on a database system. While preventing this is challenging, there are a couple of approaches to mitigating such attacks.

The simplest is to employ a per-user layered encryption mechanism so that each user has their own encryption. Other users can still access the data, but they cannot get any valuable information from it as the encryption key is different. However, this creates more problems in terms of the practicality of the database system.

Another possible option is to use user-access profiling techniques. Once a user is defined with the database system, their profile can be monitored with the help of machine learning techniques to detect behavior that is different from their regular activities. If someone is accessing unauthorized content, it can be detected.

We've now discussed data protection schemes that can be used in practical deployments and how various attacks can target data confidentiality and privacy. In chapter 10, we will be using these concepts to explain how to design a practical privacy-preserving data management solution. But first, in chapter 9 we'll look at compressive privacy for machine learning, which is an alternative approach to perturbing the data.

Summary

- Sometimes the k-anonymity privacy model is not the best solution for protecting privacy in data mining applications.
- The susceptibility of k-anonymity to homogeneity and background knowledge attacks can be mitigated with l-diversity by making l distinct sensitive records in each group of attributes.
- The idea behind t-closeness is to ensure the distribution of sensitive records in each group (equivalence class) is close enough to the corresponding distribution in the original dataset. This prevents attribute disclosure from distribution skewness.
- The output of a data mining algorithm can be modified to protect privacy for some data mining applications.
- There are many different security and privacy threats and vulnerabilities in database systems, targeting confidentiality and the privacy of data.

- We can categorize attacks on database systems into two main classes: attacks on the confidentiality of data and attacks on data privacy.
- Privacy preservation techniques in statistical database systems can be used to mitigate most of the privacy threats in today's database systems.
- Most modern database systems are not designed from the standpoint of data privacy; they generally focus on the performance of the database.

Compressive privacy
for machine learning

9

This chapter covers

- Understanding compressive privacy
- Introducing compressive privacy for machine learning applications
- Implementing compressive privacy from theory to practice
- A compressive privacy solution for privacy-preserving machine learning

In previous chapters we've looked into differential privacy, local differential privacy, privacy-preserving synthetic data generation, privacy-preserving data mining, and their application when designing privacy-preserving machine learning solutions. As you'll recall, in differential privacy a trusted data curator collects data from individuals and produces differentially private results by adding precisely computed noise to the aggregation of individuals' data. In local differential privacy, individuals privatize their own data by perturbation before sending it to the data aggregator, which eliminates the need to have a trusted data curator collect the data from individuals. In data mining, we looked into various privacy-preserving techniques and operations that can be used when collecting information and publishing the data. We also discussed strategies for regulating data mining output. Privacy-preserving synthetic data generation provides a promising solution for private data sharing, where synthetic yet representative data can be generated and then shared among multiple parties safely and securely.

As you can see, most of the techniques we have discussed are based on the definition of differential privacy (DP), which does not make any assumptions about the abilities of the adversaries, thus providing an extremely strong privacy guarantee. However, to enable this strong privacy guarantee, DP-based mechanisms usually add excessive noise to the private data, causing a somewhat inevitable utility drop. This prevents DP approaches from being applied for many real-world applications, and especially for practical applications using machine learning (ML) or deep learning. This prompts us to explore other perturbation-based approaches to privacy preservation. Compressive

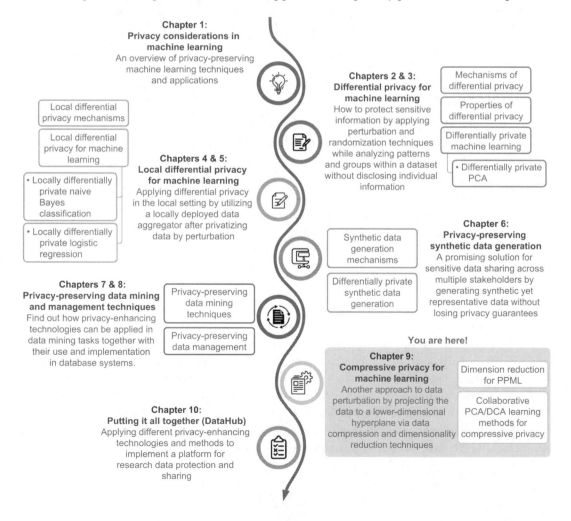

privacy (CP) is one alternative approach we can look into. In this chapter we will explore the concept, mechanisms, and applications of compressive privacy.

9.1 Introducing compressive privacy

Compressive privacy (CP) is an approach that perturbs the data by projecting it to a lower-dimensional hyperplane via compression and dimensionality-reduction (DR) techniques. To better understand the concept and benefits of CP, let's compare it with the idea of differential privacy (DP), which we discussed in chapter 2.

According to the definition of DP, a randomized algorithm M is said to be ε-DP of the input data if it satisfies $\Pr[M(D) \in S] \leq e^{\varepsilon} \cdot \Pr[M(D') \in S]$ for all $S \in Range(M)$ and all datasets D and D' differing by one item, where $Range(M)$ is the output set of M. In other words, the idea behind DP is that if the effect of making an arbitrary single change or substitution in a database is small enough, the query result cannot be used to infer much about any single individual, and it therefore provides privacy. As you can see, DP guarantees that the distribution of the query result from a dataset should be indistinguishable (modulo by a factor of e^{ε}) whether or not any single item in that dataset is changed. The DP definition does not make any assumptions about adversaries in advance. For instance, adversaries could have unbounded auxiliary information and unlimited computing resources, and DP mechanisms can still provide privacy guarantees under this definition of DP.

This shows the bright side of DP—it provides strong privacy guarantees via rigorous theoretical analysis. However, the DP definition and mechanisms do not make any assumptions about utility. As such, DP mechanisms usually cannot promise good performance in terms of utility. This is particularly true when applying DP approaches to real-world applications that require complex calculations, such as data mining and machine learning. That's why we also need to explore other privacy-enhancing techniques that consider utility while relaxing the theoretical privacy guarantees somewhat. CP is one such alternative that can be used with practical applications.

Unlike DP, the CP approach allows the query to be tailored to the known utility and privacy tasks. Specifically, for datasets that have samples with two labels, a utility label and a privacy label, CP allows the data owner to project their data to a lower dimension in a way that maximizes the accuracy of learning for the utility labels while decreasing the accuracy of learning for the privacy labels. We will discuss these labels when we get into the details. It is also noteworthy that, although CP does not eliminate all data privacy risks, it offers some control over the misuse of data when the privacy task is known. In addition, CP guarantees that the original data can never be fully recovered, mainly due to the dimensionality reduction.

Now let's dig into how CP works. Figure 9.1 illustrates the threat model of CP. The adversaries are all the data users with full access to the public datasets (e.g., background and auxiliary information).

In this scenario, let's assume that the privacy task is a two-class {+,−} classification problem (utility tasks are independent of the privacy task), and X_+, X_- are two public

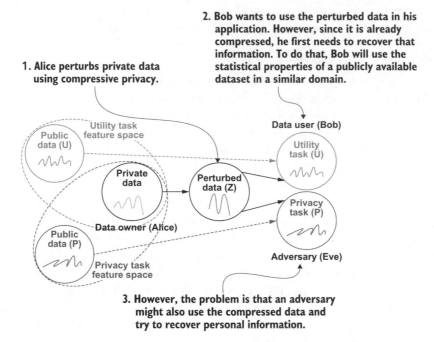

1. Alice perturbs private data using compressive privacy.

2. Bob wants to use the perturbed data in his application. However, since it is already compressed, he first needs to recover that information. To do that, Bob will use the statistical properties of a publicly available dataset in a similar domain.

3. However, the problem is that an adversary might also use the compressed data and try to recover personal information.

Figure 9.1   The threat model of compressive privacy. The real challenge is balancing the utility and privacy tradeoff.

datasets. Suppose X_S is the private data of the data owner, where $s \in \{+,-\}$ is its original class (privacy task) and $t \in \{+,-\}$ is its expected class (privacy task) after applying the CP perturbation. The data owner could publish z (the perturbed version of X_S) using the CP mechanisms. However, there could also be an adversary out there, using their approach $z' = A(z, X_+, X_-)$ to inference the original (privacy task) class s. Thus, what we want to achieve here is to minimize the probability difference, $|Pr(z' = + \mid z) - Pr(z' = - \mid z)|$, so that the adversary cannot learn any valuable information.

In figure 9.1 Alice (the data owner) has some private data, and she wants to publish it for a utility task. Let's say the utility task is to allow a data user to perform an ML classification with the data. Since it contains personal information, Alice can perturb the data using CP. Whenever Bob (the data user) wants to use this compressed data, he needs to recover the information, which he can do using the statistical properties of a publicly available dataset in a similar domain (which we call the *utility task feature space*). The problem is that someone else, Eve (an adversary), might also use the compressed data and try to recover it using another publicly available dataset, which might lead to a privacy breach. Thus, the real challenge with CP is balancing this utility/privacy tradeoff. We can compress data to perform the utility task, but it still needs to be challenging for someone to recover the data to identify personal information.

The following section will walk you through several useful components that enable CP for privacy-preserving data sharing or ML applications.

9.2 The mechanisms of compressive privacy

An important building block of CP is the supervised dimensionality reduction technique, which relies on data labels. Principal component analysis (PCA) is a widely used method that aims to project the data on the principal components with the highest variance, thus preserving most of the information in the data while reducing the data dimensions. We briefly discussed this in section 3.4.1, but let's recap it quickly.

9.2.1 Principal component analysis (PCA)

Let's first understand what principal components are. *Principal components* are new variables constructed as linear combinations of the initial variables in a dataset. These combinations are created in such a way that the new variables are uncorrelated, and most of the information within the initial variables is compressed into the first components (which is why we call it *compressive*). So, for instance, when 10-dimensional data gives you 10 principal components, PCA tries to put the maximum possible information in the first component, the maximum remaining information in the second component, and so on. When you organize information in principal components like this, you reduce dimensionality without losing much of the critical information.

Let's consider a dataset with N training samples $\{x_1, x_2, \ldots, x_N\}$, where each sample has M features ($x_i \in \mathbb{R}^M$). PCA performs something called *spectral decomposition of the center-adjusted scatter matrix $\bar{s}$* such that

$$\bar{S} = \sum_{i=1}^{N} (X_i - \mu)(X_i - \mu)^T = U \Lambda U^T$$

where μ is the mean vector, and $\Lambda = \mathrm{diag}(\lambda_1, \lambda_2, \ldots, \lambda_M)$ is a diagonal matrix of eigenvalues with eigenvalues arranged in a monotonically decreasing order (i.e., $\lambda_1 \geq \lambda_2 \geq \cdots \geq \lambda_M$).

Here, the matrix $U = [u_1, u_2, \ldots, u_M]$ is an $M \times M$ unitary matrix where u_j denotes the jth eigenvector of the scatter matrix mentioned previously. For PCA, we retain the m principal components corresponding to the m highest eigenvalues to obtain the projection matrix U_m. Once the projection matrix is found, you can find the reduced dimension feature vector as follows:

$$\tilde{X}_i = U_m^T X_i$$

As you can see, the parameter m determines to what extent the signal power is retained after dimensionality reduction.

> **Decomposing eigenvalues**
>
> In linear algebra, eigenvalue decomposition (EVD) is the factorization of a matrix into a canonical form, whereby the matrix is represented in terms of its eigenvalues and eigenvectors. Basically, it aims to find eigenvalues (called λ's) and eigenvectors (called u's) of a matrix A that satisfies the equation: $Au = \lambda u$.

> **(continued)**
> In general, EVD can be performed in a variety of ways. Some methods, such as the QR algorithm, find all the eigenvectors and eigenvalues at once. However, PCA reduces the dimensions, so not all the eigenvectors are needed. For this reason, we can rely on methods that only find a subset of the eigenvalues and eigenvectors to avoid the extra computation associated with finding unneeded eigenvectors.
>
> To that end, one of the most notable algorithms for EVD is the power iteration method. This method finds the dominant eigenvalue (the largest value) with its associated eigenvector. A matrix deflation method can be used afterward to remove the effect of the already found dominant eigenvalue while leaving the remaining eigenvalues unchanged. We can find the required number of eigenvectors by repeatedly applying the power iteration method and matrix deflation.

9.2.2 *Other dimensionality reduction methods*

Now that you know how PCA works, by projecting the data on principal components, let's look at a few other approaches that can be used for different ML classification tasks. Because the same dataset could be utilized in different classification problems, let's define a classification problem as c which has a unique set of labels associated with the corresponding training samples x_i. Without loss of generality, the dataset could be utilized for a single utility target U and a single privacy target P.

For example, suppose an ML algorithm is trained with a dataset of face images. The utility target is to identify the faces, whereas the privacy target is to identify the person. In this case, each training sample x_i has two labels $\in \{1, 2, ..., L^u\}$ and $\in \{1, 2, ..., L^p\}$. L^u and L^p are the numbers of classes of the utility target and the privacy target, respectively.

Based on Fisher's linear discriminant analysis [1], [2], given a classification problem, the within-class scatter matrix of its training samples contains most of the *noise information*, while the between-class scatter matrix of its training samples contains most of the *signal information*. We can define the within-class scatter matrix and the between-class scatter matrix for the utility target as follows,

$$S_{W_U} = \sum_{l=1}^{L^u} \left(\sum_{i=1}^{N_l^u} x_i x_i^T - N_l^u \mu_l \mu_l^T \right)$$

$$S_{B_U} = \sum_{l=1}^{L^u} (N_l^u \mu_l \mu_l^T - N \mu \mu^T)$$

where $\mu = \frac{1}{N} \sum_{i=1}^{N} x_i$, μ_l is the mean vector of all training samples belonging to class l, and N_l^u is the number of training samples belonging to class l of the utility target.

Similarly, for the privacy target, the within-class scatter matrix and the between-class scatter matrix are defined as

$$S_{W_P} = \sum_{l=1}^{L^p} \left(\sum_{i=1}^{N_l^p} x_i x_i^T - N_l^p \mu_l \mu_l^T \right)$$

$$S_{B_P} = \sum_{l=1}^{L^p} (N_l^p \mu_l \mu_l^T - N \mu \mu^T)$$

Suppose we let W be a $K \times M$ projection matrix, in which $K < M$. Given a testing sample x, $\hat{x} = x^T \cdot W$ is its subspace projection. The framework that we are going to explore here combines the advantages of two eigenvalue decomposition-based dimensionality reduction (DR) techniques: DCA (utility-driven projection) [3] and MDR (privacy emphasized projection) [4]. Let's quickly look into those:

- *Discriminant component analysis (DCA)*—DCA involves searching for the projection matrix $W \in R^{M \times K}$,

$$DCA = \frac{\det(W^T S_{B_U} W)}{\det(W^T (\bar{S} + \rho I) W)}$$

where $\det(.)$ is the determinant operator, ρI is a small regularization term added for numerical stability, and $\bar{S} = S_{W_U} + S_{B_U} = \sum_{i=1}^{N} x_i x_i^T - N \mu \mu^T$.

The optimal solution to this problem can be derived from the first K principal generalized eigenvectors of the matrix pencil $(S_{B_U}, \bar{S} + \rho I)$.

- *Multiclass discriminant ratio* (MDR)—MDR considers both the utility target and the privacy target, which is defined as

$$MDR = \frac{\det(W^T (S_{B_U}) W)}{\det(W^T (S_{B_P} + \rho I) W)}$$

where ρI is a small regularization term added for numerical stability. The optimal solution to MDR can be derived from the first K principal generalized eigenvectors of the matrix pencil $(S_{B_U}, S_{B_P} + \rho I)$.

With those basics and mathematical formulations, let's look at how we can implement CP techniques in Python.

9.3   *Using compressive privacy for ML applications*

So far we've discussed the theoretical background of different CP mechanisms. Let's implement these techniques in a real-world face-recognition application. Face recognition has been a problem of interest in machine learning (ML) and signal processing for over a decade due to its various use cases ranging from simple online image searches to surveillance.

With the current privacy requirements, a real-world face-recognition application has to ensure that there won't be any privacy leaks from the data itself. Let's investigate a couple of different CP methods to see how we can ensure both the utility of the face recognition application and the privacy of the reconstructed image. We'll need to compress the face image before submitting it to the facial-recognition application such that the application can still identify the face. However, someone else should not be able to distinguish the image simply by looking at it or be able to reconstruct the original image. For our experiments, we will employ three different face datasets. The source code for these hands-on experiments is available for download at the book's GitHub repository: https://github.com/nogrady/PPML/tree/main/Ch9.

- *Yale Face Database*—The Yale Face Database contains 165 grayscale images of 15 individuals and is publicly available from http://cvc.cs.yale.edu/cvc/projects/yalefaces/yalefaces.html.
- *Olivetti faces dataset*—This dataset contains 400 grayscale face images of 40 different people taken between April 1992 and April 1994 at AT&T Laboratories Cambridge. The dataset can be downloaded from https://scikit-learn.org/0.19/datasets/olivetti_faces.html.
- *Glasses dataset*—We derived this dataset from a combination of the Yale and Olivetti datasets by selectively choosing the subjects who are wearing glasses. In this case, the dataset contains 300 images. Half of the images are of people with glasses, and the other half are people without glasses.

For the Yale and Olivetti datasets, the task of recognizing individuals from the face images will be our utility (our target application), whereas reconstructing the image will be our privacy target. One use case scenario would be an "entity" that wants to build a face recognition algorithm using sensitive face images provided by users for training. But in this scenario, people are usually hesitant to share their face images unless they are changed so that no one can recognize the person in the image.

For simplicity, we can assume that the entity wishing to build the face recognition classifier is a service operator, but this operator could be malicious and could be trying to reconstruct the original images from the training data received from users.

For the glasses dataset, we have two different classes (with and without glasses). The utility of our application will be to identify whether the person is wearing a pair of glasses or not; the privacy target will again be the reconstruction of the image.

9.3.1 *Implementing compressive privacy*

Now let's get to work! We'll use the Yale dataset and see how we can use CP techniques in our facial recognition application. First, you'll need to load some modules and the dataset. Note that discriminant_analysis.py is a module that we developed for PCA and DCA methods. Refer to the source code for more information.

NOTE You can just use the cleaned version of the Yale dataset, which is available in the code repository: https://github.com/nogrady/PPML/tree/main/Ch9.

Listing 9.1 Loading modules and the dataset

```
import sys
sys.path.append('..');
import numpy as np
from discriminant_analysis import DCA, PCA
from sklearn.svm import SVC
from sklearn.model_selection import GridSearchCV
from sklearn.model_selection import train_test_split
from matplotlib.pyplot import *

data_dir = './CompPrivacy/DataSet/Yale_Faces/';   ⟵——— Load the dataset.
X = np.loadtxt(data_dir+'Xyale.txt');
y = np.loadtxt(data_dir+'Yyale.txt');
```

You can run the following command to see what the dataset looks like:

```
print('Shape of the dataset: %s' %(X.shape,))
```

As you can see from the output, the dataset contains 165 images, where each image is 64 x 64 (which is why we get 4,096).

```
Shape of the dataset: (165, 4096)
```

Now let's review a couple of images in the dataset. Because the dataset contains 165 different images, you can run the code in the following listing to pick four different images randomly. We are using the `randrange` function to randomly choose images. To show the images in the output, we are using the `displayImage` routine and `subplot` with four columns.

Listing 9.2 Loading a few images from the dataset

```
def displayImage(vImage,height,width):      ⟵          Define a function to
    mImage = np.reshape(vImage, (height,width)).T       show the images.
    imshow(mImage, cmap='gray')
    axis('off')
                          | Randomly select four different
for i in range(4):      ⟵—| images from the dataset.
    subplot(1,4,i+1)
    displayImage(X[randrange(165)], height, width)

show()
```

The output will look something like figure 9.2, though you will get different random face images.

Now that you know what kind of data we are dealing with, let's implement different CP technologies with this dataset. We are particularly looking at implementing

Figure 9.2   A set of sample images from Yale dataset

principal component analysis (PCA) and discriminant component analysis (DCA) with this dataset. We have developed and wrapped the core functionality of PCA and DCA into the discriminant_analysis.py class, so you can simply call it and initialize the methods.

> **NOTE**   Discriminant_analysis.py is a class file that we developed to cover the PCA and DCA methods. You can refer to the source code of the file for more information: https://github.com/nogrady/PPML/blob/main/Ch9/ discriminant_analysis.py.

The DCA object is initialized with two parameters: rho and rho_p. You'll recall that we discussed these parameters (ρ and updated ρ) in section 9.2.2. The code we use will first define and initialize these values along with a set of dimensions that we'll need to project the image data in order to see the results.

We'll start by setting rho = 10 and rho_p = -0.05, but later in this chapter you'll learn about the important properties of these parameters and how different values will affect privacy. For now we'll just focus on the training and testing part of the algorithm.

Setting ntests = 10 means that we will do the same experiment 10 times to average the final result. You can set this value to any number, but the higher, the better. The dims array defines the number of dimensions that we will use. As you can see, we will be starting with few dimensions, such as 2, and then move to more dimensions, such as 4,096. Again, you can try setting your own values for this.

```
rho = 10;
rho_p = -0.05;
ntests = 10;
dims = [2,5,8,10,14,39,1000,2000,3000,4096];

mydca = DCA(rho,rho_p);
mypca = PCA();
```

Once these values are defined, the mypca and mydca objects are trained with the following code, after the dataset is split into train and test sets. Xtr is the training data matrix (training set), while ytr is the training label vector. The fit command learns some quantities from the data, particularly the principal components and the explained variance.

```
Xtr, Xte, ytr, yte = train_test_split(X,y,test_size=0.1,stratify=y);
mypca.fit(Xtr);
mydca.fit(Xtr,ytr);
```

Thereafter, the projections of the data can be obtained as follows:

```
Dtr_pca = mypca.transform(Xtr);
Dte_pca = mypca.transform(Xte);
Dtr_dca = mydca.transform(Xtr);
Dte_dca = mydca.transform(Xte);
print('Principal and discriminant components were extracted.')
```

For each dimension that we are interested in (2, 5, 8, 10, 14, 39, 1000, etc.), the projection matrix D can be found, and then the image data can be reconstructed as Xrec:

```
D = np.r_[Dtr_pca[:,:dims[j]],Dte_pca[:,:dims[j]]];       ◁─── Reconstruct the data
Xrec = np.dot(D,mypca.components[:dims[j],:]);                  using PCA technique.

D = np.r_[Dtr_dca[:,:dims[j]],Dte_dca[:,:dims[j]]];       ◁─── Reconstruct the data
Xrec = mydca.inverse_transform(D,dim=dims[j]);                 using DCA technique.
```

When we put all this together, the complete code looks like the following listing.

Listing 9.3 The complete code to reconstruct an image and calculate the accuracy

```
import sys
sys.path.append('..');
import numpy as np
from random import randrange
from discriminant_analysis import DCA, PCA
from sklearn.svm import SVC
from sklearn.model_selection import GridSearchCV
from sklearn.model_selection import train_test_split
from matplotlib.pyplot import *

def displayImage(vImage,height,width):
    mImage = np.reshape(vImage, (height,width)).T
    imshow(mImage, cmap='gray')
    axis('off')

height = 64
width = 64

data_dir = './CompPrivacy/DataSet/Yale_Faces/';
X = np.loadtxt(data_dir+'Xyale.txt');
y = np.loadtxt(data_dir+'Yyale.txt');

print('Shape of the dataset: %s' %(X.shape,))

for i in range(4):
    subplot(1,4,i+1)
    displayImage(X[randrange(165)], height, width)
show()


rho = 10;
rho_p = -0.05;
```

```
ntests = 10;
dims = [2,5,8,10,14,39,1000,2000,3000,4096];

mydca = DCA(rho,rho_p);
mypca = PCA();

svm_tuned_params = [{'kernel': ['linear'], 'C':
    [0.1,1,10,100,1000]},{'kernel':
    ['rbf'], 'gamma': [0.00001, 0.0001, 0.001, 0.01], 'C':
        [0.1,1,10,100,1000]}];

utilAcc_pca = np.zeros((ntests,len(dims)));
utilAcc_dca = np.zeros((ntests,len(dims)));
reconErr_pca = np.zeros((ntests,len(dims)));
reconErr_dca = np.zeros((ntests,len(dims)));

clf = GridSearchCV(SVC(max_iter=1e5),svm_tuned_params,cv=3);

for i in range(ntests):
    print('Experiment %d:' %(i+1));
    Xtr, Xte, ytr, yte = train_test_split(X,y,test_size=0.1,stratify=y);
    mypca.fit(Xtr);
    mydca.fit(Xtr,ytr);
```
                                                         ⟵─┘ Precompute all
                                                              the components.
```
    Dtr_pca = mypca.transform(Xtr);
    Dte_pca = mypca.transform(Xte);
    Dtr_dca = mydca.transform(Xtr);
    Dte_dca = mydca.transform(Xte);
    print('Principal and discriminant components were extracted.')

    subplot(2,5,1)
    title('Original',{'fontsize':8})
    displayImage(Xtr[i],height,width)

    subplot(2,5,6)
    title('Original',{'fontsize':8})
    displayImage(Xtr[i],height,width)

    for j in range(len(dims)):
        clf.fit(Dtr_pca[:,:dims[j]],ytr);
```
                                                         ⟵── Test the accuracy of PCA.
```
        utilAcc_pca[i,j] = clf.score(Dte_pca[:,:dims[j]],yte);
        print('Utility accuracy of %d-dimensional PCA: %f'
              %(dims[j],utilAcc_pca[i,j]));
```
                                                         ┌─ Test the
                                                         │ reconstruction
                                                         │ error of PCA.
```
        D = np.r_[Dtr_pca[:,:dims[j]],Dte_pca[:,:dims[j]]];  ⟵┘
        Xrec = np.dot(D,mypca.components[:dims[j],:]);
        reconErr_pca[i,j] = sum(np.linalg.norm(X-Xrec,2,axis=1))/len(X);
        eigV_pca = np.reshape(Xrec,(len(X),64,64))
        print('Average reconstruction error of %d-dimensional PCA: %f'
              %(dims[j],reconErr_pca[i,j]));

        clf.fit(Dtr_dca[:,:dims[j]],ytr);
```
                                                         ⟵── Test the accuracy
                                                              of DCA.
```
        utilAcc_dca[i,j] = clf.score(Dte_dca[:,:dims[j]],yte);
        print('Utility accuracy of %d-dimensional DCA: %f'
              %(dims[j],utilAcc_dca[i,j]));
```

Test the reconstruction error of DCA. ▷

```
D = np.r_[Dtr_dca[:,:dims[j]],Dte_dca[:,:dims[j]]];
Xrec = mydca.inverse_transform(D,dim=dims[j]);
reconErr_dca[i,j] = sum(np.linalg.norm(X-Xrec,2,axis=1))/len(X);
eigV_dca = np.reshape(Xrec,(len(X),64,64))
print('Average reconstruction error of %d-dimensional DCA: %f'
      %(dims[j],reconErr_dca[i,j]));
```

Show the reconstructed image. ⟵

```
subplot(2,5,j+2)
title('DCA dim: ' + str(dims[j]),{'fontsize':8})
displayImage(eigV_dca[1],height,width)

subplot(2,5,j+7)
title('PCA dim: ' + str(dims[j]),{'fontsize':8})
displayImage(eigV_pca[i],height,width)

show()

np.savetxt('utilAcc_pca.out', utilAcc_pca, delimiter=',')   ⟵
np.savetxt('utilAcc_dca.out', utilAcc_dca, delimiter=',')
np.savetxt('reconErr_pca.out', reconErr_pca, delimiter=',')
np.savetxt('reconErr_dca.out', reconErr_dca, delimiter=',')
```

Save the accuracy and reconstruction error of each cycle as a text file.

As you can see in listing 9.3, we are running the PCA and DCA reconstructions 10 times (remember we set `ntests = 10`), and for each case it randomly splits the dataset for training and testing. In the end, we are calculating the accuracy and reconstruction error for each dimension for both PCA and DCA. That will let us evaluate how accurately the compressed image can be reconstructed.

When you run the code, the results may look like the following. The complete output is too long to include here—we've just included the first few lines of the output and the reconstructed images of the first two runs in the loop.

```
Experiment 1:
Principal and discriminant components were extracted.
Utility accuracy of 5-dimensional PCA: 0.588235
Average reconstruction error of 5-dimensional PCA: 3987.932630
Utility accuracy of 5-dimensional DCA: 0.882353
Average reconstruction error of 5-dimensional DCA: 7157.040696
Utility accuracy of 14-dimensional PCA: 0.823529
Average reconstruction error of 14-dimensional PCA: 4048.247986
Utility accuracy of 14-dimensional DCA: 0.941176
Average reconstruction error of 14-dimensional DCA: 7164.268844
Utility accuracy of 50-dimensional PCA: 0.941176
Average reconstruction error of 50-dimensional PCA: 4142.000701
Utility accuracy of 50-dimensional DCA: 0.941176
Average reconstruction error of 50-dimensional DCA: 6710.181110
Utility accuracy of 160-dimensional PCA: 0.941176
Average reconstruction error of 160-dimensional PCA: 4190.105696
Utility accuracy of 160-dimensional DCA: 0.941176
Average reconstruction error of 160-dimensional DCA: 4189.337999
...
...
```

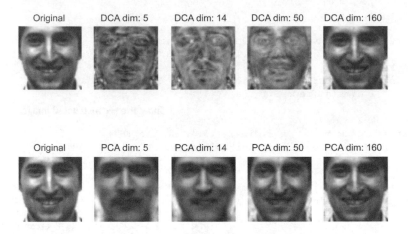

```
Experiment 2:
Principal and discriminant components were extracted.
...
...
```

If you look closely at the reproduced images in the output, compared with the originals, you'll see that when the reduced dimensions are low, it is difficult to identify the person. For instance, if you compare the original image and the version with 5 (either PCA or DCA), it is pretty hard to identify the person from the compressed image. On the other hand, when dims = 160, you can see that the reconstructed image is getting better. That means we are preserving the privacy of sensitive data by reducing the dimensions. As you can see, in this case, DCA works much better than PCA for the dimensions 5 to 50, making it close to the original but still hard to recognize.

9.3.2   *The accuracy of the utility task*

You now know that when the dimensions are reduced, privacy is improved. But what about the accuracy of the utility task? If we cannot get considerable accuracy for the utility task, there is no point in using CP techniques in this scenario.

To examine how the accuracy of the utility task changes along with the reduced dimensions, we can simply increase the value of the ntests variable to the maximum value (which is 165 because we have 165 records in the dataset) and average the utility accuracy results for each dimension.

Figure 9.3 summarizes the accuracy results. If you look carefully at the DCA results, you will notice that after the dimension becomes 14, its accuracy saturates somewhere around 91%. Now look at the face image where the dimension is 14 for DCA. You will notice that it is hard to identify the person but the graph shows that the accuracy of the utility task (the facial recognition application in this case) is still high. That is how CP works, ensuring the balance between privacy and utility.

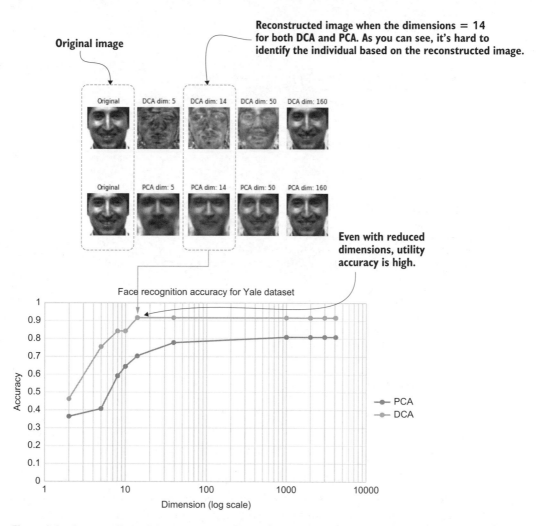

Figure 9.3   A comparison of the accuracy of the reconstructed images for different dimension settings

Now that we've investigated the accuracy of the utility, let's see how hard it is for someone else to reconstruct the compressed image. This can be measured by the reconstruction error. To determine that, we need to go through the whole dataset, not just a couple of records. Thus we'll modify the code a little bit, as shown in the following listing.

Listing 9.4   Calculating the average reconstruction error

```
import sys
sys.path.append('..');
import numpy as np
from discriminant_analysis import DCA, PCA

rho = 10;
```

```
rho_p = -0.05;

dims = [2,5,8,10,14,39,1000,2000,3000,4096];

data_dir = './CompPrivacy/DataSet/Yale_Faces/';
X = np.loadtxt(data_dir+'Xyale.txt');
y = np.loadtxt(data_dir+'Yyale.txt');

reconErr_pca = np.zeros((len(dims)));
reconErr_dca = np.zeros((len(dims)));

mydca = DCA(rho,rho_p);
mypca = PCA();
mypca.fit(X);
mydca.fit(X,y);
```

Precompute all the components.

```
D_pca = mypca.transform(X);   ⟵
D_dca = mydca.transform(X);
print('Principal and discriminant components were extracted.')
```

Test the reconstruction error of PCA.

```
for j in range(len(dims)):
    Xrec = np.dot(D_pca[:,:dims[j]],mypca.components[:dims[j],:]);  ⟵
    reconErr_pca[j] = sum(np.linalg.norm(X-Xrec,2,axis=1))/len(X);
    print('Average reconstruction error of %d-dimensional PCA: %f'
            %(dims[j],reconErr_pca[j]));
```

Test the reconstruction error of DCA.

```
    Xrec = mydca.inverse_transform(D_dca[:,:dims[j]],dim=dims[j]);  ⟵
    reconErr_dca[j] = sum(np.linalg.norm(X-Xrec,2,axis=1))/len(X);
    print('Average reconstruction error of %d-dimensional DCA: %f'
            %(dims[j],reconErr_dca[j]));
```

Save the results to a text file.

```
np.savetxt('reconErr_pca.out', reconErr_pca, delimiter=',')   ⟵
np.savetxt('reconErr_dca.out', reconErr_dca, delimiter=',')
```

Figure 9.4 shows the results of listing 9.4 plotted against different dimensions. As you can see, when the dimensions are lower, it is hard for someone to reconstruct the image accurately. For example, the DCA datapoint at dimension 14 has a very high value for the reconstruction error, making it very hard for someone to reconstruct the image. However, as you saw before, it still provides good accuracy for the face recognition task. This is the whole idea of using CP technologies for ML applications.

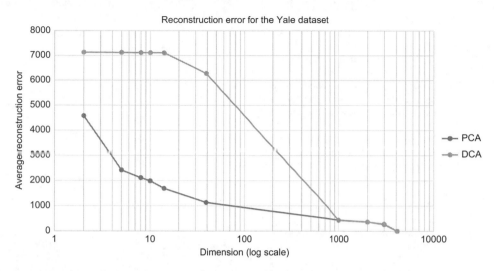

Figure 9.4   Comparing the average reconstruction error for different dimension settings

9.3.3   The effect of ρ' in DCA for privacy and utility

We have experimented with how dimension reduction can help determine privacy. When the number of dimensions is lower, more information is lost, yielding better privacy. But in DCA we have another parameter, ρ'. So far we have only changed the number of dimensions and kept ρ' as rho_p = -0.05. Now we will look at the importance of this parameter in determining the level of privacy by keeping the number of dimensions fixed.

The following listing is almost the same as listing 9.3, except that instead of going through several dimensions, now we'll change the rho_p parameter to different values: [–0.05, –0.01, –0.001, 0.0, 0.001, 0.01, 0.05]. We'll fix the dimensions at 160 (you can also try this with a different value).

Listing 9.5   Changing ρ' in DCA and determining the effect on privacy

```
import sys
sys.path.append('..');
import numpy as np
from discriminant_analysis import DCA
from matplotlib.pyplot import *
from random import randrange

def displayImage(vImage,height,width):
    mImage = np.reshape(vImage, (height,width)).T
    imshow(mImage, cmap='gray')
    axis('off')

height = 64
width = 64
```

```
rho = 10;
rho_p = [-0.05,-0.01,-0.001,0.0,0.001,0.01,0.05]
selected_dim = 160
image_id = randrange(165)

data_dir = './CompPrivacy/DataSet/Yale_Faces/';
X = np.loadtxt(data_dir+'Xyale.txt');
y = np.loadtxt(data_dir+'Yyale.txt');

subplot(2,4,1)
title('Original',{'fontsize':8})
displayImage(X[image_id],height,width)

for j in range(len(rho_p)):
    mydca = DCA(rho,rho_p[j]);
    mydca.fit(X,y);
    D_dca = mydca.transform(X);
    print('Discriminant components were extracted for rho_p: '+str(rho_p[j]))

    Xrec = mydca.inverse_transform(D_dca[:,:selected_dim],dim=selected_dim);
    eigV_dca = np.reshape(Xrec,(len(X),64,64))

    subplot(2,4,j+2)
    title('rho_p: ' + str(rho_p[j]),{'fontsize':8})
    displayImage(eigV_dca[image_id],height,width)

show()
```

The results are shown in figure 9.5. The top-left image is the original, and the rest of the images are produced with different rho_p values. As you can see, when the rho_p value changes from –0.05 to 0.05, the resultant image changes significantly, making it hard to identify. Thus, we can deduce that ρ' is also an important parameter in determining the level of privacy when DCA is used. As you can see, positive values of ρ' provide a much greater level of privacy than negative values.

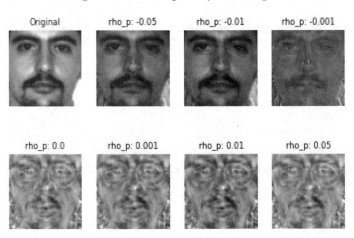

Figure 9.5   Effect of ρ' on privacy with dimension fixed at 160 on the Yale dataset

We have now explored the possibility of integrating CP technologies into ML applications. You've seen that with a minimum number of dimensions, maximum face recognition accuracy is obtainable, and the privacy of the reconstructed image is still preserved. In the next section we'll extend the discussion further with a case study on privacy preservation on horizontally partitioned data.

First, though, here are a few exercises you can explore to see the effect of ρ' on improving accuracy and to play with the different datasets.

EXERCISE 1

You now know that positive values of ρ' help to improve privacy. How about the accuracy of the face recognition task? Do positive values of ρ' help accuracy as well? Change the code in listing 9.3 and observe the utility accuracy and the average reconstruction error for each different ρ' value. (Hint: You can do this by adding another for loop that goes through the different rho_p values.)

Solution: In terms of the accuracy of the face recognition task, the value of ρ' has no significant effect. Try to plot ρ' against the accuracy, and you will see this clearly.

EXERCISE 2

All the experiments we have explored so far were based on the Yale dataset. Switch to the Olivetti dataset and rerun all the experiments to see whether the observations and patterns are similar. (Hint: This is quite straightforward. You just need to change the dataset name and the location.)

Solution: This solution is provided in the book's source code repository.

EXERCISE 3

Now change the dataset to the glasses dataset. In this case, remember that the utility of the application will be identifying the person whether they wear a pair of glasses or not. The privacy target is still the reconstruction of the image. Change the code and see how PCA and DCA help here.

Solution: The solution is provided in the book's source code repository.

9.4 Case study: Privacy-preserving PCA and DCA on horizontally partitioned data

As you already know, machine learning (ML) can be classified into two different categories or tasks: supervised tasks like regression and classification, and unsupervised tasks like clustering. In practice, these techniques are widely used in many different applications such as identity and access management, detecting fraudulent credit card transactions, building clinical decision support systems, and so on. These applications often use personal data, such as healthcare records, financial data, and the like, during the training and testing phases of ML.

While there are many different approaches, dimensionality reduction (DR) is an important ML tool that can be used to overcome different types of problems:

- Overfitting when the feature dimensions far exceed the number of training samples
- Performance degradation due to suboptimal search
- Higher computational costs and power consumption resulting from high dimensionality in the feature space

We've discussed a couple of DR methods in this chapter already: PCA and DCA.

As you'll recall, PCA aims to project the data on the principal components with the highest variance, thus preserving most of the information while reducing the data dimensions. As you can see in figure 9.6 (a), most of the variability happens along with the first principal component (shown as PC-1). Hence, projecting all the points on that new axis could reduce the dimensions without sacrificing much data variability.

Compared to PCA, DCA is designed for supervised learning applications. The objective of DCA is not recoverability (for reducing the reconstruction error like PCA) but rather is improving the discriminant power of the learned classifiers so that they can effectively discriminate between different classes. Figure 9.6 (b) shows an example of a supervised learning problem where PCA would choose PC-1 as the principal component on which the data would be projected, because PC-1 is the direction of most variability. In contrast, DCA would choose PC-2, since it provides the highest discriminant power.

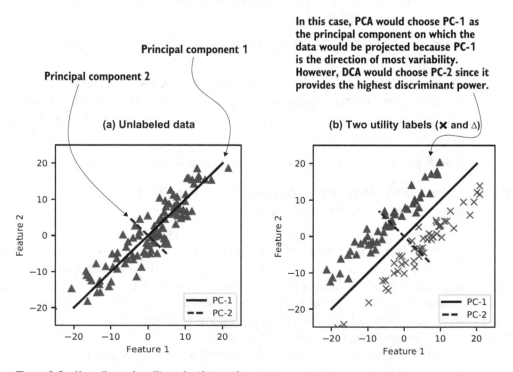

Principal component 1

Principal component 2

In this case, PCA would choose PC-1 as the principal component on which the data would be projected because PC-1 is the direction of most variability. However, DCA would choose PC-2 since it provides the highest discriminant power.

(a) Unlabeled data

(b) Two utility labels (✗ and △)

Figure 9.6 How dimensionality reduction works

Traditionally, PCA and DCA have been performed by gathering data in a centralized location, but in many applications (such as continuous authentication [5]), the data is distributed across multiple data owners. In such cases, collaborative learning is done on a joint dataset formed of samples held by different data owners, where each sample contains the same attributes (features). Such data is described as *horizontally partitioned*, since the data is represented as rows of similar features (columns), and each data owner holds a different set of rows in the joint data matrix.

In this situation, suppose a central entity (the data user) wants to compute a PCA (or DCA) projection matrix using the data distributed across multiple data owners in a privacy-preserving way. The data owners could then use the projection matrix to reduce the dimensions of their data. Such reduced dimensional data could then be used as the input to specific privacy-preserving ML algorithms that perform classification or regression.

In the case study in this section, we will be looking at the problem of a data user computing PCA and DCA projection matrices without compromising the privacy of the data owners. When it comes to distributed ML with PCA, privacy was not considered at all in early approaches. Later on, different privacy-preserving methods were proposed for PCA [6], but when it came to the implementation, they required all the data owners to remain online throughout the execution of the protocol, which was not very practical. In this case study, we'll provide a solution to this problem by proposing and implementing a practical DR method using PCA and DCA in a privacy-preserving way.

In contrast to earlier approaches, the protocol that we are about to explore does not reveal any intermediate results (such as scatter matrices) and does not require data owners to interact with each other or remain online after submitting their individual encrypted shares. This newer approach can be utilized as a privacy-preserving data preprocessing stage before applying other privacy-preserving ML algorithms for classification or regression. Thus, it ensures both privacy and utility while applying ML algorithms to private data.

9.4.1   Achieving privacy preservation on horizontally partitioned data

Before we get into the details, let's quickly walk through the key things that we'll look at in this case study. Computing projection matrices to facilitate distributed privacy-preserving PCA (or DCA) requires computing the scatter matrices in a distributed fashion. We will use additive homomorphic encryption to compute the scatter matrices.

In addition to the data owners (who hold the data) and the data user (who aims to compute the projection matrix), we will assume the existence of a third entity, a crypto service provider (CSP), that will not collude with the data user. When data owners send the data, they need to compute their individual shares, encrypt them using homomorphic encryption with the CSP's public key, and, finally, send these shares to the data user, who will aggregate these shares. After that, the CSP can build a garbled circuit that performs Eigen-decomposition on the scatter matrices computed from the aggregated shares (see the sidebar for a discussion of garbled circuits). Neither the data user nor the CSP can see the aggregated shares in their cleartext form, so data exchange protocols in this solution do not reveal any intermediate values, such as the user shares or scatter matrices. Moreover, this approach does not burden data owners with interacting with other data owners, and it does not require them to remain online after sending their encrypted shares, making these protocols practical.

What is a garbled circuit?

A garbled circuit (introduced by Andrew Yao) is a way to encrypt a computation such that it reveals the output of the computation but reveals nothing about the inputs or any intermediate states or values. The idea is to enable two mistrusting parties to communicate securely and execute a computation over their private inputs without the presence of a trusted third party.

Let's explore this in a simple example. Suppose that Alice has a private input x and Bob has a private input y. They agree on some computation function f (called the circuit) and both want to learn $f(x, y)$ but do not want the other party to learn anything more than that, such as intermediate values or the other's input. This is what they will do:

- Both parties need to agree on how to express f. Then Alice converts the circuit f to its garbled version and sends that to Bob with the garbled version of her input $\hat{x}$.
- Bob wants to create the garbled version of his input $\hat{y}$ without Alice learning what the original value y was. To do that, they use oblivious transfer (OT) techniques. The oblivious transfer is a two-party protocol between a sender and a receiver by which the sender transfers some information to the receiver, but the sender remains oblivious to what information the receiver actually obtains.
- Now that Bob has the garbled circuit and the garbled inputs $\hat{x}$ and $\hat{y}$ for that circuit, he can evaluate the garbled circuit and learn $f(x, y)$ and reveal it to Alice. Therefore, the protocol reveals no more than $f(x, y)$.

9.4.2 *Recapping dimensionality reduction approaches*

Later in this chapter we'll use the dimensionality reduction (DR) techniques that we discussed earlier and other privacy-enhancing techniques to achieve privacy preservation for PCA and DCA. Let's quickly recap the DR methods that we discussed.

PCA is a DR method that is often used to reduce the dimensionality of large datasets. The idea is to transform a large set of variables into a smaller set in a way that still contains most of the information in the large set. Reducing the number of variables in a dataset naturally comes at the expense of accuracy. However, DR techniques trade a little accuracy for the simplicity of the approach. Since smaller datasets are easier to explore and visualize, and because they make analyzing data much easier and faster for ML algorithms, these DR techniques play a vital role.

While PCA is an unsupervised DR technique (it does not utilize data labels), DCA is a supervised method of DR. DCA selects a projection hyperplane that can effectively discriminate between different classes. At a high level, the key difference between these two techniques is that PCA assumes a linear relationship to the gradients, while DCA assumes a unimodal relationship.

In addition to PCA and DCA, many other DR techniques rely on two different steps discussed at the beginning of this chapter: computing a scatter matrix and computing eigenvalues. In general, these DR methods can be distinguished in terms of which scatter matrices are needed and which eigenvalue problems need to be solved. For instance, linear discriminant analysis (LDA) is a method similar to DCA (both are utility driven). We will not be going into the details here, but the main difference is that LDA solves eigenvalues utilizing a within-class scatter matrix, whereas DCA uses a between-class scatter matrix.

While DCA and LDA are utility-driven DR techniques, another class of DR approaches concentrates on utility-privacy optimization problems such as the multiclass discriminant ratio (MDR) [4]. We looked into the details of MDR at the beginning of this chapter. At a high level, MDR aims to maximize the separability of the utility classification problem (the intended task), while minimizing the separability of the privacy-sensitive classification problem (the sensitive task). It assumes that each data sample has two labels: a utility label (for the intended purpose of the data) and a privacy label (for specifying the type of sensitive information). Hence, we can obtain two between-class scatter matrices: one that is based on the utility labels and a second that is computed using the privacy labels.

9.4.3   Using additive homomorphic encryption

To facilitate the crypto service provider's (CSP's) function, additive homomorphic encryption will be an essential building block in our protocols. In section 3.4.1 we discussed homomorphic encryption. As you know, there are multiple semantically secure additive homomorphic encryption schemes. We will look at how the Paillier cryptosystem [7] can be used as an example of such encryption schemes. Let's say function $E_{pk}[\cdot]$ is an encryption operation indexed by a public key pk, and suppose $D_{sk}[\cdot]$ is a decryption operation indexed by a secret key sk. The additive homomorphic encryption can be represented as $E_{pk}[a+b] = E_{pk}[a] \otimes E_{pk}[b]$, where $\otimes$ is the modulo multiplication operator in the encrypted domain. In addition, scalar multiplication can be achieved by $E_{pk}[a]^b = E_{pk}[a \cdot b]$. If you are interested in more details of the Paillier cryptosystem, you can refer to the original paper. You'll need to understand the basic functionality of the homomorphic encryption scheme because we'll use it in the next section.

Such encryption schemes only accept integers as plain text, but in most use cases, you'll be dealing with real values when you are implementing ML applications. When dealing with ML, the typical approach is to discretize the data (the feature values) to obtain integer values.

9.4.4   *Overview of the proposed approach*

In this study, we'll consider the case of horizontally partitioned data across multiple data owners. The system architecture is shown in figure 9.7. Suppose there are N data owners where each data owner n holds a set of feature vectors $Xi^n \in \mathbb{R}^{k \times M}$ with M number of features (dimensions) and $i = 1, ..., k$. Here, k is the total number of feature vectors. Thus, each data owner n will have a data matrix such that $X^n \in \mathbb{R}^{k \times M}$. In addition, in supervised learning, each sample x has a label y indicating that it belongs to one of the classes.

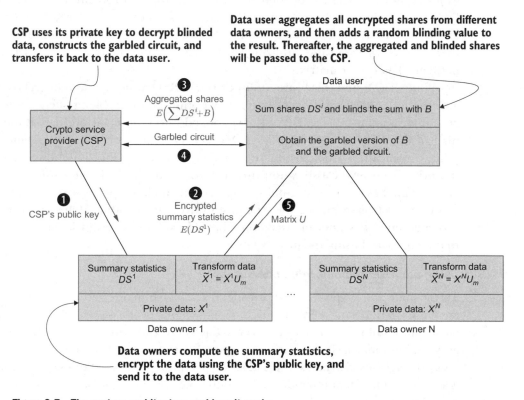

CSP uses its private key to decrypt blinded data, constructs the garbled circuit, and transfers it back to the data user.

Data user aggregates all encrypted shares from different data owners, and then adds a random blinding value to the result. Thereafter, the aggregated and blinded shares will be passed to the CSP.

Data user

❸ Aggregated shares
$E\left(\sum DS^i + B\right)$

Sum shares DS^i and blinds the sum with B

Crypto service provider (CSP)

Garbled circuit
❹

Obtain the garbled version of B and the garbled circuit.

❶ CSP's public key

❷ Encrypted summary statistics
$E(DS^1)$

❺ Matrix U

Summary statistics DS^1

Transform data $\tilde{X}^1 = X^1 U_m$

Summary statistics DS^N

Transform data $\tilde{X}^N = X^N U_m$

Private data: X^1

...

Private data: X^N

Data owner 1

Data owner N

Data owners compute the summary statistics, encrypt the data using the CSP's public key, and send it to the data user.

Figure 9.7   The system architecture and how it works

In this system, data users want to utilize the data and compute the PCA (or DCA) projection matrix from the data, which is horizontally partitioned among multiple data owners. There are many practical applications that fall under this data-sharing model. For example, with continuous authentication (CA) applications, a CA server needs to build authentication profiles for a group of registered users using ML algorithms, including DR techniques like PCA. Hence, the CA server (the data user) would need to compute PCA (or DCA) projection matrices using data that's distributed (horizontally) across all registered users (the data owners).

We will look into the details of each step later, but let's say there are two data owners, Alice and Bob, who would like to share their private data for a collaborative ML task. In this case, the ML task will be the data user. From a privacy standpoint, the most important concern is that any computation party, such as a data user or CSP, should not learn any of Alice's or Bob's input data or any intermediate values in cleartext format. That's why we need to encrypt the data first. But when the data is encrypted, how can the ML algorithm learn anything? That's where the homomorphic properties come into play, allowing you to still perform some calculations, like addition or subtraction, even with encrypted data.

Traditionally, PCA and DCA were only used in a centralized location on joint datasets (formed of data contributed by multiple data owners), but computing the projection matrix U requires the data owners to reveal their data. In this case study, we will modify the computation of the projection matrix to make it distributed and privacy-preserving. To facilitate this privacy-preserving computation, we'll utilize a third party (the crypto service provider), which will engage in a relatively short one-round information exchange with the data user to compute the projection matrix. The data owners can then use the projection matrix to reduce the dimensions of their data. This reduced dimensional data can later be used as input to certain privacy-preserving ML algorithms that perform classification or regression.

When designing a security architecture, it is important to identify the threats that could be potentially harmful or vulnerable to the solution we are developing. Therefore, let's quickly review the types of threats that we may face, so we can mitigate them in our solution. The main privacy requirement of our protocols is enabling data owners to preserve the privacy of their data. We'll consider the adversaries to be the computation parties: the data user and the crypto service provider (CSP). Neither of these parties should have access to any of the data owner's input data or any intermediate values (such as data owner shares or scatter matrices) in cleartext format. The data user should only learn the output of the PCA or DCA projection matrix and the eigenvalues.

The CSP's primary role is to facilitate the scatter matrices' privacy-preserving computation. To do that, the CSP is assumed to be an independent party, not colluding with the data user. For instance, the data user and the CSP could be different corporations that would not collude, if only to maintain their reputation and customer base. In addition, we'll assume all participants are honest but curious (this is the semi-honest adversarial model). This means that all parties will correctly follow the protocol specification, but they could be curious and try to use the protocol transcripts to extract new information. Hence, both the data user and the CSP are considered semi-honest, noncolluding, but otherwise untrusted servers. We will also discuss extensions that could account for a data user colluding with a subset of the data owners to glean private information pertaining to a single data owner.

All communication between the data owners, the data user, and the CSP are assumed to be carried out on secure channels using well-known methods like SSL/TLS, digital certificates, and signatures.

9.4.5   *How privacy-preserving computation works*

Now that we've covered all the necessary background information, let's proceed with the privacy-preserving computation of the scatter matrices and the PCA or DCA projection matrix. We'll suppose that N data owners are willing to cooperate with a certain data user to compute the scatter matrices.

PRIVACY-PRESERVING PCA

The first step in PCA is to compute the total scatter matrix in a distributed way. Let's say the total scatter matrix is $\bar{S}$ and that it can be computed in an iterative fashion. We have N data owners, and each data owner n carries a set of training samples, which we'll denote as P^n. Each data owner computes a set of values, which we'll call *local shares*, as shown in the following equations:

$$R^n = \sum_{i \in P^n} X_i X_i^T$$

$$V^n = \sum_{i \in P^n} X_i$$

$$Q^n = |P^n|$$

The total scatter matrix can be found by summing the partial contributions from each party as follows,

$$\bar{S} = \sum_{i=1}^{Q} (X_i - \mu)(X_i - \mu)^T = \sum_{i=1}^{Q} X_i X_i^T - Q\mu\mu^T = \sum_{n=1}^{N} R^n - \frac{1}{Q} V V^T = R - \frac{1}{Q} V V^T$$

where

$$R = \sum_{n=1}^{N} R^n, \quad V = \sum_{n=1}^{N} V^n, \quad Q = \sum_{n=1}^{N} Q^n$$

It is important that the data owners should not send their local shares to the data user in cleartext, since they include statistical summaries of their data. The local shares can be encrypted using an additively homomorphic encryption scheme (such as Paillier's cryptosystem) where the CSP provides the public key.

Upon receiving these encrypted shares, the data user can aggregate them to compute the encrypted intermediate values (namely R, V, and Q) and send them to the CSP for decryption after blinding the values. The data user can then use these aggregate values to compute the scatter matrix and the PCA projection matrix by using garbled circuits and oblivious transfer. Here, the *blinding* refers to adding random numbers to the encrypted values to prevent the CSP from learning anything about the data even in its aggregated form. (The values are blinded using an equivalent of a one-time pad.)

Let's look at how this protocol works step by step to ensure privacy while preserving PCA:

1   *Setting up the users*—During setup, the CSP sends its public key *pk* for Paillier's cryptosystem to the data owners and the data user based on their requests. This step could also include the official registration of the data owners with the CSP.

2   *Computing local shares*—Each data owner n will compute its own share $DS^n = \{R^n, V^n, Q^n\}$ using the equations we discussed earlier. After discretizing all the values to obtain integer values, the data owners will encrypt R^n, V^n, and Q^n using the CSP's public key to obtain $E_{pk}[DS^n] = \{E_{pk}[R^n], E_{pk}[V^n], E_{pk}[Q^n]\}$. Finally, each data owner sends $E_{pk}[DS^n]$ to the data user.

3   *Aggregating the local shares*—The data user receives $E_{pk}[DS^n] = \{E_{pk}[R^n], E_{pk}[V^n], E_{pk}[Q^n]\}$ from each data owner and proceeds to compute the encryption of R, V, and Q. More explicitly, the data user is capable of computing $E_{pk}[R]$, $E_{pk}[V]$, and $E_{pk}[Q]$ from the encrypted data owner shares as follows:

$$E_{pk}[R] = \otimes_{n=1}^{N} E_{pk}[R^n]$$

$$E_{pk}[V] = \otimes_{n=1}^{N} E_{pk}[V^n]$$

$$E_{pk}[Q] = \otimes_{n=1}^{N} E_{pk}[Q^n]$$

The data user adds some random integers to these aggregated values to mask them from the CSP, thus obtaining the blinded aggregated shares $E_{pk}[R']$, $E_{pk}[V']$, and $E_{pk}[Q']$, which can be sent to the CSP for decryption.

4   *Using garbled circuits for eigenvalue decomposition (EVD)*:

   a   Once the blinded aggregated shares are received from the data user, the CSP will use its private key to decrypt them, $E_{pk}[R']$, $E_{pk}[V']$, and $E_{pk}[Q']$. Since CSP does not know the random values added by the data user, the CSP cannot learn the original aggregated values.

   b   The CSP will then construct a garbled circuit to perform EVD on the scatter matrix computed from the aggregated shares. The input to this garbled circuit is the garbled version of the blinded aggregate shares that the CSP decrypted and the blinding values which are generated and held by the data user.

   c   Since the CSP constructs the garbled circuit, it can obtain the garbled version of its input by itself. However, the data user needs to interact with the CSP using the oblivious transfer to obtain the garbled version of its input: the blinding values. Using oblivious transfer, we can guarantee that the CSP will not learn the blinding values held by the data user.

   d   The garbled circuit constructed by the CSP takes the two garbled inputs and computes the scatter matrix from the shares R', V', and Q' after subtracting the data user's blinding values added in the previous steps. The CSP follows that by performing Eigen-decomposition on the scatter matrix to obtain the PCA projection matrix.

- e   The data user will receive the garbled circuit as its evaluator. This garbled circuit already has the CSP's garbled input (decrypted and blinded aggregate shares), and the data user obtains the garbled version of the blinding values using oblivious transfer.
- f   Finally, the data user executes the garbled circuit and obtains the projection matrix and eigenvalues as output.

That is how privacy-preserving PCA can be implemented and computed in practical applications. We will look at the efficiency of this method later in the chapter. Now let's look at how privacy-preserving DCA works.

PRIVACY-PRESERVING DCA

As we discussed in section 9.2, DCA computation requires the computation of the total scatter matrix $\bar{S}$ and the signal matrix S_B. Furthermore, some other DCA formulations also use something called the *noise* matrix S_W. We will first quickly outline the distributed computation of S_B and S_W, and then we'll move on to the protocol implementation details.

The computation of S_B and S_W could be different depending on whether the data owner has data that belongs to a single class or multiple classes. For instance, consider a spam email detection application where each data owner has spam and non-spam emails. This case represents two classes (spam and non-spam), and it is an example of a multiple-class data owner (MCDO). On the other hand, sometimes each data owner represents one class, as in continuous authentication systems. In this case, all their data would have the same label. This is an example of a single-class data owner (SCDO).

We will first review the equations for computing the scatter matrices S_B and S_W in a distributed way, and then we'll present the protocol that performs the DCA computation in a privacy-preserving way. Let's say each sample X_i has a label y_i indicating it belongs to one of the K classes $C_1, C_2, \ldots, C_k$. We'll let μ denote the mean vector of the training samples in class C_k, and M_k denote the number of samples in class C_k. With that, the noise matrix S_W can be calculated as follows,

$$S_W = \sum_{k=1}^{K} \sum_{i:y_i=c_k} (X_i - \mu_k)(X_i - \mu_k)^T = \sum_{k=1}^{K} \left(\sum_{i:y_i=c_k} X_i X_i^T - M_k \mu_k \mu_k^T \right) = \sum_{k=1}^{K} O_k$$

where the matrix O_k represents the share that pertains to class k. Since each data owner n maps to a single class k (in the SCDO case), we can write $O_k = O^n$ and have $S_W = \sum_{k=1}^{K} O_k = \sum_{k=1}^{K} O^n$.

As for the case of multiple-class data owners (MCDO), each data owner n will hold data belonging to different classes. We'll denote P_n^k as the set of training samples held by data owner n that belong to class k. For each class k, a data owner can locally compute

$$V_k^n = \sum_{i \in P_k^n} X_i$$

In addition, M_k^n can be computed as $M_k^n = |P_k^n|$, and the data owner would also compute the R^n similar to PCA, as it is not restricted to a certain class. Now the S_W can be arranged as follows in terms of the partial contributions from data owners,

$$S_W = \sum_{n=1}^{N} R^n - \sum_{k=1}^{K} \frac{1}{M_k} V_k V_k^T = R - \sum_{k=1}^{K} \frac{1}{M_k} V_k V_k^T$$

where

$$R = \sum_{n=1}^{N} R^n, \quad V_k = \sum_{n=1}^{N} V_k^n, \quad M_k = \sum_{n=1}^{N} M_k^n$$

Now let's look at how we can compute the signal matrix S_B. Both the single class (SCDO) and multiple classes (MCDO) are computed similarly. Moreover, the signal matrix can be computed directly from the aggregate data (V_k, M_k, V, M) described in previous equations as follows:

$$S_B = \sum_{k=1}^{K} M_k (\mu_k - \mu)(\mu_k - \mu)^T = \sum_{k=1}^{K} N_k \left(\frac{V_k}{M_k} - \frac{V}{M} \right) \left(\frac{V_k}{M_k} - \frac{V}{M} \right)^T$$

Unlike the scatter matrix, both the noise and signal matrices use class mean values in their computations. This will require the data owners to send per-class shares to the data user. If a data owner only sends the shares related to the classes the data owner has, this will leak knowledge of which classes belong to which data owner. Hence, it is recommended that all data owners send shares representing all classes, and when a data owner does not own certain class data, they can set that class share to all zeros.

Let's look at how the privacy-preserving DCA protocol works step by step:

1 *Setting up the users*—This step is very similar to what we did for PCA. The CSP sends its public key *pk* for Paillier's cryptosystem to the data owners and the data user based on their requests.

2 *Computing local shares*—Each data owner n computes R^n from its data, and for each class labeled k, the data owner computes V_k^n and M_k^n. As noted earlier, if a data owner does not have samples pertaining to class k, they still generate V_k^n and M_k^n but set them to zeros. After discretization and obtaining integer values, the data owner will encrypt R^n using the CSP's public key to obtain $E_{pk}[R^n]$, and will also encrypt the class-based shares (V_k^n and M_k^n) to obtain $\{k, E_{pk}[V_k^n], E_{pk}[M_k^n]\}$ for each class k. Finally, the data owner will send their own encrypted share DS^n to the data user.

3 *Aggregating the local shares*—From each data owner, the data user receives DS^n, which includes $E_{pk}[R^n]$, and for each class k, it also includes $\{k, E_{pk}[V_k^n], E_{pk}[M_k^n]\}$.

The data user then proceeds to reconstruct the encryption of R, the values of V_k, and the values of M_k as follows:

$$E_{pk}[R] = \otimes_{n=1}^{N} E_{pk}[R^n]$$

And for each class $k \in 1, \ldots, K$, the data user computes

$$E_{pk}[V_k] = \otimes_{n=1}^{N} E_{pk}[V_k^n]$$

$$E_{pk}[M_k] = \otimes_{n=1}^{N} E_{pk}[M_k^n]$$

Thereafter, the data user adds some random integers to these aggregated values to mask them from the CSP, thus obtaining the blinded shares $E_{pk}[R']$ in addition to the values of E_{pk} and E_{pk}. These blinded values are then sent to the CSP.

4   *Performing the generalized eigenvalue decomposition (GEVD):*

a   The CSP will use its private key to decrypt the blinded shares $E_{pk}[R']$ and the values of $E_{pk}[V_k']$ and $E_{pk}[M_k']$ received from the data user. Without knowing the random values that were added by the data user, the CSP cannot learn the aggregated values.

b   The CSP will then construct a garbled circuit to perform GEVD on the signal and the total scatter matrices computed from the aggregated shares. The input to this garbled circuit is the garbled version of the blinded aggregate shares that the CSP decrypted and the blinding values that were generated and held by the data user.

c   As we discussed in the PCA case, since the CSP constructs the garbled circuit, it can obtain the garbled version of its input by itself. However, the data user needs to interact with the CSP using the oblivious transfer to obtain the garbled version of its input: the blinding values. This oblivious transfer guarantees that the CSP will not learn the blinding values held by the data user.

d   The garbled circuit constructed by the CSP takes the two garbled inputs and removes the blinding values from the aggregated shares and uses the shares V_k' and M_k' to compute V and M. It then computes the total scatter matrix $\bar{S}$, and the signal matrix S_B, Finally, it performs the generalized eigenvalue decomposition to compute the DCA projection matrix.

e   The data user will receive the garbled circuit as its evaluator. We know that this garbled circuit already has the CSP's garbled input (decrypted and blinded aggregate shares), so they obtain the garbled version of the blinding values using oblivious transfer.

f   Finally, the data user executes the garbled circuit and obtains the projection matrix and eigenvalues as output.

This is how privacy-preserving DCA can be implemented in your applications and use cases.

> ### What is generalized eigenvalue decomposition (GEVD)?
> Given the matrices A and B, the GEVD aims to find the eigenvalues (called λ's) and eigenvectors (called u's) that satisfy the equation $Au = \lambda Bu$.
>
> You might think of reducing this problem to the regular EVD by computing the inverse of B and attempting to solve $B^{(-1)}Au = \lambda u$. However, $B^{(-1)}A$ is not always guaranteed to be a symmetric matrix. An important property of the scatter matrices is that they are symmetric. Eigenvalues of a symmetric matrix are always real, thus enabling us to have a simpler implementation of the power method that does not involve complex values.

You have now gone through the equations showing how to transform data using encrypted shares and how to execute eigenvalue decomposition to work with PCA and DCA in meaningful ML tasks while preserving privacy. In the next section we will evaluate the efficiency and accuracy of these different approaches.

9.4.6 *Evaluating the efficiency and accuracy of the privacy-preserving PCA and DCA*

So far in this chapter, we've discussed the theoretical background and different methods of implementing CP (particularly PCA and DCA) in real-world ML applications. Here we'll evaluate efficiency and accuracy of the implementations discussed in the previous sections of this case study (particularly in section 9.4.4). As we already discussed, when we integrate privacy into our ML tasks, it is important to maintain a balance between privacy and utility. Thus, we'll evaluate this to see how effective the proposed approaches are for practical ML applications.

In this case study, the datasets we used for the experiments are from the UCI machine learning repository [8]. While PCA and DCA work for any type of ML algorithm, we chose classification, since the number of datasets available for classification, which was 255, far outnumbered those available for clustering or regression (around 55 each). Moreover, as the efficiency of the proposed protocols depends on the data dimensions (the number of features), we chose datasets with varying numbers of features: 8–50. Tables 9.1 and 9.2 summarize the number of features and classes for each dataset. The SVM is used as the classification task for these evaluations, and the number of data owners is set to 10 in all cases.

ANALYZING THE EFFICIENCY

Tables 9.1 and 9.2 show the timing data for performing privacy-preserving PCA and DCA on different datasets using Paillier's key length of 1,024 bits. You can try this with different key sizes to see how it will affect the performance—you'll find that when the key length is longer, performance is affected adversely.

The average time cost for the data owner refers to the total time it took the data owner to compute the individual shares and encrypt them. The average time cost for data users represents the time needed to collect each share from each data owner and add it to the current sum of these shares (in the encrypted domain).

The tables also show the time it took the CSP to decrypt the blinded aggregated values received from the data user. Finally, they show the time needed to run the eigenvalue decomposition using garbled circuits to compute the PCA or DCA projection matrices. The values in brackets refer to the number of principal components generated using the garbled circuit. Naturally, reducing this number would decrease the computation time for a given dataset. As we will be discussing in the next section, even 15 principal components for the SensIT Vehicle (Acoustic) dataset is enough to achieve adequate accuracy.

Finally, you'll notice that increasing the dimension of the data will increase the computation time for all stages of the protocols, especially the eigenvalue decomposition.

Table 9.1   Efficiency of the distributed PCA

Dataset	Features	Classes	Avg. time cost for data owner (sec)	Avg. time cost for data user (ms)	CSP decryption time (sec)	Eigenvalue decomposition using garbled circuits
Diabetes	8	2	0.63	10	0.67	13.8 sec (8)
Breast cancer	10	2	0.93	11	1.0	20.7 sec (8)
Australian	14	2	1.7	12	1.8	37.4 sec (8)
German	24	2	5.0	17	5.0	3.28 min (15)
Ionosphere	34	2	9.8	24	9.9	6.44 min (15)
SensIT Vehicle (Acoustic)	50	3	22.5	40	22.7	13.8 min (15)

Table 9.2   Efficiency of the distributed DCA

Dataset	Features	Classes	Avg. time cost for data owner (sec)	Avg. time cost for data user (ms)	CSP decryption time (sec)	Eigenvalue decomposition using garbled circuits
Diabetes	8	2	0.7	12	0.8	4.0 sec (1)
Breast cancer	10	2	1.2	13	1.3	5.8 sec (1)
Australian	14	2	2.1	15	2.2	12.1 sec (1)
German	24	2	5.6	22	5.8	46.6 sec (1)
Ionosphere	34	2	11.2	29	11.6	1.9 min (1)
SensIT Vehicle (Acoustic)	50	3	26.2	48	26.9	6.7 min (2)

ANALYZING THE ACCURACY OF THE ML TASK

Figure 9.8 and table 9.3 summarize the results of performing experiments to test the accuracy of the classification tasks after using our privacy-preserving protocols compared to results obtained using the Python library NumPy.

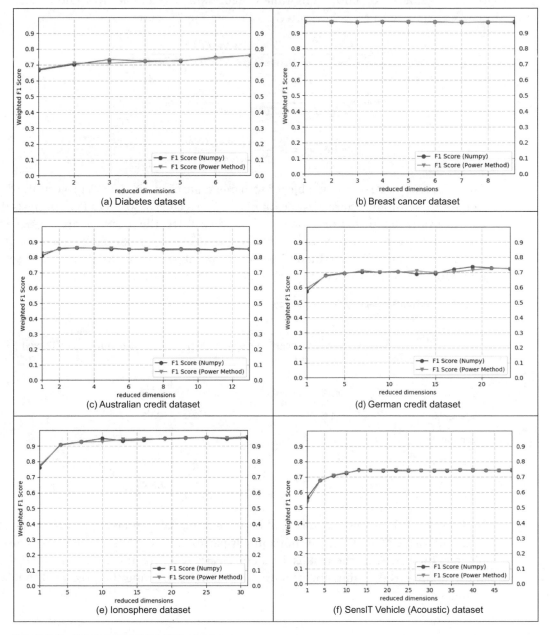

Figure 9.8   Privacy-preserving PCA accuracy

Here we are using the weighted F1 score to test the accuracy of the classifiers. The F1 score can be thought of as a weighted average of the precision and recall scores; a classifier is at its best when its F1 score is 1 and at its worst when the score is 0. The F1 score is one of the primary metrics utilized in ML applications to compare the performance of two classifiers. For more on how the F1 score works, refer back to section 3.4.3.

As a reminder, here is how you can calculate the F1 score:

$$Precision = \frac{TruePositive(TP)}{TruePositive(TP) + FalsePositive(FP)}$$

$$Recall = \frac{TruePositive(TP)}{TruePositive(TP) + FalseNegative(FN)}$$

$$F1\ Score = 2 \cdot \frac{Precision \cdot Recall}{Precision + Recall}$$

The DCA results are shown in table 9.3 with one value each, since DCA projects the data to $K-1$ dimensions (where K is the number of class labels), whereas PCA projects the data to a variable number of dimensions. As you can see, the protocols are correct and their results are equivalent to those obtained using NumPy. It should be noted that the slight fluctuation in the weighted F1 score is primarily due to the SVM parameter selection. However, the accuracy of both methods is almost the same.

Table 9.3   Privacy-preserving DCA accuracy

Dataset	F1 score % (with proposed implementation)	F1 score % (using the NumPy library)
Diabetes	76.5	76.4
Breast cancer	96.9	96.8
Australian	86.1	85.5
German	72.7	73.8
Ionosphere	84.3	83.4
SensIT Vehicle (Acoustic)	67.8	68.4

In this case study, we discussed how to implement privacy-preserving protocols for ML (particularly PCA and DCA) on horizontally partitioned data distributed across multiple data owners. From the results, it can be clearly seen that the approach is efficient, and it maintains the utility for data users while still preserving the privacy of the data owner's data.

Summary

- The main problem with DP-based privacy preservation techniques is that they usually add excessive noise to the private data, resulting in a somewhat inevitable utility drop.

- Compressive privacy is an alternative approach (compared to DP) that can be utilized in many practical applications for privacy preservation without significant loss in the utility task.

- Compressive privacy essentially perturbs the data by projecting it to a lower-dimensional hyperplane via compression and DR techniques such that the data can be recovered without affecting the privacy.

- Different compressive privacy mechanisms serve different applications, but for machine learning and data mining tasks, PCA, DCA, and MDR are a few popular approaches.

- Compressive privacy technologies like PCA and DCA can also be used in the distributed setting to implement privacy-preserving protocols for machine learning.

Putting it all together: Designing a privacy-enhanced platform (DataHub)

10

This chapter covers

- Requirements for a privacy-enhanced platform for collaborative work
- The different components of a research collaboration workspace
- Privacy and security requirements in real-world applications
- Integrating privacy and security technologies in a research data protection and sharing platform

In previous chapters we've looked at privacy-enhancing technologies that serve different purposes. For instance, in chapters 2 and 3 we looked into differential privacy (DP), which covered the idea of adding noise to data query results to ensure the individual's privacy without disturbing the data's original properties. In chapters 4 and 5 we looked at local differential privacy (LDP), which is a local setup for differential privacy, utilizing a locally deployed data aggregator. In essence, LDP eliminates the trusted data curator that we used in the original DP techniques. Then, in chapter 6 we discussed techniques and scenarios where synthetic data generation would be helpful instead of the aforementioned privacy techniques. In chapters 7 and 8 we looked into protecting data privacy, particularly in data mining and management, when data is stored in database applications and released for different data mining tasks. Finally, in chapter 9 we walked you through different compressive privacy (CP) strategies that project the data into a lower-dimensional space. We also discussed the benefits of using CP approaches, particularly for machine learning (ML) algorithms.

Now we are at the final chapter in this book. Here we'll walk you through applying privacy-enhancing technologies and methods to implement a real-world application, a platform for research data protection and sharing—we'll call it *DataHub*. In this chapter we'll look at the functions and features of this hypothetical system. Our goal here is to walk you through the design process of a practical application where privacy and security enhancement technologies play a vital role.

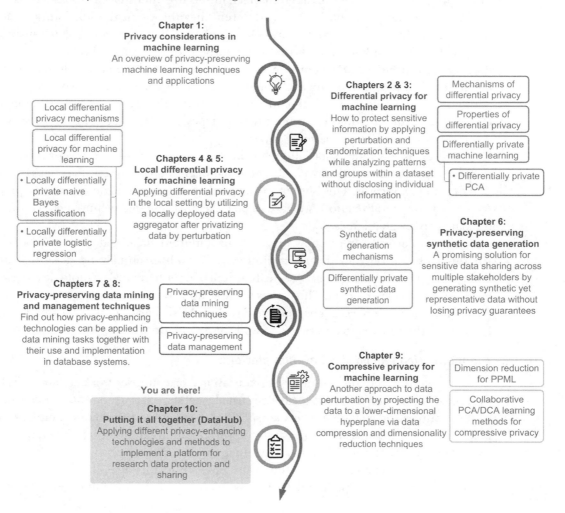

10.1   The significance of a research data protection and sharing platform

There are many application scenarios where privacy-enhancing technologies need to be applied to real-world applications to protect the privacy of individuals. For example, as we discussed in previous chapters, private data, such as age, gender, zip code, payment patterns, and so on, collected from e-commerce or banking applications needs to be protected so that it cannot be traced back by other parties to identify the original users.

Similarly, in a healthcare application you must ensure all the necessary privacy protections. Patient records and medication details must not be exposed, even for research purposes, without the patient's consent. In such situations, the best approach when utilizing this private information for purposes such as research is to apply some sort of privacy-enhancing mechanism and perturb the original data. But which mechanism works best? Can we use any mechanism in all the different use cases? This chapter will answer those questions by putting the different mechanisms together in a collaborative task.

Let's consider a scenario where different healthcare institutions work independently on finding a cure for a particular disease, such as skin cancer. Each institution works closely with its patients to develop advanced research studies. Let's assume that they are using an ML algorithm to classify skin cancer based on dermoscopic images to aid the research process. However, instead of each institute working independently, they could work collaboratively to improve the accuracy of the ML model. Different institutions could contribute varying types of data, which provides a more diverse dataset and, hence, better accuracy.

However, as you know, data collected from human subjects specifically for research purposes must be maintained securely and usually cannot be shared with other parties due to privacy concerns. This is where privacy-enhancing technologies come into play. As this is a collaborative effort, we have to pick the most suitable technology to ensure the data privacy guarantees.

This chapter will explore how we can allow different stakeholders to collaborate (in this case, various healthcare institutions). We will essentially be designing an end-to-end platform using a set of security and privacy-enhancing technologies to protect and share research data. The idea is to show how you can apply the technologies we've discussed in previous chapters in a real-world scenario. Our use case will be DataHub—the research data protection and sharing platform.

10.1.1   The motivation behind the DataHub platform

Researchers from different institutes, organizations, or countries work collaboratively to achieve a common scientific goal. They usually collect a large amount of data from various sources and analyze it to answer specific research questions. For example, suppose a cancer institute is doing research to prevent and treat mesothelioma, a type of cancer rarely seen in the US population. Since this is a rare cancer type, the data provided by mesothelioma patients at the institute is minimal. Hence, the researchers in this institute need more patient data from other cancer institutes, but other institutes may not be willing to share patient data due to privacy policies. Aggregating private data from multiple data owners is a significant problem in collaborative research.

Let's consider another scenario. Let's say a researcher is surveying individuals' political attitudes. The researcher may conduct a traditional face-to-face survey or use an online survey tool, but in either case the researcher obtains raw data containing private information about individuals. This raw data is vulnerable to misuse, as happened in the Facebook–Cambridge Analytica data scandal, which we briefly discussed in chapter 1—the data collected by Cambridge Analytica was used to attempt to influence voter opinions. As a result, there is increasing demand for systems that allow data sharing and aggregation while protecting security and privacy.

This chapter's DataHub is a hypothetical system that will accomplish those objectives. In such a system, we need to provide data storage security, eliminate data misuse, and maintain the integrity of research processes. Since human beings are the subjects of many research fields, such as medicine, biology, psychology, anthropology, and sociology, protecting the privacy of individuals is a fundamental requirement for researchers using data containing personal information. The DataHub platform we will design will solve this problem by providing privacy-preserving mechanisms for analyzing aggregated data from multiple data owners. Moreover, this platform will contain tools for conducting privacy-preserving surveys that collect perturbed data from individuals, with privacy guarantees. Essentially, we can improve survey participation and eliminate privacy breaches with these privacy guarantees.

10.1.2 DataHub's important features

There will be many different stakeholders for this application—data owners, data users, algorithm providers, and so on—so collaboration between the platform users needs to be facilitated through data or technology contributions and sharing, with privacy access controls specified by the data owners.

Let's look at the key features that we need in such an application:

- *Ensure the protection of data.* The collected data needs to be protected through security and privacy-enhancing techniques. Security can be ensured through data encryption/decryption and integrity checks during data storage and retrieval. Integrity verification can guarantee that the data is not altered unintentionally or maliciously. Privacy can be ensured by perturbing the data or analysis results using the privacy protection techniques, including synthetic data generation and privacy-preserving ML, that we discussed in previous chapters.
- *Allow the application to scale.* Once deployed, the system should leverage the advances in cloud computing and emerging distributed data processing techniques in database systems to scale the computations with the growing data and application requirements. The security and privacy techniques should be implemented through the data protection as a service deployed on virtual machines (VMs). More VM resources could be deployed dynamically as the amount of data and number of users increases.

- *Enable collaboration and participation of stakeholders*. The platform should facilitate collaboration through at least four roles: data owner, data provider, data user, and algorithm provider. In addition to research data, algorithms for data analytics and protection can be gathered and shared across institutes. Accessing the data and algorithms can be enabled through different role-based access control mechanisms.

Even within the context of data protection and sharing, there are many different application use cases. We already mentioned two: an application for data aggregation across multiple collaborating institutions, and an online survey tool to facilitate the data collection process. There could be many other use cases involving storing, analyzing, collecting, and sharing research data.

If you are wondering whether there are any established solutions similar to this, the answer is yes. For example, BIOVIA ScienceCloud (www.sciencecloud.com) is a cloud-based infrastructure that enables solutions for research collaboration. HUBzero (https://hubzero.org) is another open source software platform for hosting analytical tools, publishing data, sharing resources, collaborating, and building communities. Open Science Data Cloud (OSDC; www.opensciencedatacloud.org) is another cloud platform facilitating storing, sharing, and analyzing terabyte- and petabyte-scale scientific datasets. However, none of the existing solutions allow privacy-preserving queries or the analysis of protected data from multiple sources, which is what we are looking for. In addition, none of them provides a tool for conducting privacy-preserving surveys, which is a fundamental way of collecting information from individuals, especially in social sciences. This lack of privacy-preserving technologies means that the current platforms do not sufficiently support research collaboration. We will fill this gap by facilitating a secure, shared workspace where multiple organizations and the scientific research community can collaboratively work on a cloud-based system that caters to all the needs of the scientific community under one roof, with privacy assurances.

10.2   Understanding the research collaboration workspace

We'll now elaborate on the design of the research collaboration workspace. DataHub will facilitate four different user groups on the platform: the data owner, data provider, data user, and algorithm provider, as depicted in figure 10.1. These different users can be configured through different user roles with a role-based access control mechanism. A platform user may also have more than one role in the system. For instance, a data owner may want to utilize the data of other data owners. In that case, the data owner could run a privacy-preserving algorithm as a data user.

As you can see in figure 10.1, data owners aim to allow researchers to use their datasets while protecting the security and privacy of these datasets. One way to achieve the security and privacy of a dataset is by integrating a scalable cloud-based secure NoSQL database solution called SEC-NoSQL [1] into the architecture.

Whenever a data owner submits their data to DataHub, it is stored securely in a database. To facilitate that, one solution would be for the data owner to encrypt that

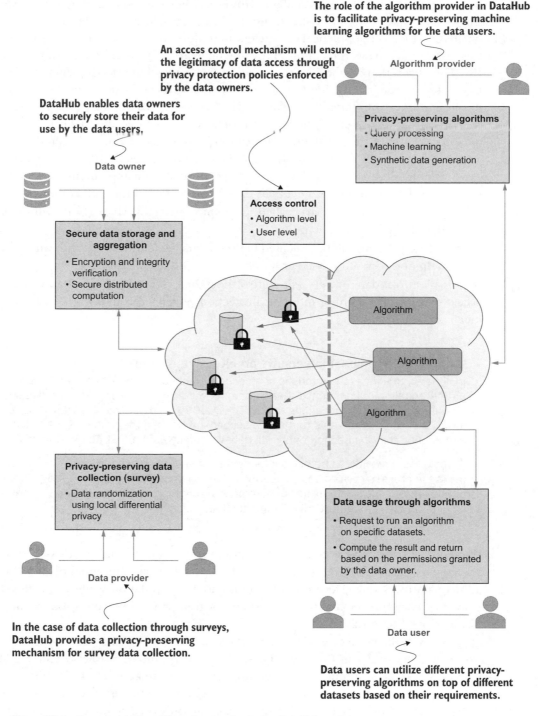

The role of the algorithm provider in DataHub is to facilitate privacy-preserving machine learning algorithms for the data users.

An access control mechanism will ensure the legitimacy of data access through privacy protection policies enforced by the data owners.

Algorithm provider

DataHub enables data owners to securely store their data for use by the data users,

Privacy-preserving algorithms
• Query processing
• Machine learning
• Synthetic data generation

Data owner

Access control
• Algorithm level
• User level

Secure data storage and aggregation
• Encryption and integrity verification
• Secure distributed computation

Algorithm

Algorithm

Algorithm

Privacy-preserving data collection (survey)
• Data randomization using local differential privacy

Data usage through algorithms
• Request to run an algorithm on specific datasets.
• Compute the result and return based on the permissions granted by the data owner.

Data provider

Data user

In the case of data collection through surveys, DataHub provides a privacy-preserving mechanism for survey data collection.

Data users can utilize different privacy-preserving algorithms on top of different datasets based on their requirements.

Figure 10.1   Overview of the different user roles in the DataHub system

information and put it in the database. However, whenever we wanted to query even a single data tuple from that dataset, the data owner would have to decrypt the whole database, which is not practical or efficient in multiparty applications. As a solution to this problem, the research community came up with a SQL-aware encryption concept [2]. The idea is that data will be encrypted in such a way that querying encrypted data is possible without decrypting the whole database. This can be achieved with layers of different property-preserving encryption. The SEC-NoSQL framework will provide data security through data encryption mechanisms and data integrity verification during data storage and retrieval. Integrity verification prevents data from being altered by any party unintentionally or maliciously. We will look into the details in section 10.3.1, but as a quick high-level overview, data security operations can be implemented in two trust models for data owners to protect their data from the rest of the DataHub:

- A semi-trusted third party called the crypto service provider (CSP) will provide the public key for encryption.
- The algorithms will be executed between data owners and DataHub without the help of the crypto service provider.

In this platform, data owners will control how their data can be used and who can access or use it by defining different protection policies through the access control mechanism.

What is a trust model in security architecture design?

In general, *trust* is a characteristic of a security architecture, and it can be thought of as the enabling of confidence that something will or will not occur in a predictable manner. For example, according to the ITU-T X.509 standard, trust is defined as follows: "An entity can be said to 'trust' a second entity when the first entity makes the assumption that the second entity will behave exactly as the first entity expects."

A trust model provides a framework for delivering security mechanisms. Trust modeling is the process performed by security architects to define a complementary threat profile. The result of the exercise integrates information about the threats, vulnerabilities, and risks of a particular IT architecture.

DataHub will also have a component for collecting data through privacy-preserving surveys (see figure 10.1). As we discussed in chapter 4, local differential privacy (LDP) allows data users to aggregate information about a population while protecting the privacy of each individual (the data owners) by using a randomized response mechanism (see section 4.1.2).

Moreover, data users can utilize data possessed by data owners by running privacy-preserving algorithms in DataHub. These algorithms could be privacy-preserving ML, query processing, synthetic data generation, and so on. In general, the data users will only learn the result of an algorithm if access is granted. The results of the algorithms will guarantee differential privacy, which is a commonly used standard for quantifying individual privacy, as we discussed in chapters 2 and 3.

Finally, DataHub can be extended by algorithm providers adding new algorithms (figure 10.1). This promotes collaboration between different institutions.

10.2.1 *The architectural design*

As a scalable system for the scientific community, DataHub will be a platform that manages all data and algorithms on a public cloud. As illustrated in figure 10.1, the main functionality of DataHub will be running privacy-preserving algorithms on protected datasets. NoSQL databases will be used for data storage because they provide better performance and high scalability for big data, and especially for increasing workloads. The detailed deployment architecture is shown in figure 10.2.

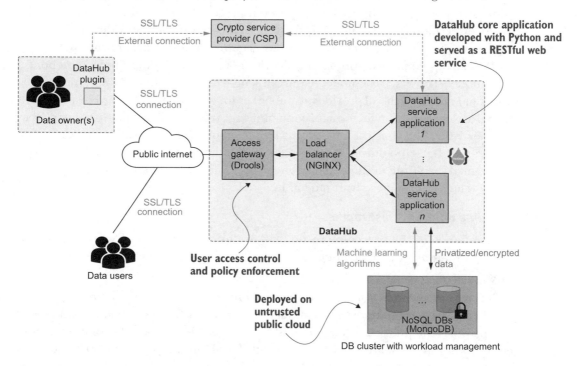

Figure 10.2   System deployment architecture of DataHub

Let's quickly go through the components shown in figure 10.2. As you can see, Data-Hub can be implemented on top of different commercially available, open source tools and technologies. The data owners and data users connect to the DataHub platform through the public internet, as they would access any web page. The access gateway will enforce the access policies during the login process to identify the privileges assigned to each user. If access is granted, the load balancer will distribute the load appropriately, and the request will be forwarded to the relevant DataHub service application based on the request type. We will be looking at the different service offerings later in the chapter. Each function performed by DataHub is offered as a service application (resource as a service). For example, ML is offered as machine learning as a service. Finally, to facilitate the secure delivery of some services, a crypto service provider is integrated.

> **NOTE**   Figure 10.2 identifies some of the most popular open source software products to give you an idea of their functions. This is just for reference. You can use your preferred software products.

In terms of deployment, we can pick the semi-honest trust model for DataHub. In the semi-honest trust model, each party in the system is assumed to follow the protocols correctly, but they might be curious about the data being exchanged and may try to obtain additional information by analyzing the values received during the execution of the protocols. Data owners cannot fully trust a cloud-based service provider, so DataHub will not require original data from data owners while running the algorithms.

We can develop privacy-preserving algorithms for two variations on the semi-honest trust model. The first trust model requires a semi-trusted third party, the crypto service provider (CSP), which will provide the public key for encryption. The algorithms for this model are more efficient in terms of communication costs. The second trust model does not need the CSP, but the algorithms require more communication between data owners and DataHub during their execution. In both models, it is possible to analyze aggregated data from multiple data owners, promoting collaborative research.

Now let's look at these trust models in detail.

10.2.2 Blending different trust models

As mentioned in the preceding section, we are using two different semi-honest trust models in our design architecture.

CSP-BASED TRUST MODEL

In this model, the idea is to use a semi-trusted third party, the crypto service provider (CSP) [3], to develop more efficient algorithms. The CSP first generates a key pair and provides the public key to be used by data owners for encryption. Since data owners do not want to share their raw data with DataHub, they encrypt their data and share the encrypted data with DataHub.

To perform computations over the encrypted data, we can use encryption schemes such as homomorphic encryption (we discussed a similar protocol in section 9.4). When DataHub performs the computation over several encrypted datasets for an algorithm, it needs to decrypt the results by interacting with the CSP before sharing them with the data user. This approach is practical since it does not require data owners to be online during the execution of the algorithms. However, it involves some assumptions, such as there being no collusion between the CSP and DataHub.

Figure 10.3 shows how an algorithm is executed in DataHub with the CSP. Each data owner first encrypts their data with the CSP's public key and sends it to the DataHub platform. Whenever a data user wants to access the data, such as to run an ML task on that data, DataHub will run the task on the encrypted data and obtain the results. Those results will then be blinded and sent to the CSP for decryption. Since the data is blinded, there is no way for the CSP to infer the data. Once the decrypted data is received, DataHub will remove the blind and send it back to the data user to fulfill the request.

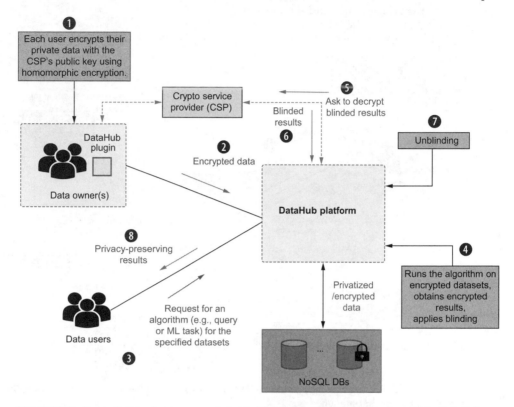

Figure 10.3   Executing a privacy-preserving algorithm for the CSP-based trust model in DataHub

NON-CSP-BASED TRUST MODEL

This model does not require the CSP to execute the algorithms. When an algorithm is being executed, DataHub directly interacts with data owners. There can be several solutions for this model. For instance, secure multiparty protocols between DataHub and the data owners can be developed, or each data owner can use their own keys for encryption and decryption.

We could use distributed differential privacy (discussed in chapter 3) as another possible solution for this model. When there is a request from a data user to run an algorithm over several datasets, DataHub could distribute the request among the owners of these datasets. Using the DataHub plugin, each dataset owner would compute its own share locally and apply differential privacy to the computed share. When Data-Hub collects all the differentially private shares from data owners, the result for the data user's request could be computed using private shares.

Figure 10.4 illustrates the execution of this distributed differentially private algorithm. Compared to the CSP-based model, this approach requires the data owners to be online during the execution of the algorithm, which requires more communication between DataHub and data owners.

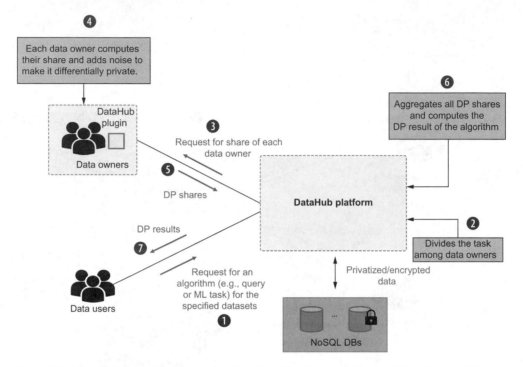

Figure 10.4   Executing a privacy-preserving algorithm (distributed DP approach) for the non-CSP-based trust model in DataHub

10.2.3   Configuring access control mechanisms

Identity and access management is an extremely vital part of any system for information security. Generally, an access control mechanism is a framework that helps manage an application's identity and access management. It is important that we use a proper access control mechanism in this system both to protect the system assets (the data and privacy-preserving algorithms) from unauthorized external parties and to manage how different assets can be accessed by internal users (the data owner, data provider, data user, or algorithm provider).

Access control policies usually can be described with reference to objects, subjects, and operations. The *object* represents specific assets to be protected in the system, such as the data owner's data and the algorithms. The *subject* refers to particular system users. The *operation* describes specific actions performed by the system users (subjects) on system assets (objects), such as CREATE, READ, UPDATE, and DELETE. One access control policy defines how a subject operates on a certain object.

Four main types of access control are employed in today's applications:

- *Discretionary access control (DAC)*—In the DAC model, the resource owner specifies which subjects can access specific resources. For instance, in operating systems like Windows, macOS, or Ubuntu, when you create a folder, you can easily add, delete, or modify the permissions (like full control, read-only, etc.) that you want to give to other users. This model is called *discretionary* because the access control is based on the discretion of the owner of the resource.
- *Mandatory access control (MAC)*—In the MAC model, users cannot determine who can access their resources. Instead, the system's security policies will determine who can access the resources. This is typically used in environments where the confidentiality of the information is of utmost importance, such as in military institutions.
- *Role-based access control (RBAC)*—In the RBAC model, instead of granting each subject access to different objects, access is granted to a *role*. Subjects associated with roles will be granted the corresponding access to those objects.
- *Attribute-based access control (ABAC)*—The ABAC model is an advanced implementation of RBAC, where access is based on different attributes of the objects in the system. These attributes can be almost any characteristic of users, the network, devices on the network, and so on.

DataHub is a role-based collaborative data sharing platform (as you saw earlier in figure 10.1), and it involves a large number of users (the subjects) accessing data (the objects). It would not be practical to individually manage the access of each subject to the many different objects. As such, we will design and implement an RBAC mechanism in our platform.

Now let's look at how RBAC can help us implement access control policies in DataHub. As shown in figure 10.5, there is a set of objects (e.g., dataset D_1, algorithm A_1), a set of subjects (e.g., user U_1, U_2, and U_3), and a set of operations (e.g., query processing, performing ML algorithms). For each object, we define different access control policies with different roles (e.g., R_1, R_2). Each role is described with certain attributes and rules. The attributes define the subjects associated with the corresponding role, and the rules define the corresponding policies. For instance, in figure 10.5 U_1 and U_2 are associated with R_1 defined within D_1, which also defines the rule "allow access to query processing." In this case, U_1 and U_2 are allowed to perform query processing on D_1. Similarly, U_3 is allowed to perform an ML algorithm A_1 on the dataset D_1.

In this design, an access control policy can also be submitted to DataHub by the corresponding users (e.g., data owners or data providers) along with their data. In this way, the data owners and data providers can have full control over their submitted data. They also have the option to control and monitor the algorithms that have access to their data. When new data users are added to DataHub, they can request access permission to a particular dataset. The data owner of the requested dataset can decide whether to add that user to one of the roles associated with that dataset. This is how the access gateway in figure 10.2 is facilitated.

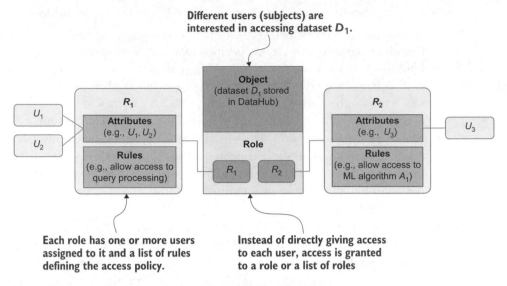

Figure 10.5   How role-based access control (RBAC) works

Now that you have a basic understanding of DataHub's architecture, let's look at how the privacy technologies work together to protect this platform.

10.3   *Integrating privacy and security technologies into DataHub*

As we mentioned earlier in this chapter, our goal is to show you how to combine different privacy-enhancing technologies in a real-world scenario. In this section we are going to look into the technical aspects of integrating these different technologies. First, we'll cover the data storage options, and then we'll extend our discussion to the ML mechanisms.

10.3.1   *Data storage with a cloud-based secure NoSQL database*

In chapters 7 and 8 we discussed how privacy-enhancing technologies can be used in data mining tasks and in database applications. As a quick recap, regardless of the data model we are using (whether relational or non-relational), security is a major concern in any datastore. But most modern database systems (especially NoSQL database systems) are more concerned about performance and scalability than about security.

Security-aware database systems based on different approaches have been researched for many years [2], [4]. One approach to ensure security for sensitive data in a cloud environment is to encrypt the data on the client side. CryptDB [2] is one such system developed for a relational database. It utilizes a middleware application to rewrite the original query issued by the client, so those queries are executed on the encrypted data at the database level. With this approach as a basis, we have explored the possibilities and implemented a framework called SEC-NoSQL [1], as depicted in figure 10.6. It ensures the security and privacy of NoSQL databases while preserving database performance for big data analytics.

The proxy server works as the middleware application. Upon receiving a request from the client, the proxy will rewrite the query such that it can be executed directly on encrypted data.

The data is stored in the cloud in encrypted format.

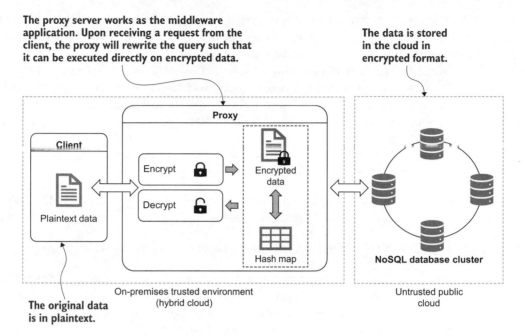

The original data is in plaintext.

On-premises trusted environment (hybrid cloud)

Untrusted public cloud

Figure 10.6   The architecture of SEC-NoSQL

The main idea behind the SEC-NoSQL framework is to implement a practical and security-aware NoSQL database solution that operates on the cloud with a guaranteed level of performance and scalability. In this design, clients only communicate with the proxy server as they would when directly storing data to or retrieving it from the database. First, the data owner issues a request to the proxy for database schema creation. The proxy transforms the schema by anonymizing the column names and executes that schema in the database. When a request appears at the proxy for a data write, it goes through the encryption mechanism, and the proxy generates a hash value (HMAC) of that record using the HMAC-SHA256 algorithm. This value will then be stored in a hash table maintained by the proxy. In the event of a read request, the proxy retrieves the encrypted record from the database, generates the hash value, and compares the corresponding entry in the hash table to ensure data integrity. If the integrity check is passed, the record will then be decrypted, and the corresponding results will be sent back to the client.

To facilitate queries over encrypted records, we need to implement cryptographic techniques that allow us to perform basic read/write operations over encrypted data. Different encryption algorithms provide different security guarantees. A more secure encryption algorithm can ensure indistinguishability against a powerful adversary, and some schemes allow different operations to be performed over encrypted data.

By following the approach suggested by CryptDB, we have implemented a different set of encryption algorithms to facilitate a different set of SQL queries over encrypted data. Based on different cryptographic operations such as random encryption, deterministic encryption, order-preserving encryption, and homomorphic encryption, SEC-NoSQL can operate and process various queries over encrypted data without much affecting the level of database performance.

With that basic understanding of how SEC-NoSQL works, let's quickly look at a simple example of how the query operations work. Suppose we are using MongoDB as our backend database, and we need to insert the ID and name of an employee in the table_emp table in the database. In MongoDB, we can do so by executing something like the following:

```
db.table_emp.insertOne({col_id: 1, col_name: 'xyz'})
```

However, when this query is received by the middleware application in SEC-NoSQL, it will be translated to something like the following:

```
db.table_one.insertOne({col_one: DET(1), col_two: RND('xyz')})
```

As you can see, all the table and column names will be anonymized, and the data will be encrypted (here, DET means deterministic encryption). This is how a simple INSERT operation works. A similar approach can be followed to implement the READ, UPDATE, and DELETE operations.

10.3.2 *Privacy-preserving data collection with local differential privacy*

We discussed the fundamentals and applications of local differential privacy (LDP) in chapters 4 and 5. One potential use case for LDP is for online surveys. Researchers use surveys for various purposes, such as analyzing behavior or assessing thoughts and opinions.

Collecting survey information from individuals for research purposes is challenging for privacy reasons. Individuals may not trust the data collector enough to share sensitive information. Although an individual may participate in a survey anonymously, it is still be possible to identify the person by using the information provided [5]. LDP is one solution to this problem. As you'll probably recall, LDP is a way of ensuring individual privacy when the data collector is not trusted. LDP aims to guarantee that when an individual provides a value, it should be difficult to identify what the original value is.

So how can we use LDP in our DataHub platform? Before we answer that, let's quickly revisit the fundamentals of LDP. LDP protocols consist of three main steps. First, each user encodes their values (or data) using an encoding scheme. Then, each user perturbs their encoded values and sends them to the data collector. Finally, the data collector aggregates all the reported values and estimates privacy-preserving statistics. Figure 10.7, which you saw earlier in chapter 4, illustrates this LDP process.

We will design an online survey tool for our DataHub platform, as shown in figure 10.8, by implementing the existing LDP methods for collecting data from individuals (data providers) and estimating statistics about the population. Since each value will be perturbed before it is sent to DataHub, the data providers will not be concerned about their privacy.

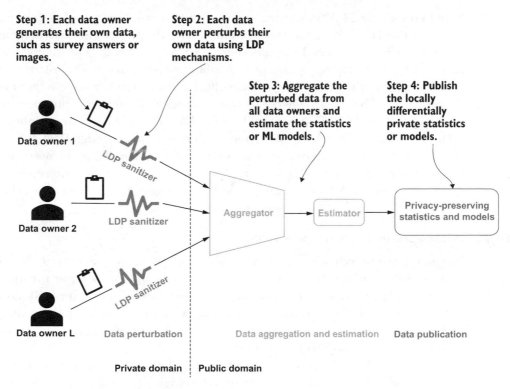

Figure 10.7   How local differential privacy works

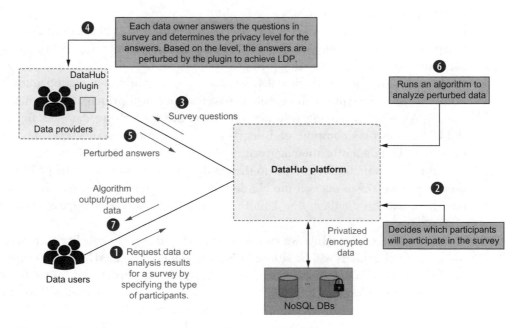

Figure 10.8   Privacy-preserving survey mechanism of DataHub

Most of the existing LDP implementation schemes assume that a single ϵ value is determined by the data collector and used by individuals. However, individuals may have different privacy preferences. In our approach, we plan to allow data providers to select a privacy level for each piece of information submitted to DataHub. For instance, an individual may share their age with the data collector, while another may prefer to hide it. Researchers will be able to collect data from individuals for different purposes by guaranteeing each individual's privacy under LDP. Each individual will control the level of their privacy when they share information with researchers through DataHub.

The same architecture can be used not just for fundamental problems such as frequency estimation but also for other analyses such as classification and regression. As discussed in section 5.3, we can use the perturbed data to train a naive Bayes classifier, which can then be used for different tasks.

10.3.3 *Privacy-preserving machine learning*

Machine learning relies heavily on the underlying data, and data privacy becomes a critical concern when that data is coming from multiple parties. For instance, data may be distributed among several parties, and they may want to run an ML task without revealing their data. Or a data owner may want to run an ML task on their data and share the learned model with other parties. In that case, the model shouldn't reveal any information about the training data.

There are different approaches to addressing this problem, and these approaches can be broadly grouped into two categories: cryptographic-based approaches and perturbation-based approaches.

CRYPTOGRAPHIC-BASED APPROACHES

In cryptographic-based privacy-preserving machine learning (PPML) solutions, homomorphic encryption, garbled circuits, and secret-sharing techniques are the widely used mechanisms for protecting privacy.

In the case study in section 9.4, we discussed a hybrid system utilizing additive homomorphic encryption and garbled circuits to perform principal component analysis (PCA) without leaking information about the underlying data. As figure 10.9 shows, data owners compute and encrypt summary statistics and send them to the data user. The data user then aggregates all the encrypted shares from the data owners, adds a random blinding value to the results, and passes them to the CSP. The CSP uses its private key to decrypt the blinded data, constructs garbled circuits, and transfers them back to the data user. Finally, the data user executes the garbled circuits to obtain outputs.

In the case of DataHub, we can slightly modify this protocol. For instance, since the encrypted datasets will be stored in NoSQL databases, DataHub can compute the local share of each data owner using homomorphic properties and follow the protocol. In the trust model with the CSP, DataHub does not need to interact with the data owners and can decrypt the results with the help of the CSP.

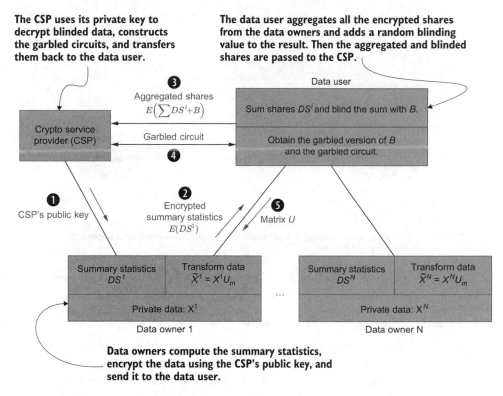

The CSP uses its private key to decrypt blinded data, constructs the garbled circuits, and transfers them back to the data user.

The data user aggregates all the encrypted shares from the data owners and adds a random blinding value to the result. Then the aggregated and blinded shares are passed to the CSP.

Data user

Aggregated shares
$E\left(\sum DS^i + B\right)$

Sum shares DS^i and blind the sum with B.

Crypto service provider (CSP)

Garbled circuit

Obtain the garbled version of B and the garbled circuit.

CSP's public key

Encrypted summary statistics
$E(DS^1)$

Matrix U

Summary statistics DS^1

Transform data $\tilde{X}^1 = X^1 U_m$

Summary statistics DS^N

Transform data $\tilde{X}^N = X^N U_m$

Private data: X^1

Private data: X^N

Data owner 1

Data owner N

Data owners compute the summary statistics, encrypt the data using the CSP's public key, and send it to the data user.

Figure 10.9   Privacy-preserving ML protocol for cryptographic-based approach

PERTURBATION-BASED APPROACHES

We discussed the use of differential privacy (DP) in chapters 2 and 3. As a quick recap, DP aims to protect the privacy of individuals while releasing aggregate information from the database, preventing membership inference attacks by adding randomness to the algorithm's outcome. We will use DP with our perturbation-based approaches.

Several different privacy-preserving ML algorithms have been developed to satisfy DP. Among these, the research community has investigated differentially private PCA with different approaches. Some approaches estimate the covariance matrix of the data by adding a symmetric Gaussian noise matrix, while others have used the Wishart distribution to approximate the covariance matrix. Both approaches assume the data has already been collected. In section 3.4 we explored a highly efficient and scalable differentially private distributed PCA protocol (DPDPCA) for horizontally partitioned data. We will use that protocol here in DataHub.

As shown in figure 10.10, each data owner encrypts their share of data and sends it to the proxy, a semi-trusted party between the data user and data owners. The proxy aggregates the received encrypted share from each data owner. To prevent the inference from PCA, a noise matrix is added to the aggregated result by the proxy, which makes the approximation of the scatter matrix satisfy (ε, δ)-differential privacy. The

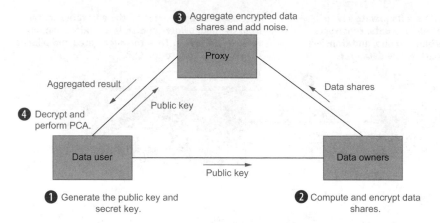

Figure 10.10   Privacy-preserving ML protocol for the perturbation-based approach

aggregated result is sent to the data user, which decrypts the result, constructs an approximation of the scatter matrix, and proceeds to PCA.

10.3.4   *Privacy-preserving query processing*

Now let's look at how query processing can be facilitated with DataHub. As we discussed in section 10.2.2, the DataHub platform will support two trust models: the CSP-based trust model and the non-CSP-based trust model, where the CSP is a semi-honest third party. Therefore, we will develop algorithms to process queries on one or more protected datasets for both trust models. This query-processing functionality can be enabled with two different approaches. The first enables query processing through the SEC-NoSQL framework, while the other enables differentially private query processing. Each approach has its own merits and demerits, so let's review the technical aspects of these approaches in detail.

Our current SEC-NoSQL framework supports the main CRUD operations (CRE-ATE, READ, UPDATE, and DELETE). By using other encryption schemes, such as homomorphic and order-preserving encryption, we can extend this framework to support different types of statistical queries, such as SUM, AVERAGE, and ORDER BY. In the CSP-based trust model, data owners will encrypt their data using homomorphic encryption with the CSP's public key and submit the encrypted data to DataHub, which can process aggregation queries with the help of the CSP. Using the SEC-NoSQL framework for processing queries under the non-CSP-based trust model is also possible. Each data owner can use their own public key and send the encrypted data to DataHub. However, when a data user wants to process a query, DataHub will need to interact with the data owners for decryption. This will reduce the practicality of query processing because data owners need to be online during query processing, and more communication between DataHub and each data owner is required.

A CSP is not required for differentially private query-processing approaches in the distributed setting. To satisfy differential privacy in numeric queries, we just need to add the required level of noise to the query results. However, when the data is distributed among several parties, deciding how much noise each party should add is not trivial. We discussed this matter in section 3.4.2. As a solution, Goryczka et al. [6] introduced a distributed differentially private setting for the secure sum aggregation problem. In the distributed Laplace perturbation algorithm (DLPA), each data owner generates a partial noise sampled from a Gauss, Gamma, or Laplace distribution, and the accumulated noise in the aggregator will follow the Laplace distribution, which satisfies DP. In practice, using the Laplace distribution for partial noise is more efficient for secure distributed data aggregation with privacy, and it adds less redundant noise. Therefore, DataHub will use DLPA for differential privacy in the distributed model.

10.3.5 *Using synthetic data generation in the DataHub platform*

In chapter 6 we discussed different use cases for synthetic data generation and why synthetic data is so important. Privacy-preserving query processing and ML algorithms are important, but sometimes researchers want to execute new queries and analysis procedures. When there is no predefined algorithm for the operation, we have to request original data from data owners so we can utilize it locally. That's where privacy-preserving data sharing methods such as *k*-anonymity, *l*-diversity, *t*-closeness, and data perturbation come into play. We discussed these privacy-preserving data sharing and data mining techniques in chapters 7 and 8. However, another promising solution for data sharing is to generate synthetic yet representative data that can be safely shared. Sharing a synthetic dataset in the same format as the original data gives us much more flexibility in how data users can use the data, with no concerns for data privacy. Let's look at how synthetic data generation mechanisms can be utilized in the DataHub platform.

DataHub will include a private synthetic data generation algorithm as a service, as was shown in figure 10.11. This algorithm will combine attribute-level micro-aggregation [7] and a differentially private multivariate Gaussian generative model (MGGM) to generate synthetic datasets that satisfy differential privacy. As discussed in chapter 6, the noise required to achieve DP for synthetic data is less than for other algorithms. Data users will be able to perform aggregation queries on a synthetic dataset, or they can use synthetic data with ML algorithms in DataHub.

To better capture the statistical features from the actual data, we can divide the attributes into independent attribute subsets. Attributes in the same subset will be correlated to each other and uncorrelated to the attributes in different attribute subsets. For each attribute subset, we can assign a synthetic data generator that includes micro-aggregation and differentially private MGGM. You can refer to section 6.4 for more about the implementation and technical details.

Our solution will be well suited for both trust models (with the CSP and without), which we discussed earlier. In the CSP-based trust model, DataHub generates the synthetic data with the help of the CSP. In the non-CSP-based trust model, the data owners generate the synthetic data and release it to DataHub. Figure 10.11 shows the steps involved in generating and using the synthetic data in DataHub for the non-CSP-based trust model.

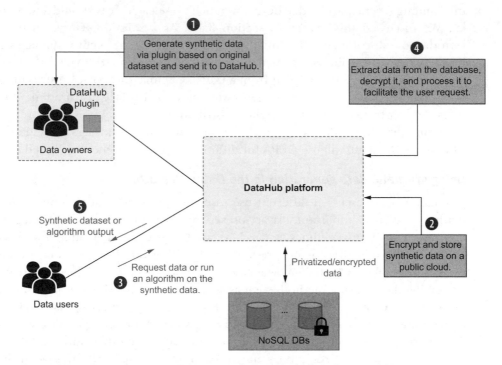

Figure 10.11   DataHub's synthetic data generation mechanism without a CSP

This concludes our discussion of the different features in the DataHub platform. We have explored possible ways of implementing and productionizing the privacy-enhancing techniques we discussed throughout this book by deploying them in a real-world scenario. DataHub is just one application scenario. You can use the same concepts, techniques, and technologies in your application domain. The relevant source code for each chapter is available in the book's GitHub repository, so you can apply any of the concepts we've discussed. Implement them, experiment with them, and make good use of them. Good luck!

Summary

- Throughout the book we've discussed various privacy-enhancing technologies that can serve privacy protection as a whole.
- These different concepts have their own merits, demerits, and use cases. When you want to implement privacy, it is important to look at the broader picture and choose the appropriate technologies wisely.

- Our privacy-enhanced platform for research data protection and sharing (Data-Hub) is a real-world application scenario that showcases how we can align different privacy-enhancing technologies toward a common goal.

- There are two main trust models—CSP-based and non-CSP-based—that we can integrate into DataHub's architectural design.

- Data privacy and security are essential when designing an application, especially for distributed, collaborative environments.

- We can store data in the DataHub platform with a cloud-based secure NoSQL database.

- DataHub can facilitate privacy-preserving data collection with local differential privacy and privacy-preserving machine learning in two different settings: using cryptographic-based and perturbation-based approaches.

- DataHub also provides synthetic data generation in both trust models (with CSP and without).

appendix
More details about
differential privacy

As we discussed in chapter 2, differential privacy (DP) is one of the most popular and influential privacy protection schemes. It is based on the concept of making a dataset robust enough that any single substitution in the dataset does not reveal private data. This is typically achieved by calculating the patterns of groups within the dataset, which we call *complex statistics*, while withholding information about individuals in the dataset. The beauty of differential privacy is its mathematical provability and quantifiability. In the following sections, we will introduce the mathematical foundations and the formal definition of DP. If you are not interested in these mathematical foundations, you can bypass this now and come back to it when necessary.

A.1   *The formal definition of differential privacy*

Before we introduce the formal definition of DP, let's look at some essential terms originally defined by Dwork and Roth [1]:

- *Probability simplex*—Let B denote a discrete set. The probability simplex of B, denoted $\Delta(B)$, is defined to be $\Delta(B) = \{x \in \mathbb{R}^{|B|} : x_i \geq 0 \text{ for all } i \text{ and } \sum_{i=1}^{|B|} x_i = 1\}$. You can consider the probability simplex to be the space of a given probability distribution.
- *Randomized algorithm*—A randomized algorithm M with domain A and discrete range B is associated with the mapping $M: A \rightarrow \Delta(B)$. Given an input $a \in A$, the algorithm M outputs $M(a) = b$ with probability $(M(a))_b$ for each $b \in B$. The probability space is over the coin flips of the algorithm M. We discussed how randomization in the algorithm happens with two coin flips in section 2.2.1.
- *Database*—A database x is a collection of records that form a universe X.

For instance, let the universe X define the set of unique elements in the database. Then a database could be represented by the histograms of the elements within the database, $x \in \mathbb{N}^{|X|}$, where each entry x_i represents the number of elements in the database x of type $i \in X$.

- *Distance between databases*—The l_1 norm of a database x is denoted $\|x\|_1$ and is defined to be $\|x\|_1 = \sum_{i=1}^{|x|} |x_i|$. Thus, the l_1 distance between two databases x and y is $\|x - y\|_1$.

- *Neighboring databases*—Two databases, x, y, are defined to be neighboring databases if they differ only in one row. For instance, for a pair of databases $x, y \in \mathbb{N}^{|X|}$, if $\|x - y\|_1 \leq 1$, we consider x, y to be neighboring databases.

Now we are ready to introduce the formal and most general definition of DP. It provides the mathematical guarantee of a randomized algorithm that will behave similarly on neighboring databases.

- *(ϵ, δ)-differential privacy*—A randomized algorithm M is (ϵ, δ)-DP if for every two neighboring databases, x, y, and for all $S \subseteq Range(M)$, we have

$$\Pr[M(x) \in S] \leq e^{\epsilon} \cdot \Pr[M(y) \in S] + \delta$$

where $\Pr[\cdot]$ denotes the probability of an event, and $Range(M)$ denotes the set of all possible outputs of the randomized algorithm M. The smaller ϵ and δ are, the closer $\Pr[M(x) \in S]$ and $\Pr[M(y) \in S]$ are, and the stronger the privacy protection is. When $\delta = 0$, the algorithm M satisfies ϵ-DP, which is a stronger privacy guarantee than (ϵ, δ)-DP with $\delta > 0$. Usually people call ϵ the *privacy budget* in the definition of DP. A higher value of ϵ means that one has more privacy budget and thus can tolerate more privacy leakage. A lower value of ϵ means stronger privacy protection is required or provided. The privacy parameter, δ, represents a "failure probability" for the definition. With a probability of $1 - \delta$, we will get the same guarantee as pure DP (i.e., ϵ-DP, where $\delta = 0$). With a probability of $\delta > 0$, we get no guarantee. In other words,

- With probability $1 - \delta$, we have $\Pr[M(x) \in S] \leq e^{\epsilon} \cdot \Pr[M(y) \in S]$.
- With probability δ, we get no guarantee at all.

A.2   *Other differential privacy mechanisms*

Chapter 2 discussed three of the most popular differential privacy mechanisms: binary, Laplace, and exponential. To recap, randomization in the binary mechanism comes from the binary response (the coin flip), which helps us to perturb the results. The Laplace mechanism achieves DP by adding random noise drawn from a Laplace distribution to the target queries or functions. The exponential mechanism helps us cater to scenarios where the utility is to select the best response but where adding noise directly to the output of the query function would fully destroy the utility. In this section we'll discuss some other DP mechanisms.

A.2.1 Geometric mechanism

The Laplace mechanism (discussed in section 2.2.2) adds real-value noise to a query function's outputs. It works best for query functions that output real values, because adding the noise directly to the outputs won't make the outcomes meaningless. For query functions that output integers, you can still add Laplace noise but apply a discretization mechanism after that. However, this could reduce the outcomes' utility.

This is where the geometric mechanism comes in [2]. It is designed to add the discrete counterpart of Laplace noise (drawn from the geometric distribution) to query functions that have only integer output values. These are the definitions of geometric distribution and geometric mechanism:

- *Geometric distribution*—Given a real number $\alpha > 1$, the geometric distribution denoted as $Geom(\alpha)$ is a symmetric distribution that takes integer values such that the probability mass function at k is $\frac{\alpha-1}{\alpha+1} \cdot \alpha^{-|k|}$.

  The geometric distribution has properties similar to the Laplace distribution. The variance of random variables drawn from $Geom(\alpha)$ is $\sigma^2 = 2\alpha/(1-\alpha)^2$.

- *Geometric mechanism*—Given a numerical query function $f: \mathbb{N}^{|X|} \to \mathbb{Z}^k$, the database, $x \in \mathbb{N}^{|X|}$, and the privacy budget ϵ, the geometric mechanism is defined as

$$M_{Geo}(x, f(\cdot), \epsilon) = f(x) + (Y_1, Y_2, \ldots, Y_k)$$

where Y_1 are independent and identically distributed random variables drawn from $Geom\left(\frac{\epsilon}{\Delta f}\right)$, and Δf is the l_1-sensitivity of query function f.

THEOREM A.1 The geometric mechanism satisfies $(\epsilon, 0)$-DP.

The geometric mechanism could be applied to all the examples involving the Laplace mechanism in section 2.2.2, giving slightly better utility.

A.2.2 Gaussian mechanism

The Gaussian mechanism [1] is another alternative to the Laplace mechanism. Instead of adding Laplace noise, the Gaussian mechanism adds Gaussian noise and provides a slightly relaxed privacy guarantee.

The Gaussian mechanism scales its noise to the l_2 sensitivity (compared with the Laplace mechanism, which scales to the l_1 sensitivity), defined as follows:

- *l_2-sensitivity*—Given a numerical query function $f: \mathbb{N}^{|X|} \to \mathbb{R}^k$, for all pairs of databases, $x, y \in \mathbb{N}^{|X|}$, its l_2-sensitivity is $\Delta f = \max_{\|x-y\|_1=1} \|f(x) - f(y)\|_2$.

We can define the Gaussian mechanism based on Gaussian distribution and l_2-sensitivity as follows:

- *Gaussian mechanism*—Given a numerical query function $f: \mathbb{N}^{|X|} \to \mathbb{R}^k$, the database, $x \in \mathbb{N}^{|X|}$, and the privacy budget ϵ and δ, the Gaussian mechanism is defined as

$$M_{GM}(x, f(\cdot), \epsilon, \delta) = f(x) + (Y_1, Y_2, \ldots, Y_k)$$

where Y_i are independent and identically distributed random variables drawn from the Gaussian distribution $\tau = \Delta f \sqrt{2\ln(1.25/\delta)}/\epsilon$, and Δf is the l_2-sensitivity of query function f.

THEOREM A.2 The Gaussian mechanism satisfies (ϵ, δ)-DP.

Compared with other random noise, adding Gaussian noise has two advantages:

- Gaussian noise is the same as many other sources of noise (e.g., white noise in communication channels).
- The sum of Gaussian random variables results in a new Gaussian random variable.

Those advantages make it easier to analyze and correct privacy-preserving machine learning algorithms that apply the Gaussian mechanism.

A.2.3 *Staircase mechanism*

The staircase mechanism [3] is a special case of the Laplace mechanism. It aims to optimize the error bounds of the classic Laplace mechanism by tuning the tradeoff between the Laplace mechanism (whose probability density function is continuous) and the geometric mechanism (whose probability density function is discrete).

In the staircase mechanism, we usually define a loss function $L(\cdot) : \mathbb{R} \to \mathbb{R}$, that is a function of the additive noise, where given additive noise n, the loss becomes $L(n)$. Let $t \in \mathbb{R}$ denote the output of the query function $f(\ )$, and P_t denotes the probability distribution of the random variable that generates the additive noise. Then, the expectation of the loss function would be

$$\int L(n) \cdot P_t(dn)$$

The staircase mechanism aims to minimize the worst-case cost among all possible query output $t \in \mathbb{R}$:

$$minimize \sup \int L(n) \cdot P_t(dn)$$

For more information about how to formulate and solve such optimization problems, please refer to the original paper by Geng and Viswanath [3].

The staircase mechanism can be specified by three parameters: ϵ, Δf, and γ^*, which is determined by ϵ and the loss function $L(\ )$. Figure A.1 illustrates the probability density functions of the Laplace and staircase mechanisms.

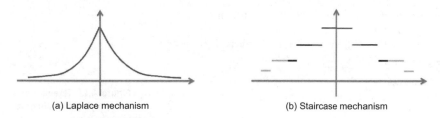

(a) Laplace mechanism   (b) Staircase mechanism

Figure A.1   Probability density functions of the Laplace and staircase mechanisms

A.2.4   Vector mechanism

The vector mechanism is designed to perturb vector-valued functions, such as the convex objective functions of many ML algorithms (linear regression, ridge regression, support vector machines, etc.).

The vector mechanism scales its noise to the l_2 sensitivity of a vector-valued function defined as follows:

- l_2-*sensitivity of a vector-valued function*—Given a vector-valued query function f, its l_2-sensitivity is defined as the maximum change in the l_2 norm of the value of the function when one input changes:

$$\Delta f = \max_{i} \max_{z_1, z_2, \dots, z_n, z_i'} \| f(z_1, z_2, \dots, z_i, \dots, z_n) - f(z_1, z_2, \dots, z_i', \dots, z_n) \|_2$$

Once the l_2-sensitivity of a vector-valued function has been defined (even though formulating such sensitivities in real scenarios, such as ML algorithms, is non-trivial), we could define the vector mechanism using independent and identically distributed random variables drawn from any other mechanisms, such as $Lap\left(\frac{\Delta f}{\epsilon}\right)$, where Δf is the l_2-sensitivity of the vector-valued function f.

A.2.5   Wishart mechanism

The Wishart mechanism [4] is designed to achieve DP on second moment matrices, such as covariance matrices. The basic idea is to add a Wishart noise matrix generated from a Wishart distribution to the second moment matrices. Since a Wishart matrix is always positive semidefinite, and can be considered as the scatter matrix of some random Gaussian vectors, it is a natural source of noise to generate the differentially private covariance matrix while maintaining its meaning and utility (because covariance matrices are always positive semidefinite and are also scatter matrices). Figure A.2 illustrates pseudocode for applying the Wishart mechanism on covariance matrices, where $W_d(\cdot, \cdot)$ is the Wishart distribution.

Input: Raw data matrix $X \in \mathbb{R}^{d \times n}$; Privacy parameter ϵ;
Number of data n;
1. Draw a sample W from $W_d(d + 1, C)$, where C has d same
    eigenvalues equal to $\frac{3}{2n\epsilon}$;
2. Compute $A = \frac{1}{n} X X^T$;
3. Add noise $\hat{A} = A + W$;
Output: $\hat{A}$;

Figure A.2   Pseudocode for applying the Wishart mechanism

A.3   *Formal definitions of composition properties of DP*

One very important and useful property of DP is its composition theorems. The rigorous mathematical design of DP enables the analysis and control of cumulative privacy loss over multiple differentially private computations. There are two main composition properties, and we discussed them in detail in section 2.3.3. In this section we'll explore the mathematical definitions of these properties.

A.3.1   *The formal definition of sequential composition DP*

The sequential composition property of DP confirms that the cumulative privacy leakage from multiple queries on data is always higher than the single query leakage (figure A.3). For example, if the first query's DP analysis is performed with a privacy budget of $\epsilon_1 = 0.1$, and the second has a privacy budget of $\epsilon_2 = 0.2$, the two analyses can be viewed as a single analysis with a privacy loss parameter that is potentially larger than ϵ_1 or ϵ_2 but at most $\epsilon_3 = \epsilon_1 + \epsilon_2 = 0.3$.

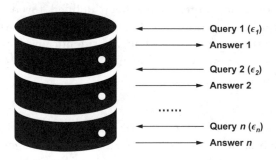

Query 1 (ϵ_1)
Answer 1

Query 2 (ϵ_2)
Answer 2

......

Query n (ϵ_n)
Answer n

Figure A.3   Sequential composition

We'll start with a simple case, where there are two independent DP algorithms, an $(\epsilon_1, 0)$-DP algorithm M_1 and an $(\epsilon_2, 0)$-DP algorithm M_2. If one applies M_1 and M_2 sequentially (where the output of M_1 becomes the input of M_2), then it follows the two-sequential composition theorem that follows.

> **THEOREM A.3**   Two-sequential composition: Let $M_1 : \mathbb{N}^{|X|} \rightarrow R_1$ denote a randomized algorithm that is $(\epsilon_1, 0)$-DP, and let $M_2 : \mathbb{N}^{|X|} \rightarrow R_2$ denote a randomized algorithm that is $(\epsilon_2, 0)$-DP. The sequential composition of these two, denoted as $M_{1,2} : \mathbb{N}^{|X|} \rightarrow R_1 \times R_2$ by the mapping $M_{1,2}(x) = (M_1(x), M_2(x))$, satisfies $(\epsilon_1 + \epsilon_2, 0)$-DP.

Having seen the two-sequential composition theorem, it should not be hard to extend it to a multi-sequential composition theorem that works for multiple independent DP algorithms that cascade sequentially, as follows.

THEOREM A.4 Multi-sequential composition 1.0: Let $M_i : \mathbb{N}^{|X|} \to R_i$ denote a randomized algorithm that is $(\epsilon_i, 0)$-DP. The sequential composition of k DP algorithms, M_i, $i = 1, 2, \dots, k$, denoted as $M_{[k]} : \mathbb{N}^{|X|} \to \prod_{i=1}^{k} R_i$ by the mapping $M_{[k]}(x) = (M_1(x), M_2(x), \dots, M_k(x))$ satisfies $\left(\sum_{i=1}^{k} \epsilon_i, 0\right)$-DP.

What if $\delta \neq 0$? What would the sequential composition look like? Take a look at the following theorem.

THEOREM A.5 Multi-sequential composition 2.0: Let $M_i : \mathbb{N}^{|X|} \to R_i$ denote a randomized algorithm that is (ϵ_i, δ_i)-DP. The sequential composition of k DP algorithms, M_i, $i = 1, 2, \dots, k$, denoted as $M_{[k]} : \mathbb{N}^{|X|} \to \prod_{i=1}^{k} R_i$ by the mapping $M_{[k]}(x) = (M_1(x), M_2(x), \dots, M_k(x))$ satisfies $\left(\sum_{i=1}^{k} \epsilon_i, \sum_{i=1}^{k} \delta_i\right)$-DP.

A.3.2 The formal definition of parallel composition DP

Now let's move to the parallel composition of DP. To summarize, if algorithm $F_1(x_1)$ satisfies ϵ_1-DP, and $F_2(x_2)$ satisfies ϵ_2-DP, where (x_1, x_2) is a nonoverlapping partition of the whole dataset x (figure A.4), the parallel composition of $F_1(x_1)$ and $F_2(x_2)$ satisfies $max(\epsilon_1, \epsilon_2)$-DP.

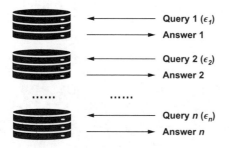

Figure A.4 Parallel composition

Suppose a single database x has been portioned into k disjoint subsets, x_i. Here, "disjoint" ensures that any pair of the subsets, x_i, x_j are independent of each other. In this context there may be k independent DP algorithms, but all of them satisfy the same $(\epsilon, 0)$-DP, and each algorithm M_i exclusively takes care of one subset x_i. The following parallel composition theorem will allow us to combine those k DP algorithms.

THEOREM A.6 Parallel composition 1.0: Let $M_i : \mathbb{N}^{|X|} \to R_i$ denote a randomized algorithm that is $(\epsilon, 0)$-DP, where $i = 1, 2, \dots, k$. The parallel composition of k DP algorithms, M_i, $i = 1, 2, \dots, k$, denoted as $M_{[k]} : \mathbb{N}^{|X|} \to \prod_{i=1}^{k} R_i$ by the mapping $M_{[k]}(x) = (M_1(x_1), M2(x_2), \dots, M_k(x_k))$, where x_i, $i = 1, 2, \dots, k$, represent k disjoint subsets of database x, satisfies $(\epsilon, 0)$-DP.

What if all the DP algorithms use DP budgets, thus satisfying different levels of DP in the parallel composition scenario? The following theorem provides the solution to this situation.

THEOREM A.7 Parallel composition 2.0: Let $M_i : \mathbb{N}^{|X|} \to R_i$ denote a randomized algorithm that is $(\epsilon_i, 0)$-DP, where $i = 1, 2, \ldots, k$. The parallel composition of k DP algorithms, M_i, $i = 1, 2, \ldots, k$, denoted as $M_{[k]} : \mathbb{N}^{|X|} \to \prod_{i=1}^{k} R_i$ by the mapping $M_{[k]}(\mathrm{x}) = (M1(x_1), M_2(x_2), \ldots, Mk(x_k))$, where x_i, $i = 1, 2, \ldots, k$, represent k disjoint subsets of database x, satisfies $(\max \epsilon_i, 0)$-DP.

references

Chapter 1

[1] J. Feng and A.K. Jain, "Fingerprint Reconstruction: From Minutiae to Phase," *IEEE Trans. Pattern Anal. Mach. Intell.*, vol. 33, no. 2, pp. 209–223, 2011, doi: 10.1109/TPAMI.2010.77.

[2] M. Al-Rubaie and J.M. Chang, "Reconstruction Attacks Against Mobile-Based Continuous Authentication Systems in the Cloud," *IEEE Trans. Inf. Forensics Secur.*, vol. 11, no. 12, pp. 2648–2663, 2016, doi: 10.1109/TIFS.2016.2594132.

[3] S. Garfinkel, J.M. Abowd, and C. Martindale, "Understanding Database Reconstruction Attacks on Public Data," *Commun. ACM*, vol. 62, no. 3, pp. 46-53, March 2019, doi: 10.1145/3287287.

[4] M. Fredrikson, S. Jha, and T. Ristenpart, "Model Inversion Attacks that Exploit Confidence Information and Basic Countermeasures," *Proc. ACM Conf. Comput. Commun. Secur.*, October 2015, pp. 1322–1333, 2015, doi: 10.1145/2810103.2813677.

[5] R. Shokri, M. Stronati, C. Song, and V. Shmatikov, "Membership Inference Attacks Against Machine Learning Models," *Proc. - IEEE Symp. Secur. Priv.*, pp. 3–18, 2017, doi: 10.1109/SP.2017.41.

[6] A. Narayanan and V. Shmatikov, "Robust de-anonymization of large sparse datasets," *Proc. - IEEE Symp. Secur. Priv.*, pp. 111–125, 2008, doi: 10.1109/SP.2008.33.

[7] M. Barbaro and T. Zeller, "A Face Is Exposed for AOL Searcher No. 4417749," *New York Times*, August 9, 2006, pp. 1–3, 2006, [Online]. Available: papers3://publication/uuid/33AEE899-4F9D-4C05-AFC7-70B2FF16069D.

[8] A. Narayanan and V. Shmatikov, "How To Break Anonymity of the Netflix Prize Dataset," 2006, [Online]. Available: http://arxiv.org/abs/cs/0610105.

[9] B. Cyphers and K. Veeramachaneni, "AnonML: Locally Private Machine Learning Over a Network of Peers," *Proc. - 2017 Int. Conf. Data Sci. Adv. Anal.*, pp. 549–560, doi: 10.1109/DSAA.2017.80.

[10] M. Hardt, K. Ligett, and F. McSherry, "A Simple and Practical Algorithm for Differentially Private Data Release," *Nips*, pp. 1–9, 2012, [Online]. Available: https://papers.nips.cc/paper/4548-a-simple-and-practical-algorithm-for-differentially-private-data-release.pdf.

[11] V. Bindschaedler, R. Shokri, and C.A. Gunter, "Plausible deniability for privacy-preserving data synthesis," *Proc. VLDB Endow.*, vol. 10, no. 5, pp. 481–492, January 2017, doi: 10.14778/3055540.3055542.

[12] J. Soria-Comas and J. Domingo-Ferrer, "Differentially Private Data Sets Based on Microaggregation and Record Perturbation," *Lect. Notes Comput. Sci.*, LNAI, vol. 10571, pp. 119–131, 2017, doi: 10.1007/978-3-319-67422-3_11.

[13] K. Liu, H. Kargupta, and J. Ryan, "Random projection-based multiplicative data perturbation for privacy preserving distributed data mining," *IEEE Trans. Knowl. Data Eng.*, vol. 18, no. 1, pp. 92–106, 2006, doi: 10.1109/TKDE.2006.14.

[14] X. Jiang, Z. Ji, and S. Wang, "Differential-Private Data Publishing Through Component Analysis," *Bone*, vol. 23, no. 1, pp. 1–7, 2014, doi: 10.1038/jid.2014.371.

[15] S.Y. Kung, "Compressive Privacy : From Information/Estimation Theory to Machine Learning," *IEEE Signal Process. Mag.*, vol. 34, no. 1, pp. 94–112, January 2017, doi: 10.1109/MSP.2016.2616720.

Chapter 2

[1] X. Shen, B. Tan, and C. Zhai, "Privacy protection in personalized search," *ACM SIGIR Forum*, vol. 41, no. 1, pp. 4–17, 2007, doi: 10.1145/1273221.1273222.

[2] A. Narayanan and V. Shmatikov, "Robust De-anonymization of Large Sparse Datasets," *Proc. - IEEE Symp. Secur. Priv.*, pp. 111–125, 2008, doi: 10.1109/SP.2008.33.

[3] C. Dwork, "Differential Privacy," in *International Colloquium on Automata, Languages, and Programming, 2006*, LNTCS, vol. 4052, pp. 1–12, 2006, doi:10.1007/11787006_1.

[4] C. Dwork, A. Roth, et al., "The Algorithmic Foundations of Differential Privacy," *Found. Trends Theor. Comput. Sci.*, vol. 9, no. 3–4, pp. 211–407, 2014, doi: 10.1561/0400000042.

[5] S.L. Warner, "Randomized Response: A Survey Technique for Eliminating Evasive Answer Bias," *J. Am. Stat. Assoc.*, vol. 60, no. 309, pp. 63–69, 1965.

[6] C. Dwork, F. McSherry, K. Nissim, and A. Smith, "Calibrating Noise to Sensitivity in Private Data Analysis," in *Theory of Cryptography Conference, 2006*, vol. 3875, pp. 265–284, 2006, doi: https://doi.org/10.1007/11681878_14.

[7] F. McSherry and K. Talwar, "Mechanism Design Via Differential Privacy," in *48th Annual IEEE Symposium on Foundations of Computer Science* (FOCS'07), 2007, pp. 94–103, doi: 10.1109/FOCS.2007.66.

Chapter 3

[1] C. Dwork, A. Roth, et al., "The Algorithmic Foundations of Differential Privacy," *Found. Trends Theor. Comput. Sci.*, vol. 9, no. 3–4, pp. 211–407, 2014, doi: 10.1561/0400000042.

[2] M. Hardt and E. Price, "The Noisy Power Method: A Meta Algorithm with Applications," *Adv. Neural Inf. Process. Syst.*, vol. 27, pp. 2861–2869, 2014, doi: 10.48550/arXiv.1311.2495.

[3] M. Abadi et al., "Deep learning with differential privacy," in *Proceedings of the 2016 ACM SIGSAC Conference on Computer and Communications Security*, pp. 308–318, 2016, doi: 10.48550/arXiv.1607.00133.

[4] J. Vaidya, B. Shafiq, A. Basu, and Y. Hong, "Differentially Private Naive Bayes Classification," in *2013 IEEE/WIC/ACM International Joint Conferences on Web Intelligence (WI) and Intelligent Agent Technologies (IAT)*, vol. 1, pp. 571–576, 2013, doi: 10.1109/WI-IAT.2013.80.

[5] K. Chaudhuri, C. Monteleoni, and A.D. Sarwate, "Differentially Private Empirical Risk Minimization," *J. Mach. Learn. Res.*, vol. 12, no. 3, 2011, 10.48550/arXiv.0912.007

[6] O. Sheffet, "Private Approximations of the 2nd-moment Matrix Using Existing Techniques in Linear Regression," *arXiv Prepr.* arXiv1507.00056, 2015.

[7] S. Lloyd, "Least squares quantization in PCM," *IEEE Trans. Inf. theory*, vol. 28, no. 2, pp. 129–137, 1982, doi: 10.1109/TIT.1982.1056489.

[8] D. Su, J. Cao, N. Li, E. Bertino, and H. Jin, "Differentially Private K-means Clustering," in *Proceedings of the Sixth ACM Conference on Data and Application Security and Privacy*, 2016, pp. 26–37 doi: 10.1145/2857705.2857708.

[9] S. Wang and J.M. Chang, "Differentially Private Principal Component Analysis Over Horizontally Partitioned Data," in *2018 IEEE Conference on Dependable and Secure Computing (DSC)*, 2018, pp. 1–8, doi: 10.1109/DESEC.2018.8625131.

[10] H. Imtiaz, R. Silva, B. Baker, S.M. Plis, A.D. Sarwate, and V. Calhoun, "Privacy-preserving source separation for distributed data using independent component analysis," in *2016 Annual Conference on Information Science and Systems (CISS)*, 2016, pp. 123–127, doi: 10.1109/CISS.2016.7460488.

[11] H. Imtiaz and A.D. Sarwate, "Symmetric matrix perturbation for differentially-private principal component analysis," in *2016 IEEE International Conference on Acoustics, Speech and Signal Processing (ICASSP)*, 2016, pp. 2339–2343, doi: 10.1109/ICASSP.2016.7472095.

Chapter 4

[1] Ú. Erlingsson, V. Pihur, and A. Korolova, "RAPPOR: Randomized Aggregatable Privacy-Preserving Ordinal Response," *Proc. ACM Conf. Comput. Commun. Secur.*, pp. 1054–1067, 2014, doi: 10.1145/2660267.2660348.

[2] J.C. Duchi, M.I. Jordan, and M.J. Wainwright, "Local Privacy and Statistical Minimax Rates," *Proc. - Annu. IEEE Symp. Found. Comput. Sci. FOCS*, pp. 429–438, 2013, doi: 10.1109/FOCS.2013.53.

[3] T. Wang, J. Blocki, and N. Li, "Locally Differentially Private Protocols for Frequency Estimation," *USENIX Secur.*, 2017.

[4] E. Yilmaz, M. Al-Rubaie, and J. Morris Chang, "Naive Bayes Classification Under Local Differential Privacy," *Proc. - 2020 IEEE 7th Int. Conf. Data Sci. Adv. Anal. DSAA 2020*, pp. 709–718, 2020, doi: 10.1109/DSAA49011.2020.00081.

Chapter 5

[1] N. Wang et al., "Collecting and Analyzing Multidimensional Data with Local Differential Privacy," *2019 IEEE 35th International Conference on Data Engineering (ICDE)*, 2019, pp. 638-649, doi: 10.1109/ICDE.2019.00063.

[2] J.C. Duchi, M.I. Jordan, and M.J. Wainwright, "Minimax Optimal Procedures for Locally Private Estimation," *J. Am. Stat. Assoc.*, vol. 113, no. 521, pp. 182–201, 2018, doi: 10.1080/01621459.2017.1389735.

[3] E. Yilmaz, M. Al-Rubaie, and J.M. Chang, "Locally Differentially Private Naive Bayes Classification," *arXiv*, pp. 1–14, 2019, 10.48550/arXiv.1905.01039.

[4] D. Dheeru and E.K. Taniskidou, "UCI Machine Learning Repository," 2017, http://archive.ics.uci.edu/ml (accessed Jan. 18, 2021).

Chapter 6

[1] D.C. Barth-Jones, "The 'Re-Identification' of Governor William Weld's Medical Information: A Critical Re-Examination of Health Data Identification Risks and Privacy Protections, Then and Now," *SSRN Electron. J.*, pp. 1–19, 2012, doi: 10.2139/ssrn.2076397.

[2] L. Sweeny, "k-ANONYMITY: A MODEL FOR PROTECTING PRIVACY 1," *Int. J. Uncertainty, Fuzziness Knowledge-Based Syst.*, vol. 10, no. 5, pp. 557–570, 2002, doi: 10.1142/S0218488502001648.

[3] P. Samarati and L. Sweeney, "Protecting Privacy When Disclosing Information: K Anonymity and its Enforcement Through Suppression," *Int. J. Bus. Intelligents*, vol. 001, no. 002, pp. 28–31, 1998, doi: 10.20894/ijbi.105.001.002.001.

[4] D. Su, J. Cao, N. Li, and M. Lyu, "PrivPfC: differentially private data publication for classification," *VLDB J.*, vol. 27, no. 2, pp. 201–223, 2018, doi: 10.1007/s00778-017-0492-3.

[5] K. Taneja, "DiffGen: Automated Regression Unit-Test Generation," in *IEEE/ACM International Conference on Automated Software Engineering*, 2008, pp. 407-410, doi: 10.1109/ASE.2008.60.

[6] S.C. Johnson, "Hierarchical clustering schemes," *Psychometrika*, vol. 32, no. 3, pp. 241–254, 1967, doi: 10.1007/BF02289588.

[7] J. Domingo-Ferrer, "Microaggregation," L. Liu and M.T. Özsu (eds.), *Encyclopedia of Database Systems*, Springer, Boston, MA., 2009, doi:10.1007/978-0-387-39940-9_1496.

[8] D. Dheeru and E.K. Taniskidou, "UCI Machine Learning Repository," 2017, http://archive.ics.uci.edu/ml (accessed Jan. 18, 2021).

Chapter 7

[1] C. of Massachusetts, "Group Insurance Commission," 1997, https://www.mass.gov/orgs/group-insurance-commission (accessed Jan. 05, 2020).

[2] R. Kohavi and B. Becker, "Adult Data Set," 1996, http://archive.ics.uci.edu/ml/datasets/Adult (accessed Apr. 26, 2020).

[3] P. Samarati and L. Sweeney, "Protecting Privacy When Disclosing Information: K Anonymity and its Enforcement Through Suppression," *Int. J. Bus. Intelligents*, vol. 1, no. 2, pp. 28–31, 1998, doi: 10.20894/IJCOA.101.001.001.004.

[4] CryptoNumerics, "CN-Protect for Data Science," 2019.

Chapter 8

[1] A. Machanavajjhala, D. Kifer, J. Gehrke, and M. Venkatasubramanian, "*L*-diversity: Privacy beyond k-anonymity," *ACM Trans. Knowl. Discov. Data*, vol. 1, no. 1, 2007, doi: 10.1145/1217299.1217302.

[2] L. Ninghui, L. Tiancheng, and S. Venkatasubramanian, "t-Closeness: Privacy beyond k-anonymity and ?-diversity," *Proc. - Int. Conf. Data Eng.*, no. 3, pp. 106–115, 2007, doi: 10.1109/ICDE.2007.367856.

[3] R. Kohavi and B. Becker, "Adult Data Set," 1996. http://archive.ics.uci.edu/ml/datasets/Adult (accessed April 26, 2020).

[4] N. Prabhu, "Anonymization methods for network security," 2018. https://github.com/Nuclearstar/K-Anonymity (accessed May 12, 2020).

[5] G.D. Samaraweera and M.J. Chang, "Security and Privacy Implications on Database Systems in Big Data Era: A Survey," *IEEE Trans. Knowl. Data Eng.*, vol. 33, no. 1, pp. 239-258, January 2021, doi: 10.1109/tkde.2019.2929794.

[6] B. Fuller et al., "SoK: Cryptographically Protected Database Search," *Proc. - IEEE Symp. Secur. Priv.*, pp. 172–191, 2017, doi: 10.1109/SP.2017.10.

[7] G. Kellaris, G. Kollios, K. Nissim, and A. O'Neill, "Generic Attacks on Secure Outsourced Databases," *Proc. 2016 ACM SIGSAC Conf. Comput. Commun. Secur. - CCS'16*, pp. 1329–1340, 2016, doi: 10.1145/2976749.2978386.

[8] P. Grubbs, T. Ristenpart, and V. Shmatikov, "Why Your Encrypted Database Is Not Secure," *Proc. 16th Work. Hot Top. Oper. Syst. - HotOS '17*, pp. 162–168, 2017, doi: 10.1145/3102980.3103007.

[9] M.S. Lacharite, B. Minaud, and K.G. Paterson, "Improved Reconstruction Attacks on Encrypted Data Using Range Query Leakage," *Proc. - IEEE Symp. Secur. Priv.*, pp. 297–314, 2018, doi: 10.1109/SP.2018.00002.

[10] M. Hosenball, "Swiss spy agency warns U.S., Britain about huge data leak," *Reuters*, December 4, 2012. https://www.reuters.com/article/us-usa-switzerland-datatheft/swiss-spy-agency-warns-u-s-britain-about-huge-data-leak-idUSBRE8B30ID20121204 (accessed January 15, 2019).

[11] C. Terhune, "Nearly 5,000 patients affected by UC Irvine medical data breach," *Los Angeles Times*, June 18, 2015. https://www.latimes.com/business/la-fi-uc-irvine-data-breach-20150618-story.html (accessed Jan. 15, 2019).

[12] J. Vijayan, "Morgan Stanley Breach a Reminder of Insider Risks," *Security Intelligence*, January 8, 2015. https://securityintelligence.com/news/morgan-stanley-breach-reminder-insider-risks/ (accessed Jan. 15, 2019).

Chapter 9

[1] F. Douglas, L. Pat, and R. Fisher, "Methods of Conceptual Clustering and their Relation to Numerical Taxonomy," *Ann. Eugen.*, vol. 7, no. 2, pp. 179–188, 1985.

[2] B. Scholkopft and K. Mullert, "Fisher Discriminant Analysis with Kernels," *Neural Networks Signal Process.* IX, pp. 41–48, 1999.

[3] S.Y. Kung, "Discriminant component analysis for privacy protection and visualization of big data," *Multimed. Tools Appl.*, vol. 76, no. 3, pp. 3999–4034, 2017, doi: 10.1007/s11042-015-2959-9.

[4] K. Diamantaras and S.Y. Kung, "Data Privacy Protection by Kernel Subspace Projection and Generalized Eigenvalue Decomposition," *IEEE Int. Work. Mach. Learn. Signal Process. MLSP*, 2016, doi: 10.1109/MLSP.2016.7738831.

[5] J. Šeděnka, S. Govindarajan, P. Gasti, and K.S. Balagani, "Secure Outsourced Biometric Authentication with Performance Evaluation on Smartphones," *IEEE Trans. Inf. Forensics Secur.*, vol. 10, no. 2, pp. 384–396, 2015, doi: 10.1109/TIFS.2014.2375571.

[6] M.A. Pathak and B. Raj, "Efficient protocols for principal eigenvector computation over private data," *Trans. Data Priv.*, vol. 4, no. 3, pp. 129–146, 2011.

[7] P. Paillier, "Public-Key Cryptosystems Based on Composite Degree Residuosity Classes," *International conference on the theory and applications of cryptographic techniques*, pp. 223–238, Springer, Berlin, Heidelber, 1999.

[8] D. Dheeru and E.K. Taniskidou, "UCI Machine Learning Repository," 2017. http://archive.ics.uci.edu/ml (accessed Jan. 18, 2021).

Chapter 10

[1] G.D. Samaraweera and J.M. Chang, "SEC-NoSQL: Towards Implementing High Performance Security-as-a-Service for NoSQL Databases," *arXiv*, 2019, [Online]. Available: https://arxiv.org/abs/2107.01640.

[2] R. Popa and C. Redfield, "CryptDB: Processing queries on an encrypted database," *Communications of the ACM*, vol. 55, no. 9, p. 103, 2012, doi: 10.1145/2330667.2330691.

[3] V. Nikolaenko, U. Weinsberg, S. Ioannidis, M. Joye, D. Boneh, and N. Taft, "Privacy-Preserving Ridge Regression on Hundreds of Millions of Records," *Proc. - IEEE Symp. Secur. Priv.*, pp. 334–348, 2013, doi: 10.1109/SP.2013.30.

[4] E. Pattuk, M. Kantarcioglu, V. Khadilkar, H. Ulusoy, and S. Mehrotra, "BigSecret: A Secure Data Management Framework for Key-Value Stores," *IEEE Int. Conf. Cloud Comput. CLOUD*, pp. 147–154, 2013, doi: 10.1109/CLOUD.2013.37.

[5] A. Narayanan and V. Shmatikov, "Robust De-anonymization of Large Sparse Datasets," *Proc. - IEEE Symp. Secur. Priv.*, pp. 111–125, 2008, doi: 10.1109/SP.2008.33.

[6] S. Goryczka, L. Xiong, and V. Sunderam, "Secure multiparty aggregation with differential privacy: A comparative study," *ACM Int. Conf. Proceeding Ser.*, pp. 155–163, 2013, doi: 10.1145/2457317.2457343.

[7] J. Domingo-Ferrer and V. Torra, "Ordinal, Continuous and Heterogeneous K-anonymity Through Microaggregation," *Data Min. Knowl. Discov.*, vol. 11, no. 2, pp. 195–212, 2005, doi: 10.1007/s10618-005-0007-5.

Appendix

[1] C. Dwork and A. Roth, "The algorithmic foundations of differential privacy," *Foundations and Trends in Theoretical Computer Science*, vol. 9, no. 3-4, pp. 211-407, 2014, doi: 10.1561/0400000042.

[2] A. Ghosh, T. Roughgarden, and M. Sundararajan, "Universally Utility-Maximizing Privacy Mechanisms," SIAM Journal on Computing, vol. 41, no. 6, pp. 1673-1693, 2012.

[3] Q. Geng and P. Viswanath, "The Optimal Mechanism in Differential Privacy," *2014 IEEE International Symposium on Information Theory*, 2014, pp. 2371-2375, doi: 10.1109/ISIT.2014.6875258.

[4] H. Imtiaz and A.D. Sarwate, "Symmetric Matrix Perturbation for Differentially-Private Principal Component Analysis," *2016 IEEE International Conference on Acoustics, Speech and Signal Processing*, 2016, pp. 2339-2343, doi: 10.1109/ICASSP.2016.7472095.

index

A

ABAC (attribute-based access control) 229, 279
access control
  implementing fine-grained 229
  supporting attribute-level 228
  types of 279
accuracy 218–219
additive homomorphic encryption 255
adult dataset 66, 69
age attribute 213
agglomerative hierarchical clustering 168
AI (artificial intelligence) 3–5
AMI (adjusted mutual information) score 75
anonymization 151–155
  beyond k-anonymity 154–155
  private information sharing vs. privacy
    concerns 151–152
  using k-anonymity against re-identification
    attacks 152–154
ARI (adjusted rand index) 75
association rule hiding 20, 217–218
attacks 8–16
  challenges of privacy protection in big data
    analytics 15–16
    correlation attacks 16
    identification attacks 16
  de-anonymization or re-identification attacks 15
  membership inference attacks 13–15
  model inversion attacks 12–13
  on database systems 222–225
    targeting data confidentiality 223–224
    targeting data privacy 224–225
  problem of private data in 9

reconstruction attacks 9–12
  attacker's perspective of 10–11
  real-world scenario involving 11–12
attribute-based access control (ABAC) 229, 279
attribute-level access control 228
Australian dataset 172
AVERAGE query 286

B

big data analytics 15–16
  correlation attacks 16
  identification attacks 16
binary mechanism (randomized response) 35–37
binary response 35
binning method 138
bins 138
blinding 258
breast cancer dataset 172
budget, privacy 31–32

C

CA (continuous authentication) applications 256
categorical values 191
cloud-based storage 280–282
CNAE dataset 86, 88
complex statistics 25
composition properties 51–55, 296–298
  parallel composition 54–55, 297
  sequential composition 51–52, 296–297
compressive privacy 21–22, 237
concrete attacks 224
confidence parameter 217
confidentiality of data 223–224

RELATED MANNING TITLES

Data Privacy
by Nishant Bhajaria
Foreword by Neil Hunt

ISBN 9781617298998
384 pages, $49.99
January 2022

Interpretable AI
by Ajay Thampi

ISBN 9781617297649
328 pages, $59.99
May 2022

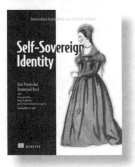

Self-Sovereign Identity
by Alex Preukschat and Drummond Reed
Foreword by Doc Searls

ISBN 9781617296598
504 pages, $49.99
May 2021

OpenID Connect in Action
by Prabath Siriwardena

ISBN 9781617298974
281 pages (estimated), $59.99
November 2023 (estimated)

For ordering information go to www.manning.com

A new online reading experience

liveBook, our online reading platform, adds a new dimension to your Manning books, with features that make reading, learning, and sharing easier than ever. A liveBook version of your book is included FREE with every Manning book.

This next generation book platform is more than an online reader. It's packed with unique features to upgrade and enhance your learning experience.

- Add your own notes and bookmarks
- One-click code copy
- Learn from other readers in the discussion forum
- Audio recordings and interactive exercises
- Read all your purchased Manning content in any browser, anytime, anywhere

As an added bonus, you can search every Manning book and video in liveBook—even ones you don't yet own. Open any liveBook, and you'll be able to browse the content and read anything you like.*

Find out more at www.manning.com/livebook-program.

*Open reading is limited to 10 minutes per book daily

MANNING

The Manning Early Access Program

Don't wait to start learning! In MEAP, the Manning Early Access Program, you can read books as they're being created and long before they're available in stores.

Here's how MEAP works.

- **Start now.** Buy a MEAP and you'll get all available chapters in PDF, ePub, Kindle, and liveBook formats.

- **Regular updates.** New chapters are released as soon as they're written. We'll let you know when fresh content is available.

- **Finish faster.** MEAP customers are the first to get final versions of all books! Pre-order the print book, and it'll ship as soon as it's off the press.

- **Contribute to the process.** The feedback you share with authors makes the end product better.

- **No risk.** You get a full refund or exchange if we ever have to cancel a MEAP.

Explore dozens of titles in MEAP at www.manning.com.